LIVING DEATH IN M
FRENCH AND EN
LITERATUR_

Medieval literature contains many figures caught at the interface between life and death – the dead return to place demands on the living, while the living foresee, organize or desire their own deaths. Jane Gilbert's original study examines the ways in which certain medieval literary texts, both English and French, use these 'living dead' to think about existential, ethical and political issues. In doing so, she shows powerful connections between works otherwise seen as quite disparate, including Chaucer's *Book of the Duchess* and *Legend of Good Women*, the *Chanson de Roland* and the poems of François Villon.

Written for researchers and advanced students of medieval French and English literature, this book provides original, provocative interpretations of canonical medieval texts in the light of influential modern theories, especially Lacanian psychoanalysis, presented in an accessible and lively way.

JANE GILBERT is Senior Lecturer in French at University College London.

CAMBRIDGE STUDIES IN MEDIEVAL LITERATURE

GENERAL EDITOR
Alastair Minnis, *Yale University*

EDITORIAL BOARD
Zygmunt G. Barański, *University of Cambridge*
Christopher C. Baswell, *University of California, Los Angeles*
John Burrow, *University of Bristol*
Mary Carruthers, *New York University*
Rita Copeland, *University of Pennsylvania*
Simon Gaunt, *King's College London*
Steven Kruger, *City University of New York*
Nigel Palmer, *University of Oxford*
Winthrop Wetherbee, *Cornell University*
Jocelyn Wogan-Browne, *Fordham University*

This series of critical books seeks to cover the whole area of literature written in
the major medieval languages – the main European vernaculars, and medieval
Latin and Greek – during the period *c.*1100–1500. Its chief aim is to publish and
stimulate fresh scholarship and criticism on medieval literature, special emphasis
being placed on understanding major works of poetry, prose and drama in relation
to the contemporary culture and learning which fostered them.

A complete list of titles in the series can be found at the end of the volume.

LIVING DEATH IN MEDIEVAL FRENCH AND ENGLISH LITERATURE

JANE GILBERT

CAMBRIDGE
UNIVERSITY PRESS

CAMBRIDGE
UNIVERSITY PRESS

University Printing House, Cambridge CB2 8BS, United Kingdom

Cambridge University Press is part of the University of Cambridge.

It furthers the University's mission by disseminating knowledge in the pursuit of
education, learning and research at the highest international levels of excellence.

www.cambridge.org
Information on this title: www.cambridge.org/9781107449251

© Jane Gilbert 2011

First published 2011
First paperback edition 2014

A catalogue record for this publication is available from the British Library

Library of Congress Cataloguing in Publication data
Gilbert, Jane, 1964–
Living death in medieval French and English literature / Jane Gilbert.
p.   cm. – (Cambridge studies in medieval literature ; 84)
Includes bibliographical references and index.
ISBN 978-1-107-00383-5 (hardback)
1. English literature – Middle English, 1100–1500 – History and criticism.   2. French literature – To
1500 – History and criticism.   3. Death in literature.   4. Dead in literature.   5. Death – Political
aspects.   6. Death – Moral and ethical aspects.   7. Existentialism in literature.   8. Ethics in
literature.   I. Title.
PR275.D43G56   2011
820.9'3548 – dc22   2010041740

ISBN 978-1-107-00383-5 Hardback
ISBN 978-1-107-44925-1 Paperback

Contents

Acknowledgements

When the princess Melisande was born, her mother, the queen, wished to have a christening party, but the king put his foot down and said he would not have it.

'I've seen too much trouble come of christening parties,' said he. 'However carefully you keep your visiting book, some fairy or other is sure to get left out, and you know what *that* leads to . . . I'll be her godfather, and you shall be her godmother, and we won't ask a single fairy; then none of them can be offended.'

'Unless they all are,' said the Queen. (Nesbit, 'Melisande', pp. 161–2)

Unlike Melisande's parents, I have not been able to resist at least a small party. Mistrusting my memory, I can only beg the pardon of those I omit, for so many people have contributed to this book over a long period that I cannot possibly name all. Although I have distinguished between the kinds of support for which I am grateful – emotional, intellectual, professional – I have of course benefited from more than one of these in most cases.

Moral support has been dispensed mainly in various cafes. I am grateful for much coffee, advice and encouragement as well as academic ideas and discussion to Elizabeth Archibald, Anne Cobby, Marilynn Desmond, Paola Filippucci, Samantha Rayner and Shelagh Sneddon.

Chapters have been read by Bill Burgwinkle, Ardis Butterfield, Elizabeth Edwards, Helen Phillips, Jim Simpson, Diane Watt and Nicolette Zeeman. For their generosity with their time, expertise and ideas I am enormously grateful. Mention must be made also of the anonymous readers for Cambridge University Press. Should they ever read this book again, I hope they will feel that their work on the manuscript was worthwhile. Others for Cambridge University Press have invested a great deal of time in my projects, and I thank them, particularly Alastair Minnis and Linda Bree.

Some debts are so diffuse and long-standing as to be difficult to articulate. Sarah Kay was the most inspiring and exacting teacher I could have hoped for, Simon Gaunt has been a true friend and the best of mentors, Jim Simpson the most original of contemporaries. Among medievalists not so far mentioned, some names stand out for the long friendship and inspiration I owe to them: Sylvia Huot, Nicola McDonald, Finn Sinclair.

This book first came to completion thanks to a grant under the AHRC Research Leave scheme. I am grateful to the AHRC, and also to the Department of French at UCL, for periods of leave. These have been made more productive by the knowledge that teaching was in the extremely capable hands of my former colleague, Sally Burch. I am indebted to her, and also to other UCL colleagues for many forms of support.

All the chapters below had outings as papers, and I thank those who invited, attended or commented on them. UCL students at undergraduate and postgraduate level have also joined in the debates in this book and have helped shape its argument. My thanks go especially to Natasha Romanova, who as my PhD student taught me much.

A number of people have worked on the domestic front, allowing my husband and me to pursue careers. Tabitha Buck, Kathy Jones, Tessa Hill and Justine Parker have looked after the children, Tessa Hill and Neil Johnson the garden, Maureen Wallace and others the house. I thank them all most gratefully for their assistance over the years.

My family has been living with this book for as long as I have. It has impinged on some more than others. My husband Dan Elliott, my children Sam and Nanon, and my mother Norma, have borne much; but my father, Malcolm, has borne most, as reader, editor and interlocutor. His only fault has been that his commitment to understanding my prose exceeds what anyone not related to me is ever likely to share. It is to him that I dedicate this book.

Melisande, by the way, grew up bald; all the fairies were offended.

Parts of Chapter 1 appeared as 'The *Chanson de Roland*' in Simon Gaunt and Sarah Kay (eds.), *The Cambridge Companion to Medieval French Literature* (Cambridge University Press, 2008), pp. 21–34.

An earlier version of Chapter 5 appeared in Nicola F. McDonald and W. M. Ormrod (eds.), *Rites of Passage: Cultures of Transition in the Four-teenth Century* (York Medieval Press; Woodbridge: Boydell Press, 2004), pp. 109–29 (reproduced by kind permission of Boydell and Brewer).

Note on translations

Throughout this book I have provided translations of medieval works. For modern secondary material in French, I have given English translations alone where I judge that the original wording is not significant to my argument. Translations are reproduced or silently adapted from published translations where available, as referenced; other translations are my own.

Introduction: living death

This book is about the ways in which certain medieval literary texts use death, dying and the dead to think about problems relating to life – problems political, social, ethical, philosophical or existential. More specifically, it is about the dynamic interface between life and death and about figures caught at that interface, hence 'living death'. There are ghosts and revenants who, although dead, actively speak and will, disturbing the properly living. And there are those who while alive exist under a deathly shadow that forecloses their engagement with life and isolates them from their fellows. Vampires, ghosts and zombies are currently fashionable in popular culture; in literary criticism, tropes of the interstitial, the intermediary or the 'third' are in vogue. What I have attempted to do in this book is to use some of the latter – in particular, Lacan's notion of *l'entre-deux-morts* – to think through some medieval examples of phenomena related to the former: dead who return to place demands on the living; living who foresee, organize or desire their own deaths.

LIFE AND DEATH

Death, dying and the dead, as Lévi-Strauss might have said, are good to think with. But surely this assertion is paradoxical? The modern philosophical tradition with which I engage in this book is shaped by Epicurus' affirmation that death 'is nothing to us; since, when we exist, death is not yet present, and when death is present, then we do not exist'.[1] Epicurus' rhetorical opposition between life and death is reflected in modern rejections of personal immortality in an afterlife; however, his insistence on death's nothingness for the living is transformed. In a tradition borne most influentially by Hegel and Heidegger, death has become the negative which constitutes humanity as such, distinguishing it from animals on one side and from immortals on the other.[2] Awareness of mortality, of finitude, makes possible that freedom from compulsion which is the highest human capacity. Modern life, in Heidegger's phrase, is 'being towards death' where the simple fact that death is nothing to us frees me 'for possibilities before death, my own possibilities, not everyday trivia or the menu offered to me by the They'; this freedom compels me to make my own meaning.[3]

In the Middle Ages, things were different. As regards the dead, first of all. Patrick Geary asks us to imagine a 'movement in support of the dead's rights' parallel to those which today demand 'women's rights, children's rights, minorities' rights, and even animal rights'.[4] Dying is seen as ceasing to be one kind of person and becoming another, significantly altering but by no means destroying social roles and relations. The medieval dead and living had reciprocal obligations and complementary spheres of activity as members of a greater community.[5] Geary relates how the deceased Stephen of Grammont was approached when he failed in his duty to protect the tranquility of his monastery: 'Miracles worked at [Stephen's] tomb resulted in a pilgrimage that threatened the peace and isolation of the community. The prior approached his tomb and solemnly commanded him to cease his miracles, or else, he was told, his body would be disinterred and cast into the nearby river.'[6] Saints formed a special case in several ways, but the ordinary dead also retained a social role safeguarding the communities and places in which they found themselves and shielding those who were special to them. These might be the communities, places and people they knew when alive, or equally those among whom they found themselves when dead. In return, the living owed them reverence, commemoration and the prayers which might advance their souls through purgatorial pains.

Most dead persons remained quietly in their place. Those who rose from the grave in dreams, visions, apparitions or even vivid memories did so to intervene in the existence of the living and in this sense were troubled and troublesome even where their intervention was appreciated, and much more so when not. Schmitt relates the case of the knight's son who inherits his dead father's profits from usury. One night the deceased comes calling to reclaim his goods. Since the son refuses to open the door, the spirit eventually goes away, leaving behind him a gift of fish. Come the dawn, the young man finds instead toads and snakes, 'hellish food cooked in the sulphurous fire' according to Caesarius of Heisterbach, who recounts this *exemplum*. Schmitt comments:

The intense ambivalence of these gifts and of this revenant who offers, in the guise of fish, hell's deadly fare – symbol of the ill-gotten inheritance – equals the son's ambivalence towards his father. Only too happy to accept the inheritance, he does not want to know its origin, just as he refuses to recognize his father and open the door to him. The repressed returns in the figure of the father, whose hammering on the door expresses metaphorically – even the *exemplum*'s vocabulary recalls it (*fortiter pulsans*) – Freud's 'repetition compulsion', so characteristic of ghost stories.[7]

The obvious enforcing of social and ethical order in this tale does not prevent the dead man from appearing unusual and disturbing; even when playing their proper role by warning or advising, revenants depart from the norm for death. Others are deliberately obstreperous and obstructive. Welcome or unwelcome, the dead possess authority, agency and urgency; they threaten the living, making explicit or implicit demands or heralding imminent demise. Death in this perspective, then, is very much something to medieval people.

Relations between life and death were also different in the Middle Ages, and most intimate in Christianity. 'You have filled the whole world with tombs and sepulchres', Julian the Apostate complained, protesting against such Christian practices as the cult of bodily relics and the location of burial spaces within inhabited areas.[8] From the earliest period onwards, Christian writings play on the opposition between 'life' and 'death' in such a way as to make the two share quarters. Innocent III's influential *De miseria condicionis humane* [*De contemptu mundi*] illustrates the characteristic ideas and the biblically grounded rhetoric that mingles while it divides:

We are therefore always dying while we live, and we only stop dying at such time as we stop living. It is better to die for life than to live for death, because mortal life is nothing but a living death. Solomon: 'I praised the dead rather than the living, and I judged him happier in both ways that is not yet born.'[9]

Life in the body is a long process of dying that begins with conception and ends only with death's consummation. Metaphorical uses of the terms as well as massive emphasis on the afterlife add to the complexity.[10] Earthly life is not only a shadow of the life to come, it is very much more deathly than the post-mortem condition enjoyed by the blessed. In an extremist but recurrent Christian tradition championed by St Paul, corporeal and spiritual life are placed in inverse relation: 'God's ecstasy-in-Incarnation, his leaping down from heaven, demonstrates once and for all that self-preservation leads to death, while self-oblation leads to eternal life.'[11] In this way of thinking, life in the material body is an ethical concept:

The gospel message of life through self-oblation and sacrificial death cuts clean through the assumptions of the present age. The world lives by the law of the flesh and strives wherever possible to consolidate self. The world believes that power and glory come through calculating self-preservation. The world can make no sense of the word of the cross, of Christ-wisdom-crucified, and so regards it as 'insanity' (*mōría*, 1 Cor. 1: 18ff.).[12]

By aiming to minimize as far as possible the impulses of the flesh and the importance of its various conditions, including its demise, the ascetic attempts to die to sin and to the flesh and thus to actualize the life of the spirit on earth.

Conversely, pursuing the life of the flesh leads to, and indeed constitutes, the death of the soul. The damned are condemned to what is sometimes referred to as a 'second death' (the phrase derives from St John's Apocalypse) whose magnitude dwarfs that undergone on earth (and note that the first death is envisaged for most Christians as a physically painful and spiritually trying experience).[13] Although in early Christianity the second death which was the fate of non-Christians may arguably have been envisaged as simple ceasing to be, by the period with which I am concerned damnation, for Christians and others, had become an eternity of torment actively suffered by a conscious, sentient being whose awareness formed an essential element of his torture. From this perspective there is no final cessation of or for the spirit, hence in one important sense no death. Spiritual 'death' is rather a kind of negative life, characterized by duration, existence, consciousness and intensity.[14] Death is thus everything to us.

If damnation may be taken to be an important notion in the minds of medieval people, it by no means dominates medieval literature in French and English. Issues of salvation, and the extremist ideology according to which worldly life equates to spiritual death, govern only one of the texts I foreground, the Middle English *Pearl*, and even there it is put into question. Among the other texts I discuss, secular concerns predominate in relation to mortality and immortality, questions of fame, influence and potency in this world. This is a function not only of my own literary preferences but in part also of ideas of what constitutes 'literature'; modern literary studies often pays scant attention to the vast body of medieval theological, devotional or simply pious writing. (I am not the critic to redress this imbalance, which is more marked in French than in English studies, in part due to the nature of the extant material.) On the other hand, while the latter massively outnumber those works that qualify today as literary, it cannot claim to define medieval culture as a whole. The writers whose works are discussed in this book inevitably belong to educated cultural elites (which may coincide with a socially marginal position, as famously in Villon's case, or to a much lesser degree in the self-presentations of Chaucer or the *Pearl*-poet; marginality is a feature of late medieval poetics). Their audiences, insofar as we can recover information about them, are more diverse, and usually not identical socially or culturally to the writers, even where there is substantial crossover. But it is evident that both writers and audiences availed themselves of a variety of discourses. The names by which medievalists refer to these discourses depend on the contexts within which they have come to critical attention: genres such as romance, epic or fabliau; social milieux such as courtly, chivalric, clerical or vulgar; intellectual distinctions such as learned or popular; moral attitudes such as pious, secular or irreverent. Most medieval poets for whom we can identify an oeuvre show (display, even) a range of formal, rhetorical and ideological modes. Those who are sometimes pious are not always, only or uniformly pious. A single writer may use themes relating to death in ways which imply quite divergent views on the philosophical, social or literary issues involved. While numerous aspects of medieval thinking in relation to death, dying and the dead are foreign to modern Western subjects, many others are familiar, including the ability to hold or at least express contradictory opinions on those subjects. In this book I have not attempted a cultural history of the medieval 'way of death';[15] my field is literary criticism, my subject the ways in which certain topoi are exploited in particular literary texts.

Fine recent work has been done on the themes of death, suicide and sacrifice in medieval literature; however, my subject is different.[16] I have selected my texts to fulfil a number of criteria. Each foregrounds the shifting frontier between life and death, and shows human subjects and cultural systems confronting that problematic division. All are particularly embedded in medieval networks of reading and writing. All are notably high quality; almost all enjoy canonical status today. Widely studied and researched, they influence modern academic perceptions of medieval literary norms and therefore provide excellent places from which to re-examine such perceptions. One of my aims has been to investigate whether and how these important French and English literary works can be said to be normative.[17] I argue that the works analysed in this book deploy the ideas of death's presence in life and life's in death in such a way as to place in suspension or abeyance certain expectations, rules and ideals of what they represent as everyday life. These norms are thereby extracted from the ideological or customary contexts which give them meaning, force and vigour, to be examined from new and disorienting perspectives. It is therefore important to appreciate that the figures and situations through which this examination takes place are not themselves in conflict with normal expectations; the literary texts work to make cultures strange to themselves by highlighting problematic aspects of normal practice, whether 'normal' is taken to mean banal or ideal. The living dead present an ethical challenge to the ordinarily living.

I have sought meaningful representation rather than exhaustive coverage. The first three chapters, which focus on masculinity, encompass works from different genres and periods in the long development of medieval literature in French, from early *chanson de geste* (the *Chanson de Roland*) through mid-period Arthurian prose romance (the non-cyclic prose *Lancelot do Lac*) to late ballades by Deschamps and Villon, in the latter's case set into a satirical mock-will. In English I have concentrated on the flowering of high literary discourse under Richard II. The final two chapters develop the analysis of idealized femininity begun in relation to Villon's ladies, in Middle English poems mourning dead females: *Pearl*, read in relation to Middle French marguerite poetry in Chapter 4; Chaucer's *Book of the Duchess* and Prologue to the *Legend of Good Women* in Chapter 5. In discussing these English-language texts in the context of French-language ones I place them in one proper context. Such Ricardian works belong to a period and milieu in which English literature enjoyed an especially close and well-documented association with French, exemplified here by the use of French models and the adaptation of continental poetic practices and projects to insular media.[18] These poems therefore form a privileged site for comparative study.

ENTRE-DEUX-MORTS

Central to my project is the distinction between corporeal death and what may be called 'symbolic' death, by which I mean the community's formal recognition of a person as dead. Symbolic death may follow bodily death, as in the funeral or the memorial ceremony. Symbolic may also precede corporeal death, as when such phenomena as religious commitment or mental illness make a person 'dead to the world'.[19] A different understanding of non-corporeal death might be termed 'subjective', referring to subjects' sense of being set on an inevitable course towards death, and attending to the ways in which that awareness affects their engagement with life. Symbolic and subjective deaths refer respectively to collective and individual aspects of human experience; although I would not wish to lose sight of the distinction completely, these two aspects interpenetrate. All death is importantly subjective until formally ratified by the collective (though it may be objective enough in the criteria it relies on to determine the extinction of life). Similarly, a particular subject's sense of being effectively already dead ('effectively' invites exploration) necessarily refers to the wider social order with its norms of life and death – what characterizes life and death, how they are to be recognized, accessed and organized.

The condition of those whose subjective or symbolic deaths seem to have come adrift from bodily death, I shall term *entre-deux-morts* or 'between-two-deaths': 'mort empiétant sur le domaine de la vie, vie empiétant sur la mort' ('death encroaching on the domain of life, life encroaching on death', my translation).[20] These much-discussed expressions, drawn from psychoanalyst Jacques Lacan's Seminar VII of 1959–60 on the ethics of psychoanalysis, have been widely used in modern literary studies where they are understood in varied ways, therefore any use requires explication and particularization. Before embarking on a preliminary overview, I emphasize that my use of Lacan does not entail rigorously Lacanian analyses of the medieval texts, for two reasons. In the first place, I treat Seminar VII here not as the exposition of a system but as a complex text: fragmentary, teasing, elusive, its constituent parts suggesting divergent, sometimes contradictory directions of inquiry. My chapters take this heterogeneous text as a starting point in order to develop different directions in relation to the medieval material. If my theoretical expositions are sometimes pedagogical in tone, it is not because I wish to restrict my readers' responses but rather, by clarifying the ideas, assumptions and logical steps that guide my arguments, to invite critical engagement with those arguments. In the second place, I explore alternative explanations of similar phenomena, with a view to contextualizing and thus reconceptualizing Lacan's account (the distinction between 'symbolic' and 'subjective' death is not Lacanian, for instance). Different chapters highlight different aspects of and approaches to these phenomena, dialoguing around their common theme of death's overlap with life and its ethical and political effects. I have drawn in my analyses on Freudian psychoanalysis for its accounts of the death drive, mourning and repetition; on (post)structuralist phenomenology and rhetorical theory for their challenges to human subjectivity; on gender studies and queer theory for their critiques of the famously contentious psychoanalytical accounts of gender and sexuality; and on anthropological discussions of burial and memorialization practices in different cultures. Each chapter can be read independently, but the approaches and questions treated in any one chapter will enrich those discussed in others, material from Lacan's Seminar VII providing both continuity and variety.

Unlike many theoretical medievalists, I do not justify my practice by appealing to continuities between medieval and modern culture; though it never fails to surprise me how many points of contact there are. It not infrequently seems, to adapt Slavoj Žižek's *jeu d'esprit*, that medieval writers have read Lacan; conversely Lacan, like some other thinkers, at times appears to be more in sympathy with medieval writers than with modern readers. This enjoyable illusion is not the basis of my method, however. I subscribe to the principle of ethnographic study according to which the explanatory model employed in the analysis should not be internal to the culture being analysed. Deploying modern critical theory in juxtaposition with medieval texts avoids the circularity risked by, for instance, reading in the light of Lacan's writings modern writers themselves influenced by having read those writings. The model of the medievalist as anthropologist has been influentially disputed, embraced by R. Howard Bloch and rejected by Sarah Kay, who points out that the past is not, in fact, a foreign country and cannot be visited by participant-observers.[21] I defend the model on three counts. In the first place, the impossibility of inhabiting the medieval world fully is a positive condition of medievalist study insofar as it aids the critical distance essential to insightful analysis. In the second, although many ethnographers participate in the living cultures they study in a way strictly impossible to modern literary medievalists, we can, by our practices of reading and research, aim to enter sympathetically and imaginatively into the ethos of the literary works we read. The imaginary is a valid heuristic tool and dimension of knowledge, though naturally scholarly observation and analysis also require drawing on documented external sources. Finally, an equally vital element in the ethnographic investigative model is the principle that investigators should not only refer to explanatory terms familiar from their own cultures, but should adapt those and formulate new ones as the material requires; thus the encounter between cultures, *entre-deux*, ideally generates both the analysis and its terms, and provides a new perspective on the analyst's original as well as target culture.[22] This goal of conceptual innovation, its purpose to discover more about medieval cultures than can be supplied by the terms within which modern cultures predominantly think about themselves or about more familiar others, is shared by many medievalists of both 'theoretical' and 'non-theoretical' persuasions. In pursuit of this innovation, critical theory (which may more helpfully be considered philosophy employed in the practical context of the study of literary and other cultural artefacts) stimulates by its bold questioning of modern mindsets and by the creative tensions which arise from placing its determined modernity and avant-gardism into dynamic interaction with a serious effort to imagine and to inquire into the past. My use of theory, therefore, aims to open up new questions, to find new angles on old ones, and to test contemporary ideas against other kinds of evidence.

For Lacan, as for many thinkers influential in recent times, death is the negation of existence. It is one manifestation of what he calls the Real: those aspects of human life that cannot be mastered because they defy symbolization (which may be glossed as the process of translation into one of the many artificial patterned and structured communicative forms which make up human reality).[23] Lacan, again like others, does not consider death's nothingness as one among a number of historical and philosophical responses to a perennial existential crisis facing human beings but as an ontological reality – the crisis itself.

Although death in its Real dimension can never be tamed (*pace* Ariès, whose influential cultural history *The Hour of Our Death* entitles its opening, medieval chapter, 'The Tame Death'), this does not mean that it has no impact on human life. On the contrary, the unassimilable trauma of the Real stimulates endless responses, which show the futility of efforts to tame it. Thus the Real lies at the heart of human culture, even though that culture by definition excludes it. Lacan distinguishes two other registers within cultural and psychic experience: the imaginary and the symbolic. However distinct in theory, these registers nevertheless intertwine in complex ways. Any attempt to represent death figuratively involves the imaginary, 'the realm of image and imagination, deception and lure', whose 'principal illusions . . . are those of wholeness, synthesis autonomy, duality and, above all, similarity'.[24] Visual examples can include the *transi* or decaying corpse of late medieval tomb-sculpture; the skeleton representing death or the dead person; the soul going to heaven or hell, and indeed the characteristic rewards and punishments of the afterlife. Dying may be conceived, under its imaginary aspect, as reunion and return, as the recovery of loss and the end of lack, as ultimate fulfilment and peace. Hence the blessed expect repose in Abraham's bosom and everlasting bliss in the presence of the Lord. For the wicked, death brings a painful and humiliating dismantling: dismemberment, impalement, suffocating, burning, violation, explosion, turbulent and uncontrolled movement – a permanent process of dying which never achieves its final denouement (this providing its principal distinction from purgatorial regimes).[25] Since the symbolic aspect relates to social, political, cultural and linguistic order as systems abstracted from content or actual realization (which belong to the imaginary), symbolic death concerns whether or not someone is considered to exist as a person. There is a potential confusion here. On the one hand, 'symbolic death' can refer to the rites by which a person moves from the society of the living to that of the dead, a process which keeps that person within society's remit. Thus medieval anchorites, officially dead to secular society, were empowered by their unworldly position to exercise in some cases considerable political influence.[26] Even marginal categories such as the mad or the leprous – made up of subjects incapable of fulfilling their proper social roles – have a place: as to receive charity or to remind the more fortunate to be humble; or to criticize and thus improve the social order, like the unquiet dead. On the other hand, there is a more radical sense, in which death under its symbolic aspect appears as non-personhood, manifested either by social placelessness (the Wandering Jew, the Flying Dutchman) or conversely by too-perfect assimilation of, or into, the symbolic order. Fantasy figures corresponding to this latter condition include the living doll, the zombie, and figures of possession or hollowness, the apparently human shell animated by a non-human, automatic force. Metaphors rather than figurations of death, these figures refer to the symbolic, structural aspects of death (though clearly they also have imaginary aspects).

If death in its Real aspect resists symbolization absolutely, nevertheless Lacan argues that imaginary and symbolic responses to death can conjure up a sense of the Real. He considers this to be the special vocation of art, explaining via an elaboration of that classic metaphor of creation and paternity, the pot.[27] Considered from one point of view, a pot is a container for some substance, such as water, and is therefore logically secondary to the thing it contains. Viewed in another perspective, however, a pot gives shape to the emptiness within it prior to any filling. Thanks to the pot – and beyond it, to the potter – this emptiness acquires a kind of presence, coming into conceptual being as a void; which then cries out to be filled. We may choose to fill it with God the Potter or with some other transcendent stabilizer of meaning; however, for Lacan (as for many other thinkers) the mystery is final. The void thus produced is not the Real, but is a response to and place-holder for it, and genuinely if inadequately communicates a sense of its alterity. Thus the void dwarfs the artefact that projects it. Lacan insists on the heroism of human making: when the potter creates the pot he introduces into the world a no-thing (the void) which is man-made yet beyond making, indicative of the threatening, creative emptiness of the cosmos, and dwarfs into insignificance any human effort within that vast context. Our response to this *au-delà* ('beyond') will be one of awe and horror, in various measures. Lacan emphasizes that such images as the pot (both as object and as analogy) are ontologically entirely distinct from the Real, yet insists equally that the contact between them is a valid one. By means of this special artistry, which lies as much in the beholder's response as in the artisan's craft, a pressure point is set up such that the Real becomes almost – but never quite – accessible to signification. Any product in which this pressure can be felt renders 'ce qui du réel pâtit du signifiant' ('that which in the [R]eal suffers from the signifier').[28] In an endless dialectic of revelation and concealment, art takes away with one hand what it gives with the other, since each work of the sort that interests Lacan can gesture towards the Real which dissipates the imaginary only by itself privileging an image.

The purpose of art, according to Lacan, is therefore to 'projeter une réalité qui n'est point celle de l'objet représenté' ('to project a reality that is not that of the object represented').[29] This alternative reality is the Real, which makes us question the ontological status of the reality within which the object ordinarily has meaning for us. Lacan focuses on figurative but non-realistic art forms which, by treating the objects represented in an obviously artificial manner, allow us to see beyond the imaginary shapes and symbolic patterns within which we live. His major themes are anamorphosis in early modern painting, courtly love in the medieval lyric, and Sophoclean tragedy, principally *Antigone*; the expression *l'entre-deux-morts* occurs in this last context.

Lacan defines anamorphosis by the experience of becoming legible: 'c'est tout espèce de construction faite de telle sorte que, par transposition optique, une certaine forme qui n'est pas perceptible au premier abord se rassemble en une image lisible' ('any kind of construction that is made in such a way that by means of an optical transposition, a certain form that wasn't perceptible at first sight transforms itself into a readable image').[30] This shift from unintelligible to intelligible image has a purpose : 'il s'agit, d'une façon analogique, ou anamorphique, de réindiquer que ce que nous cherchons dans l'illusion est quelque chose où l'illusion elle-même se transcende en quelque sorte, se détruit, en montrant qu'elle n'est là qu'en tant que signifiante' ('it is a matter of indicating anew, through an analogy or an anamorphosis, that what we seek from the illusion is something in which the illusion itself somehow transcends itself, self-destructs, showing that it is there only as a sign-post', my translation).[31] Baroque anamorphosis, by distorting the perspectival constructions which conventionally render three-dimensional space onto a two-dimensional surface, pushes us to recognize the factitious quality of figurative art per se, a quality that we tend to forget when faced with more straightforwardly mimetic works.

Courtly love similarly highlights its own artificiality and its investment in not achieving union, by a rhetoric and an attitude of prostration before the beloved Lady which jar with medieval reality (Lacan insists on the brutality of medieval women's social position). In Sophocles' *Antigone*, the figure of the protagonist overcome by Ate (a goddess inducing folly and thence ruin) reveals the workings of the death drive, indifferent to the interests of a fragile social order and of the organism itself.

Each of the art forms that Lacan discusses is conceived as a means of projecting this haunting other dimension, reminding audiences that the reality within which they live is contingent, a mere symbolic and imaginary order, and reconnecting them with that Real dimension which is the birthplace of fertility and meaning, as well as their negation. What works through art is thus the death drive, displacing man from his position as master of the universe and belittling his achievements. This primary work of art, although inevitably lost sight of by artists and audiences – since it is not an intuition that can be tolerated long-term – can be reactivated by departures from figurative traditions.[32] The Real may be projected in 'l'entre-deux de deux champs symboliquement différenciés' ('the in-between of two symbolically differentiated fields', my translation).[33] This *entre-deux* is not an intermediate place or space (although that may act as a trigger or vessel), but the consciousness that the existence of plural distinct fields implies a further field external to any that can be delimited or identified. This further field may be considered a metaphysical dimension; Lacan bids us be wary of giving it that ontological status.

LACANIAN ETHICS AND POLITICS

A good deal of this book will be occupied with exploring the *entre-deux* connecting death and life, both within and without Lacan's conception of it. I approach death as a crisis confronting humanity at collective and individual levels, and concentrate on the responses of societies and subjects who face the challenge of integrating death, dying and the dead into their lives. My analyses therefore highlight different ethical and political dimensions of the *entre-deux-morts* in various texts. I do not limit my understanding of ethics to Lacan's account of the 'ethics of psychoanalysis' in Seminar VII; however, my analyses throughout this book are in dialogue with that account. The next two sections explain my broad understanding of that ethical stance and its political consequences, preliminary to more detailed analysis of particular points in the chapters below.

Lacan argues that certain psychoanalytic theories are significant both in psychoanalytic practice and in ethical theory more broadly. His primary reference is to Freud's identification of 'the sense of guilt as the most important problem in the development of civilization', or more precisely: 'the price we pay for our advance in civilization is a loss of happiness through the heightening of the sense of guilt'.[34] However, a major intellectual influence in Seminar VII, in my opinion, is existentialism; Lacan's themes and approach are consonant with Steven Crowell's characterization of existentialist thinking:

Heidegger's 1927 *Being and Time*, an inquiry into the 'being that we ourselves are' (which he termed 'Dasein', a German word for existence), introduced most of the motifs that would characterize later existentialist thinking: the tension between the individual and the 'public'; an emphasis on the worldly or 'situated' character of human thought and reason; a fascination with liminal experiences of anxiety, death, the 'nothing' and nihilism; the rejection of science (and above all, causal explanation) as an adequate framework for understanding human being; and the introduction of 'authenticity' as the norm of self-identity, tied to the project of self-definition through freedom, choice, and commitment. Though in 1946 Heidegger would repudiate the retrospective labelling of his earlier work as existentialism, it is in that work that the relevant concept of existence finds its first systematic philosophical formulation.[35]

The dialogue with this concept of existence conducted within Seminar VII makes it a particularly appropriate text for my purposes. The 'ethics of psychoanalysis' on which this Seminar focuses relates to mortality and to death as 'nothing', and to the limit experiences which confrontation with these induces.

Drawing a highly selective history of ethical thought from Aristotle through Kant and Bentham, Lacan makes three general points against which psychoanalytic ethics must distinguish itself. Firstly, he claims that ethical theory traditionally treats 'the good' as something known, measurable and common, essentially the same for all ethical subjects. Thus the Golden Rule, 'do as you would be done by', is a valid principle and the notion of welfare a rational one: material needs and conditions for contentment adequately met but not indulgently exceeded. Secondly, traditional ethics subordinates the individual's freedom to maximize his or her good to collective interests ('the greatest good for the greatest number', in Bentham's phrase). This principle, according to Lacan, entails envisaging happiness as what economists call a limited good (if one person has more then another must have less), posing problems relating to distribution. Finally, ethical tradition has emphasized the role of pleasure in reinforcing our attachment to the good, but with a proviso: human beings must be taught to restrain baser pleasures in order to appreciate the finer rewards offered by goodness and self-discipline.[36]

Psychoanalysis, by contrast, introduces the idea of the unconscious and rests on a Hobbesian philosophy of human nature as greedy, competitive and irrational but restrained by civilization, whose job is both to limit and to sublimate human impulses into socially acceptable paths. Freud refines by making guilt itself, together with its agent the superego, at once the moral force and the social glue. Guilt is originary, implanted in humankind by the primordial murder of the father and, unlike remorse, needing no prior action or even intention on the subject's part. Following Freud, Lacan refuses to consider unconscious desires within a framework of evolutionary usefulness. Self-preservation itself cannot be taken to be a goal of the human organism; Lacan sees the organism as tending towards its own death and (following Freud's analogy between individual and collective processes) civilization towards its own destruction.[37] Human desires do not relate to biological need, cannot be rationalized, and are essentially singular, hence unpredictable, unintelligible and potentially illegitimate in the eyes of others. They can never form the basis for a social system. This conception allows Lacan to critique certain accepted ethical notions as hegemonic (because they serve the interests of particular groups) and/or unworkable (because they neglect or conceal a fundamental aspect of human nature). For instance, he considers the tale of St Martin sharing his cloak with the beggar as an exemplary fable of the 'good' in its utilitarian, communal, distributive sense, and suggests that the beggar's desires might lie elsewhere.[38] Or he discusses a problem put by Kant, in which a man is offered sex with a woman he desires on condition that he be put to death immediately afterwards. Whereas (according to Lacan) Kant presents this bargain as exemplifying the inconceivable, Lacan points out that the promised execution might actually heighten the allure; for some the opportunity of dying might increase exponentially the pleasure gained from what is otherwise another banal sexual encounter. *Jouissance*, the ultimate pleasure sought by each human subject under an irreducibly personal form, involves a kind of dying – temporary self-dissolution if not literal bodily death – which itself is only part of the vicious pleasure of destruction. Civilization at once denies us this, implants in us a guilty sense of having effectively already done it, and maintains our desires in relation to it. Lacan develops elements of Freud's text to invert the usual picture according to which human desire is ruled by a drive to destroy ourselves and others, society, the whole known world, and which further claims that as social animals we are impelled to suppress that drive, to behave altruistically and communally, to sublimate our desires into art or other displacements, while as moral beings we suffer from our dual nature. For psychoanalysis in the Lacanian tradition, patriarchal civilization thrives on a transgressive urge to unbridlement which it also restrains, through the conscience as well as through external constraints, thus doubly manifesting the death drive: via the unleashing of the destructive urge and via the organism's collapse under the tension between competing forces.

In spite of the emphasis on singular desire, it would be incorrect to label Lacan's ethics individualistic or egocentric. In the first place, its field of application is psychoanalytic practice. From one perspective its import is therefore narrow. The question 'As-tu agi en conformité avec ton désir?' ('Have you acted in conformity with your desire?')[39] posed to the analysand marks a divergence between psychoanalytic and general practical ethics. The case of Antigone, who does not 'give ground relative to [her] desire', is both mythical and tragic.[40] Lacan admires her authenticity and comments on the function of her beauty but notes that her position is adopted *in extremis*, her life being intolerable, and uses her to exemplify the destructive nature of desire.[41] From another point of view, the non-utilitarian ethic of psychoanalysis has far-reaching implications. Lacan rejects the notion that psychoanalysis aims to make subjects either happy or normal. Lacanian analysis (at least the training analysis that qualifies analysts) will not enable analysands to attain their desire (which is by definition unattainable), though it may help them to achieve an accommodation with that desire and their own chronic lack of fulfilment. Nor will it encourage them to submit pragmatically to normative social ideals; rather, it teaches a critical method designed to challenge intellectually those ideals and the social, cultural and political conditions that dictate them. Conditioned conformity to a normative code is a suppressive mechanism unworthy of psychoanalytic sanction. Civilization ought to produce discontents, and Lacanian analysis aims not to reconcile the subject to its discontentment, but to carry that discontentment to a further, reflexive level. This leads me to a second important disjunction between Lacan's ethics and either individualism or voluntarism: the subject acting in accordance with the 'désir qui [l']habite' ('the desire that inhabits it', my translation) is ruled neither by the ego nor by any conscious self but by the unconscious (in Lacanian thinking, absolutely inaccessible to consciousness).[42] This is the dimension that Lacan seeks to restore to philosophy. Lacan's Antigone is not a hero in any normal sense: 'Victime et holocauste, c'est malgré elle qu'elle est là' ('victim and holocaust, it is in spite of herself that she is there').[43] Dissenting from the idea that autonomous, atomic individuals act with intention, will and cognizance or can assume their own unwilled acts in this spirit, Lacan attacks liberal and Enlightenment ideas of the person and the morality that addresses those ideas. His 'hero' inverts the traditional form.[44]

Finally, his ethics may be considered a politics of resistance or revolution, even though Lacan's own expressed views on the possibility of revolution altered over his career, and his political engagement was rarely more than lukewarm. The singular desire driving the subject produces a stance which defies hegemonic collective orders, based as these are on notions of the general good. Correspondingly, civilization's internal dynamic, similarly impelled by the death drive, will inevitably lead to political and cultural upheaval on a large scale. These impulsions may – however contingently – lead to new social forms. While Lacan himself, elevating only certain theoretical constructs to the status of Real, mostly forgoes the notion of social progress through this dialectical process, thinkers such as Ernesto Laclau and Slavoj Žižek have found room in his theory for positive, Marxist-inspired revolutionism. As Terry Eagleton insists, 'there is a redemptive face to the Real as well as a destructive one':[45] it can regenerate as well as devastate, and devastation may be a step on the path to regeneration. Thus in the medieval texts with which I am concerned, some individuals faced with their own or others' death find renewed impetus in life. Where the collective is concerned, at times an old order is reasserted, at others change may be initiated or a new order founded. For Eagleton and others, there is a politics as well as an ethics of the Real. For Lacan, contrastingly, such appropriations belong to the realms of the imaginary or symbolic, and are to be maintained as analytically distinct.

The politically disruptive and constructive uses to which death may be put are a major theme of the book. *Entre-deux-morts* in my understanding of it serves at once and in varying degrees as crisis and partial solution; it powerfully undercuts ideological constructs, but that very power can be exploited in the service of other ideologies. My principal guide in this area is Žižek, to whom I refer throughout this book as at once a witty and illuminating expositor of Lacan, a Lacanian revolutionary revisionist, and an analyst of ideology, of the Real, and of the relations between the two. One example of how Lacan's Seminar VII facilitates and limits ideological analysis is through the concept of the 'second death'. Terminological confusion with 'between two deaths' is inevitable, and indeed, as Lacan uses them, these concepts are related. Numerous interpretations circulate; as I use it here, the second death is not to be identified with that death (symbolic, subjective or bodily) which brings to an end the state 'between two deaths'. The 'deaths' in the latter refer to 'deux champs symboliquement différenciés' in the *entre-deux* between which the Real arises: two states whose definition, place in the world and relationship to each other are regarded as closed or 'dead' questions. To be *entre-deux-morts* is therefore to disturb a settled vision of the world. In contrast, the 'second death' is, as mentioned above, an ancient and important idea within Christian tradition, signifying eternal damnation within an apocalyptic framework. In one sense, therefore, the second death has an established place within Christianity as salvation's complement; it is a powerful imaginary support for the Christian regime. Differently viewed, however, it is a source of perpetual outrage. Thus Charles Péguy, before his conversion, writes: 'This is what I find most hateful, this is barbaric, this is what I shall never consent to . . . : that strange combination of life and death which we call damnation . . . An eternity of living death is a perverted, inverted imagining.'[46] Péguy's objection responds to the excessive nature of second death, extravagantly over and above any rational ethical norm. The second death offends. In this perspective, it represents death in its Real aspect. Its profligacy places it ethically *entre-deux-morts*; politically, however, it is evidently open to exploitation by various interested forces. It is the former rather than the latter aspect which attracts Lacan, who is not concerned with the economic and material bases of power. He nevertheless not only emphasizes the potential for ideological appropriations of the *entre-deux-morts* but over the course of his life's work analyses various psycho-political positions adopted in the public sphere by different forms of power, thus sharing in the debate over the political that occupies French post-war thinking.[47] Lacan's thinking about power does pay attention to historical specificity, though not in the mode of a historian.[48]

His scepticism of causes and emancipations, of sacrifices and salvations, is a useful reminder to be cautious about our investments. On the other hand, Lacan himself is of course not free of such investments – nor does his analysis of the human allow for such purity. He too allows the Real regenerative potential. For all the dramatic rhetoric of Seminar VII, the ethical position 'beyond the second death' with which it resolves permits the common man through being-for-death to borrow some of the hero's glamour while remaining within the circuit of everyday life. This position bespeaks a certain redemption enabling either provisional acceptance of prevailing norms or positive commitment to changing them.[49] The scepticism that Lacan here advocates does not preclude, and may even empower ideological engagements. We cannot, therefore, except Lacan from our ethical and political critique; indeed, he 'at once analyzes and symptomizes' the 'fantasy of law as insurpassable authority'.[50] In order to address in detail this last point, I turn to the potent figure of Antigone as a case study in the modern problematic of relating ethics to politics.

ANTIGONE

Antigone is a reference point throughout this book. This requires explanation, since although she has been since the nineteenth century a major Western cultural focus for thinking about certain issues under the aegis of death, she was not a figure to conjure with in medieval culture.[51] To summarize her story as found in its today most influential telling, Sophocles' *Antigone*, of 441 BCE: Antigone is one of the four children of Oedipus and Jocasta's unwittingly incestuous marriage. After Oedipus blinds and exiles himself on discovering his incest and parricide, his sons Eteocles and Polyneices agree to share power but soon embark on a civil war. Polyneices, who brings a foreign army against the city, loses. Both brothers are killed. Creon, Jocasta's brother, inherits the governance of Thebes and declares that while Eteocles will receive honourable burial, anyone undertaking to bury Polyneices' corpse will die. Antigone defies Creon's proscription to bury her brother and is condemned to be buried alive. She hangs herself in the tomb. Creon survives desolate after the consequent suicides of Haemon, his son and Antigone's fiancé, and of Eurydice, his wife.

Sophocles' Antigone is a key figure in discussions of the Lacanian *entre-deux-morts*. She forms a pendant to Polyneices: if he is physically but not yet symbolically dead, then she is symbolically dead from the moment she decides to bury her brother in defiance of Creon's edict. Her role as one who tidies up anomalies on the life/death interface – by struggling to achieve the appropriate symbolic death for her brother – leads her into a complementary (rather than opposing) condition, as she herself becomes anomalous through her inevitable, then actual condemnation. By mirroring and supplementing Polyneices' situation 'between two deaths', Antigone's example elevates the anomaly into an alternative to the norm and establishes the zone between two deaths as a distinct ethical 'place' – or more exactly, a 'no-place', for it negates 'place' as a bounded and intelligible category. This no-place has a particular relation to death in the body, which it contrasts to some worse fate which may be conceived as another form of 'death' – spiritual, moral, social or subjective – a second death. Thus for Antigone, bodily dying is the painful but justified price of a superior form of integrity. Many commentators rest here, with Antigone's heroic sacrifice or pathetic martyrdom. Lacan pursues her 'beyond the second death', and the comparison between his approach and others' is worth making.

ANTIGONE'S DRIVE

Apart from her importance to discussions of the *entre-deux-morts*, Antigone is important here for her focal role in modern thinking about the relation between ethics and politics, and particularly in the post-war French effort to go beyond Oedipus as the political and philosophical subject.[52] Hegel, the major intertext for modern philosophical interests in Antigone, is also Lacan's; his understanding of Hegel being heavily influenced by Alexandre Kojève. Hegel's famous association of Antigone as woman with divine law and with the family (realms respectively 'above' and 'below' the masculine laws of the *polis*) is only one treatment to associate her with law, and may be placed in a wider context. In her history of (principally but not only French) presentations of Antigone, Fraisse outlines an ancient strand in the reception of Sophocles' protagonist as spokeswoman for 'natural law' against 'positive law', a distinction elaborated by Aristotle, Cicero and Aquinas. Natural law (exemplified in this case by the duty to bury the dead) is eternal and immutable, the same for every human being – indeed contributes importantly to defining the meaning of the term 'human'. It takes precedence over the contingent positive laws of particular regimes. In Sophocles' play, natural law as appealed to by Antigone derives its authority from the gods; however, Fraisse notes an influential secular appropriation, according to which Antigone stands for 'the judgement of the individual conscience in revolt against collective embargos':

Antigone's protest – the protest of one who dares to act according to her heart in spite of social oppression – engenders modern individualism: that of Rousseau who believes that conscience is a divine instinct, that of Kant for whom the moral law is written in every man's heart, that of the anarchists who acknowledge neither God nor master, but each of whom believes himself to be in possession of truth, of *his* truth.[53]

If Lacan's Antigone epitomizes the subject in conflict with collective authority and its laws, nevertheless she does not stand for moral conscience in the tradition of Rousseau, Kant or the anarchists. To see her as such would be to fill the intolerable Real opened up by her actions with transcendentals that award to imaginary constructs and symbolic structures an illusory metaphysical grounding. Lacan challenges at base the contention that death – whatever, if any, significance be granted to it – gives meaning to life. Death, for Lacan, is meaningless, and the view that it renders life meaningful is a defensive reaction formation to this glimpse of the void. Confronting life's Real meaninglessness is the basis of Lacan's ethical position.

Lacan's Antigone is therefore inhuman without being divine, driven by an amoral imperative that sets her apart from everyone, including other would-be protesters, and that refuses the name of martyrdom. Lacan focuses on those same lines in Antigone's self-justification which were highlighted by Hegel to the scandal of other commentators, notably Goethe:

never, had children of whom I was the mother or had my husband perished and been mouldering there, would I have taken on myself this task, in defiance of the citizens. In virtue of what law do I say this? If my husband had died, I could have had another, and a child by another man, if I had lost the first, but with my mother and my father in Hades below, I could never have another brother.[54]

Lacan neither seeks an explanatory cultural framework for these lines nor attempts to read them as symptomatic of any principled stance but instead emphasizes their unintelligibility as indicating the radical singularity of Antigone's desire.[55] She dies for nothing else and in no other name. Antigone incarnates 'the death that is without meaning, the sheer terror of the negative that contains nothing positive, nothing that fills it with a content' – Hegel's characterization of Terror.[56] Ideological appropriations of the figure attempt, by referring to a big Other as transcendental guarantor of meaning, to evade the truth revealed in her. The 'natural law' to which Lacan's Antigone bears witness at the cost of her unliveable life is only that desire is finally autonomous, antisocial and destructive of its human host.

Lacan turns to the lament in which Antigone, on her way to be walled up, regrets all that she has lost and bids farewell to life – a key passage for such influential modern commentators as Hölderlin and Heidegger, who see in it the human consciousness become superhuman in its recognition of and refusal to yield before the nothingness of death and humanity's aloneness within the universe.[57] In my opinion Lacan's reading pays more attention to her aesthetic context in the ritual of classical tragedy (some critics would dispute this). For him, the speaking Antigone here shifts from the unconscious to the conscious and from the Real to the symbolic; past the point of no return and therefore released from the drive, she becomes recognizably, intelligibly human and regrets all that she has lost. She is pathetic and sublimely beautiful in her suffering, and it is this spectacle which leads the chorus (and with it the audience) to the catharsis that will allow them to resume their ordinary, liveable lives with their own destruction drive partly purged, partly satisfied. The *éclat* of her sacrifice dazzles, beauty (*le beau*) intervening at a higher level than, though in a similar way to, utilitarian moral concerns (*le bien*) in distracting us from the Real to redirect our own energies back into familiar paths and familiar evasions.[58] Her drama as Lacan tells it comprises two acts: the 'ethical' drive to death, followed by the 'moral' rehabilitation into, and consequent regeneration of, the established order. Lacan's assessment of the figure's capacity for enabling workable, durable resistance to that order is therefore lukewarm. Insofar as she has a social and political function, Antigone is normality's sacrifice to itself.

Thus Lacan undermines the various moralizing and political traditions that have hailed Antigone as hero or martyr. Her actions' significance in his view lies in the fact that the working of the destruction drive is revealed most clearly by the subject's choice of a course of action which is not merely disallowed but inexplicable and foreclosed. Maintaining one's choice unto death nevertheless has ethical force – more precisely, the ethical force with which Lacan is concerned lies in just that perseverance. Human living requires us to accept any number of compromises, substitutions and detours in relation to our desire. Lacan draws on Lévi-Strauss's anthropological theorizing to argue that the incest taboo formalizes a pattern in which desire is prohibited from attaining its object and sidetracked towards other goals; this pattern is that of life in society. To insist on one's desire is therefore to resist not just a given society but sociality itself. Similarly, although dying is unavoidable, the preference for death over giving up on one's desire is a short circuit which extracts the subject from the self-reproducing cycle of social existence and, further, allows it to symbolize social liberation or revolution for others. It is therefore through its structure and not primarily through its content that Antigone's demand is unassimilable for the dominant order. As Žižek comments:

With regard to this relation between drive and desire, we could perhaps risk a small rectification of the Lacanian axiom of the psychoanalytic ethic 'not to cede one's desire': is not desire as such already a certain yielding, a kind of compromise formation, a metonymic displacement retreat, a defense against intractable drive? 'To desire' *means* to give way on the drive – insofar as we follow Antigone and 'do not give way on our desire,' do we not precisely step out of the domain of desire, do we not shift from the modality of desire into the modality of pure drive?[59]

This theoretical clarification, however, raises the question, central to Lacan's work, of the intimate relation between desire as social formation and the destruction drive as absolute. Subjects do not generally go to their deaths in the name of the 'pulsion de mort' (however that drives them unconsciously) but in that of some desire locatable within the symbolic and imaginary fields: the fields of familiar, intelligible, social and political discourse. In Seminar VII Lacan judges the good for which subjects are willing to die to be a mere camouflage for the death drive, consonant with his wider analysis of 'the good' as a means of keeping us at a distance from our ultimate object of desire. The ideological effects that interest him concern the parameters that in a given culture shape our approach to the ethical sphere – responses such as guilt, ideals such as forgiveness, neighbour-love or *mesura*, goals such as happiness or the common good. In contrast, Žižek himself has been an important analyst of the psychic dimensions of, in particular, capitalism and some variants of state communism or socialism: forms of government and economic organization which reach far into the mind. Individuals' refusal or failure to give up on their desire may have far-reaching collective implications.

Žižek conspicuously revives the revolutionary potential on which Lacan's pessimism casts doubt. In the absence of a positive, intelligible moral frame-work, Žižek's Antigone becomes a figure of pure negation.[60] This figure has the potential to ground an extremist understanding of resistance or revo-lution that draws on the writings of Robespierre, Marat and revolutionary socialism, allying itself with 1793 and the Terror against the bourgeois lib-eral republicanism that has dominated leftist thought and understandings of the Revolution in recent decades.[61] In an environment where all rational discourse has been appropriated by institutional authorities, resistance will be inarticulate, even incomprehensible, but not necessarily unethical in the broader sense (compare the Newspeak of Orwell's *Nineteen Eighty-Four*). Though in one perspective negating the natural law tradition, therefore, in her inherent disruptiveness Žižek's Antigone rejoins it. As Fraisse points out, 'in the constitution of a collective, nothing is more unsettling than natural law: "It is indispensable for establishing order . . . but seems to enclose a principle that destroys all order." . . . Natural law is only ever invoked so as to resist established laws.'[62] In spite of his emphasis on the singular form it takes for each individual, Lacan's notion of *jouissance* as driving every human subject without exception beyond society is itself an instance of natural law (his and Žižek's use of Antigone as exemplar is traditional in this respect). The more inconceivable within dominant systems of meaning the desires expressed become, the more revolutionary force they contain, for revolution (as distinct from rebellion) challenges the philosophical and discursive bases of power as well as its established forms. The incomprehensible nature of Antigone's decision to bury her brother therefore enhances the political radicalism of an action that might otherwise be merely defiant and thus subservient to the hegemonic order (hence Anouilh's insubordinate heroine becomes in a Lacanian view a 'petite Antigone fasciste', a 'little fascist Antigone').[63] Antigone's is 'a decision (to kill, to risk or to lose one's own life) made in absolute solitude, not covered by the big Other . . . [although] extra-moral it is not "immoral"'.[64] Thus the unrepresentable nature of revolutionary desire functions for Žižek as a trope for a sublime which, as in Lacan's writing, is twinned with the abject. Whereas in Lacan's Seminar VII this twinning serves to divorce the notion of the sublime from the idea of the good to which it once seemed naturally wedded (hence the treatment of Kant and Sade as complementary), in Žižek's writing the abject-sublime is recuperated to a positive moral value broadly associated with the political left which he aims to regenerate. In Žižek's interpretation, Lacanian ethics rescues leftist politics from its own timorous bad faith by permitting a move from theoretical to practical anti-humanism. Thanks to Althusser the left has long had a structuralist, hence inhuman vision of man, but has supplemented that with a traditional, humanist ethics; Lacanian ethics, grounded in man's inhumanity, will allow socialism's true radical potential to emerge.[65] As the monstrous neighbour (*prochain*, *Nebenmensch*) in whom we recognize our inhumanity, Antigone is the parable for this new (in)human – and thus for the first time properly human – order.

ANTIGONE'S DESIRE

'Sophocles' *Antigone* will not suffer from Lacan,' affirms Steiner, for whom the play uniquely expresses 'all the principal constants' conditioning both conflict and 'positive intimacy' in human life.[66] The great humanist's protest against this anti-heroic Antigone is echoed by writers within other intellectual traditions, some of whom claim Lacanian heritage. Steiner's intimate conflicts are fivefold: 'the confrontation of men and of women; of age and of youth; of society and of the individual; of the living and the dead; of men and of god(s)'.[67] His list of ethical encounters is markedly apolitical, lacking the struggles which oppose class to class, people to lords, subjects to rulers, nobles to kings. He reminds us of other political aspects, however: firstly, of the fact that Antigone struggles against an antagonist – Creon, often said to be absent from Lacan's account; secondly, of dimensions of struggle not foregrounded by Lacan. I highlight here two such, championed by important thinkers: gender, in Irigaray's writing, and sexuality, in Butler's.

For both thinkers, Lacan plays a part akin to Creon's, since both argue that he sacrifices Antigone to vested interests which, for all his anti-establishment rhetoric, are institutionally entrenched. Antigone's double exclusion, from the political order by Hegel and from the symbolic order by Lacan, is thus itself a political fact to be interrogated (Butler actually distances Creon from the persecuting role, attributing it to the philosophers). Lacan consummates this exclusion. When he makes Antigone exemplify the death drive, consequently to self-destruct on the impulse of apolitical, unconscious forces, he severely restricts her potential impact on the mutually interwoven spheres of society, culture, representation and politics. Butler and Irigaray, contrastingly, view the necessity of Antigone's death not as ontological – necessary in all possible worlds – but contingent – necessary in particular worlds only. They consider Lacanian psychoanalysis to be guilty of elevating specific cultural norms to universal laws. For both, Lacan is at once enabling and frustratingly constraining: he shows how the symbolic functions 'to transcendentalize its claims', 'enforcing an appearance of its universality but having no mandate outside itself that might serve as a transcendental ground for its own functioning', yet then appears to accept at face value the transcendence of certain claims, awarding them Real or universal status.[68] Irigaray and Butler attend to the radical content of Antigone's claims, thus restoring her from the field of drive to that of desire, from Real to symbolic and imaginary, brute fact to alterable state. They urge political realignment in the 'real world' of public policy, also for the sake of Creon, whose fall is inseparable from Antigone's.

For Irigaray, Antigone is the spokeswoman of an essential femininity excluded from the twin male orders of discourse and government. Her early work highlights the figure's tragic irony.[69] Antigone acts out of fidelity to a feminine ethics represented by the maternal genealogy, burying her mother's son; however, this solidarity with the maternal will lead her to reproduce her mother's fate, hanging herself. Her self-affirmation as a woman is thus also her self-destruction, a result of the foreclosure of an alternative, feminine order. Not Antigone but patriarchy embodies the death drive. Irigaray's more recent work, however, changes this focus. In the 1997 *Être deux*, Antigone has a valid order of her own: that of 'concrete singularity' and 'a concrete collectivity'.[70] The artificial world of men, in self-imposed alienation from this natural order, is caught in near-psychosis, incoherence, violent destruction and self-destruction. Creon dies – all the men die – but Antigone lives and speaks. She institutes a language, an ethics and a politics grounded in the imaginary, ontologically prior and necessary to man's merely symbolic fabrication.[71] In Irigaray's own writing style as well as in her arguments, Antigone achieves an intelligible place from which to state what remain extraordinarily far-reaching claims on patriarchal forms.

Butler's position is closer to Irigaray's than she herself allows.[72] For Butler, Antigone's claim is to be allowed to mourn a relation based in the brother–sister incest to which Hegel and Lacan seem strangely blind. Antigone therefore argues for social recognition of a relation and a love whose transgressive nature otherwise condemns them, and those implicated in them, to the outlawry of symbolic death. Butler criticizes Lacanian psychoanalysis for its heterosexism. She points to its failure to address 'how new forms of kinship can and do arise on the basis of the incest taboo'.[73] In place of the revolutionism endorsed by Žižek, for whom Antigone is the perverse constitutive exception (foundational but excluded) of the new order to come, Butler proposes a Foucauldian variant of evolution. The incest taboo, like all prohibitions, works by inadvertently proliferating the sins and crimes it forbids. Butler envisages that these illegitimate practices may give rise to changes in actual laws if presented as Antigone articulates them, that is to say if 'the perverse or the impossible emerges in the language of the law and makes its claim precisely there in the sphere . . . that depends on its exclusion or pathologization'.[74] The ethical-political act here becomes that of the faithful traitor: Antigone enacts the law and carries out her father's orders but 'in aberrant form, transmitting them loyally and betraying them by sending them in directions they were never intended to travel'.[75] One might, then, view Antigone as a 'queer heroine'; however, Butler only partially endorses this.[76] Unlike the later Irigaray, Butler maintains Antigone's unrepresentability and impossibility even while insisting that she holds the potential for effective change. Indeed, in this account Antigone's capacity to help legitimize new forms of attachment and desire depends on her continuing to challenge the established order, thus on her marginality. If Antigone's specific predicament and claim cannot come to full realization within the present (or perhaps any) symbolic order, Butler nevertheless stresses how Sophocles' text strains linguistic and conceptual structures to achieve another order that teeters on the brink of representability. Butler's demonstration that Antigone can and does speak her unthinkable, horrifying desire importantly replaces her claim within the political sphere.[77] Where literary language innovates, cultural and legal orders may follow. Those who fail to listen, notably Hegel and Lacan, reject the intellectual and political challenges that Antigone embodies, condemning her to sterility and to death.

A MEDIEVAL ANTIGONE?

It is fair to say that the medieval Antigone has little of the immense cultural resonance with which the nineteenth and twentieth centuries invested the figure, though she is not without political significance. Medieval Antigones are drawn not primarily from Sophocles but from Euripides' *Phoenician Women* via Statius' *Thebaid*, texts which show more interest in the problems of statecraft and a greater focus on the male characters. Antigone here does not die, nor is she always the instigator of Polyneices' burial, and the obligations to which she responds are typically those of a daughter as much as or more than of a sister.[78] Her relative marginality is illustrated by her omission from the major retelling of the Statian Theban story that is Boccaccio's *Teseida*. In these predominantly political narratives, what place is there for the Lacanian ethical?

We cannot assert that versions in which Antigone does not act or die necessarily lack either a place between two deaths or the death drive. In the mid twelfth-century *Roman de Thèbes*, for instance, Antigone plays no part in the burial episode, where the focus is on the Greek king Adrastus' two daughters, married to princes slain in the battle against Thebes (the elder sister being Polyneices' wife). These women decide to commit suicide, before consenting instead to the prayers of the assembled bereaved Greek women to lead them to find and bury their menfolk's bodies. The burial episode thus takes place under the shadow of a suspended suicide, with the exhausted women dragging themselves to the battlefield; however, it is also a mass event and one which earns official protection in the shape of Theseus duke of Athens, whom the women (led by Adrastus) meet on their way. Only 'Creon le vieil, qu'est assotez' (l. 10008; 'Senile old Creon') rejects their claims, and he is swiftly defeated by Theseus. All the bodies are buried, but the earth itself rejects Eteocles and Polyneices. It proves impossible to prevent them from fighting each other even once dead: their very ashes attempt combat, and Theseus finally has them buried in a single sarcophagus to struggle eternally (ll. 10187–90). More strikingly still, the entire history of the *Roman de Thèbes* is one of *entre-deux-morts* after the baby Oedipus, whom his father has ordered to be killed, is secretly abandoned alive by servants who tell their king, 'Se vos poez des vis guarder, / Ne vos estuet les morz doter' (ll. 127–8; 'If you can keep yourself safe from the living, you need not fear the dead'), thus identifying the child as a *mort vivant*, and placing the story arising from his survival 'between two deaths'. Whereas the passage between ethics and politics may be contested within modern treatments of the

Theban story, in this medieval account it is an urgent and unavoidable question.

No medieval 'Antigone' as such, then. However, in this book I shall argue that figures comparable to the modern Antigone arise *entre-deux-morts* in numerous medieval literary works: Roland, Galehot, the lords and ladies of *ubi sunt* works, the Pearl-Maiden, Blanche and Alceste. Ethics and politics intertwine in various ways, suggestive of different aspects of the Antigones I have discussed above. My explorations, though broadly held together by a Lacanian approach, will therefore not be limited to Lacan's own questions or answers on the subject.

THE STRUCTURE OF THIS BOOK

I end this introduction with a brief overview of the structure and contents of the following chapters. Chapters 1 and 2 discuss the relationship between the death drive and heroic desires – what the masculine hero desires and what is desired of him – in narratives belonging to the two major secular narrative genres current in the early period of French literature, *chanson de geste* in the first chapter, chivalric romance in the second. 'Roland and the second death' focuses on the eleventh-century Anglo-Norman Oxford *Chanson de Roland*, today the most iconic of medieval French works, comparing it to other redactions. After discussing the 'second death' and its link to revolution and to apocalypse, this chapter explores the hero's route towards death as a Lacanian ethical act that shatters existing symbolic and political structures, but which is afterwards appropriated for ideological use by a particular political order. Chapter 2, 'The knight as Thing: courtly love in the non-cyclic prose *Lancelot*', concentrates on an early thirteenth-century version of the story of Lancelot and Guinevere, one of the most developed romance narratives. I discuss how this version differs from other major accounts, primarily *Le Chevalier de la Charrette* and *La Mort le roi Artu*. This chapter foregrounds the parallel between the love of Lancelot and Guinevere and that of Galehot and Lancelot. It incorporates extensive reflection on what is meant by 'courtly love', and an exploration of how that love models homosocial relationships within the text without imposing pseudo-heterosexual norms on them. In the third chapter I examine how the official message of mortality, mutability and vulnerability carried by the widespread *ubi sunt* topos is shadowed by a second one affirming the subject's immortality and sovereignty. I concentrate on particular Middle French fixed-form lyrics: Eustache Deschamps's late fourteenth-century courtly Ballade 1457 and François Villon's celebrated mini-sequence, the three 'Ballades du temps jadis' inset in his *Testament* of 1461. Here I show how Villon's ballades progressively bring disintegration upon the sovereign masculine subject which other examples sustain – often, like Deschamps's, in complex ways. A debate between Derrida and Barthes over the phrase 'Je suis mort' completes the perspective.

The remaining two chapters turn to dream poems in Middle English, and to the analysis of the desires expressed by female figures *entre-deux-morts* within male dreams. These poems offer an opportunity to consider male–female relations in a context wider than the heterosexual; they also examine the relationship between the court poet and the prince. Chapter 4, 'Ceci n'est pas une marguerite: anamorphosis in *Pearl*', considers the English poem in the light of the fashionable marguerite topos employed in contemporary and slightly earlier French-language court writing, arguing that these writings share a discursive field regardless of language difference. Through Lacan's discussion of anamorphosis or distorted perspective, I examine *Pearl*'s problematic negotiation of religious and courtly ideologies. Chapter 5, 'Becoming woman in Chaucer: on ne naît pas femme, on le devient en mourant', contrasts the dead ladies at the centre of Chaucer's *Book of the Duchess* and Prologue to the *Legend of Good Women* in the light of anthropological discussions of memorialization rites. This chapter links the difficulties of reading the notoriously monotonous *Legend* to its identification of the poetic project as a living death.

One definition that Lacan advances of the Real is 'ce qui revient toujours à la même place' ('that which always comes back to the same place').[79] Though I treat here of the Real – among other things – that is not my aim for this book.

CHAPTER I

Roland and the second death

Reading medieval French writing, one is struck by how widely known and how influential was the story of Roncevaux. Other *chansons de geste* return tirelessly to the subject; Roland's death is the foundational event of the *cycle du roi*, the group of around twenty *chansons* centred on Charlemagne's foreign campaigns. The conventional dating of the Oxford text to the end of the eleventh century makes it one of the earliest surviving works of French literature, while the rhymed tradition was still being recopied in the fifteenth century. Roland himself epitomizes a powerful and disturbing conception of heroism: that of a violence mesmerizing in its ferocity, its energy and its intimate connection to death. We might have little difficulty in accepting such destructiveness in a villain (such as Ganelon), but in a hero it requires more ethical exploration. Most discussions of the *Chanson de Roland* which recognize the hero's extreme violence have taken one of two paths. Many place it within cultural contexts – Christian, warrior (Germanic, feudal), or legal – said to consider such violence familiar and justifiable though lost to us today. Numerous others show the failings of Roland's moral or strategic judgement, considering the text either critical or tragic.[1] Valuable though such readings are, I wish to concentrate on the heroic desires expressed in and by Roland. For his combination of high energy and activity with a magnetic pull towards death and general catastrophe is hardly unique, but typifies culturally significant notions of heroism and of the hero. 'Death is the lifestyle to which epic warriors are dedicated.'[2] I shall focus on Roland as a figure 'between two deaths', with particular emphasis on the destructive violence which he incarnates. Working with Lacan's distinction between two versions of the death drive, I argue for a revolutionary impulse at the heart of the *Chanson de Roland* and of the *chanson de geste* genre more widely, against the influential representation of *chansons de geste* as bastions of social and aesthetic conservatism.[3] I shall further investigate how this revolutionary position is put to various ideological uses within surviving *Roland* texts, and how they handle differently the forces of destruction, revolution and containment.[4] In his death-directed insistence Roland bears comparison with Lacan's Antigone; and in consecrating a substantial proportion of its text to the aftermath of its protagonist's death, the *Chanson de Roland* resembles Sophocles' *Antigone*.

The first section of this chapter focuses on Lacan's discussion of the death drive in Seminar VII, establishing a framework that brings to bear Sade and Freud. After this my analysis will bear on the assonanced *Roland* tradition up to and including the episode of Roland's death. This tradition, dated to the late eleventh or early to mid twelfth century, is represented by what is today much the most famous version, the so-called Oxford *Roland* preserved in the Bodleian Library's manuscript Digby 23 (hereafter O), and by the first part of Venice 4 (V4). The remaining five substantial surviving texts (six if we include V4, which begins in assonance but ends in rhyme) preserve a version in rhyme, dated after 1180 and thought to represent a *remaniement* in which the earlier, assonanced tradition was adapted to late twelfth-century tastes, interests and political imperatives. The assonanced and rhymed traditions display substantial narrative differences, in particular in the aftermath of Roland's death. Each surviving individual version also constitutes a distinct text by virtue not only of its particular wording but also of its date, provenance, dialect and the selection of other works with which it was copied or bound.[5] The third section of this chapter compares some of these different versions within the framework of a contrast between assonanced and rhymed traditions, concentrating on their distinctive uses of repetition as reflecting their dissimilar thematic concerns and relating these to the two varieties of death drive. I draw again on Freud's *Beyond the Pleasure Principle* as a work linking violence and repetition, the characteristic content and form of *chansons de geste*. The final section returns to O to focus on the narrative following Roland's death, in which various meanings are ascribed to that death. Overall, I argue that the assonanced *Roland* up to and including Roland's death (I shall refer to this as the 'first part' of the text) enshrines an open-ended destructiveness which releases energies that the latter parts of the assonanced text press into the ideological service of particular political orders representing themselves as at once innovative and traditionalist. The rhymed tradition attempts, and fails, to revise this destructiveness out of existence. When using the term '*Chanson de Roland*', I therefore envisage a work comprising both the revolutionary impetus and the response that contains and exploits that impetus. The elements of this composite are concretely realized in different ways by the various surviving texts. I therefore disagree with those critics who explain the *Roland*'s discontinuities by positing a process of textual accretion or the gradual accumulation of further episodes, as well as with those who treat the Oxford text as a seamless whole working consistently towards a single ideological end.

The core narrative of what I am calling the 'first part' of the *Chanson de Roland* goes as follows: in Charlemagne's long war against the Saracens of Spain, King Marsile of Saragossa, the last unconquered Muslim city, offers to capitulate, secretly intending to renege once the invaders have returned home. The Frankish barons wonder whom to send on the risky mission to negotiate. Roland, Charlemagne's heroic nephew, nominates his stepfather Ganelon, who promptly swears vengeance on his stepson. Ganelon plots with the Saracens to ensure that when the Franks withdraw, Roland, his friend Oliver and the twelve peers (Charlemagne's major barons) will lead the rearguard, which the Saracens will then ambush at Roncevaux. During the first assault, Oliver asks Roland to blow his horn, the oliphant, to recall the emperor and the main body; Roland refuses. The Franks repel the first Saracen wave but gradually succumb before the second. Oliver now rejects Roland's proposal that the oliphant be sounded, but Archbishop Turpin (one of the twelve peers) insists and Charlemagne returns. The Saracens are put to flight but all the Franks are dead, including Roland and Oliver.

The second part shows much greater variation in the different texts. In O, Charlemagne mourns and takes revenge on the fleeing Saracens and on the African emir Baligant, Marsile's overlord, who arrives with a large army. On his return to Aix-la-Chapelle, Charlemagne informs Aude, Roland's betrothed and Oliver's sister, of Roland's death; she laments and dies. At trial, Ganelon's plea that he is innocent of treachery is accepted by Charlemagne's council. He is nevertheless convicted and sentenced to death after a judicial combat between his kinsman Pinabel and Charlemagne's champion Thierry d'Anjou, who wins with divine assistance. The rhymed tradition will be discussed further below.

DEATH DRIVE AND LIFE CYCLE

Lacan returns on many occasions to claims advanced by Freud in *Beyond the Pleasure Principle*: that '*the aim of all life is death*' and that organisms consequently seek to die.[6] His engagement with the ensuing hypothesis of a 'death drive' or 'death instinct' runs over many years, and he continues throughout his career to redefine both terms. In Seminar VII, his discussion centres on a lengthy quotation from Pope Pius VI's harangue to the heroine in Sade's *Juliette*, in which the pontiff expounds the necessity of vice in the universe.[7] Sade's speaker distinguishes three possible ratios of vice to virtue, and explains their cosmic consequences. He firstly contemplates the common ideal in which war, conflict and crime are abolished. This state he dismisses as 'une trop parfaite harmonie' ('a too perfect harmony') bringing about a loss of cosmic vitality – 'repos absolu', in Lacan's phrase ('absolute rest'). A better alternative is the 'parfait équilibre' ('perfect balance') of Horace's *rerum concordia discors*, where crime and disorder provide a necessary counterweight to peace and harmony, troubling the universe sufficiently to maintain dynamism and hence life. This second notion is linked to the life cycle; personal death and such destructive phenomena as war and famine allow room for and give rise to new life, and are therefore conceived as normal and useful parts of that cycle. Building on the relation between conflict and vitality, however, Sade's text poses a third possibility, namely a destructiveness represented by the notion of an ideal murder that would obliterate even the victim's 'seconde [vie]' ('second life'), beyond the possibility of regeneration. This destructiveness, Sade's pontiff asserts, represents the true will of Nature; serving that will requires 'des destructions bien plus entières... bien plus complètes que celles que nous pouvons opérer' ('far more total destructions... destructions much more complete than those we are able to accomplish'). The everyday life cycle is thus encapsulated conceptually within another, apocalyptic and ideal, by definition outside human ken since it would involve the destruction of mankind. This super-cycle Sade hopes to conjure up by committing what the dominant order deems 'unnatural' acts, their sterility blocking the normal cycle's self-reproduction. In fact, however, it is the super-cycle that represents Nature's essential will which is (according to Sade) to exercise her highest faculty, that of creation; a faculty which human virtue and social management, by preserving *rerum concordia discors*, impede. In this context 'death' is reconceived as a qualitative concept referring to the stagnation of Nature's creative faculty. For organic growth and development to move only within known patterns equates to mortal stasis; this must be opposed by the vivifying desire to torch the earth in order that in this newly made-virgin territory an entirely novel form of life may take root.

Lacan uses the Sade passage to illustrate how Freud's work on the death drive contains two distinct modes.[8] Thus, of the three conditions differentiated in Sade's text, Lacan distinguishes only two, conflating Sade's 'trop parfaite harmonie', in which cosmic dynamism is lost, with the *rerum concordia discors*, the dynamic interaction of forces in equilibrium (this conflation is entirely in spirit with Sade's polemical thrust). Both are aligned with the pacifying 'principe de Nirvâna, ou d'anéantissement' ('Nirvana or annihilation principle'), a reference to a theory advanced by Freud, who puts it thus: 'The dominating tendency of mental life, and perhaps of nervous life in general, is the effort to reduce, to keep constant or to remove internal tension due to stimuli (the "Nirvana principle", to borrow a term from Barbara Low) – a tendency which finds expression in the plea-sure principle.'[9] According to Lacan's analysis, Sade's 'repos absolu' and 'équilibre universel' can be equated in their opposition to Freud's 'pulsion de destruction' ('destruction drive'), which 'doit être au-delà de la tendance au retour à l'inanimé' ('must be beyond the instinct to return to the state of equilibrium of the inanimate sphere'). This is a truly active principle, crackling with energy. Sade's imagined heroic vice finds echoes in Lacan's terminology, as he refers to 'une volonté de destruction directe' which 'met en cause tout ce qui existe' ('a direct will to destruction' which 'challenges everything that exists'). It is simultaneously a 'volonté de recommencer à nouveaux frais' and a 'volonté d'Autre-chose' ('will to make a fresh start' and a 'will for an Other-thing'), for something outside the known world. I shall return below to Lacan's interpretation of the destruction drive's regenerative urge and to the notion of a super-cycle. For the moment I observe only that Sade's characteristic climactic rhetoric and sexual themes highlight the element in the destruction drive of what Lacan calls *jouissance*: understood in this case to indicate an enjoyable pain or unbearably painful satisfaction, a paradox incompatible with the pleasure principle, which works to keep our stimulations and frustrations at a manageable level, and us at a distance from our desires and hence from death. Leading the subject it inhabits towards *jouissance*, towards an inhuman *Autre-chose* beyond the paths of liveable life, the destruction drive introduces that subject into the *entre-deux-morts*. But not into death or Nirvana; as that which impels one who is dead nevertheless to go on, the destruction drive is, according to Žižek, 'the Freudian term for immortality', 'that which prevents you from dying'.[10]

ROLAND BETWEEN TWO DEATHS: THE ASSONANCED *CHANSON DE ROLAND*

Roland in the assonanced texts can be considered to be 'between two deaths' in the sense of passing beyond the bounds of normal life and committing himself to death, although it is disputable at what point passage occurs.[11] From one perspective he has always been there, for his brand of heroism commits him to risking and defying death. As Ganelon tells Blancandrin, 'chascun jur de mort si s'abandunet' (O, 390; 'every day he gives himself up to death').[12] Daily provocation of the grim reaper is bound to meet a response sooner or later, thus all Ganelon has to do to make Roland die is to let the hero have his head.[13] He goes further by providing his nephew with what appears (and, in a double irony, in the second part of the work ultimately turns out) to be a gratifying scenario inviting him to fulfil fantasies of his grandeur, a stage on which to perform and enhance the *los* ('reputation') he has constructed through his previous activities and declarations. On the other hand, dying does not seem to feature on Roland's horizon early in the poem. Death's role in the scenarios he imagines occurring is rather to demonstrate his immunity from dying than finally to crown his career. If Roland fails to understand that he may actually die, then it is debatable whether his heroism per se places him 'between two deaths'. For Lacan, however, Antigone's *éclat* is determined by her refusal or inability to let death divert her from her goal, combined with the audience's knowledge that she is fated to die. In these respects Roland too is condemned from his first appearance in the poem.

Or perhaps it is in the first horn scene, when Roland refuses Oliver's request to call Charlemagne back to rescue the rearguard, that he crosses 'la limite que la vie humaine ne saurait pas trop longtemps franchir', beyond Ate ('the limit that human life can only briefly cross').[14] Oliver appears to think that this was their last chance of escaping death, commenting immediately afterwards that 'Ki ceste fait, jamais n'en ferat altre' (O, 1105; 'whoever serves in this rearguard will never take part in another'). Oliver's words focus on the warriors' inability to live to fight another day, referring to a cycle associated with the return of Charlemagne. He envisages the preferable outcome of the present conflict not as the final annihilation of the enemy but as an ongoing pattern of skirmishes where the priority is to husband one's resources for the next encounter. Time stretches forward in endless variations on the present situation; a pattern broken by Roland's disastrous resolve. Oliver's challenge to Roland represents the hero's behaviour as unorthodox and transgressive, underlining the problems it poses to the established political order inasmuch as that depends on repeat performances. Roland has gone too far.

Roland's own interest in the first horn scene is couched in quite other terms. Each speech in which he rejects Oliver's proposal begins by referring to an impossible dishonour expressed in negative conditionals and subjunctives, before moving on to contemplate violence in the indicative with a variation between future and present tenses which suggests both immediacy and resolve. Against these Oliver's future-tense assurances of Charles's return seem weakly hypothetical. Roland's concern during the first horn scene is not with corporeal or cyclic survival but with his *los*, a concept in which the prestige and potency of such collectives as his kin group and country, *France dulce*, are harnessed to his grandiose self-construction. This extended *los* is embodied in an apparently indestructible sword as well as in a physical body which seems impervious to outside forces, as witness his repeated miraculous feats in the text's back story. He views the Saracen attack as an undeclinable invitation to re-perform this *los*. Roland both invests fully in the present situation and moment ('Nus remeindrum en estal en la place', O, 1108; 'We shall stand firm in the field') and (relatedly) inhabits some ethically if not metaphysically other place, neither of which fits with Oliver's vision. Thus Roland's very rejection of the possibility of dying where dying is taken to mean defeat, as it does for Oliver, places him *entre-deux-morts*.

Roland's desire correlates with various collective reference points. Reputation and word, and the ability to sustain those in action, are central cultural values in a range of medieval texts. Roland does not distinguish between his personal fame and the prestige of his kin, country, emperor or religion. (I leave aside for the moment the fact that Roland's deeds will finally be recuperated in the public interest thanks to those to which they inspire Charlemagne.) From another perspective, however, Roland's desire denies the collective. He recognizes only his personal *los* as the master-signifier for the various values he claims to represent. Oliver's intervention makes clear that Roland's pursuit of this *los* exceeds the broad cultural value system and baronial norms, whether through the absolute priority he accords *los* or because of the strategies by which he pursues it. Roland's *los* is, in Lacan's terms, the singular desire through which the destruction drive operates in Roland. We would therefore expect the dominant culture to view it as an ethical anomaly: 'C'est parce que l'homme prend le mal pour le bien, parce que quelque chose d'au-delà des limites de l'*Atè* est devenu pour Antigone son bien à elle, un bien qui n'est pas celui de tous les autres, qu'elle se dirige πρὸς ἄταν' ('It is because man mistakes evil for the good, because something beyond the limits of Ate has become Antigone's good, namely, a good that is different from everyone else's, that she goes toward, πρὸς ἄταν').[15] Correspondingly, Roland's concern with *los* exceeds the cultural systems that give *los* meaning. His desire is therefore given no coherent rationale within the text. We can understand Oliver, Turpin and Charles, but concerning Roland we must ask, with generations of critics, 'What does he really want?' According to Žižek, we pose this question only when what the subject claims to want is fundamentally unintelligible within established norms, so that the question already precludes the asker's identification with the subject about whom the question is posed.[16] Roland cannot, surely, want only the escalating destruction, the intensified conflict and violence which his every decision calls forth? Critical debates over the ethical and strategic value of Roland's actions often refer decisively to the fact that both Roland himself and his collective ultimately benefit from his decisions; but I wish here to emphasize actions and moments as they occur, without the valuation accorded by retrospection. The point in a Lacanian framework is the rich destructiveness which affects both the hero and his environment. Self-destruction is the final logic of the death drive, the sapping of established norms its ethical effect.[17]

Hence in the second horn scene Roland chooses, as he always does, the option which offers the maximum potential for continuing violence and conflict. The specificity of his position emerges when we compare it to Oliver's and Turpin's. Oliver interprets the situation facing the rearguard as not only personal death and the ruin of Charles's army, but the end of an epoch:

> Vostre proëcce, Rollant, mar la veïmes!
> Karles li magnes de nos n'avrat aïe.
> N'ert mais tel home desqu'a Deu juïse.
> Vos i murrez e France en ert hunie.
> Oi nus defalt la leial cumpaignie:
> Einz la vespree ert gref la departie.
>
> (O, 1731–6)

(Your prowess, Roland, in an evil hour we saw it! Charlemagne will never have aid from us. There will be no such man till Judgement Day. You will die here and France will be dishonoured for it. Now our loyal comradeship is failing us: before evening the parting will be grievous.)

Oliver claims that an entire order has been destroyed by Roland's insistence on performing his 'proëcce'. There will be no further fighting, no re-cycling, for the soldiers who die at Roncevaux. This is the end of an era not to be renewed, since the man at its centre is unique (O, 1733). This devastation has been wrought by Roland's 'folie' or 'estultie', which, whatever their more positive senses, are contrasted by Oliver to the 'vasselage par sens' (O, 1724; 'wise baronage') which would have enabled the warriors to continue their established pattern of serving Charlemagne.[18] Oliver's criticism is clarified by a notion that Freud floats in *Beyond the Pleasure Principle*, a text rooted in the psychic and social aftermath of extreme military violence: that of an improper 'short circuit' in the organism's natural and necessary path towards death (see p. 224 below, n. 37). Roland, by short-circuiting the Christian soldiers' natural trajectory, has broken the cycle which (according to Oliver) would otherwise have led to their renewal in a future guard. Roland's actions, in his companion's perspective, have precluded not only personal survival and biological progeny, but also the more significant possibility of a future generation of symbolic sons, since Oliver implies that no adequate substitutes will step forward to take the place of the deceased. By refusing to allow Roland to conclude the contracted marriage with his sister Aude (O, 1719–21), Oliver expresses his sense of Roland's sterility, his opposition to (re)generation and reproduction: he has achieved the destruction to which Sade aspired, destroying 'la régénération résultant du cadavre' ('the regeneration resulting from the corpse'), its second earthly life.[19] Roland has broken the bond between them, fatally. 'Quant je'l vos dis, n'en feïstes nïent' (O, 1708; 'When I told you to do it, you did nothing at all'). Oliver's famous pragmatism therefore articulates a sense that the special kind of death to which Roland has brought the Franks represents final collective ending and defeat – a form of apocalypse. This sense of life's trajectory short-circuited, with consequent denial of renewal, is an important aspect of the *entre-deux-morts*. Compare Butler's discussion of Antigone, the *anti-generation*, condemned to sterility no less by Creon than by Lacan, for whom her demand to restructure kinship will have no progeny, and who denies her heroism and her tragedy.[20] This enforced sterility at once fuels, contrasts with and gives the lie to the political and ethical fertility that Antigone's reception history demonstrates. The same is true of Roland: Oliver's challenge is an essential element in his legend.

Archbishop Turpin like Oliver focuses on maintaining a cycle and like Roland imagines continuing violence:

> Li arcevesques les ot cuntrarïer,
> Le cheval brochet des esperuns d'or mer,
> Vint tresqu'a els, si's prist a castïer:
> 'Sire Rollant, e vos, sire Oliver,
> Pur Deu vos pri, ne vos cuntralïez!
> Ja li corners ne nos avreit mester,
> Mais nepurquant si est il asez melz
> Venget li reis, si nus purrat venger:
> Ja cil d'Espaigne n'en deivent turner liez!
> Nostre Franceis i descendrunt a piéd,
> Truverunt nos e morz e detrenchez;

> Leverunt nos en bieres sur sumers,
> Si nus plurrunt de doel e de pitét,
> Enfüerunt en aitres de musters;
> N'en mangerunt ne lu ne porc ne chen.'
> Respunt Rollant: 'Sire, mult dites bien.'
>
> (O, 1737–52)

(The archbishop hears them arguing. He urges on his horse with his pure gold spurs, came up to them and began to rebuke them: 'Lord Roland, and you, Lord Oliver, for God's sake I beg you, do not quarrel! Blowing the horn will be of no help to us, nevertheless it is much better that the king come, and he can avenge us: the men of Spain must not turn away from this spot in gladness! Our Franks will dismount here and find us dead and cut to pieces; they will lift us on biers onto packhorses, and will weep for us in sorrow and pity. They will bury us in churches' hallowed ground; no wolf, pig or dog will eat of us.' Roland replied, 'Lord, you speak very well.')

Turpin, unlike either hero, is concerned for the warriors' souls, whose passage into the afterlife seemingly requires proper ritual burial and military revenge. The further fighting he advocates is required to bring about closure, a settling of debts with the enemy. While Oliver looks back to a lost life, Turpin looks forward to a death which is certain in all senses. Though one character is concerned with bodily and the other with spiritual 'second life', both refer to established ideological orders whose goal is self-renewal: military in Oliver's version, religious in Turpin's.

During the second horn scene, the heroes reverse their positions, Roland arguing for Charlemagne's recall while Oliver opposes him in terms that satirize Roland's former insouciance and indict his reckless sacrifice of himself and others by mimicking the arguments, tenses and moods that the latter used in the first horn scene:

> Dist Oliver, 'Vergoigne sereit grant
> E reprover a trestuz voz parenz;
> Iceste hunte dureit al lur vivant.'
>
> (O, 1705–7)

(Said Oliver, 'It would be great dishonour and reproach to all your kin, this shame would last their whole lives.')

This rhetorical change serves to highlight ironically the continuity in each character's position. While Oliver continues to mourn a lost cause, Roland consistently envisages and works towards the renewal of violence and destruction. He observes the dead, expresses sympathy for France which now stands bereft of barons of quality, and regrets that the king is not there:

> E! reis, amis, que vos ici nen estes!
> Oliver, frere, cum le purrum nus faire?
> Cum faitement li manderum nuveles?
>
> (O, 1697–9)

(Oh king, friend, that you are not here! Oliver, brother, how can we do it, how shall we send him word?)

His expression of regret – in the indicative and accompanied immediately by the question of how his new desire may be realized – is entirely different from Oliver's subjunctive lament, 'S'i fust li reis, n'i oüsum damage' (O, 1717; 'Had the king been here we should have suffered no harm' / 'Were the king here we would suffer no harm'). Nor, when faced with Turpin's reasoned justification, does Roland do more than agree with this proposal which suits the desire inhabiting him. His speech may be compared to Antigone's famous lament on her way to the tomb. In Lacan's reading, the conscious human mind speaks here to regret the predictable life and intelligible desires that it might otherwise have had, and that its own unconscious has stolen from it by setting it irretrievably on the path to death. Lacan argues that Antigone at this stage is released from the drive (the plot, once set in motion, carries the death drive for her) to become a figure of sublime pathos: 'pour Antigone, la vie n'est abordable, ne peut être vécue et réflechie, que de cette limite où déjà elle a perdu la vie' ('from Antigone's point of view life can only be approached, can only be lived or thought about, from the place of that limit where her life is already lost').[21] In his ethics of tragedy, the moment that presents audiences with a figure become suddenly, belatedly and movingly human offers them an aesthetic *jouissance* in place of the Real thing, and thus reconciles themselves to their ordinary lives. Roland's moment of reflection is comparable, though unlike Antigone's, his lament precedes an intensifying of the drive to destruction working on and through him.

Whatever his earlier relation to death, Roland definitively commits himself to dying when he cracks his brainpan while blowing the oliphant to recall Charlemagne; he cannot physically recover from this self-inflicted wound. No longer one of the living, he awaits the physical event that will translate him into death proper ('Sans être encore morte, [Antigone] est déjà rayée du monde des vivants'; 'Without yet being dead, [Antigone] is already eliminated from the world of the living').[22] This event, when it occurs, will be exemplary in baronial-Christian terms: self-administering field communion and confessing his sins, Roland is received as God's heavenly vassal by the archangel Michael. Roland's assimilation into an established ideological framework may be considered to close his period between two deaths, a possibility that will be discussed in the final section of this chapter. However, in many other medieval literary works, divine intervention not only fails to resolve but actually gives impetus to questions posed in the course of the text; similarly God's endorsement here crowns the questionable hero's ambiguity and thus perpetuates his *entre-deux-morts* status. Hence the fresh destructive energy released into the poem.[23] Roland's summons will lead to renewed slaughter in the later parts of the narrative and instil new passion into Charlemagne's sluggish person and army ('Par grant irur chevalchet Charlemagnes', O, 1842; 'Charlemagne rides in high fury'). Roland himself is invigorated by his injury. His next assault calls forth Turpin's approval:

> Si cum li cerfs s'en vait devant les chiens,
> Devant Rollant si s'en fuient paiens.
> Dist l'arcevesque: 'Asez le faites ben!
> Itel valor deit aveir chevaler
> Ki armes portet e en bon cheval set.'
>
> (O, 1874–8)

(Just as the stag runs before the hounds, so the pagans flee before Roland. The archbishop says, 'You do very well! A knight who bears arms and sits astride a good horse ought to have such valour.')

The transgressive excess of Roland's prowess sustains the idealized norm of knighthood, with the epic simile at once crowning his achievement and dehumanizing him. The ideal itself lies outside accepted human bounds, in a quasi-animal ferocity. This is the space that Lacan calls the sublime, at once greater and lesser than the ordinary human world. It is in this sense, rather than in one which assimilates him into Christianity or into some acknowledged good, that I would argue for Roland's sublimity.

Roland's insistence carries the entire Frankish army with him:

> Home ki ço set que ja n'avrat prisun
> En tel bataille fait grant defension:
> Pur ço sunt Francs si fiers cume leüns.
>
> (O, 1886–8)

(A man who knows that no prisoners will be taken puts up a stout defence in battle: for this reason the Franks are as fierce as lions.)

Oliver and Turpin both enjoy their own moment between two deaths:

> Oliver sent qu'il est a mort nasfrét,
> De lui venger ja mais ne li ert sez.
> En la grant presse or i fiert cume ber.
> (O, 1965–7)

(Oliver feels that he is mortally wounded, he will never be sated on vengeance. Now he strikes like a baron in the great fray.)

> Turpins de Reins, quant se sent abatut,
> De .IIII. espiez par mi le cors ferut,
> Isnelement li ber resailit sus.
> (O, 2083–5)

(When Turpin of Rheims feels himself struck down, pierced through the body with four spears – instantly the baron springs back up.)

For each subject a mortal wound produces a new lease of ultra-violence. Neither seems to be thinking in terms of cycles or second life here; unlimited destruction occupies the whole horizon of their desire. These *morts vivants*, suspended in their moment of short circuit and wreaking appalling havoc, are Roland's achievement.

The above analysis of the assonanced *Roland* before the hero's death demonstrates that in the Sadean-Lacanian choice between ways in which to die – gently, or otherwise – Nirvana principle and destruction drive are not paths to the same ethical and ideological ends. Sade's discourse has implications beyond the individual or the biological. His life cycles relate also to human societies. The 'normal' cycle, with its emphasis on organic growth, on balance and the avoidance of extremes, implies that human change will occur only slowly through minor variations on established forms: evolution. Sade presents this condition, or ideal, as the projection of the dominant ideology, which proposes it to be necessary if the world is to go on reproducing itself from generation to generation. The hegemonic political order has an interest in identifying itself with the conditions under which it is possible to live at all. Similarly, the ultimate object of his ideal destructiveness is the order regulating social, cultural, moral and spiritual expectations and presenting itself as at once normal and natural. Sade's radical destruction aims to bring down that order in an act of violent revolution. For Sade, therefore, whereas the path of radical destruction leads to the birth of a new order of being, that of the status quo condemns the organism to a lifeless half-existence incapable of true regeneration. In this living death, the 'second death' – the goal at which Sade's ferocities and multiple rejections of reproductive sexuality aim – represents a utopian ideal. 'L'impossible mort' stands for life's lost meaningfulness:[24] death as Real in its regenerative aspect. In this way of thinking, the ethical category of spiritual and moral 'death' is associated with the peaceable rituals of the quotidian, rituals which, by helping to make life liveable, ensure the preservation and reproduction of the dominant order.

Lacan only partly espouses this view and its implications. He exploits Sade for the ideological identification linking the 'natural' human life cycle to the hegemonic order as jointly deathly, and connects both to a redefined version of Freud's Nirvana principle. If he represents equilibrium as stagnation and encourages the connection between destruction, intellectual challenge and psychic perturbation, nevertheless he dismisses faith in the regenerative teleology of the destruction drive. For Lacan, such faith is a 'sublimation créationniste' ('creationist sublimation') by means of which Sade, Freud and indeed all human subjects evade the truth that they themselves have glimpsed.[25] Lacan distinguishes two movements here. On the one hand, Freud's hypothesis of the death drive has an important heuristic function. As the ultimate exception to human order, the death drive can be articulated only by positing a position outside that order. It therefore forces us to reconceive human reality not as the totality of being but as only one among its larger possibilities. We glimpse a beyond to the human world:

La pulsion de mort est à situer dans le domaine historique, pour autant qu'elle s'articule à un niveau qui n'est définissable qu'en fonction de la chaîne signifiante, c'est-à-dire en tant qu'un repère, qui est un repère d'ordre, peut être situé par rapport au fonctionnement de la nature. Il faut quelque chose d'au-delà, d'où elle-même puisse être saisie dans une mémorisation fondamentale, de telle sorte que tout puisse être repris, non pas simplement dans le mouvement des métamorphoses, mais à partir d'une intention initiale.[26]

(The death drive is to be situated in the historical domain; it is articulated at a level that can only be defined as a function to the signifying chain, that is to say, insofar as a reference point, that is a reference point of order, can be situated relative to the functioning of nature. It requires something from beyond whence it may itself be grasped in a fundamental act of memorization, as a result of which everything may be recaptured, not simply in the movement of the metamorphoses but from an initial intention.)

True revolutionary potential, therefore, requires creationist sublimation; it alone is capable of radically eliminating God from the universe, for the Creator paradigm encourages *homo faber* to similarly radical acts of innovation.[27] On the other hand, we must beware of our instinct to transform this logical position into a metaphysical Other Place occupied by a transcendent subject (God, Nature), endowed with purpose and agency, and directing human life and death. This is a fantasy with which we veil both the gulf of the Real and the unacceptable fact (itself an aspect of the Real) that it is only human activity which veils that gulf. Lacan insists on the foreclosure of any forward-looking vision, thereby divorcing the second death (and the destruction drive of which it is an image) from a redemptive 'seconde vie', whether on earth or in the afterlife. At the same moment he notes, ambivalently, the human tendency towards sublimation in this special sense. Intuitions of death's nature and humanity's meta-physical isolation bring detachment and creeping disillusionment under one aspect; under another they vitalize the further ideological engagement which generates further chimeras as well as real, and sometimes valuable, change. Lacan's complex stance is both receptive to revolutionism and wary of endorsing calls to political renewal, especially when backed up by apoc-alyptic violence. This ambivalence must be seen in the context of the Cold War with its nuclear threat, to which Lacan refers several times in Seminar VII. His position is that of one who refuses to love the bomb, in defiance of its promotion by various states. Apocalypse nevertheless represents a crucial mental discipline; as the *mise en cause* of 'all that exists', it gives the measure of Lacan's intellectual ambitions. Unlike Anouilh's Antigone and Charles de Gaulle, he refuses merely to 'dire non'. Negativity has greater reach.

It is self-evident that an emancipated consciousness cannot be achieved without adventuring psychically and ethically beyond the cycle of everyday living and everyday dying sponsored by the hegemonic order. In princi-ple, however, the radical destructiveness of the second death cannot be maintained as such but will give way (or birth) to a new order. Once the revolution achieves a form in which it can be recognized as such – in other words, once a new system has successfully replaced the old – then the prop-erly revolutionary moment is past. Its radical openness has been exchanged for closure, its inchoate swirl by new forms which, however different (or not), nevertheless represent an incipient settled order. It is this openness which Lacan exhorts his audience to cherish in the momentary flashes of it afforded them; this is the touchstone of a secular and non-idealist ethics, to which humans should aspire. Lacan terms this philosophical position, committed to demolishing the status quo and sceptical about the possibil-ity of authentic innovation arising from any revolutionary act, 'beyond the second death'. Insofar as he cherishes a revolutionary spirit which must be perpetually beyond any attempt to represent it concretely, Lacan may be compared to such a classic French revolutionary thinker as Robespierre. However, his objections to 'creationist sublimation' distinguish him from political thinking in this vein, and warn of its dangers.[28] Revolution and apocalypse frame Lacan's ethical thinking and psychoanalytic teaching, and allow for political engagements and actions quite other than those he himself endorsed.

ASSONANCE AND RHYME

Roland's *entre-deux-morts* quality makes his value difficult to assess. The early parts of the assonanced poem are animated by the debate over Roland's worth, a debate which focuses on the contested significance of his (then hypothetical) death. Oliver, Ganelon and the Saracens question (while also, in their different ways, reinforcing) his status as military hero. The Saracens portray him as a hollow man, Ganelon as quarrelsome, rash and irresponsible, Oliver as something perhaps worse. This uncomfortable aspect is, in fact, eradicated from the *Chanson de Roland* after the assonanced account of Roland's death. In the aftermath of that death in both O and V4, tensions generated during the personal crisis of the living hero 'between two deaths' are turned to political advantage by forces that expel the hero's problematic destructiveness from their literally official account of the narrative. I shall discuss in the final section of this chapter how this process of internal revisionism appears in O, the only text to conclude in assonance. In the present section, I compare the assonanced tradition with the rhymed *Roland*, which throughout presents Roland as normative ideal and martyr. I read this aspect of the rhymed tradition as an extended response to the disruptive Roland of assonance, along the same lines as that found in the later sections of the assonanced works, though more thorough-going in revision and appropriation. Roland's *entre-deux-morts* is not only inscribed in his characterization, but also enacted formally and thematically through the early parts of the assonanced poem. Its erasure is correspondingly thorough. In Lacanian terms, the rhymed response shifts the death drive from destruction to Nirvana.

Although the individual manuscripts vary in presentation, the assonanced and rhymed traditions display substantial narrative differences, in particular after Roland's death. The rhymed tradition, that death accomplished, greatly expands the treatment of both Aude and Ganelon. Aude's protracted anxiety and anticipatory mourning enhance Roland's status, while Ganelon's escape and the comic and cruel pursuit which follows emphasize his wickedness and whet the audience's appetite for his brutal punishment.[29] Thematic differences are also evident, and these run throughout the texts. The heroes of the assonanced tradition are much more divided, quarrelsome and destructive, their treatment by the texts less straightforwardly laudatory. All the main characters including Ganelon and the Saracens are treated as worthy barons, while no individual is wholly righteous. These phenomena reflect a fissuring of the ideological domain in the assonanced poem. Actions are set within an assortment of sometimes overlapping, sometimes contradictory ethical and strategic frameworks. In short: up until Roland's death, the assonanced *Roland*s ambiguously encourage discord as well as unity within the Christian community of audience and characters, and maintain an uneasy tension between those forces (the repeated use of collective first-person plurals highlights this tension). In conspicuous contrast, the rhymed versions harmonize the conflicting values of the assonanced tradition into a comprehensive ideology in which the Christian God, Carolingian emperor and French king, country, family and military unit, form a single allegiance. All its characters are carefully placed on one ethical scale stretching from an idealized Roland to Ganelon, a pantomime villain.[30] The Saracens are uncomplicatedly demonized, with little evidence of the similarities which in the assonanced tradition cut across distinctions between faithful and infidel.[31]

These thematic differences of approach correspond to formal distinctions worth pausing over. I rehearse Simon Gaunt's analysis of the first horn scene in O and P, which contrasts the handling of Oliver's challenge to show how the rhymed tradition proleptically resolves questions about Roland's value that the assonanced tradition keeps in suspension until after his death.[32] In order to demonstrate that the textual features discussed do not belong only to O as an individual masterpiece, I shall concentrate on the little-known V4; I use Duggan's composite CV7 as the fullest rhymed text. In V4, *laisses* 79, 80 and 81 (compare O, *laisses* 83, 84 and 85), Oliver appeals three times in very similar terms to Roland to summon Charlemagne, and Roland responds with dissimilar refusals. This is an example of the technique known as *laisses similaires* in which successive *laisses* depict what appears to be numerically a single event in qualitatively different ways.[33] The effect is one of narrative disturbance, since the audience is unsure how to make sense of what it has heard. *Laisses similaires* are associated in the assonanced tradition with moments in which Roland's death is foreseen and its significance discussed. Audience members are thus obliged to decide not only which interpretation of Roland's character, but which version of events to credit. The scene culminates with the claim that 'Rollant est proç, Oliver est saçe' (V4, 1038;

'Roland is valiant, Oliver is wise'; compare O, 1093), an interpretative crux. Elsewhere in the assonanced texts, lines on this model sometimes imply complementarity or opposition: 'Alti son li poi e le val tenebror' (e.g., V4, 765; 'The hills are high and the valleys in shadow'; compare O, 814); 'Païn ont tort et cristïans lo dres' (V4, 950; 'The pagans are wrong and the Christians right'; compare O, 1015). On other occasions, however, the same framework contains mutually reinforcing and harmonious elements: 'Bel est li çorno el sol est mol cler' (V4, 601; 'The day is beautiful and the sun is very bright'; compare O, 157). Contrast and comparison use a single paratactic structure. Further complication is introduced by the following line: 'Ambes dos ent bon vassalaçe' (V4, 1039; 'Both have good vassalic qualities'; compare O, 1094), a pronouncement which may either offset Roland and Oliver's difference or further intensify their similarity. The audience is faced with a complex ethical and aesthetic challenge: to assess the relative claims of valour and prudence and each's relation to the standard of vassalage, and to determine the relationship between lines 1038 and 1039. Weighing the alternatives requires us to reflect on the question of what will be (has been) lost or achieved by Roland's death, a problem which the assonanced texts do not allow us to answer with finality – except in far off hindsight. By contrast, in the rhymed *remaniement* the equivalent couplet reads: 'Rollanz fu proz et Oliver fu ber; / per igal furent et compeignon et per' (CV7, 1887–8; 'Roland was valiant and Oliver valorous; they were absolutely equal and companions and peers'). The virtually synonymous adjectives *proz* and *ber* uniformly denote martial qualities, the second line unambiguously reinforces the first and no division is created in the audience response. As Gaunt points out, there is no longer any difference of principle to ground the quarrel between Roland and Oliver and thereby to unsettle the audience's attachment to its hero.

Significantly, the rhymed tradition emphasizes the fact that Oliver repeats his request to blow the horn ('Sire compeing, car sonez la menee; / je le vos ai autre fois rovee', CV7, 1839–40; 'Sir companion, sound the blast; I have asked you before to do so'). The provocative *laisses similaires* of the assonanced tradition are thus replaced with *laisses parallèles*, a technique in which numerically different events are described in qualitatively similar terms, buttressing a single interpretation. Roland is the greatest of heroes, a paragon among men and among leaders, whose tragic demise we can mourn wholeheartedly, following the examples of Aude and Charlemagne in adding lustre to his image. Roland's death here does not mean his loss as an ideal or the end of his influence; on the contrary, it consecrates him as the incarnation of the ideals of leadership and vassalage.

In line with its streamlined, positive interpretation of Roland's character and death, the rhymed version makes very different use of the space between two deaths from that found in the assonanced version. Roland, who has previously shown no signs of the flirting with death which characterized his assonanced counterpart, here steps consciously into the *entre-deux-morts* at a precise point in the narrative: before the first horn scene, when he first sees the Saracen army (which he does before Oliver): "'Deus,' dist Rollant, "qui feïs mer salee, / men esïent, ma mort est hui juree"', CV7, 1532–3; "'God,' said Roland, "who made the salt sea, to my knowledge, my death is sworn today"'). Believing it too late to call for help, Roland reasons that his task is to ensure that his troops make of their final battle and of the *chanson* that will be sung of it an inspiration to generations yet to come. (In the assonanced version he is more concerned to avoid a 'male cançon', V4, 1439, a 'bad song', than to rouse others.) He is contrasted to Oliver who, faced with the same realization, wishes to call for help – an unambiguous and futile breach in his courage. Oliver's later opposition to the blowing of the oliphant will be based on personal rancour and on the misapprehension that there would have been time to call Charlemagne back; there is none of the righteous anger nor the valid different perspective that the character voices in the assonanced *Roland*. Moreover, the Oliver of rhyme cannot match the piety that distinguishes Roland, whose repeated recourse to prayer emphasizes that he submits to God's will and accepts his own role as a pawn in the cosmic struggle against evil.[34] Roland has become the exemplar of both *sagesse* and *prouesse*, Oliver his foil.

A more unquestionably virtuous hero, Roland in the rhymed version is also in an important sense more dispensable. In spite of demonstrating his pre-eminence, the poem insists on the absolute equality, not only of the two heroes, but of all its Christian characters. As Roland himself exhorts the Franks, 'As colps doner soiez tuit par ingal' (CV7, 1594; 'may you all be absolutely equal in dealing blows'). At once a sacrificial victim and a self-sacrifice, his death is eagerly embraced for the impetus it gives to future undertakings. Thus Charlemagne urges his men on:

> Ferez, baron! Ne vos atargez mie!
> Ge ai grant droit, tort a la paienie!
> Il m'ont tolu tant de ma compeignie
> dont dolce France est lasse et apovrie!
> Rollant m'ont mort, mon nevo, par envie,
> et Oliver a la chiere hardie.
>
> (CV7, 5566–71)

(Strike, barons! Do not delay! I have great right, the pagan people has the wrong. They have deprived me of so many of my retinue, by which sweet France is wretched and impoverished! They have killed my nephew Roland out of envy, and Oliver of the bold face.)

France may have lost its champions but their exalted memory will be translated into glorious undertakings inspired by their example. The Roland of these texts lacks altogether the awkward singularity which distinguishes the hero of the assonanced versions, this lack forming an important part of his value. Hence the rhymed texts repeatedly compare the surviving warriors to the lost hero: 'Dist l'uns a l'autre: "Cist fiert bien par vigor! / Unques Rollant ne dona cop meillor!"' (CV7, 5677–8; 'One says to another, "This man strikes with great force! Roland never delivered a better blow!"').[35] Not Roland but his idealized memory is to be kept alive, a resource for moulding future generations in his socially useful image. Heroism here is a much less challenging concept.

We can read the thematic and formal repetition in the *Chanson de Roland* in the light of two contrasting forms of repetitive action that Freud analyses in *Beyond the Pleasure Principle*. One he illustrates by what has become known as the *fort/da* game: a small boy repeatedly throws out of his curtained cot, and retrieves, a cotton reel on a string, at the same time articulating sounds that Freud interprets to mean *fort* ('gone') and *da* ('there'). Freud hypothesizes that the child is playing out the everyday situation of his mother's coming and going, and that the frustration, humiliation and pain encountered when passively suffering this situation are transformed into pleasure when the boy awards himself the active, masterly role, 'disappearing' and 'reappearing' his mother at will. The other form of repetition offers no such pleasurable yield; Freud exemplifies this by the shell-shocked survivors of World War I whose recurrent dreams of their terrible experiences fail to put the subjects in control of their experiences and instead deepen their trauma.[36] He suggests that in this latter form particularly we witness a repetition compulsion which lies 'beyond the pleasure principle', and links it instead to death. His account is complex and, if not contradictory, leaves open multiple possible interpretations. Thus one reading would align the ultimately pleasurable, mastering repetition with the Nirvana principle, which renders death as peace, return, reunion and equilibrium. The repetition associated with shell-shock recalls rather the destruction drive, and refers to death as violent agitation and fragmentation. Repetition is therefore a crux at which these two conflicting interpretations meet and diverge.

The moments of unsettling conflict over the value of Roland and his death that mark the assonanced texts attract *laisses similaires*. Most critics read such *laisses* in ways that make rational, cumulative sense: each *laisse* in a set moves the action on or opens new avenues of interpretation. This is to focus on variation rather than on repetition, and thus to neglect an important effect of *laisses similaires*. Repeating a word too often, as everyone knows by experience, produces the vertiginous effect not only of making it seem meaningless but of making one doubt language as a vehicle of sense. *Laisses similaires* as a stylistic strategy invoke that kind of repetition which, for Freud, shatters the illusion of mastery, in part through the destruction of coherent meaning. The recurrent and bewildering accounts of critical moments deepen the trauma of Roland's loss for the audience. Such a strategy indicates the destruction drive at work. In contrast, *laisses parallèles*, which encourage a univocal interpretation, partake of Freud's other kind of repetition, permitting mastery and comfort. They are reserved in the first half of the assonanced texts for combats between Christian and Saracen. Whatever the similarities between the two sides, they are opposed in combats presented with a repetition which is unthreatening, indeed reassuring to Christian ears. Thus the sequence of *laisses* in which the Saracen peers proclaim in turn their intention to kill Roland (V4, *laisses* 64–74) enhances their villainy and his reputation, encouraging a limited moral certainty. *Laisses parallèles* alone continue in the second half of O, and in the rhymed texts, as Gaunt shows, replace *laisses similaires*. These *laisses parallèles* work to defuse the possibility of trauma over Roland's death. Death now follows the Nirvana principle, for Roland, a secular saint, unquestionably deserves the heaven into which he is finally received. No less than his absence, his presence is here a morally unifying force within the Christian ranks and against the infidel. Critics who consider Roland to be 'the ideal knight submitting himself body and soul to his feudal lord, and by extension to his country and God' describe the rhymed rather than the assonanced hero; or view the latter wholly within the perspective established in the assonanced texts' developments after his death.[37] This idealized hero is 'dead' even during his life inasmuch as his meaning is fixed and assimilated into a particular order represented within the text itself. This pacific 'living death' or Nirvana reworks and responds to the disruptive *entre-deux-morts* of the living assonanced hero.

We might expect that the rhymed tradition's unequivocal elevation of Roland would constitute the more successful and politically effective memorial tradition. Certainly its survival in six manuscripts (including V4) and three fragments suggests a respectable level of popularity. (The relative paucity of manuscript evidence for the assonanced tradition does not allow us to assume that it was unpopular. There is a huge rise in the number of manuscripts of all sorts surviving after the mid twelfth century, and the Oxford *Roland* is one of a tiny handful of *chansons de geste* surviving in earlier manuscripts, the majority of them Anglo-Norman.) However, each of the extant rhymed texts departs in some way from the 'rhymed tradition' as it can be pieced together from other witnesses, and there is a noticeable tendency for such departures to disturb the smooth handling of Roland's death. Both C and V7, for example, include assonanced as well as rhymed material in the first horn scene, disorienting the audience with a narrative discord comparable to *laisses similaires* but with the added jolt of the formal shift from rhyme to assonance. V7 includes only two extraneous *laisses* (printed in Appendix A as 92A and 108A by Duggan) but in C the effect is carried to a grand scale, the text containing first the assonanced account of the whole first horn episode (*laisses* 90–9) and then the rhymed (*laisses* 100–27). Both versions of the couplet comparing Roland and Oliver, discussed earlier as emblematizing the two traditions' different conceptions, are found in C (1465–6 and 1939–40).

Such indifference to strict coherence is typical of medieval textuality. Although often edited out of modern published texts, textual inconsistencies of this kind repay close attention. They invite speculation on the conditions of textual production; where multiple versions of a story were circulating, individual redactors might be unable or unwilling to choose between alternatives.[38] They also allow us to consider the effect on readers or audiences of the end product regardless of the intentions or accidents which brought it about. Thus, in manuscripts C and V7, the idealized Roland of rhyme is periodically and inconsistently cut through with the problematic figure of assonance as if the former, however rationally desirable, lacked some quality that only the more disturbing persona could bestow; yet the texts' primary allegiance to the rhymed tradition is clear. The archaic material and form intrude on the 'official' text as indices of Roland's troubling past and of the past as troublesome: the return of a kind of textual unconscious.[39] Reintroducing in these slippages a confusion and ambiguity which the rhymed tradition consciously works to erase, C and V7 reanimate the debate over Roland and thereby refuse his passing. His uncanny, repetitive return re-establishes the protagonist *entre-deux-morts*.

This may be compared to manuscripts L and T, which open up the Roland question by omission: L commences its narrative in the middle of the first battle just after the horn scene; T, whether intentionally or accidentally,[40] starts in the middle of Roland's nomination to the rearguard and thereafter loses much of the first horn scene to a lacuna in the manuscript between lines 411 and 412. P, which has lost a quire, now begins just before the first horn scene.

Before moving on, it is worth observing that the rhymed tradition represents only one possible response to the cultivated ambiguity of the assonanced tradition. We find a complementary response in such *chansons de geste* as *Girart de Vienne* (late twelfth century) and *Gui de Bourgogne* (early thirteenth century), both prequels to the *Roland*;[41] the former relates the first encounters between Roland and Oliver in the war which opposes Oliver's uncle Girard to Charlemagne, the latter how the sons of Charlemagne's army, grown to adulthood during their fathers' long absence, come to Spain to help the militarily and spiritually bankrupt older generation. Both these texts expand on and polarize the *prouesse/sagesse* distinction, contrasting a pugnacious, arrogant Roland to an idealized counterfoil (Oliver and Gui, respectively). They emphasize that the hero's military usefulness is offset by the imprudence which leads him unnecessarily to risk his men's lives and by his willingness to quarrel with fellow Christians and thus weaken the social order. This Roland's death, when it comes in the narrative future (but intertextual past), will inspire mainly relief at the passing of a source of too often inappropriate conflict. These texts conclusively bury Roland while resisting the loss of an ideal threatened in the assonanced tradition, for they provide alternative candidates for the role of model hero and leader – better men, they imply, than Roland ever was. Killing Roland allows text and society to move on from an unsatisfactory past to a brighter future: heading for Nirvana.

To summarize: the texts examined offer three distinct treatments of Roland's death. In the rhymed tradition (and in some *chansons de geste* not examined here) he dies an unquestioned hero, the text making of itself a memorial to Roland's enhanced and clarified reputation, harnessed to the surviving social order. Those works which reject Roland or refuse to lionize him view his death as the possibility of a new beginning for a society in which he is made to represent the main real principle of internal conflict. In its first part, in contrast, the assonanced *Roland* tradition rejects either form of closure and emphasizes the uncertain value of what is lost in Roland, thus keeping him uncomfortably 'between two deaths'.

THE SUBLIME OBJECT OF IDEOLOGY

I turn now from the revolutionary act and figure to the revolutionary institution in the assonanced *Roland*: the new dispensation which replaces that
which Roland destroys.[42] As I noted earlier, Lacan understands the *entre-
deux-morts* to be defined by its externality in relation to order (strictly,
to two orders) and not by its propositional content. He interprets the
destruction drive, with its relation to the Real, as a challenge to the symbolic and imaginary registers, hence to the intelligible order of the world.
Strictly speaking, therefore, the 'between two deaths' is beyond ideology.
This raises a question mark over instances where institutions or ideologies dramatize their claims using an *entre-deux-morts* topos. For instance,
Sarah Kay argues that hagiography depicts saints 'between two deaths' in
Christian apologetic.[43] Apocalyptic discourse too lent itself to different
political messages throughout the medieval period.[44] Lacan accounts for
such instances by emphasizing the role of the imaginary. As Seminar VII
has it, we access the Real through an image which simultaneously veils and
displaces it.[45] The ideological content of revolutions therefore both gestures towards and obscures the Real of the destruction drive. This duality
can be illustrated by the tension between theatricality and inexpressibility
in propaganda following the Great Revolution of 1789; the revolutionary
institution was torn between a need to represent itself and an insistence on
the defectiveness of representation per se.[46] Thanks to its designation of
any concrete equivalent as inadequate, the Real, to which Lacan links the
sublime, may itself become a motor of ideological inflation, its pressure
detected in the proliferation and intensification of imaginary constructions
purporting to conceal or contain it. Equally important is the burst of vital
energy issuing from the *jouissance* of the unleashed destruction drive. Thus
Roland's destructiveness in the first part of the assonanced *Roland*, which
I have been arguing is a manifestation of the Real, attracts and energizes
numerous ideological investments. Whereas Lacan is primarily interested
in urging us to look beyond the fantasies in which the *entre-deux-morts* is
dressed to the Real beyond, other critics – notably Žižek, interested as he
is in pressing psychoanalysis into the service of Marxist politics and revolutionary socialism – regard the fantasies themselves as objects of significance,
for they are the stuff of ideology.[47] The subject of this final section will be
the ideological content of the Oxford *Chanson de Roland*, the sole surviving
text to relate in assonance the aftermath of Roland's death.

Roland in the Oxford text repeatedly refers to certain ideological values
or figures: *los*, family, *France dulce*, the emperor who will love his warriors

for their blows, the Christian God and Christian community. I argued earlier that the assonanced poem stages his invocation so as to emphasize ideological fracturing and dissonance. In another perspective, however, these values if not examined carefully are sufficiently widely acknowledged and imprecise to function like 'motherhood and apple pie': hearers may accept them as defining a collective which many can, however temporarily or loosely, support, and which gives a provisional unity to their diverse political goals. The values that Roland proclaims perhaps confine the *Chanson de Roland*'s usefulness to a Christian framework; however, the text's cultural history is evidence of the practical flexibility of the interpellations it permits within that limit. It was for medieval writers and audiences a bearer of imaginary investments in community and struggle, different from but analogous to those it has borne in modern France.[48] Just as Gaston Paris and Raoul Mortier invoked the *Roland* to give courage in modern times of war, twelfth-century historians felt inspired to report that a *cantilena Rollandi* was sung to lead Duke William's troops into the Battle of Hastings.[49] Norman conquests were thus ennobled by absorption into a communal heroic tradition.[50] Rendered helpfully indeterminate by its territorial extent as well as by its temporal distance, 'Frankish' identity lent itself to multiple appropriations.[51] Mandach describes the rash of new Charlemagnes: 'The glorification of Charlemagne and the ambition to equal him were a kind of disease among the great medieval princes.'[52] The *Roland* circulated well beyond modern France; neither of the two substantial manuscripts in which the assonanced tradition survives can be considered unproblematically 'French', O being written in Anglo-Norman, the dialect of post-Conquest England, and V4 (which follows the assonanced tradition only until the end of the Baligant episode) in a particularly difficult form of Franco-Venetian, a koine devised for the diffusion of French works in Northern Italy.[53] Within what would become modern France, but outside the sphere of Old French, Roland is more frequently cited in the Occitan lyric tradition than are such major figures as Tristan, Alexander, Charlemagne and Arthur.

Evidently the *Chanson de Roland*'s appeal was significant to various medieval communities, not limited to those which we today would call French. Its future as a symbol of French nationalism was not, in medieval times, an obvious one. My view of the ideological values invoked by Roland in the first part of the assonanced *Roland*, therefore, is that they do not in themselves encapsulate many firm identifications. Even the opposition of Christian and pagan is not at this point as energetically invested or as energizing as is sometimes argued.[54] Hence Roland's infamous declarations of religio-moral hierarchy (O, 1015, 1212) in the assonanced texts are not shored up by the consistent denigration of Saracens individually and collectively that is found in the rhymed tradition. More significant in the assonanced version are the structure of opposition and the ethic of collective struggle, both repeated at multiple levels throughout the text. To put it another way, Roland's singular desire and destruction drive, from which the poem's energy derives, are not represented by this vague ideological collection. While the pannier of values invoked works as an imaginary crutch enabling the protagonist's drive towards the second death, it does not adequately explain or limit it. Nevertheless, these categories will be expanded, specified and invested in responses to the poem. Like the rhymed *remaniements* and other *chansons de geste* discussed above, the episodes which follow Roland's death in the Oxford *Roland* exemplify one such response – a binding of the largely free-floating energy that accumulates around Roland's destructiveness. Exploiting this energy to specific political ends, the latter part of the text provides an ideologically bound 'second life' to complement the hero's focus on the second death. This second life, as Sade feared, knits him back into the social and political hegemony from which the destruction drive temporarily extracted him.

The main ideological thrust of the second part of the Oxford *Roland* centres on the figure of Charlemagne as divinely empowered king and emperor.[55] This is evident in the arguments put forward in Ganelon's trial. For Ganelon, Roland was just another baron where all are equal and private conflicts no affair of the king's. For Thierry, Roland was something quite different: the right arm of a king who is not to be considered first among equals (the paradox denies royal authority a firm basis), but a ruler by divine decree. The representation of a reluctant and weakened king with which the poem ends strengthens this mandate, of course; Charlemagne's legitimacy now rests neither on his ability to fulfil his duties nor on his support from his barons, but directly on God. In case anyone be deceived about the way in which it intends to wield power, the new order founded on the debris of Roncevaux is confirmed by a series of crushing victories owed to God's direct intervention; it will not be satisfied with 'moral victories' such as Roland's. In the same movement, the barons on whom Charles may call are diminished in stature. Roland and Oliver are replaced in the vanguard by Rabel and Guinemant, characters who might as well be anonymous for all the distinction their names carry. Like Thierry, they never exceed the definition of the barony as instruments of the king. Despite the sanctions that attend dissenters such as Ganelon, the power of the king is now represented as internalized by the baron himself. Charlemagne's lesser ability to coerce his barons is compensated for by the entrenchment of his authority in the baronial psyche.

Charlemagne's pain at Roland's death and his terrible, wide-ranging revenge confirms Roland's own assertion earlier in the poem that 'por itels colps nos eimet li emperere' (O, 1377; 'for such blows the emperor loves us'). The exemplary bond between king and baron is that of love, and whatever it means in the first part of the Oxford text, as it is read in the second half the conception of love recalls that described by Žižek in an analysis of Christianity:

love is, as Lacan pointed out, an interpretation of the desire of the Other: the answer of love is 'I am what is lacking in you; with my devotion to you, with my sacrifice for you, I will fill you out, I will complete you.' The operation of love is therefore double: the subject fills in his own lack by offering himself to the other as the object filling out the lack in the Other – love's deception is that this overlapping of two lacks annuls lack as such in a mutual completion.[56]

Roland's death is interpreted retrospectively as a sacrifice for Charlemagne's sake, a superlative attempt to earn his love. Charles's love would then be what Roland really wanted: an intelligible, ideological desire to replace the incomprehensible, singular drive towards death. Although this sacrifice reveals Charles's lack by depriving him of his 'right arm', it also completes him as a king by relieving him of the need to admit a source of weakness other than Roland's death and its scapegoat, Ganelon. Converted into a lack, Charlemagne's loss becomes the essential ground of his authority and the guarantee of the political order established through the poem (compare the discussion of *Pearl*, Chapter 4 below). Haidu comments that the Oxford *Roland* plays out the Oedipal myth in reverse, the father killing the son, but this action can be recuperated to a more orthodoxly Freudian interpretation.[57] At his trial, Ganelon's quarrel with Roland is reinterpreted as an attack on Charlemagne, the king-father, and the text in its later parts labours to stress how Charlemagne is weakened by the resulting loss. At the end of the narrative he feels the full weight of his two hundred years, an age which previously testified to his superhuman power to resist time. 'Murdered' by his son-baron, Charlemagne can for the first time access the unassailable authority of the symbolic father.[58] His real suffering over Roland therefore has a yield of ideological gratification. Roland, ironically, becomes the founding figure of an order in which the king lays claim to considerably greater control over his barons than he exercised over Roland himself.

The monarchy is further legitimized and extended by the Baligant episode. Prior to this point Charles was only a king of France, his pagan counterpart similarly a king, Marsile. When Baligant enters the poem as Charles's new double, his status as overlord of merely national kings elevates Charles to imperial eminence. The introduction of Baligant also broadens the sense of the emperor's Christian mission, since it results in the extirpation of the Saracen presence in Spain and presumably its unsettling in its heartland. Like the taming of independent barons, this is achieved in Roland's name, in revenge for his death and thus as a completion of the revolution which he began. In the revision performed by the second half of the poem, Roland's *estultie* aimed at this previously unimagined annihilation. His destructiveness is provided with a horizon, albeit one not visible at the time. Charlemagne's revenge makes of Roland a Christian visionary. In comparison Turpin himself, however ready he was to follow Roland, appears now to have been too entrenched in the established order to see beyond it. (Contrast this with the earlier parts of the text, where Turpin possessed a wider Christian vision than did Roland. The latter, though naturally pious, showed little concern with either the afterlife or the political condition of Christianity as a dominant world religion.) In the Oxford *Roland* we find an organization similar to that of hagiography, in which the saint is represented as a revolutionary force disrupting secular society in the name of Christ's new order.[59] Whereas in saints' lives that new order is aligned with the Church in some form, here the Christian revolutionary is a secular baron, and the arch-churchman Turpin is one representative of the limited, compromised status quo from which he must break away. Even if Turpin is of all men the closest to Roland and most willing to support him, the difference of ethical status is established. By claiming to follow Roland's star, Charles can legitimately claim a degree of independence from the Church, as presumably can a later ruler who identifies with him. The question of empire is a related one. Medieval French kings periodically laid claim to the status of Holy Roman Emperor, and were concerned at least to establish equal rank with, and therefore independence of, the Empire; the legend of Charlemagne played a key role in such claims.[60] Roland's disturbingly motiveless death is confiscated to provide a shot in the arm for a religious and political order which bears little relation to what appears to have been his original inspiration, in spite of the redeployment of terms creating a link at once superficial and crucial.

This much strengthened monarchy nevertheless presents itself as an improved incarnation of feudalism, and in this respect as traditionalist.[61] By adopting Roland as its patron it proclaims its allegiance to baronial values and professes to fulfil baronial ideals. In the early part of the poem Roland may be viewed as no less guilty than Ganelon in flaunting a baronial competitiveness which both weakens the king and discredits the barony. But in the trial scene, this is conveniently forgotten, the official record rewritten (not without difficulty); Thierry establishes that Ganelon, not Roland, has enacted what Haidu calls feudalism's self-destruction.[62] Since the feudal system has clearly failed adequately to prevent such destructive competition – and may even have encouraged it – the king needs to step in to ensure that the system can work properly. The greater the need for collective unity – provided by the expansion of the battle against Marsile into a global crisis – the more authority the king needs to hold and the more his barons need to subordinate their personal interests to the Crown. Roland's idealization and Ganelon's demonization are complementary parts of a symbolic fiction designed to unite king and barony against their mutual enemies internal and external; and significantly, it wards off the disruptive power possessed by every baron, the very thin line between the loyal and the rebellious baron being as evident in many *chansons de geste* as it is in Charles's own council.[63]

The second half of the poem, therefore, consists of an attempt to attach the large and fairly free-floating ideological terms invoked by Roland, together with the significant charge that they gain from Roland's death (retrospectively reinterpreted as sacrifice or martyrdom), to a specific political order: that of a Christian monarchy wishing to enhance its power in a variety of domains and with imperial ambitions. This order presents itself as novel, sweeping away an older regime; in this it draws on the revolutionary force of Roland's destructive, second-death-directed actions earlier in the poem, awarding those a teleology which, in my view, they did not have. Thus I interpret as rhetorical strategy what are often considered signs of actual historical change. The rhetoric of change in the poem I read as the programmed creation of an order that wishes to increase its ideological standing in a competitive field by injecting itself with the sublime and by representing itself as at once rooted in a unique past event (Roncevaux), and visionary in the political programme it proposes to implement. It is possible, of course, to consider the early stages of the text in the same light, and Roland's revolution an artificial one. Basing myself on the discussion of repetition above, however, I affirm that Roland's act in the assonanced poem is an authentic one, an instance of the Real; that its later opportunistic exploitations are not incidental, for instances of the Real cannot but provoke efforts to bind them to meanings; and that both the multiplicity of appropriations and their failure are intrinsic, since they result from the

Real's resistance to meaning. There is a genuine difference between the disruptive forces of the early part of the assonanced *Roland* and the palliative influences that dominate the later sections of the Oxford text, and which bear comparison with the techniques of the rhymed *remaniement*; the latter's deployment in V4 is thus congruent with the O development, as is V4's incorporation of further empire-building through a *Prise de Narbonne* episode.

The revolutionism of the Oxford *Roland* thus falls into two parts: the phase of destruction – performed by Roland – and that of new beginning – performed by Charlemagne. If we take the work to promote continuously a single message, destructiveness being performed with an eye to the radical renewal it enables, then it conforms rather to Sade's than to Lacan's model. However, Lacan's insistence that the initial impulse to destruction should be detached in theory from the later movement to a new order is valuable. His discussion of the second death in the context of *entre-deux-morts*, hence as ethically unplaceable, captures the destructive passion and energy not only of Roland in the assonanced tradition but also of other *chanson de geste* heroes such as Raoul de Cambrai. Turning to Christian monarchy and imperialism as improved feudalism and construing the hero as a martyr in that cause, the second half of O indeed appears as both a *sublimation créationniste* and a retrospective ideological appropriation, following Lacan's suggestion that creationism incorporates a revolutionary urge absent from evolutionism. This sublimating response does not, however, either account for or exhaust Roland's purely destructive energy. Thus Roland's death engenders in different retellings various responses which all in their way aim to resolve that death's problematic aspect. They retrospectively endow the protagonist's horizonless destructiveness with a final aim, defined in terms of the 'common good'. Wasteful destruction, an evil, is ascribed to the villains who attack that good. Within the *Roland* narrative this is effected by the aftermath of Roncevaux: Charlemagne's immediate revenge and subsequent war with Baligant, the massacre of the Saracens and Bramimonde's conversion, Charlemagne's and Aude's mourning, Aude's death, Ganelon's trial and execution. However, all the surviving versions of the *Chanson de Roland* are also themselves part of the 'aftermath'. None represents the original version of the story and each brings its own solution, and therefore must be considered along with other *chansons de geste* among the reactions to Roland (this is not to posit an 'original' version lacking in self-reflexivity). The story of Roncevaux is reworked, with episodes added or omitted and with shifting emphases; it is furnished with sequels and prequels and is inserted into manuscript compilations with other works whose selection invites us to read it in particular ways.[64] All these responses constitute so many explanations which attempt to render Roland's death-directed actions acceptable according to some literary, historical, spiritual or moral logic, and thereby to remove their outrageous, offensive, traumatic quality. Their effect is not only palliative, for such responses also exploit the energies generated by Roland's destruction drive. The ideological claims formulated derive considerable force from the aesthetic and psychic dynamics issuing from that drive and from the *entre-deux-morts* to which it brings the protagonist. That this position is intolerable for either protagonist or audience to maintain for long may explain why O's early encouragement of controversy over Roland's worth does not lead to a more discriminating or detached pose in the heavily ideological sections following his death. Moreover, it is crucial to the legend's literary life that Roland's death should meet no final resolution; hence the potential for future action stressed at the ending of all the extant *Roland* texts. It seems that the vitality of the *Chanson de Roland* tradition – its ability to generate further textual responses – is best served precisely by the destruction drive enshrined within Roland's revolutionary act.

CHAPTER 2

The knight as Thing: courtly love in the non-cyclic prose Lancelot

I closed Chapter 1 with the claim that the Oxford *Chanson de Roland* ends by interpreting Roland's death as a loving sacrifice for Charlemagne's sake; and that this was a misreading of the protagonist's desire. In this second chapter I turn to an unquestionable instance of a male character dying for love of another, whose own love in turn brings him close to death. These are, respectively, Galehot and Lancelot. Again I shall foreground a Lacanian analysis while exploring other ways of conceiving the ethical relation between love and death, that classic pairing. In human meditation, death provides a kind of yardstick to measure love, the affirmation 'I would die for my beloved' defining a horizon which is a constitutive element of love itself. Love often leads narratively to death, which is sometimes seen as successful consummation. It may persist beyond death. To love another person is to experience a kind of death of the self, which may then be reborn in a new guise as a lover. Love is therefore commonly associated with the *entre-deux-morts*. Parental love and the love of God will be considered in later chapters. The present chapter focuses on the tragic passion of noble lovers, the intensity of whose loves threatens calamity both for the lover, whose life, mental health, reputation and morals are placed in jeopardy, and for the society he heads.

It is clear enough how Galehot falls *entre-deux-morts*, doomed as he is from his first meeting with Lancelot, his grand passion. Lancelot's situation is more disputable, for he is destined to outlive the Arthurian order. His case can be clarified through a comparison with Tristan, the great exemplar of fateful passion in medieval literature and Lancelot's prototype. Tristan and Lancelot are ideal chivalric figures whose adulterous loves at once confirm and undermine their hyperbolic social value. Each's passion is implicated in the establishment and maintenance of a kingdom. However, Tristan's brings about only a personal tragedy, whereas Lancelot's heralds the final collapse of a cultural, social and political order in the bloodbath of Salisbury Plain. Responding to and reworking the story of Troy and its prince Paris (as well as that of Tristan), Lancelot's love story highlights political and historical questions. Moreover, insofar as the love of Tristan and Ysolt is potion-induced it is not freely chosen, and its status is therefore equivocal. Lancelot and Guinevere's love entertains no such weakened links with the social and cultural mechanisms within which they operate; on the contrary, their love is shown to lie at the very heart of those mechanisms. While the *Tristan* narratives pose large questions of guilt, intention, impulse, conscious or unconscious knowledge, regret and the consequences of one's actions (foreseen and unforeseen, intended and unintended), those concentrating on Lancelot test to (literal) destruction-point the internal logic and rigorous functioning of the chivalric order. Love in Lancelot's connection is therefore implicated in the greatness and the ending of the Arthurian order; a collective death drive works itself out through him, and his fascinating *éclat* reflects a whole culture *entre-deux-morts*. What is so intriguing about Lancelot is that he is not only, as the Demoiselle d'Escalot describes him in *La Mort le roi Artu*, 'li plus vilains chevaliers el monde et li plus vaillanz' ('the most uncourtly knight in the world and the worthiest'), but a figure in whom *vilains* and *vaillanz* are shown to be near-anagrams, and therefore appear to be only different ways of organizing the same material.[1] In him Arthurian chivalry's sublime and its abject overlap to crystallize an ethical crux, *entre-deux*. Significantly, this undecidable creation is posited as the chief object of desire in all those romances where he appears. The paradoxes associated with him make him, even more than the Grail, an impossible object of Arthurian desire. Complementarily Galehot, I shall argue, represents the exemplary subject of this desire, equally though differently *entre-deux-morts*.[2]

My discussion will bear primarily on the romance known as the non-cyclic prose *Lancelot*, a version said to minimize the problematic dimension of Lancelot's passion.[3] In the first parts of this chapter I examine this claim through an analysis of Lancelot as courtly lover in the non-cyclic prose *Lancelot*, *Le Chevalier de la Charrette* and *La Mort le roi Artu*, basing my conceptual framework on the chapter on courtly love in Lacan's seventh seminar. Lacan's notion of courtly love, which owes a considerable debt to literary studies of the medieval love lyric, now appears both narrow and dated, for modern medievalist scholarship considers more varied relationships, objects and texts under the heading of *fine amor*. It remains nevertheless the most influential modern theorization of the phenomenon (there are, of course, numerous non-theoretical accounts). In order to contextualize Lacan's account as a tool of medievalist literary analysis, I shall begin by comparing it to two classic accounts of the ethics of courtly love:

those of Gaston Paris and C. S. Lewis. I shall then turn to more recent critical developments of Lacan's account in the hands of Slavoj Žižek and Sarah Kay, developments which elucidate loves dissimilar to as well as corresponding with the Lacanian paradigm. I aim to show the ways in which Lacanian accounts do and do not fit the love between Lancelot and Guinevere in the non-cyclic prose *Lancelot*, and to suggest why both fit and lack of fit illuminate this and other loves in their special relation to death and to the death drive. The later parts of the chapter will therefore explore the *entre-deux-morts* in the non-cyclic prose *Lancelot* through the figure of Galehot, Lancelot's passionate lover, prince of the Distant Isles and son of the Fair Giantess. Deathly features which other works attach to Lancelot's love for Guinevere are here associated instead with Galehot's love for Lancelot; and hence with Lancelot as object rather than subject of love, or with him as reciprocator rather than initiator. Thus (as is commonly observed) the erotic triangle which connects Lancelot, Guinevere and Arthur is paralleled by another linking Guinevere, Lancelot and Galehot. I shall end by drawing out the implications of this reconfigured infidelity for Lancelot's moral stature. My view is that the non-cyclic prose *Lancelot* does not diminish the importance of Lancelot's transgressive actions by shifting the grounds of his transgression away from his adulterous affair with Guinevere. Among the many characters who wish to win Lancelot's love in the non-cyclic romance, Galehot stands out. Situated as the lover of the truly impossible object, he represents Arthurian desire – a desire shared by Arthurian knights, ladies and readers – in its starkest form.

THE NON-CYCLIC PROSE *LANCELOT*

The so-called non-cyclic prose *Lancelot* is a short form of the lengthy cyclic *Lancelot* which is the central panel of the Vulgate or Lancelot-Grail cycle of early thirteenth-century French prose romances. In its entirety this cycle encompasses the history of the Grail, the genealogy and life of Lancelot, and the rise and fall of Arthur's kingdom and the order associated with it.[4] Both cyclic and non-cyclic versions begin with the dispossession by the ruthless King Claudas of Lancelot's father, King Ban of Benoyc, and with the baby Lancelot's abduction by the Lady of the Lake.[5] The narratives broadly agree until the end of the 'Marche de Gaule' section; both then cover, but with distinct emphases and at different length, the second voyage to Galehot's kingdom of Sorelois, the False Guinevere episode and the death of Galehot.[6] The cyclic version goes on to recount many further adventures and to prepare the way for the Grail quest, with its emphasis on sexual purity and Christian redemption, and for the tragic turn of the *Mort*. Apparently neglecting these themes, the non-cyclic prose *Lancelot* instead details Lancelot's progress towards the public recognition which is a necessary part of knighthood. It concentrates on his constitution, not so much as loving subject (having fallen in love with Guinevere early in the narrative, he alters little as a lover), but as the desired or beloved object of a variety of other characters. Two events mark the ending of the non-cyclic narrative: Lancelot's establishment at court as Guinevere's lover and Arthur's principal knight, and Galehot's death. It is difficult not to see these events as interrelated.

The relationship between the non-cyclic and cyclic *Lancelot* romances is the subject of a controversy illustrating characteristic features of medieval textuality. For some critics, most notably Elspeth Kennedy, the non-cyclic form represents an earlier and independent work from a pre-cyclical stage in the legend's development, while for others it is an abridgement of the cyclic version.[7] Further complexities are created by substantial divergences between the manuscripts of each 'version', by what may be considered cross-currents (some manuscripts classified as one recension following the other at various points), and by the characteristic intertextuality of Arthurian works which means that even non-cyclic texts give the impression of drawing on a shared resource.[8] In writing about the shorter prose recension, I accept the text as a romance within the Arthurian corpus, and consider it to be significantly constituted around the figure of Galehot. I take its representations to be significant within the horizon of the eventual collapse of the Arthurian world. Whether composed before or after the Vulgate, it gives an alternative perspective of that collapse and consequently of Arthurian ethics: one which situates the Arthurian death drive not in questionable sexual morality but in admirable chivalric love between men.

'COURTLY LOVE' AND ITS DISCONTENTS

The notion of 'courtly love' has had an immensely influential, if uneven history. In spite of scholarly criticisms and revisions it remains a central term in discussions of the ethics, aesthetics and rhetoric of desire, sexuality and love in medieval literature. If we cannot live with it in the sense of accepting its valency, neither, it seems, can we do without it; to adapt Winston Churchill's famous remark on democracy, 'courtly love' is the worst way of organizing the forms it purports to regulate except all those other ways that have been tried from time to time. Churchill's quip is a staple resource of Žižek's for illustrating certain kinds of paradox. He modifies it, for instance, when explaining how 'woman' is the symptom of 'man': 'unbearable – thus, nothing is more agreeable; impossible to live with – thus, to live without her is even more difficult'.[9] Correspondingly, 'courtly love', and the view of the Middle Ages that it encapsulates, may be considered to be among modernity's symptoms.

Its recent resurgence – as 'love', till late neglected in favour of 'desire', has returned to the forefront of medievalist study – revises earlier content, but does not escape symptomatic status.[10] Researchers have emphasized the links between courtly love and the death drive, pondering its passive-aggressive masochism (Cohen, Krueger), its interest in self-sacrifice ((Lefay-)Toury, Fradenburg, Gaunt) and the madness or social ostracism to which it leads (Huot, Kay).[11] In this chapter I consider that death provides a significant horizon against which medieval courtly texts question the values and behaviours involved in love, but that its value is variable and often unclear, multiple or ambiguous. Thus, although dying for love is proof of superlative devotion, it is typically not allowed to stand as a finite event. Take *La Chastelaine de Vergi*, one of the most concise expressions in narrative of the lyric theme of dying for love, which nevertheless ends by extending the story into the history of the Templars and the Crusades, thus pursuing on a large social scale the outcome of what is presented as a very private affair. Moreover, love is not deadly for all noble lovers in courtly texts. If, as a way of life, courtly love involves a certain set of relations to the death drive, nevertheless these relations may be negotiated in different ways and give rise to varying outcomes. Later courtly texts will emphasize the life-oriented aspects of courtly love, which also deserve to be called 'ethical', but numerous early romances allow their lovers happy endings, at least in the sense of surviving at the end of the narrative in union or hope of union with their beloveds. (Lyrics, arguably, imply survival.) A number of these romances engage positively with debates over married love widely propagated in the twelfth century, and to consider that courtly love is entirely distinct from marriage is no less reductive than to consider it as only about that. 'The literature of courtly love could be defined as an explanation of marriage and adultery', asserts Virginie Greene, highlighting its exploratory dimension.[12] Some critics argue that such successful, socially integrated loves – and in particular married love – should be assigned to a different category from the courtly; this has the regrettable effect of narrowing our discussion of medieval texts, in ways, moreover, that the texts themselves do not justify. Categorizing marriage-oriented thirteenth-century romances like *L'Escoufle* or *Guillaume de Dôle* as 'bourgeois', 'realist' or 'idyllic', or dismissing as 'moralizing' later rewritings of the sort sponsored by the Burgundian court, may have some critical relevance, but such works should also be regarded as entering into debate over courtly love while reorienting its terms to suit their own concerns and values.[13] For very different reasons, Tristan's 'amour sauvage, indomptable et passionné' is also often considered to lack the characteristic features of 'courtly love' and excluded from consideration under this rubric.[14] This restriction of what in medieval texts is a very broad field in one sense justifies the frequently reiterated criticism that 'courtly love' is an exclusively modern concept. *Fine amor* is traditionally suggested as an authentically medieval substitute, yet the two are hardly interchangeable. *Fine amor* can be viewed as a prescription, code or ideal brought into repeated comparison and contrast with antithetical principles, among them *haür* and *ire* ('hatred'; 'pain'/'anger'), *raison* ('reason'), *fole amor* and *folie* ('mad/foolish love'; 'madness'/'folly'). 'Courtly love' may be taken to name the field allowing for this wide-ranging ethical debate, which tests central as well as limit-case and exceptional courtly values – it is 'a vehicle for dealing with love-trouble'.[15] Hence, when the narrator of Thomas's *Tristan* worries at the problem of whether his protagonist's love for Ysolt can be considered *fine amor*, the complex interweaving of terms rather enmeshes than disentangles the ideas of love, hatred, pain and revenge.[16] Love within the courtly field is necessarily not *fine* ('pure') but includes its negation. Whether generated spontaneously or by some external event, an antithesis or underside manifests itself, not always fully acknowledged, to threaten and fragment the official construction and aspirational norm. In Lancelotian terms: *vilains* and *vaillanz* endlessly contrast, intermingle and re-emerge as moral terms.

By comparing Lacan's Seminar VII account of *l'amour courtois* to two influential earlier paradigms, I aim to map the former's relation to core traditions in medieval studies (whether or not Lacan knew these earlier accounts is immaterial to this mapping), to elucidate the specificity of courtly love in Lacan's account, and to illustrate some distinctive features of Lacanian ethics. We begin with Gaston Paris, founder of this particular discourse in an article published in 1883. Paris's seminal definition, which draws primarily on Chrétien de Troyes's Lancelot romance, *Le Chevalier de la Charrette*, deserves revisiting.[17] I want to draw attention to two aspects. In the first place, Paris's conception of courtly love posits it as highly normative and rule-bound, a discipline as well as a discourse, and in this respect similar to other aspects of society's organization: love 'a ses règles tout comme la chevalerie ou la courtoisie, règles qu'on possède et qu'on applique mieux à mesure qu'on a fait plus de progrès' ('has its rules, like chivalry and courtliness; rules that the subject masters and applies the better as he progresses'). Having a structured progression incorporating advancements and regressions, courtly love forms a kind of ladder of perfection, requiring constant striving, anxious self-surveillance and careful mannerism on the part of its adepts. Those who fail to conform to its precepts having once entered on its path are punished by loss of privileges and the threat of ejection from the order. Paris thus asserts the internal rationality of courtly love, in which everything tends towards the same end. Even the lady's capricious behaviour represents an effort to improve her lover's acquisition of 'un art, une science, une vertu' ('an art, a science and a virtue'). In the second place, Paris places the system of courtly love in a complex relationship to the established social order of chivalry and courtesy, as variably overlapping with, out of joint with or antagonistic to that order. Thus, although the courtly lover 'accomplit toutes les prouesses imaginables' ('accomplishes all imaginable deeds of prowess') and love makes him 'mieux valoir' ('more worthy'), his love is nevertheless 'illégitime, furtif' ('illegitimate, stealthy') and 'ne peut se concilier avec la possession calme et publique' ('irreconcilable with tranquil, public possession'). The lovers cannot, therefore, be married. Love brings the lover prowess and prestige in the wider world but also a timidity that to the uninitiated seems anomalous in a warrior. This timidity Paris explains as deriving from the lover's fear of losing the lady owing to her dominant position, itself rationalized as compensation for the risks she runs in giving herself to the lover due to the different sexual morals of the wider world and to medieval sexual double standards.[18] Three ethical orders intertwine: feudal marriage, chivalric court society and courtly love. Noting the ethical nature of *l'amour courtois* and its complex relationship to other contemporary systems, Paris yet appears careful not to pronounce it either a fully independent system or a straightforward inversion of the public norms, and documents its contributions to as well as its departures from those norms.

Paris has common ground with Lacan. Both writers, in spite of their different approaches, have noticeably similar senses of the social norms relating to marriage, sexuality and femininity. For both, 'troubadour love' represents a highly regulated ethical system that diverges from the public organization of erotic desire in the patriarchal, north-west European regime of monogamy, and yet epitomizes certain hidden principles underlying that regime. In Lacan's case, this forms part of an overarching theory of desire. According to him, for humans to achieve the object of our desire would be an experience of pleasure so intense as to be unbearably painful and so shattering as to be unsustainable within the human sphere; this is *jouissance*.

Our relation to our own desires is a fraught one, divided between the urge towards a fulfilment that would be devastating (one manifestation of the death drive) and the preference to continue a normal human life, only possible if we remain at a certain distance from the object of our desire. Everyday life is organized so as to maintain our pleasures at a manageable level in accordance with the pleasure principle or, as Freud also called it, the 'unpleasure principle' – 'principe de déplaisir, ou de moindre-pâtir', adds Lacan ('unpleasure principle, or least-suffering principle') – which enjoins us to 'enjoy as little as possible'.[19] This principle's function is to 'faire que l'homme cherche toujours ce qu'il doit retrouver, mais ce qu'il ne saurait atteindre' ('make man always search for what he has to find again, but which he will never attain');[20] a succinct analysis of the romance quest. Inspired by Lacan, Žižek proposes a taxonomy of erotic relationships according to which marriage provides a liveable and toned-down, moral alternative both to courtly love and to all-consuming, death-directed romantic passion on the model of Wagner's *Tristan and Isolde*.[21] Whereas the last-mentioned relation offends both society and individuals by its isolation (such love may, of course, be more positively damaging), marriage grafts us into the social order by giving us enough satisfaction to prevent us becoming wreckers, and enough frustration and fear to encourage us to redirect surplus sexual energies to socially constructive, civilized ends – to sublimate them, in Freud's sense of the term (on the Lacanian sense, see pp. 14–15, above).

Courtly love too operates to regulate desire in accordance with the (un)pleasure principle and consequently imposes sublimation. Hence the constant striving for moral and social improvement on which Paris insists. Its mechanism, however, is quite different from that of marriage. According to Lacan, courtly love is an *amor interruptus* which defers union with the beloved object indefinitely in favour of extending and elaborating what would usually be called the preliminary stage of courtship.[22] As Leo Spitzer puts it in his essay on Jaufré Rudel's 'amour lointain' ('love from afar'), courtly love is grounded in a 'paradoxe amoureux' ('amorous paradox'). It is 'a love which wants not to possess, but to joy in [jouir de] this state of non-possession, a *Minne*-love containing both the sensual desire to touch the true woman [de "toucher" à la femme vraiment "femme"] and also chaste distancing, Christian love transposed onto the secular plane, which wants to "have *and* have not"'.[23] Courtly love pre-empts the pleasure principle by aiming never to reach the goal of union that would signal desire's demise.[24] Extended frustration, itself often expressed in lyrics as a protracted dying, is nevertheless preferable to the end of desire, for that implies a subjective dissolution more terrifying than mere mortality. Any moments of fulfilment are furtively, fleetingly snatched in order to enflame rather than sate, thus avoiding the certainties of either the Wagnerian or marital states. The obstacles which Paris considers to be structurally necessary to courtly love permit, in Lacan's version, the lover to remain at a safe distance from, but still in creative tension with, the desired object.

This 'scolastique de l'amour malheureux' ('scholastics of unhappy love') not only allows the lover to evade the disappointment of consummation but paradoxically offers a route to *jouissance* which may be compared to the looking-glass advice given to Alice:[25] walk in the opposite direction from your goal. Courtly love differs from marriage, that other authorized system of regulating sexual love, by the nature and degree of the sublimations it enables. Unsatisfied desire elevated to an art form places the lover on a different path which, by breaking out of the well-trodden substitute fulfilments of everyday life, comes closer to *jouissance* in its refined, perverse rewards: in masochism, in surplus enjoyment, in the debt incurred by the beneficiary, in the moral high ground that the lover comes to occupy (since typically the lady reneges on the debt) and, not least, in poetry.[26] Courtly love may not enable the lover to have what he purports to want most, but it does grant him significant compensations which find their place within the courtly œuvre. As Spitzer puts it, for the troubadour, 'to experience amorous pain is itself a joy [une jouissance]'.[27] The never-ending disciplines of courtly love do not, like marriage, limit the lover to the symbolic register but bring him into relation also with the Real. According to Lacan, troubadour lyric's 'paradoxe amoureux' reflects an admission, not necessarily conscious, that true fulfilment is unattainable within the human sphere. On the one hand, the incest taboo forbids us access to our primordial object of desire, the mother, thus forcing us to turn to substitute objects which can never satisfy a demand not really addressed to them. On the other hand and much more fundamentally, this prohibition on the mother is merely a retroactive rationalization concealing the essential impossibility of satisfaction which is a primordial, Real fact of life. One would thus expect that the various barriers to the lover's desire would function as a smokescreen encouraging him to believe that the object is in principle attainable if only he can overcome these impediments. And we find in fact that the various impediments permit the lover to cherish fictions supporting ideologies relative to, for instance, social position and gender, such as that the jealous husband, his brother-rivals or the Lady herself – or rather the misogynistically conceived woman – is responsible for his privation. More significantly, however, in troubadour love lyric 'des détours et des obstacles ... s'organisent pour faire apparaître comme tel le domaine de la vacuole' ('detours and obstacles . . . are organized so as to make the domain of the vacuole stand out as such');[28] that is, so as to emphasize the Real void or vacuum at the centre of the structure of desire, and consequently the facticity of its symbolic and imaginary evasions. The 'paradoxe amoureux' means that the lover can maintain the fantasy of union as totally fulfilling, but also that the (un)pleasure of deferment is offset by a deeper and unbearable awareness that the object of desire is not lacking but lost, unobtainable in the Real and not merely in the symbolic register. A major theme of troubadour lyric is therefore 'celui du deuil, et même d'un deuil jusqu'à la mort' ('mourning, and even mourning unto death').[29]

The 'vacuole' at the centre of the structure of desire is a kind of black hole created by the incessant orbiting around the object of those who desire it and who are at once drawn towards it and repelled by the fatal implications. The tension between centripetal and centrifugal forces makes itself felt in the desiring subjects who therefore project into the place of the void (human nature abhorring a vacuum) a creation that is at once charismatically attractive and magnificently repulsive; this Lacan terms the Thing. Not the final object of desire, the Thing nevertheless occupies the place of that object – it is the only possible presentable face of the unrealizable. It provides a focus for the bafflement and frustration provoked by the impossibility of fulfilment which founds the human domain, and in this sense may be seen as 'ce qui du réel pâtit du signifiant' ('that which in the [R]eal suffers from the signifier'), indicating the Real's forceful pressure on the psyche.[30] The Thing is therefore itself *entre-deux*, between two domains, even though one of those domains – the Real – is strictly unbindable; the Thing's mutability transmits some of the special terror that this inspires. The Lady of troubadour lyric is one instance of the Thing, her supposedly arbitrary and unpredictable behaviour expressing the lover's prior ambivalence.

This depiction of the Lady takes us some way from Paris's rationalizing account, but brings us close to another great medievalist. In his 1936 account, C. S. Lewis enumerates courtly love's essential characteristics: 'Humility, Courtesy, Adultery and the Religion of Love'.[31] Where Paris is concerned to understand *l'amour courtois* as a good in its own right (albeit a specialized and restricted one), Lewis presents it as parasitically dependent on established values. It shares some of the dominant culture's standards (humility, courtesy), others it contravenes. Courtly love is an erotic anti-religion that 'arises [partially but most significantly] as a rival or a parody of the real religion and emphasizes the antagonism of the two ideals'.[32]

Lewis draws attention to the element of scandalous transgression: courtly love's special pleasures rely on a perverse incitement to intermingle piety with blasphemy in a 'revolting' manner.[33] Adultery is structurally necessary for Lewis as for Paris, but for different reasons. Marital law stands for a much deeper-seated prohibition on loving or desiring anything other than in and through God; thus, whereas sexuality can be theologically innocent, 'romantic passion' is always wrong.[34] Lewis connects what he deems courtly love's repellent qualities not to animal need but to cultivation and sublimation: the lady's married status poses an obstacle whose overcoming promises the sought after blend of thrill and revulsion. Lewis thus agrees with Lacan in analysing an intimate relation between idealization and abjection in courtly love.[35] The practice of courtly love poetry represents more than just a redefined honour; courtly love is, in Lewis's term, always 'dishonourable'.[36]

Lewis's analysis supplies an element of unattractiveness missing from Paris's coherent pursuit of a good. With some exaggeration, this may be compared to the way in which Sade makes available for Lacan something implied by but suppressed in Kantian ethics: discipline's perverse yield. The programmatic violation of taboos in courtly love forges a path towards the *jouissance* which ordinary rules are designed to keep at bay. In Lacan's words: 'Si les voies vers la jouissance ont en elles-mêmes quelque chose qui s'amortit, qui tend à être impracticable, c'est l'interdiction qui ... sert, si je puis dire, de véhicule à tout terrain, d'autochenille, pour sortir de ces boucles qui ramènent toujours l'homme, tournant en rond, vers l'ornière d'une satisfaction courte et piétinée' ('If the paths to *jouissance* have something in them that dies out, that tends to make them impassable, prohibition, if I may say so, becomes its all-terrain vehicle, its half-track truck that gets it out of the circuitous routes that lead man back in a roundabout way toward the rut of a short and well-trodden satisfaction').[37] Where *jouissance* is considered to be an evil, the role of moral law is to 'servir d'appui à cette jouissance, à faire que le péché devienne ce que saint Paul appelle démesurément pécheur' ('support ... the *jouissance* involved; ... so that the sin becomes what St Paul calls inordinately sinful').[38] Discipline, whether enacted in self-castigation and renunciation or in programmatic indulgence in the disgusting, becomes a kind of slingshot towards *jouissance*.

The sensitivity to courtly love's shock value that Lewis and Lacan, for all their differences, share, measures the difference between Lacan's ethics and the tradition from which he claims to depart, namely that in Lacanian ethics the 'good' is not considered primarily as an end engendering an ideal of conduct, but as a structural barrier keeping us within the pleasure principle's circuit of frustration and away from the ugly *jouissance* that we seek in spite of our civilized selves.[39] The internal division resulting from this antagonism is one aspect of the Real, and Lacanian ethics is designed to analyse the subject's relation to the Real, independent of the symbolic and imaginary anchors that keep us within the circuit of 'real life'. Positive moral value is awarded to phenomena or initiatives that advance this analysis, thus serving our 'devoir de vérité' ('duty of truth').[40] Courtly love comes closer than does traditional ethics to humanity's secret heart inasmuch as it elevates an unconventional 'good' which is singular, antisocial and unconcerned with utilitarian considerations of need or moral requirements of 'bienfaisance' ('philanthropy').[41] It thus allows for a more accurate understanding of the Real; however, it also brings complicated imaginary and symbolic configurations of the sort which recent Lacanian thinkers in particular have explored. In the next section, I turn to such elaborations of courtly love operating in relation to all three Lacanian registers, showing how these illuminate the love relation between Lancelot and Guinevere in the non-cyclic prose *Lancelot*.

LANCELOT AND GUINEVERE: LACANIAN COURTLY LOVERS?

Žižek explains how the Lacanian concept of the 'other' includes imaginary, symbolic and real aspects, corresponding to the classification Lacan puts on psychic experience:

First there is the imaginary other – other people 'like me', my fellow human beings with whom I am engaged in mirror-like relationships of competition, mutual recognition, and so on. Then there is the symbolic 'big Other' – the 'substance' of our social existence, the impersonal set of rules that coordinate our existence. Finally there is the Other qua Real, the impossible Thing, the 'inhuman partner', the Other with whom no symmetrical dialogue, mediated by the symbolic Order, is possible.[42]

He adds that the other 'perhaps provides the ultimate case of the Lacanian notion of the "Borromean knot" that unites these three dimensions', emphasizing that although these different aspects can be distinguished conceptually in this manner, in any actual instance they will interlink and interweave with different biases and in different proportions to produce a distinct and complex compound. Sarah Kay elaborates a parallel analysis of troubadour love lyric, summarizing the lover's relation to the object of desire as being 'both traumatic and paradoxical because it is at the same time imaginary (aspiring to delusional exaltation), symbolic (a product of the poet's linguistic and institutional codes) and [R]eal (powered by its relation to the Thing)'.[43]

Following these thinkers, we can detect the same three dimensions to the courtly lover's experience in a key passage halfway through the non-cyclic prose *Lancelot*: the decisive scene in which, at a tryst negotiated by Galehot, Lancelot admits his love to Guinevere, leading to the couple's first kiss:

'Or me dites, [said the queen,] totes les chevaleries que vos avez faites, por cui les feïstes vos?'

'Dame,' fait il, 'por vos.'

'Commant?' fait ele, 'amez me vos tant?'

'Dame,' fait il, 'ge n'ain tant ne moi ne autrui.' ...

'Dites moi,' fait ele, 'd'ou cest anmors mut dont ge vos demant?' ...

'Dame,' fait il, 'vos lo me feïstes faire, qui de moi feïstes vostre ami, se vostre boche ne me manti.'

'Mon ami,' fait ele, 'et comant?'

'Dame,' fait il, 'ge ving devant vos qant ge oi pris congié de monseignor lo roi, toz armez fors de mon chief et de mes mains, si vos commandai a Deu et dis que j'estoie vostre chevaliers an quel qe leu que ge fusse. Et vos deïstes que vostre chevaliers et vostres anmis voloiez vos que ge fusse. Et ge dis: "A Deu, dame." Et vos deïstes: "A Deu, biaus douz amis." Ne onques puis do cuer ne me pot issir. Ce fu li moz qui prodome me fera se gel suis. Ne onques puis ne vign an si grant meschief que de cest mot ne me manbrast. Cist moz m'a conforté an toz mes anuiz, cist moz m'a de toz mes maus garantiz et m'a gari de toz periz; cist moz m'a saolé an totes mes fains, cist moz m'a fait riche an totes mes granz povretez.' (pp. 345–6)

('Now, tell me, [said the queen,] all the knightly deeds that you have done, for whom did you do them?' 'Lady,' he said, 'for you.' 'What?' she said, 'do you love me so much?' 'Lady,' he said, 'I do not love myself or anyone else as much.' ... 'Tell me,' she said, 'from where did this love which I am asking you about spring?' ... 'Lady,' he said, 'you made me do it, for you made me your *ami*, if your mouth did not lie to me.' 'My *ami*?' she said, 'and how was that?' 'Lady,' he said, 'I came before you when I had taken leave of my lord the king, fully armed except for my head and my hands, and I commended you to God and said that I was your knight wherever I might be. And you said that you wished that I might be your knight and your *ami*. And I said: "Goodbye, lady." And you said: "Goodbye, fair, sweet *ami*." And never since could that go out of my heart. That was the word which will make me a man of valour, if I am one. And never since have I been in such dire straits that that word did not come to my mind. That word has comforted me in all my troubles, that word has protected me against all ills and saved me from all dangers; that word has filled me full whenever I have been hungry, that word has made me rich in my moments of great poverty.')[44]

The imaginary aspect of courtly love relates to the idealization of the Lady which, for Lacan as for Freud before him, is narcissistic. The Lady is the mirror surface onto which the courtly lover projects his ideal ego, and her love is sought, in part, to confirm that he is the epitome of knightly and courtly values.[45] Lancelot links his adulation of Guinevere to his own idealized self-image by his claim that it is out of love for Guinevere that he has performed the exploits which have earned his peerless chivalric reputation, an assertion acknowledged in Guinevere's response, 'si vos en est bien venu, que prodome vos ai fait' ('and good has come to you because of it, for I have made you a man of valour'). This process is performative in the sense that chivalry needs always to be re-established, as indicated by the tenses Lancelot employs: 'Ce fu li moz qui prodome me fera se gel suis'. Chivalry can only be asserted in the present by promising future and ever greater deeds. As the lover progresses ethically (following Paris's analysis) his task becomes more demanding, his path more rigorous, and his object, to become the ideal knight and worthy of his lady, recedes, requiring ever greater discipline. Lacan emphasizes Freud's interest in the fact that moral conscience becomes only more punctilious as we offend it less: it is 'comme un parasite nourri des satisfactions qu'on lui accorde' ('like a parasite that is fed by the satisfactions we accord it').[46]

Courtly love's symbolic dimension relates to language and society conceived as conventional and contractual systems which allow one to become a subject through using language and playing social roles, and which also alienate the subject by retaining a resistant core never wholly amenable to personal appropriation. Lancelot alleges that the 'biaus douz amis' with which the queen bade him farewell on his first adventure has sustained him ever since and that it is his effort to live up to this name which has made him the 'prodome' he may be or become. Through Lancelot's repeated emphasis on the 'mot' spoken by Guinevere, not only the beloved Lady but also the lover emerge as the creation of linguistic codes. Guinevere emphasizes that she intended her words not as the mark of a privileged, intimate relationship but as polite commonplace, 'friend' but not 'lover' (she says it to all the boys); nevertheless she accepts and even applauds the process by which Lancelot has fashioned her meaning into that appropriate to a courtly beloved:

'A foi, a foi,' fist la reine, 'ci ot mot dit de mout bone ore, et Dex an soit aorez qant il dire lo me fist. Mais ge nel pris pas si a certes comme vos feïstes, et a mainz chevaliers l'ai ge dit ou ge ne pansai onques fors lo dire. Et vostre pansez ne fu mie vilains, ainz fu douz et debonaires; si vos en est bien venu, que prodome vos ai fait.' (p. 346)

('In faith, in faith,' said the queen, 'that was a word fortunately spoken, and God be praised for having made me say it. But indeed I did not take it in the way you did, and I have said it to many knights without any thought beyond the words. And your thought was not uncourtly, but sweet and gracious; and good has come to you because of it, for I have made you a man of valour.')

When Lancelot alleges in the tryst scene that Guinevere made him her *ami*-lover, he is not claiming to have misunderstood her. His response at the time to her 'biaus douz amis' was to mutter under his breath 'Granz merciz, dame, qant il vos plaist que ge lo soie' (p. 165; 'Many thanks, lady, when it pleases you that I be that'), implying an intention already to convert her open, friendly sentiment to one of clandestine love. Earlier comments by the narrator suggest that Guinevere is indeed innocent of any equivocating intention for, although she suspects on more than one occasion that Lancelot loves her, she tries to distance herself (pp. 157–8, 161). That her intention is immaterial, however, is implied by the way Lancelot fragments her person, isolating her mouth ('se vostre boche ne me manti'). Claiming to refuse any source of meaning other than the words themselves, he invokes a supra-individual, impersonal order of language to empower the interpretation desired by the hearer. Lancelot forges the relationship between himself and the queen out of 'un sol mot' (p. 347; 'a single word').

Courtly love's contractual aspect is no less evident than its linguistic basis. Lancelot contrives to obtain the sword that completes his dubbing from Guinevere, exploiting a technicality to become her knight rather than Arthur's. The bond thus created is spelled out in the message urging Guinevere to send him the sword he lacks: 'Et li dites que ge li ment que, por moi gaaignier a tozjors, que ele me face chevalier, si m'envoit une espee com a celui qui ses chevaliers sera' (p. 174; 'And tell her that I urge her that, in order to win me forever, she make me knight, and send me a sword as to the one who will be her knight'). The power dynamic which this bond represents is not straightforward. Lancelot's actions throughout the first half of the text aim to create obligations on Guinevere's part, and the queen acknowledges that such debts must be paid:

'Certes,' fait ele, 'ge sai bien que il a fait plus por moi que ge ne porroie deservir, se il n'avoit plus fait que la pais porchaciee [between Galehot and Arthur]. Ne il ne me porroit nule chose requerre do je lo poïsse escondire bellemant.' (p. 347)

('Indeed,' she said, 'I know well that he has done more for me than I could deserve, even if he had done nothing more than bring about the peace [between Galehot and Arthur]. And there is nothing that he could ask of me that I could decently refuse him.')

Although Lancelot ascribes to Guinevere the agency powering the entire romance and she accepts the dominating role ('prodome vos ai fait'), it is evident that his actions impel her into this position. The loving contract that binds him to submission and her to command is his creation, for a long time known to and honoured by him alone. As in Deleuze's account of masochism – extended to courtly love by Žižek – the real agency remains with the suffering 'victim'.[47] Lancelot adventures under the banner of the Other's desire, but in this text at least, that banner camouflages a disregard for the other's desire.[48] Unlike in Paris's model, the knight's gift of himself, his sacrifice and his risk precede and determine the lady's apparently almost mandatory reciprocation. Her authority is a product of his fantasy, though once established it entails real consequences in the narrative, including real risks to Lancelot himself.

The imaginary and symbolic dimensions of courtly love are complemented by its Real aspect, marked by the lady's conversion into the Thing. No sooner does Guinevere assent to the imposed role of courtly beloved than she begins to torment her lover with unpredictable changes in attitude and cruel teasing:

'Et vostre sanblanz me mostre que vos amez ne sai la quele de ces dames la plus que vos ne faites moi, car vos an avez ploré de paor, ne n'osez esgarder vers eles de droite esgardeüre. Si m'aparçoif bien que vostre pensez n'est pas si a moi com vos me faites lo sanblant. Et par la foi que vos devez la riem que vos plus amez, dites moi la quel des trois vos amez tant.' . . .

Et ce disoit ele bien por veoir coment ele lo porra metre a malaise, car ele cuide bien que il ne pansast d'amors s'a lui non, ja mar aüst il fait por li se la jornee non des noires armes. Mais ele se delitoit durement an sa messaise veoir et escouter. Et cil an fu si angoissos que par un po ne se pasma. (p. 346)

('And your behaviour shows me that you love one or other of those ladies over there more than you do me, for you have wept with fear because of it and do not dare look directly at them. I can tell that your thought is not so set on me as you pretend. So by the faith that you owe to the thing you love most, tell me which of the three you love so.' . . .

And she said this to see how she could upset him, for she believed indeed that he had no thought of love except for her, even if he had done nothing for her sake but the day of the black armour. But she took great delight in seeing and hearing his discomfort. And he was so disturbed that he almost fainted.)

It is difficult to see in the queen's actions here an effort to 'rendre [Lancelot] meilleur, à le faire plus "valoir"' ('improve him, make him more "worthy"'), in Paris's terms.[49] Nor is there any evidence of fear of discovery on her part to justify Lancelot's answering fear. Taking pleasure in her power to discomfit her lover, Guinevere instead resembles the 'cold, distanced, inhuman partner' of Lacanian courtly love, as repellent as she is fascinating.[50] Lancelot's strenuous avoidance of her presence up to this point has allowed him to engage in virtuous chivalric activity which enhances his status and serves others. His first step outside this orbit towards greater intimacy with the object of desire triggers pain and anxiety, in a movement of repulsion expressed narratively by her heartlessness and his answering distress.

COURTLY LOVE ETHICS

While the above exposition has concentrated on those aspects of Lancelot and Guinevere's relationship, as presented in the non-cyclic prose *Lancelot*, that fit the Lacanian analysis of courtly love, there are also significant divergences. The handling can be clarified by comparison with other extant treatments, which approach with varying emphases the problematic of Lancelot's simultaneously ideal and transgressive status. In the following discussion, I shall concentrate attention on relatively narrow differences and subtle distinctions between works.

Chrétien de Troyes's influential verse romance *Le Chevalier de la Charrette* (*c.* 1177–81, hence perhaps one or two generations earlier than the non-cyclic prose romance) is thought to be the earliest literary treatment of the adulterous affair between Lancelot and Guinevere. For much of this text Guinevere is presented as a mysterious and terrifying creature capable not only of demanding that her lover shame himself (an action whose import it is difficult to exaggerate) by fighting 'au nouaz' ('to the worst') in a tournament and by adopting the public identity of a dishonoured criminal, but further of greeting with coldness the man thus devoted to her.[51] As Paris points out, 'Aux yeux du poète, elle est en cela dans son rôle tout aussi bien que lui [the self-abnegating Lancelot], et elle est le type accompli de la *dame* tout comme il est celui de l'*ami*' ('In the poet's eyes, she is thereby fulfilling her role as much as he, and she is the fully realized type of the *lady* just as he is of the *lover*').[52] Her swings from scorn to reciprocation keep her lover in abject fear. Reasoning by contraries, Paris analyses this fear as compensation for or transfer of the risk that the lady runs in giving herself to the knight; Lacan's suggestion that the lover's fear is primary and represents fear of the object of his desire is simpler and better fitted to the text of the *Charrette*, where Guinevere behaves with apparent callousness and life-threatening whimsy towards her would-be protector.[53] In the non-cyclic prose version, contrastingly, Guinevere's teasing of Lancelot is one of a very few episodes in which she resembles the inhuman and arbitrary Lady-Thing, and then only mildly. There her reactions to Lancelot's suffering are almost exclusively sympathetic, even empathetic. Far from blowing hot and cold, she shows great constancy, her respect for and attachment to her knight developing over the course of the romance. If 'the Lady is the Other which is not our "fellow-creature": that is to say, she is someone with whom no relationship of empathy is possible', then this particular Guinevere is no Lady.[54]

Even the teasing episode finishes with her concern for the suffering Lancelot's well-being and active intervention to ease his distress: 'Et la reine meïsmes lo dota [that he might faint], qui lo vit muer et changier; si lou prist par la cheveçaille que il ne chaïst, si apelle Galehot' (p. 346; 'And the queen herself feared it [that he might faint], when she saw him change colour and alter; and she took hold of his collar to stop him falling, and called Galehot'). Again she has taken her own words less seriously than has her lover. On the one hand, the mildness of her teasing contrasts with Lancelot's dramatic response to enhance his unanticipated seriousness and thereby to increase his stature. On the other, it is further evidence that the text encourages a distinction between the character of Guinevere and the position held by the Lady-Thing within the economy of courtly love. My point is not that Guinevere has not yet fallen in love, but that the whole complex of *l'amour courtois* is shown by the text to be gendered masculine; cultural rather than individual psychology is at stake. Sublimation, in the Lacanian sense of the elevation of an object to the dignity of the Thing (thus filling out the void of the Real, as in the creationist sublimations of Chapter 1), is shown to originate with the lover. He therefore at once takes credit and bears responsibility for it, the Lady being only the support of his ambition. Sublimation in the Freudian sense is similarly involved in this gendered paradigm; the transformation of erotic passion into social utility and into virtue is a male preserve resistant to feminine encroachment. Recall how the non-cyclic prose text insists that Guinevere's authoritative and inspiring role as well as her improving effect on Lancelot are entirely his creations, while his swoon rebukes and punishes her small attempt to appropriate the place of the Thing. The Thing's disruptiveness is minimized in Guinevere, with the effect that its Real dimension diminishes to become only a structuring device within a system.

The non-cyclic prose romance, moreover, generally correlates Lancelot's love with his honour in the conventional manner of the chivalry topos.[55] This contrasts with the *Charrette*, where his devotion to the queen exposes

Lancelot to disgrace and mockery (including in the comic scenes of his excessive love) as often as it permits him to enhance his reputation. Lancelot's humiliation in Chrétien's text is particularly ambiguous where it occurs in association with the quasi-religious treatment of his love, since the text here draws on a spiritual rhetoric which places the categories of the abject and the sacred in direct communication.[56] Pollution – all too representable in its insistent materiality – becomes a symbol of ineffable, divine purity, 'low' signifying 'high' in a trope common in hagiographic writing.[57] Thus the temporary inversion of chivalric values operates in the *Charrette* to suggest that Lancelot transcends those values, a kind of holy fool.[58] Lancelot's love would then lie outside the chivalric order, critical of it and eluding norms like the prohibition on adultery and betrayal of one's friend or lord. The affair with Guinevere could in such a case be justified according to the Christian theme of love superseding law, a numinous exemption from the common run. The *Charrette* would therefore represent a foundational document of the courtly anti-religion which so irritated Lewis.

This argument is, however, far from conclusive. Sarah Kay and Simon Gaunt have pointed recently to Lancelot's failure in the *Charrette* to reach the transcendent heights that would indicate convincingly the logic of inversion at work. For Gaunt, Lancelot's unstable knightly status suggests his personal inadequacy relative to the highest courtly standards; for Kay, it opens the question of the defectiveness of courtly ethics with reference to religious standards.[59] The death drive inherent in Lancelot's (and Guinevere's) passion falls short of the sublimity that would award it definite ethical valence. My position is somewhat different. Accepting that, in contrast to the madness and isolation experienced by Tristan or Yvain, the abjection and suffering endured by the *Charrette*'s Lancelot leave him (just) within the chivalric circuit, I consider that he stretches the ethical coverage of this circuit. Lancelot after the cart episode is permitted to join courtly gatherings and continues to function socially as a knight in spite of wounds and dishonour. In his ambivalence he figures conflicts and aberrations fundamental to the courtly, chivalric order itself. As the quintessential bearer of values desired and feared by the court he can be compared to Gauvain and to Kay. These are in many texts paired figures whose adventures and misadventures represent the Arthurian court's social, moral and spiritual achievements and weaknesses; thus they are used to define chivalry's symbolic order. Lancelot, contrastingly, undertakes exploits whose extreme nature makes them difficult to judge. The three characters' careers in the *Charrette* are a case in point. Kay is imprisoned and disabled by wounds received as a result of over-extending his prowess, Gauvain trapped due to his courtesy – the punishment in both cases fitting the crime. Neither is touched by the love which permits Lancelot to achieve feats of prowess and courtesy that extend the aspirations of the court, gesturing towards their redefinition. By attaching the best knight/worst knight trope to Lancelot and to his love, the *Charrette* initially drives a wedge between the values of *l'amour courtois* and those of public courtliness and chivalry on the one hand, and of religion on the other (to recall the distinctions made by Paris and Lewis respectively). The antagonism thus created has the effect, not of isolating courtly love, but of opening up its dialectics and paradoxes to wider ethical valence – the gift of the Real. In a secondary though foreseeable phase, the court and its chivalry themselves become caught up in this ethical extension, their values tested in the career of their doubly hyperbolic hero. 'Lancelot figures as a touchstone whose contact reveals the positive and negative alloys of the society itself.'[60]

Failure is not an unethical notion. The critical but uncertain failure to transcend (or, differently, the possible failure of transcendence) is inherent in Lancelot's structural situation as within courtly love per se.[61] Lancelot teeters on the brink of the Real, in the *entre-deux* between it and the symbolic and imaginary orders. It is not necessary for him actually to die in order to activate the critical uncertainty that characterizes the Real. Indeed, a character who actually (fictionally) dies, as Antigone does, extinguishes the audience's hesitation and doubt in awe and sometimes admiration: dying installs a settled regime and brings an end to the *entre-deux-morts*. Sacrifice enacted by dying or by withdrawing from the world is not the only way of activating ethical possibilities, as Gaunt and Kay imply. Death is a significant horizon at numerous points for the lovers in the *Charrette*, and their situation brings them into contact with the Real. Although they fail to take the final step, their choices place into question imaginary and symbolic aspects of their environment: courtly life's lies, substitutions and partial satisfactions. If there is nothing in the *Charrette* that is quite out of the courtly world, this very fact enhances the uncertainty affecting the value of the many things within that world, from its centre to its outermost margins. It forces us to question whether they 'belong' to that world, either de facto or by ethical appropriateness. The death drive inherent in Lancelot's love therefore energizes an inquiry into courtly norms. This potential of courtly love in Lacan's account relates not to whether the lover dies but to the nature of the object as Thing. Through the Thing, the Real defines the courtly space as what Spitzer, referring to troubadour lyric, calls 'the psychological in-between [*entre-deux*] in which the sentiment of love is placed; felt as real yet unreal, shifting from the *straight nothing* [*dreit nien*] to occupy our whole being'.[62] Lancelot's failure to move wholly beyond the courtly world in the *Charrette* points to an exploration of the collective psychological phenomenon that is the courtly Borromean knot: a world at once real and unreal, contradictorily caught up in symbolic, imaginary and Real registers and disturbing the grounds on which we judge. As Cohen argues, Lancelot's devotion queers courtly norms by distending them.[63] The *Charrette* interrogates the courtly by obliging us to locate its exemplary figure in precisely this critical intermediacy: the more *entre-deux* because not *mort*. The eventual outcome may be the condemnation of the Arthurian order, or the initiation of a new and better order of chivalry; my interest is rather in the problem posed than in answers that put an end to questioning. Chrétien equated (if he did not inherit the equation) the field of questions relating to Lancelot's love and chivalry with the very fullest dimensions of the Arthurian order. It is within this same agenda, defined by the limit case where 'best' turns into 'worst', 'most courtly' into 'most uncourtly', and vice versa, that later *remanieurs* frame their responses.

It is therefore notable that, compared with his counterpart in the verse romance, the hero of the non-cyclic prose work is encouraged by love into relatively familiar and 'normal' chivalric paths and suffers correspondingly less humiliation and bewilderment. Those embarrassments he does undergo are not willed by the queen. Moreover, there is never other than the most transitory ambiguity about his real pre-eminence. When, for example, Lancelot falls into a trance at the sight of Guinevere and is ludicrously captured by Daguenet lo Fol, a knight described as 'fox naïs et la plus coarde piece de char que l'an saüst' (p. 268; 'a simple idiot and the cowardliest piece of flesh known'), it is Daguenet who is the object of ridicule. When Lancelot is imprisoned by the Lady of Malohot, his imprisonment becomes a formality as she rapidly succumbs to desirous wonder at the evidence of his extraordinary chivalric prowess. In place of the moral equivocations of the *Charrette*, in the non-cyclic prose romance Lancelot's temporary setbacks and humiliations are challenges he overcomes in advancing towards a status as the greatest of knights.[64] He does not ambiguously exceed/fall below but exemplifies and carries to new heights the court's ideal norms. He occasions no radical problematization of the chivalric order. His *maître*, the Lady of the Lake, speaks for an ideal of chivalry acceptable to the establishment, and the hero pursues this ideal with distinction.[65] Piety and protection of the Church are central to this code, presented as conventional values integrated into the aristocratic class myth in order to reinforce it. They elevate the nobility's moral status without requiring nobles to abandon their life in the world, which is essential to their protective role as *bellatores*. It is not surprising, in this context, that Lancelot and Guinevere's affair in the prose version lacks the 'revolting' (to recall Lewis) quasi-religious features which characterize Chrétien's lovers; the consummation of their love, an occasion for transcendent ecstasy in the *Charrette*, is summarily rendered in the non-cyclic prose. If this Lancelot knows less humiliation as a lover, he is also ignorant of the sexual-mystical *jouissance* which brings his predecessor erotic satisfaction and the highs of moral ambiguity. In both Guinevere and Lancelot himself, love in this text withdraws from the Real that gave *l'amour courtois* its ethical dimension for Lacan.

The non-cyclic prose *Lancelot* can also be compared to narratives of the Vulgate cycle: the *Queste del saint Graal*, the *Mort le roi Artu*, and indeed the cyclic prose *Lancelot* romance. After the point where it diverges from the non-cyclic version, the cyclic *Lancelot* continues to celebrate its hero but increasingly emphasizes the values that will come to fruition in the *Queste*: condemnation of worldly chivalry and the paramount importance of sexual purity, religious faith and divine grace. Lancelot's story in this version is presented less as his gradual public acquisition of the name Lancelot than as a long decline from the potential encoded in his baptismal name of Galahad. His affair with Guinevere plays a, if not the, key role in this decline.[66] Lancelot's privileged, paradoxical position in the *Queste*, and increasingly in the cyclic prose *Lancelot*, is that of the great sinner who repents and receives grace and who fathers the Grail hero but who, because of his fault, can never rise to the spiritual heights he should have achieved. Once again he can be contrasted with Gauvain. Whereas Gauvain's limitations are those of the court and of worldly life generally, the cyclic Lancelot even in his ruin retains a greater potential which stretches courtliness to one positive (and negative) extreme. The *Mort*, in contrast and perhaps reaction to the *Queste*, restores Lancelot to splendour and makes his love story only one element in the deepening twilight of the Arthurian order. Although the sense of culpability is generalized in the *Mort*, the connection between love and death is hammered home. Bors, rebuking Guinevere for her anger with Lancelot, states as a rule: 'Onques nus hom ne s'i prist fermement qui n'en moreust' (ch. 59, ll. 59–60; 'No man ever committed himself firmly to it without dying of it'). The Demoiselle d'Escalot's fate contradicts the gender configuration that Bors intends, while Mordred's late passion for Guinevere confirms that love is a necessary element in his rush to destruction. Whether constant or inconstant, love in an imperfect world is implicated in the cataclysm of the society it also sustains. Adultery, as Elizabeth Edwards remarks, is the 'structure of structure' in the

Arthurian world, grounding and sustaining those inter-male relationships that it also damages.[67] Guinevere's rejection will destroy chivalry's sustaining norm, hence its very values: 'vos feroiz perir el cors d'un seul chevalier toutes bones graces por quoi hom puet monter en honneur terrienne et por quoi il est apelez graciex, ce est biautez et proesce, hardemenz et chevalerie, gentillesce' (ch. 59, ll. 61–6; 'you would cause to perish in the person of a single knight all good graces by which man can rise in worldly honour and for which he is called gracious, namely beauty and prowess, boldness, chivalry and nobility'). The damage will be widespread: 'vos domageroiz moult plus cest roiaume et maint autre que onques dame ne fist par le cors d'un sol chevalier' (ch. 59, ll. 80–2; 'you would harm this kingdom and many others much more than any lady ever did through the person of a single knight'). Lancelot and Guinevere are linked to multiple deaths and suffer repeated accusations of murder which confirm their love's mortiferous quality while displacing the guilt of their adultery onto acts of which they are at least partially innocent and submerging it in the general drive towards destruction.[68] Lancelot's exceptional unselfishness in returning Guinevere to Arthur after the Pope's intervention (Guinevere expresses no opinion) also offers one of the narrative's few instances of redemption, and the work ends with his salvation through as well as despite his love for both Guinevere and Arthur. These deathly, loving moments transcend as well as hasten the self-destruction of the Arthurian order, whose best and worst are again made inseparable, and ultimately equally fatal. The *Mort* recalls once again Freud's description of the organism in the grip of the death drive making its own way towards dying for strictly internal reasons. The endgame of the society he epitomizes is a cause as well as an effect of Lancelot's *vilains* and *vaillanz* characterization, encouraging readers to credit him as 'li plus vaillanz' for those actions in which he exercises free will, as opposed to those, not within his control, in which he appears 'li plus vilains'.

The spiritual, moral and social disruptiveness that the works relating to the end of the cycle ascribe to the adulterous relationship between Arthur's queen and his principal knight are weak in the non-cyclic prose *Lancelot*, which instead stresses the personally and politically constructive and integrative aspects of Lancelot and Guinevere's attachment. His love for Guinevere inspires Lancelot to deeds which establish his own greatness and enhance the prestige of Arthur's court, to which he adheres for her sake. Whatever the subversive qualities of other courtly love relationships, the present one is the primary support of the orthodox social order centring on the king. The potential problems associated with adultery are brushed aside in favour of a love which combines a manageable level of passion with creative (Freudian) sublimation. Lancelot's advances in love are correlated with his progress towards insertion in the social order by the stages of what has been called the 'identity theme': discovery of his name, acquisition of a reputation and installation as a knight of the Round Table.[69] For Lancelot to become Guinevere's lover appears as one among several events contributing to his inscription into the '"big Other", the intersubjective public space' of the Arthurian court.[70] This alliance between Lancelot's love for the queen and the regulated and regulatory order is augmented when he performs the same inscription for Guinevere, re-establishing her right to her name and rescuing both her and Arthur from the intrigue of the False Guinevere. The relationship between Lancelot and Guinevere upholds rather than opposes legal marriage, and is in this distinguished from Arthur's disastrous passions for the Saxon Maiden and the False Guinevere – both situations being rectified by Lancelot's intervention. Marriage in the work correspondingly endorses this particular adultery; Guinevere's recognition of the debt that she owes Lancelot in her capacity as Arthur's wife and queen (p. 74, above) authorizes her to accept, in recompense, his interpretation of the phrase 'biaus douz amis'. The lovers' excuse does not depend only on the morally weak argument that Arthur's conduct has been no less bad. The ideologies of marriage, queenship and feudal assistance are made to justify Lancelot and Guinevere's liaison as a necessary supplement to the power of husband and king, a concrete check and balance protecting wife, realm and people against potential tyrannical abuses.

To sum up the argument of this section: by comparison with the *Charrette*, the *Queste* and the *Mort*, the non-cyclic prose *Lancelot*'s treatment of Lancelot and Guinevere's affair diminishes those aspects of the courtly love relationship which refer to the Real while accentuating the narcissistic dimension which aligns it with the imaginary and, in Lacan's analysis, forms a defensive barrier against the Real.[71] Still more noticeably, the symbolic register is very substantially strengthened in the modes of law and contract, and as enforcement not negation. Lancelot's love for Guinevere is positioned as supportive of order, and namely of the Arthurian order, of marriage and of good kingship. The text is therefore more 'moral' than 'ethical' in the Lacanian sense. Whereas the death drive expresses itself in the *Mort Artu* in fatalism and mass destruction and in the *Charrette* in transcendent sexual pleasure and quasi-religious ecstasy, in both cases connected to the relation between Lancelot and Guinevere, the non-cyclic prose *Lancelot* detaches it from social cataclysm and also almost entirely from Lancelot's sexuality. Lancelot briefly goes mad when captured by the Saxon Maiden, Arthur's mistress, who treacherously imprisons the king and other key knights; thus a viable interpretation of his insanity is that it figures the damage inflicted on the kingdom by Arthur's sexuality, not his own. He is cured when the Lady of the Lake appears to restore his love's alignment with the Law, enabling him to rescue Arthur and restore the kingdom. Arthur's adultery may therefore be held to necessitate Lancelot's operationally, as well as to excuse it morally.

Many of the preceding remarks are true also of the cyclic prose *Lancelot*. However, the constructive aspect of Lancelot and Guinevere's love there represents only one strand in a situation that grows increasingly complex as we read on and look back. By ending early, the non-cyclic version excludes many of the most compromising events in the lovers' story and presents a more straightforwardly positive picture in which Lancelot as Guinevere's lover represents only the virtues and strengths of the chivalric order. He is the best of knights but not the worst – except very briefly in his madness, where another is to blame. This does not mean that the liaison is entirely unproblematic in the non-cyclic prose romance. A compromised air increasingly haunts Guinevere's position. If, as Kennedy claims, comparisons with Tristan work in the cyclic prose *Lancelot* to deprecate the hero, and these comparisons are lacking in the non-cyclic version, nevertheless Guinevere increasingly recalls Ysolt.[72] Thanking Lancelot publicly for his assistance in the war against the Saxon Maiden (during which war the couple have consummated their relationship), her equivocal use of conventional signs recalls that of the paradigmatic adulterous queen:

'Sire chevaliers, ge ne sai qui vos iestes, ce poise moi; ne ge ne vos sai que offrir por l'annor mon seignor avant et por la moie aprés, que vos avez hui maintenue. Mais por lui avant et por moi aprés vos otroi ge moi et m'amor, si comme leiaus dame doit doner a leial chevalier.'

Et qant li rois l'ot, si l'am prise mout de ce que ele l'a fait sanz estre anseigniee. (p. 569)

('Sir knight, I am sorry that I do not know who you are; and I do not know what to offer you for my lord's honour first and mine after, that you have upheld today. But for his sake first and for mine after I grant you myself and my love, as a loyal lady should give to a loyal knight.'

And when the king heard this, he esteemed her greatly because she had done it without being instructed.)

This scene echoes the *rendez-vous épié* and equivocal oath episodes in which Béroul's Ysolt establishes the innocence of her friendship with Tristan.

Guinevere, moreover, becomes increasingly dependent on Lancelot until, in the text's reiterated phrase, 'ele ne voit mies comment ele se poïst consirrer de lui veoir' (p. 558; 'she cannot at all see how she could do without seeing him'). Her desire to keep Lancelot close to her and her fear for his safety induce a new ambivalence in her towards his prowess:

Et li poise de ce qu'ele lo set et lo voit a si volenteïf et a si corageus, car ele ne voit mies comment sa vie poïst durer sanz la soe, s'il s'an aloit ja mais de cort. Si voudroit bien que il aüst un po mains de hardement et de proece. (p. 558)

(And it grieves her to know and see him so resolute and courageous, for she cannot at all see how her life could continue without his, in case he ever left court. And she would definitely have preferred in him a little less boldness and prowess.)

Caught between contradictory desires, Guinevere grows into the characteristics of the demanding, unprincipled courtly Lady, a role which earlier she held only in Lancelot's fantasy. Ironically, the text's treatment of her developing subjectivity ascribes to her the disturbing behaviour that Lacan detects in the courtly Lady-Thing. Whereas courtly love improves masculine behaviour, it causes the female to deteriorate. Responsibility for his moral, social and chivalric virtues remains with Lancelot, while we can foresee in Guinevere the potential for 'caprices apparents' and 'rigueurs passagères' ('seeming fits of contrariness', 'short-lived episodes of severity') arising from her love for the knight.[73] The discordant aspects of the courtly *paradoxe amoureux*, 'have and have not', are apportioned: sublimation to the male, cupidity to the female. It is therefore possible to ascribe the damaging consequences of episodes barely sketched in the narrative future to Guinevere's love, and more generally to female interference in ethical matters. At the least, the non-cyclic prose version implies one commentary on the impending events of Arthurian history. At most, its selection and treatment of episodes may be understood to reject the sequel that it refuses to tell.

GALEHOT

A significant portion of the destructive or problematic material from which Lancelot's love for Guinevere is distanced is transferred to the love for Lancelot of Galehot, a character thought to be an invention of the prose *Lancelot*.[74] Galehot is a figure clearly *entre-deux-morts* from the moment he meets and loves Lancelot, in an encounter which takes him beyond the bounds of normal life and condemns him to death. The death drive in Galehot has some similarities with the destruction drive running through

Roland and discussed in Chapter 1. Thus Galehot is repeatedly associated with threats to the Arthurian kingdom. His first intervention in the narrative recalls the giants of the chronicle tradition; like them, Galehot declares that he has conquered many kings and demands Arthur's submission in order to complete his triumph, threatening conquest and the ravishment of Guinevere if he is resisted (pp. 263–4).[75] However, the brutality, overweening pride and appetite for conquest of the chronicle giants are in Galehot partially assimilated to approved chivalric virtues, for he is spoken of as a great leader and as 'li plus gentis chevaliers et li plus deboenneres do monde et toz li plus larges' (p. 264; 'the most noble and gracious knight in the world and absolutely the most generous'). Galehot is so impressed with the anonymous hero's exemplary chivalry that he drops his belligerent challenge to Arthur and abandons destructive *jouissance* in exchange for this unknown knight's acceptance of his hospitality. This motif aligns Galehot with those pagan knights of *chanson de geste* and romance whose appreciation of Christian chivalry is assimilated to religious revelation, for they convert in order to become the companions in arms of the Christian heroes they admire. Such figures are often gigantically tall and strong and are themselves wonderful knights and shining examples of chivalry both before and after their conversion.[76] Galehot's destruction drive is transformed into loving care for Lancelot. Nonetheless, he retains ambiguous overtones that some of these chivalric rationalizations of the folk giant lose, in particular the association with excessive appetite.[77] It is Galehot who, fearing lest Lancelot die of his love for Guinevere, initiates the physical – and even the reciprocal – relationship with the queen by pressing her to kiss the knight when Lancelot himself, a true Lacanian courtly lover in this respect, asks for nothing.[78] Thus the adulterous affair may be distinguished from Lancelot's love and any culpability assigned to the former need not taint the latter. Not Lancelot's love for Guinevere but Galehot's for Lancelot can be held responsible for the *passage à l'acte* which carries socially constructive sublimation into questionable sexual liaison; the consequent destruction can therefore be taken to represent the half-giant's affection rather than the knight's. *Vaillanz* is separated from *vilains*, 'to have' from 'to have not'. Galehot joins Guinevere in responsibility for the problematic aspects of male heterosexuality. On the other hand, a contrary reading emphasizing Galehot's human and royal side allows Galehot to add stature to Lancelot's love. Thus Stäblein argues that Galehot and Guinevere together represent sacral royal power, and that Galehot's participation encourages us to interpret Lancelot's kiss not as a carnal act but as the gesture of a king.[79] Galehot's involvement therefore ambiguously either exaggerates or offsets the baser aspects of Lancelot's love, confirming that Galehot bears the *entre-deux-morts* for Lancelot as well as in his own right.[80] A consequence of this duality is that the death drive working in the figure is not a straightforward destruction drive; Galehot's loving, self-effacing melancholy has elements of the Nirvana principle also, as he goes seemingly gently into his good night. By its role in Lancelot's elevation and incorporation into the court, Galehot's death drive regenerates the collective imaginary and symbolic domains. Yet its negative aspect is not so easily contained. Although it does not match in intensity those revitalizing energies that are generated by Roland's dynamic embrace of destruction, I shall nevertheless ultimately argue that it may in the end be more detrimental to the existing order and to what the text imagines as the conditions for order per se.

Galehot's love for Lancelot is placed in insistent parallel with Lancelot's love for Guinevere, producing a comparison interesting for the differences as well as the similarities it reveals. The imaginary dimension of courtly love is expressed in the wonder and instant devotion with which Galehot greets Lancelot's chivalry when he encounters it in his second battle against Arthur. In response to Galehot's question about his identity, Lancelot gives his usual answer, 'uns chevaliers suis' ('I am a knight'). Galehot immediately perceives the normative value of this apparently modest claim: '"Certes," fait Gualehoz, "chevalieres iestes vos, li miaudres qui soit"' (p. 320; '"Indeed," said Galehot, "a knight you are, and the best there may be"'). The dimensions of Lancelot's assertion are unfolded in an early conversation with the Lady of the Lake (pp. 141–7), who presents knighthood as a supreme moral, spiritual and physical achievement to be approached in a spirit of awe, and failure in which will incur worldly dishonour and divine condemnation. The state of true knighthood has only been achieved by a handful of men before and after Christ's passion. This discussion causes Lancelot to declare his vocation for knighthood, and his self-identification as 'uns chevaliers' must be understood in this light. By his response to this epitome of chivalry, Galehot reveals with great clarity a significant aspect of the love that runs throughout romance knightly interactions, hostile and friendly. Zeikowitz analyses the identificatory aspects of this desire, while Schultz names it *aristophilia*, a gender-neutral erotic attraction to 'nobility and courtliness'.[81]

Courtly love's symbolic dimension is evident in the text's expression of Galehot's love through phrases that it presents as internal formulae, repeating them from one relationship to another. Thus Galehot calls Lancelot his 'biaus dolz amis' (e.g., p. 324), the same phrase on which Lancelot hopes to exert the pressure that will transform Guinevere's polite disinterest into love. Lancelot is consistently identified as the thing Galehot loves most in the world, 'la rien au monde que il plus aimme', an expression used also to define Lancelot's attachment to Guinevere. The verbal correspondences are multiple, as the text sets up a comparison between the two loves.[82] Galehot initially approaches the embodiment of his ideal ego by proposing a contract: 'Et ancor vos pri ge, por Deu, que vos herbergiez anuit a moi par covant que ferai a devise quant que vos m'oseroiz requiere' (p. 321; 'And I pray you again, for God's sake, that you lodge with me this night on condition that I will perform in full whatever you would dare ask of me'). The fact that he offers a *don en blanc* – an absolute, formal engagement empty of content – accentuates the contract's symbolic aspect. Like Lancelot's, Galehot's love is wedded to the symbolic order – not to any particular and therefore imaginary order, but to the empty structures of order as such.

Lancelot eventually reveals that Galehot has engaged to surrender to Arthur in the very moment of victory over him (p. 325). Galehot's love for the quintessential *chevalier* requires him to abandon the aggressive yet magnificent goals he has hitherto pursued, converting honour into humiliation in a manner which recalls the Lancelot of the *Chevalier de la Charrette* but not, I argued above, the hero of the non-cyclic prose romance.[83] This signals a major difference between Lancelot and Galehot as lovers in the later work. Galehot's love will involve him in suffering and ultimately in dying because, even though Lancelot acknowledges his obligations to Galehot, he remains an inaccessible object. This inaccessibility is not an incidental part of Galehot's love, rather he undergoes rebuff after rebuff. Prime among these is his intervention in Lancelot's affair, undertaken because he fears that Lancelot will die if he does not obtain some satisfaction from the queen. Galehot explains his anxieties when Guinevere asks him how arrangements are going for her first meeting with the hero whose name and secret love are still unknown to her:

'Dame,' fait il, 'g'en ai tant fait que ge dot que vostre proiere ne me toille la rien o monde que ge plus ain.'
    'Si m'aïst Dex,' fait ele, 'vos ne perdroiz ja rien por moi que ge ne vos rande a dobles. Mais q'an poez vos perdre por ce?'
    'Dame,' fait il, 'celui meesmes que vos demandez, que ge dot que chose n'en aveigne par qoi il se corrout, que gel perdroie a tozjorz mais.'
    'Certes,' fait ele, 'ce ne porroie ge mies randre. Mais se Deu plaist, par moi ne lo perdroiz vos ja, ne il ne seroit mie cortois se noiant vos an faisoit par ma proiere. (p. 337)

('Lady,' he said, 'I have done so much in it that I am afraid your entreaty may take from me the thing I love most in the world.' 'So help me God,' she said, 'you would never lose anything for my sake that I should not make up to you twice over. But what can you lose because of this?' 'Lady,' he said, 'the very man that you ask for, for I am afraid that something may come of it to vex him, and that I should lose him for ever.' 'Indeed,' she said, 'I could not make that up to you [return him to you]. But, please God, you would never lose him by my actions, and he would not be courtly if he did anything to you because of my entreaty.')

Although he fears losing Lancelot if Guinevere accepts him as her lover no less surely than if she rejects him, Galehot continues to ease negotiations.[84] The conscious ironies of such exchanges are a not insignificant element in the death drive working through Galehot. Notice that the text grounds Lancelot's inaccessibility in the fact that he is already in love with Guinevere rather than in the same-sex relationship. Galehot's union with Lancelot is not, like Lancelot's with Guinevere, merely forbidden by law. Laws can be broken, or transcended. Where they are regretfully respected and sacrificed to, they may help to fuel the forbidden love's elevation to an ideal persisting outside the contingent social order, as realized, perhaps, in the joint burial consecrated in the cyclic prose *Lancelot*. But for Galehot, the Other's desire does not respond to the subject's; Lancelot loves Guinevere. Lancelot's inaccessibility for Galehot pervades their interaction to such an extent that when the hero reveals the content of a second *don en blanc*, which is that Galehot has promised not to ask Lancelot his name, Galehot comments that this would otherwise have been his very first request of his new companion (p. 329), even though he has previously shown no inclination to ask. This is not mere *Vorlust*, the half-pleasurable tension that precedes sexual union and valorizes it by deferring it.[85] Much more clearly than Lancelot's love for Guinevere, Galehot's for Lancelot is an *amor interruptus*, an unhappy love in which joy, humiliation, pain and ultimately death are interlinked.[86] His inherent and multifaceted impossibility makes Lancelot for Galehot an object in the Real.

Impossible desire is central to Arthurian discourse, which elsewhere inscribes it in other modes: the quasi-mystical love for the Grail, the yearning after the ideals of Camelot and the Round Table. The non-cyclic prose *Lancelot* diverts away from the central heterosexual couple both the courtly lover's humiliation and agonizing bewilderment in the face of unjust rejection which characterized the Lancelot of the earlier *Chevalier de la Charrette*, and the personal and social destructiveness associated with the adulterous, treasonous relationship between hero and queen in the later narrative stages of the Vulgate prose romance cycle. These questionable qualities attach instead to the love for Lancelot of the newly introduced figure of Galehot, the character who in this text is placed in the nearest relation to death and is the most obvious bearer of the death drive.[87] This may represent the projection of disturbing or destructive elements onto an outsider figure so that they may be disavowed. Galehot's giant affiliation at once accounts for his excess, inhibits identifications between him and fully human subjects within or outside the text, and allows a certain sense of relief when he is finally expelled from the narrative by dying.[88] To regard Galehot as a lone homosexual in a heterosexual courtly world similarly distinguishes him from the rest of the text, making his passion a tragic exception. The clarity of both his love and the death drive means that this remains the case even if chivalry is viewed as revealing in him its own homoerotic underpinnings or, as Klosowska puts it, 'flirting with homoeroticism by heavily borrowing from the arsenal of heterosexual romance in "perfect friendship" narratives'.[89] In the remainder of this chapter I shall develop a different reading, according to which the figure of Galehot highlights problems which inhere not in Galehot himself but in Lancelot as chivalric ideal and love object. Far from distancing the hero from the notion of love as destructive, the non-cyclic prose *Lancelot* intensifies that association but relocates the relationship so that it falls centrally within the chivalric, monologically masculine sphere.[90]

THE KNIGHT AS THING

Almost all discussions of courtly love take its domain to be heterosexuality. Although it may be understood to be a means of negotiating more important male–male social relations or to be an indirect expression of male homosexuality, in such discussions its heterosexual format is usually taken for granted.[91] The lady may be only a screen object, but precisely as such she holds an essential place in the economy of desire. In Lacan's account the feminine gender of the Lady-Thing and the loving subject's masculinity are not incidental. Courtly love epitomizes heterosexuality and, indeed, masculine and feminine desire more generally, topics that he develops notably in Seminar xx. It is, of course, possible to treat this gendering of desire as mobile in relation to persons, such that male characters can adopt feminine roles and females masculine. However, if one partner's 'masculine' behaviour is held to imply the 'femininity' of the other, or vice versa, then heterosexuality is hypostatized as the essential structure of erotic desire, with binary, complementary gender difference as its fundamental framework. Such a hypostatization runs counter to the arguments put by queer theorists and medievalists over the last three decades, since back in 1984 Gayle Rubin argued that 'it is essential to separate gender and sex analytically' (where 'sex' means 'erotic desire').[92] Scholars have shown the complex interweaving of identification and objectification in many sexual forms, including those within the 'normal' range. Moreover, as Michael Warner points out, desiring heterosexually does not guarantee that the desiring subject thereby creates a relation to 'irreducible phenomenological difference', nor does homosexuality preclude such a relation.[93] If sexual difference lies within the Real, so does the fundamental singularity of human beings; 'one is one and all alone'. The Real generates endless imaginary and symbolic responses, efforts to represent and evade, to comprehend and to mediate its intractability. While accepting the Real nature of sexual difference as one among an indeterminate number of antagonisms which rend the human condition, I contend that any sex–gender system should be considered one such response to the Real.[94]

Lacan's formulations, which reflect his own time and social and cultural position, need to be seen in the same light. While they provide valuable insights for critiquing sex–gender relations in historically actual cultures, and have a particular affinity with courtly modes, the meanings that they impose on gender difference, if accepted as Real, limit their usefulness. They belong, inevitably, to a particular political field, and any decision to accept or reject that field is itself a political one.[95]

The non-cyclic prose *Lancelot* presents two, closely parallel courtly love relationships: Lancelot's with Guinevere and Galehot's with Lancelot. Its model is therefore not limited to heterosexuality: neither to the 'hetero' nor to the 'sexual'. I do not propose to consider Galehot 'feminine'; his is the masculine lover's role and it is Lancelot who occupies the feminine position. To consider Lancelot thereby 'feminized', however, would involve re-ascribing to the feminine and to heterosexuality problems that the text works to shift into the masculine domain. This would be a retrograde step that failed to take advantage of the text's radical ethical critique.[96] Lancelot is not feminized but 'Thing-ized'. Nor do I propose to read Galehot's love for Lancelot as either homosexuality or a displaced form of heterosexuality. Shifting the erotic triangle in which Arthur and Lancelot are rivals for Guinevere so that Galehot and Guinevere compete for Lancelot's erotic attention and sole devotion has the advantage of placing a 'gay' character centre-stage in a major medieval text – an important political move within modern medievalist discourse.[97] It may also, however, divert us from other questions which the text encourages us to pursue and which require us to revise established notions of gender and relationships. I shall argue that the 'Lancelot effect' is neither limited to Galehot nor addresses only his sexuality. My analysis of the non-cyclic prose *Lancelot* is advanced by Schultz's proposal that we both abandon classifying medieval love relations on grounds of gendered erotic object-choice and analyse critically and historically the heterosexual norm.[98] Refusing to instantiate what Bersani calls 'the great homo-heterosexual divide' permits us to compare patterns of love and desire and opens up the possibility of rethinking these other than as either variants on heterosexual norms or as wholly asexual.[99] This non-gendered gaze is well adapted to the non-cyclic prose *Lancelot*, with its insistently comparable love relationships. However, it would be unfortunate if we were led thereby to overlook the sexual–gender politics which permits some relationships but makes others impossible, unintelligible or excessive, distinguishing official or normative symbolic fictions from spectral fantasies; or to fail to notice what happens in a work which disregards these accepted boundaries, as I believe this text does.[100] As it is presented in this early thirteenth-century work, Galehot's love for Lancelot has some of the socially disruptive force ascribed by Bersani to homo-ness, by Edelman to the *sinthom*osexual, and by Butler to Antigone.[101] We do not need to import sexual classifications in order to be attentive to this force, though it is difficult to find a suitable language in which to analyse its sexual aspect. Thus I continue to use such shorthand terms as 'heterosexuality' against Schultz's recommendation.

Lancelot's demand that Galehot submit to Arthur after defeating him demonstrates the complex relationship between the text's two courtly loves. An obvious effect of Lancelot's choice is to emphasize his service to Arthur, whose prestige is not only preserved but increased by the homage of the conqueror of thirty kings. Since Lancelot's action is motivated by his love for Guinevere, it forms part of that love's justification through the assistance it demonstrably renders her husband and the social order he represents. This is therefore an important episode in establishing that Lancelot's love for Guinevere endorses rather than conflicts with that order. The same episode is, however, also central to the relationship between Lancelot and Galehot, since it relates what Galehot first gives in exchange for Lancelot's company. It is clear that Lancelot knows his power over Galehot: 'Et ge vos dirai orrandroit lo don par quoi ge remanrai. Et se ge ne l'ai, por noiant parleroiz de remanoir' (p. 325; 'And I shall tell you at once the gift that will make me stay. And if I do not get it, you will waste your breath to talk of my staying'). Lancelot's insistence that Galehot should willingly enact his own dramatic humiliation exceeds the rational norm for honourable enmity. It could perhaps be justified by Galehot's being half giant, but he is not fully characterized as a giant in the text, and in the scenes under discussion is not obviously so at all.[102] Lancelot's directive therefore has aspects which recall the demands conventionally imposed by the courtly Lady-Thing. Galehot's beloved requires that his lover renounce a dream which has nourished him for years. The cherished aspirations thus designated for sacrifice concern the lover's honour, of all chivalric values most crucial to a knight's sense of identity and self-worth. The enormity of Lancelot's ultimatum is heightened by the stipulation that it is only in the moment of victory over Arthur that Galehot must abandon his claim; it would be more sensible and kinder to forestall the battle by requiring instant submission. Yet it is noticeable that Lancelot's demand receives no commentary from any character except Galehot, who sees in it matter for celebration. Like Lancelot, Galehot builds his love on a 'mot':

'Cuidiez vos qe ge bee a repentir? Se toz le monz estoit miens, si li oseroie ge tot doner. Mais ge pensoie au riche mot que il a dit, que onques mais home ne dist si riche. Sire,' dist il, 'ja ne m'aïst Dex, se vos ne l'avez, lo don, que ge ne porroie rien faire por vos o ge poïsse honte avoir.' (p. 325)

('Do you think that I want to repent? If the whole world were mine still I would dare give it all to him. No, I was thinking about his noble words, that no man ever spoke so nobly. Sir,' he said, 'may God never help me if you do not have it, this gift, since nothing I could do for your sake could bring me shame.')

Galehot's open-ended pledge is viewed with dismay by his lordly vassals and with suspicion by Lancelot. To embrace such extreme demands is marginally intelligible within the framework of courtly heterosexuality – as established by the Lancelot of the *Charrette* – but in the homosocial context it appears simply extravagant. Lancelot's and Galehot's complementary roles are those of the courtly love duo: autocratic, inconsistent, cruel imposition complements gratifying ascesis. Placing this pattern in the context of relations between men restores to it the strangeness and hence the ethical force that it has largely lost within the overly familiar heterosexual context.

The spectacle of Lancelot languishing but unable or unwilling to approach Guinevere prompts Galehot to plead his friend's cause. His love compels him to serve his beloved's desire in the knowledge that this desire is for another, thus attenuating Lancelot's suffering at the price of increasing his own. That the latter would also increase were Lancelot to die elevates the altruism of Galehot's decision (compare Paris's insistence on the improving effect on her knight of the Lady's rigour). The fact that Lancelot's wishes are not always expressed explicitly does not alter the compulsion that they exercise on Galehot, an attentive reader of his beloved's desire. Galehot interprets the possibility that Lancelot may die for love as a threat on his friend's part to die for love, hence as an indirect demand addressed to himself. Pursuing the Other's desire involves Galehot in all sorts of substitutions; he must pay homage to a series of figures – Arthur, Guinevere, the Lady of Malohot – whom he desires only in the mediated sense that his desire for them has been dictated to him by Lancelot and serves the latter's aims. This kind of oblique relation to the object through a series of substitutes is not uncommon in courtly love. In one perspective it defines the symbolic order: the *objet a*, object-cause of desire, can be pursued only through surrogate objects and leads the subject to replace each actual object attained – and discovered not to be the hoped-for fulfilment – with a new, in which the same hopes may be invested until it in turn is achieved.[103] In *l'amour courtois* the substitutive string is sometimes interpreted to be tyrannically commanded by the Lady-Thing; it is she whom the lover consciously serves and pursues through his frustrations, tormented by the inadequate, proxy satisfactions that his love imposes on him. Directly or indirectly, Lancelot's lover is required to sacrifice his own hopes in love and in chivalry and to adopt substitute objects, recalling Thomas's Tristan, whose marriage to the Breton princess Ysolt aux Blanches Mains is expressive of various emotions centred on his true love, Ysolt la Blonde, and rapidly doubles his torment.[104] The non-cyclic prose *Lancelot* makes it evident that sublimation in the courtly love between Galehot and Lancelot, as in that between Lancelot and Guinevere, originates with the lover. Both the ethical prestige and the difficulties arising from Galehot's sublimation of Lancelot must therefore accrue to the former. Counter-arguments are, of course, possible: as noted above, Galehot's love works to disculpate Lancelot to some extent of the problematic sexual relationship with Guinevere; Lancelot does not ask Galehot to arrange his tryst with the queen. Moreover, Lancelot repeatedly expresses guilt for his treatment of Galehot, again signalling the importance of this particular male–male relationship (neither he nor Guinevere feels much guilt in relation to Arthur). However, Lancelot's persistence in conduct which he admits is harsh aligns him – much more closely than Guinevere – with the pattern of unpredictable shifts from humanity to inhumanity, rationality to irrationality, justice to injustice that Paris ascribes to the *dame* and Lacan to the Thing. Guilt being importantly constitutive of subjectivity in thirteenth-century prose romances, all this hardly dislodges Lancelot from his position as hero.[105] The major point is that the non-cyclic prose *Lancelot* locates the ethical space within the chivalric relation.

When, as usually, a woman occupies the position of the Thing, then medieval ideologies of sexual difference allow its heartless inconsistency to be absorbed into a feminine stereotype. It is Woman who is capricious, faithless, insensible and unworthy of the idealization accorded her, which reflects rather her lover's nobility than her own. Audiences medieval and modern can shrug off such behaviour as typical if not of women, then of a certain view of women. Where, as in the non-cyclic prose *Lancelot*, it is meted out by a knight, it becomes more difficult; what to make, then, of the one who, before all others, is 'uns chevaliers', 'li bons chevaliers', yet whose behaviour patterns him as the Thing? Knighthood's ideal is made to appear erratic and antipathetic in a context which is neither heterosexual nor heterosocial. With the figure of Galehot the text superimposes the courtly erotic relation onto the model chivalric relation of *compaignie* or privileged friendship. The value of *compaignie* is shown in this exchange between Arthur and Guinevere:

'Dame, ge voil prier Lancelot de remanor a moi et d'estre compainz de la Table Reonde, car bien sont ses granz proeces esprovees. Et s'il ne voloit por moi remanoir, si l'an cheïssiez tantost as piez.'

'Sire,' fait la reine, 'il est a Galehot et ses compainz, si est bien que vos an priez Galehot qu'il lo sueffre.'

Lors vient li rois a Galehot, si li prie en toz servises qu'il voille que Lanceloz soit de sa maisniee et qu'il remaigne a lui comme ses maistres et ses compainz. (p. 570)

('Lady, I wish to entreat Lancelot to stay with me and to be a companion of the Round Table, for his great knightly qualities have truly been proven. And if he did not wish to stay for my sake, you should fall at his feet.' 'Sire,' said the queen, 'he belongs to Galehot and is his companion, therefore it is proper that you entreat Galehot to allow it.' Then the king came to Galehot and beseeched him to allow Lancelot to be part of his [Arthur's] retinue and to stay with him as his master and companion.)

Compaignie binds Lancelot to Galehot and the knights of the Round Table to each other, and represents the egalitarian aspect of the relation that Arthur desires with Lancelot.[106] A bond of mutual support and honour, *compaignie* is the most treasured of male homosocial relations; the idea that one may be a good knight but a poor companion strains notions of chivalry. Yet Lancelot repeatedly declares his inability to fulfil his contractual obligations to Galehot and, inspired by his love for Guinevere, defaults on the behaviour which his *compainz* is entitled to expect. Witness his response to Guinevere's entreaty that he remain at court:

Et qant Lanceloz la voit a genolz, si li fait trop grant mal au cuer; si n'atant mie
tant que Galehoz lo regart, ainz saut sus et dist a la reine:
    'Ha ! dame, ge remaign a mon seignor a son plaisir et au vostre.' (pp. 570–1)

(And when Lancelot saw her on her knees it distressed his heart very greatly, and
he did not wait for Galehot to look at him but leapt up and said to the queen,
'Oh, lady! I remain with my lord at his pleasure and yours.')

Lancelot is not actually breaking a promise to Galehot, since the pair earlier
agreed that Lancelot would join Arthur's retinue if the queen asked him
to do so (though this is a forced concession on the part of Galehot who,
as so often, recognizes that his own ability to bear privation is greater than
Lancelot's). However, Lancelot's failure to solicit the formal permission that
the text implies is necessary suggests that he bears some guilt; his hinted
avoidance of Galehot's gaze further insinuates that he knows himself to
bear it. His actions here reinforce his reputation for scrupulousness as
he attempts to satisfy conflicting obligations, but also contribute to the
repeated pattern of public and private snubs that he delivers to Galehot. In
the non-cyclic prose *Lancelot*, therefore, the association in which Lancelot
can with justice be accused of betrayal is not that with Arthur, but that
with Galehot; the key relation is not the institutionally hierarchical but
the ideally egalitarian.[107] It is his behaviour in this domain that makes him
'li plus vilains chevaliers el monde et li plus vaillanz' for this particular
text, which thereby situates serious ethical disruption within the privileged
chivalric alliance of *compaignie*. And this is achieved by overlaying on
compaignie patterns derived from courtly love.

L'AMOUR CHEVALERESQUE EN ANAMORPHOSE

Lacan's discussion of courtly love includes a chapter entitled 'L'amour courtois en anamorphose'. Here he presents courtly love as an anamorphosis of
heterosexual desire – and of desire generally – in the sense that he treats
it as an exaggerated and distorted representation whose very mannerisms
nevertheless reveal commonly overlooked and therefore especially significant characteristics of more usual forms, namely the presence of the drives
that, in Žižek's terms, stand for 'the curvature of the space of desire, i.e. for
the paradox that, within this space, the way to attain the object (a) is not to
go straight for it (the safest way to miss it) but to encircle it, to "go round
in circles"', this circumnavigation being a feature of desire that courtly love
importantly exaggerates.[108] Distortion reveals not the objective social situations of love (the condition of women, patriarchy, medieval marriage, etc.)

but the Real as the trauma around which social reality is structured. I shall return more fully to anamorphosis in Chapter 4. For the moment, it should be noted that Lacan also subjects courtly love itself to anamorphosis by portraying it in the curious perspective of his own psychoanalysis. Through this presentation he emphasizes the insistent artificiality which allows his version of *l'amour courtois* to project or conjure up the spectre of a properly unrepresentable dimension. The artwork – courtly love poetry, and also Lacan's own analysis – puts the object into relation with the Thing. The courtly erotic is thus given ethical status, or, in Lacan's play on *das Ding*, its 'dignity' or *Ding*-ity is renewed.[109] Its import is limited neither to a brief flowering in Western European poetry nor to a longer one in the history of Western heterosexuality.

Most commentators agree that an extensive social, political and cultural order is implicated in the erotics of courtly love. The step implied by the non-cyclic prose *Lancelot*, in my view, is the relocation of this erotics into the strictly masculine domain of horizontal male–male relations. This move radically interrupts accepted perspectives on that domain and on its role in the general order, stressing its disturbing qualities. To designate this male–male love, overlaid with the forms of courtly heterosexuality, which is essential to and disruptive of the chivalric sphere, I borrow from Paris a term that for him is synonymous with 'l'amour courtois': in the non-cyclic prose *Lancelot* it is 'l'amour chevaleresque' which is placed *en anamorphose*.

Since his various cruelties to Galehot spring from actions undertaken out of love for Guinevere, Lancelot's behaviour as a beloved object is the correlative of his behaviour as a loving subject. However, it cannot therefore be deduced that it is first and foremost his conduct as Guinevere's illicit lover which is placed into question, or that the text merely presents one more exploration of the difficult balance to be achieved between such gendered terms as love and prowess, private and public, heterosexual and homosocial, or feminine and masculine. Because his passion for Guinevere lies at the centre of all Lancelot's chivalry, the heterosexual relation cannot be bracketed off as the sole locus of difficulty. Nor can a sexuality ascribed to Galehot alone be taken to be the problem. Galehot's love for Lancelot and Lancelot's for him are not set apart from the various desires expressed by other characters. On the contrary, an important characteristic of Lancelot in this work is that, at least where he is concerned, courtly love paradigms are read onto alliances between knights. Galehot's combination of idealization, contract and self-prostration is encountered in relationships that other male characters (and also, keeping the parallel alive, female characters such as the Lady of Malohot) establish with Lancelot, whose regretfully disappointing response is typical, though nowhere so clear or so culpable as with Galehot. His snubbing of female expectations enhances the ethical status of Lancelot's love for Guinevere by glossing it as the virtue of fidelity while underlining the disruptive force of women's excessive and unprincipled appetites; in both aspects it finds an orthodox place within courtly thinking. Were Galehot positioned as a direct sexual rival to Guinevere, he could be dismissed as easily as the amorous maidens of other Lancelot romances, and his death for love would bring to the hero's reputation only the same gloomy lustre as does that of the Demoiselle d'Escalot in the *Mort Artu*. Representing and rejecting homosexuality in this way would, obviously, be a political and ethical act; however, such a possibility is not broached within the text. Instead, Galehot's very foreclosure as a sexual suitor accentuates the wrong that Lancelot does him. Whereas letting down a *compainz* indicates a serious moral failing, causing him to die points to a truly critical inadequacy (compare the carnage that Gauvain wreaks in the ranks of the Round Table during the *Queste del saint Graal*). Thus the personally and socially disturbing and even the mortiferous qualities considered by other *Lancelot* texts to attach to the hero's defining heterosexual relationship (and thereby potentially to his relation with Arthur) are grafted in the non-cyclic prose romance not onto Galehot himself, but onto Lancelot in his relations with his male peers, his brother knights. I take this less as an exposure of the existential singularity of each human being than as an analysis of the various desires, relationships and fantasies that constitute chivalry as a collective cultural and social order.[110]

The clearest instance is the notable scene which occurs after Galehot has submitted to Arthur but before he has brought Lancelot to meet Guinevere. Galehot asks Arthur, Gauvain (gravely injured in the preceding battle) and Guinevere in turn how they value the knight they currently know as the *Noir Chevalier* (Black Knight), before himself answering the question:

'Sire, sire, veïstes vos onques plus prodome de celui au noir escu?'

'Certes,' fait le rois, 'ge ne vi onques chevalier de cui j'anmasse tant la conoissance por chevalerie qui an lui fust.'

'Non?' fait Galehoz. 'Or me distes donc, par la foi que vos devez madame qui ci est ne monseignor Gauvain, combien voudriez vos avoir doné an sa compaignie avoir a tozjorz.'

'Si voirement m'aïst Dex,' fit il, 'ge li partiroie parmi qanque ge porroie avoir fors solement lo cors a ceste dame, don ge ne feroie nule part.'

'Certes,' fait Galehoz, 'assez i metriez. Et vos,' fait il, 'messire Gauvain, se Dex vos doint ja mais la santé que vos dessirrez, quel meschief feriez vos por avoir tozjorz mais un si prodome?'

Et messires Gauvains pansa un petit, comme cil qui ja mais ne cuidoit avoir santé.

'Se Dex,' fait il, 'me doint la santé que je desir, ge voudroie orendroit estre la plus bele damoisele do mont saine et haitiee, par covant que il m'amast sor tote rien, ausin bien com ge l'ameroie.'

'Certes,' fait Galehoz, 'assez i avez offert. Et vos, dame,' fait il, 'par la rien que vos plus amez, que an feriez de meschief par covant que uns tex chevaliers fust tozjorz an vostre servise?'

'Par Deu,' fait ele, 'messires Gauvains i a mis toz les offres que dames i puent metre, ne dame ne puet plus offrir.'

Et il comancent tuit a rire. (pp. 333–4)

('Sire, sire, did you ever see a more worthy man than him with the black shield?' 'Truly,' said the king, 'I never saw a knight whose acquaintance I would sooner make on account of the chivalry that was in him.' 'No?' said Galehot. 'Now tell me, on the faith you owe my lady here and monseigneur Gauvain, how much you would be willing to give to have his company for ever.' 'So help me God,' he said, 'I would give him half of all I might have excepting only this lady's person, which I would never share.' 'Truly,' said Galehot, 'you would give a great deal. And you,' he said, 'Sir Gauvain, as God give you the health you desire, what sacrifice would you make to have such a man of valour for ever?' Sir Gauvain thought for a while, as a man who never expected to recover. 'As God,' he said, 'give me the health I desire, I should wish there and then to be the most beautiful damsel in the world, hale and hearty, on condition that he love me more than anything, as I should love him.' 'Indeed,' said Galehot, 'you have offered a great deal. And you, my lady,' he said, 'by the thing you most love, what sacrifice would you make on condition that such a knight would always be in your service?' 'By God,' she said, 'Sir Gauvain has advanced all the offers that ladies can, nor can any lady offer more.' And they all started to laugh.)

Each response posits a certain relationship between heterosexual and homosocial bonds. Arthur's answer recalls the familiar triangle in which two male friends compete for a woman's love (or other prize). In Arthur's version the woman is displaced from her central position, allowing the men to express their bond directly when one renounces her for the other's sake. Ironically, of course, reserving her in this way also situates her as precisely that trophy for which a loving friend or enemy must strive. Such a view of homosocial relations as mediated by a doubly beloved woman will allow the Arthur of some texts to interpret Lancelot's affection for his queen as care for himself, an interpretation given textual support in such works as the cyclic *Lancelot*, the *Mort Artu*, and most clearly in Malory's *Le Morte Darthur*.

In Gauvain's suggested 'meschief', courtly love relations are read onto knightly alliances in a more radical manner. We could construe this as a

version of Arthur's fantasy of male union, with the collapse of the trian-
gulating female figure into one male partner; we could equally interpret it
as an expression of homosexual fantasies underpinning chivalry. However,
the implications I wish to draw from this use of the courtly heterosexual
relation to figure the chivalric male alliance at its most intense and reciprocal, are different. On the one hand, the truly problematic nature of the
intense knightly bond is presented by casting one participant in feminine
guise, thus uncovering the complexities of 'l'amour chevaleresque': the
not only identificatory desires which his fellow knights focus on Lancelot,
chivalry's paragon. On the other, the nature of this chivalric passion means
that Lancelot can be no more devoted to Gauvain the man than he could
to Gauvain the damsel, or, to put it another way, that male Gauvain can
have Lancelot's devotion no more than could female Gauvain. Reciprocity
is as impossible in one as in the other domain.[111] Love between men is
properly unfigurable not only because the homosexual possibility is suppressed but because relations between men lie in the Real, no less than do
those with the other sex or with God; it is not forbidden but impossible.[112]
Knights must idealize and pursue, must aspire to be recognized, esteemed
and loved by the best knights as exemplars of chivalry, which is enthroned
as a regime of ideal models as early as the Lady of the Lake's description
(pp. 141–7). But according to this text, such sublimation places the paragon
in the fundamentally ambivalent position of the Thing, prone to arbitrary
cruelties and to demands which reveal its own unworthiness and require its
lover's subjective destitution. The desire ascribed to 'li bons chevaliers' is to
humiliate, reject and therefore devastate his peers as chivalric subjects, to
see them abject. And this abjection by the Other, itself a form of *jouissance*,
represents the trajectory of chivalry as a whole. It can be generalized to
other texts, being performed in the Vulgate cycle works by the slow grind-
ing towards self-destruction of the Arthurian order and by the intensifying
culpabilization of the leading characters. In the non-cyclic prose romance
it is articulated by that archetypal Arthurian personage, Gauvain, whose
aspirational offer is placed under the auspices of the death drive, linked
to the health he never expects to recover and designated a 'meschief', a
sacrifice or mutilation of self or others;[113] although it is contained by the
fact that the shadow is here temporary and by its conscious designation
as a game easily disavowed with laughter.[114] In this work, then, chivalry's
collective death drive attaches to the heroic person of Lancelot not as
Guinevere's lover but as beloved and desired lover of other great knights.
Women, we note, are banished from this relation. Guinevere's circumspect
and ironic reply to Galehot's question points up Gauvain's appropriation

of the courtly feminine position, drawing attention to that position as a rhetorical one within male discourse and distancing her once more from the figure of the Lady-Thing. Once transferred into the exclusively masculine domain, the unrequited longings of all those amorous maidens acquire a moral seriousness that chivalric discourse does not allow them in their own right.[115]

It is in the light of these prior responses that we read Galehot's answer to the question he himself posed: 'J'an voudroie avoir tornee ma grant honor a honte, par si que ge fusse a tozjorz ausi seürs de lui comme ge voudroie que il fust de moi' (p. 334; 'I should wish my great honour changed to shame, provided that I should always be as sure of him as I should wish him to be of me'). Like Gauvain, Galehot dreams of being loved by Lancelot. In his vision the conventionally feminine role has not been marginalized from the intense knightly alliance (as Arthur dreams) nor incorporated into it (as Gauvain fantasizes), but re-gendered as the fully masculine role of the loving knight. Chivalric companionship is indistinguishable henceforth from the courtly love relation in its rhetoric and its psychic economy. This conversation exposes the fundamental correspondence between Galehot's love and the desires that issue from other knights to centre on Lancelot in the work, and portrays all as problematic. The position of the incomprehensible Thing is located in the exclusively chivalric space; knights carry the Thing with and within them as knights rather than only as heterosexual lovers. Lancelot's *entre-deux* status in so many romances, as the overlapping of chivalry's best and worst, its sublime and its abject, is revealed in the non-cyclic prose romance to be that of the Thing. Whether as best or as worst, Lancelot never exits entirely from the circuit of earthly norms (see the discussion of the *Charrette*, above) because the Thing represents the point at which the Real becomes partially, wonderfully and horrifyingly accessible via the imaginary and the symbolic. Lancelot represents 'ce qui du réel pâtit du signifiant' in a specifically chivalric modulation; he is the attractive, repellent vacuole around which many romances turn. Numerous *Lancelot* works, including the *Charrette*, the *Queste* and the *Mort Artu*, address Lancelot's Thing-ness by attaching it to his reprehensible yet justifiable love for Guinevere. They thereby join the large number of medieval works that deem women or the heterosexual desire they arouse to be responsible for all kinds of ills, while the part of transcendence is allotted to men. The non-cyclic prose *Lancelot*, however, locates the difficulty as well as the sublimity with men as subjects and as objects. Women and giants remain problematic, but they are not alone – chivalry's major symptom is Lancelot himself. The split in the chivalric self which Plummer ascribes to the tension between the Mother's desire and the Father's *non/nom* is shown here to mask a strictly chivalric set of desires, prohibitions and impossibilities.[116]

The relocation of the destructive courtly love relationship into the exclusively male space renders it more subversive than it is likely to be if confined to the heterosexual or feminine spheres. By imposing onto intimate associations between knights formal patterns drawn from courtly love, and especially by elevating the knightly paradigm to the position of the callous, whimsical, treacherous Thing, the text challenges the knightly relation at its core. Courtly love is treated by Lacan as one response to the real fact that 'il n'y a pas de rapport sexuel' ('there is no relation between the sexes', in Evans's gloss) – that is, men and women are fated to a radical lack of symmetry, complementarity or harmony.[117] In the non-cyclic prose *Lancelot*, the primary failing relationship is located not between men and women nor between king and knight but between male peers, such that their loving interaction with each other is made to seem as intractable as elsewhere that between the sexes. The message of the non-cyclic prose *Lancelot* is therefore the impossibility not so much of the sexual relation as of the chivalric social contract. Galehot's death as loving subject, though in one sense it expels him from the narrative, leaves Lancelot a disturbing and guilt-stricken survivor and his future career – should he have one, as in the cyclic version – under the mark Galehot places on him, as idealized yet inadequate object of 'l'amour chevaleresque'.

CHAPTER 3

The ubi sunt *topos in Middle French: sad stories of the death of kings*

Within medieval Christianity, accepting that one had to die was an ethical and spiritual imperative involving realigning one's priorities towards God and eternity and away from earthly reality and the worldly pursuit of ease, wealth and power. A substantial effort was therefore poured into persuading and enabling subjects to acknowledge what Ariès calls 'the death of the self' (as opposed to 'the death of the other').[1] Medieval texts, like modern theorists, recognize certain challenges in the project of contemplating mortality. One is the difficulty of imagining one's own death. Thus in Guillaume de Deguileville's influential fourteenth-century dream vision, the *Pèlerinage de vie humaine* (first redaction, 1330–1), when Death arrives the narrator-Pilgrim wakes, bringing to an end both narrative and poem:

> La Mort laissa sa faus courir
> Et fist m'ame du cors partir,
> Ce me sembla si com songoie.
> Mais ainsi comme je estoie
> En tel point et en tel tourment
> J'oui l'orloge de convent
> Qui pour les matines sonnoit
> Si comme de constume estoit.
> Quant je l'oui, je m'esveillai
> Et tout tressuant me trouvai,
> Et pour mon songe fu pensis
> Mont grandement et esbahis.[2]

(Death let her scythe swing and made my soul leave my body, so it seemed to me as I dreamt. But just as I was in this circumstance and in this torment, I heard the abbey bell ringing for matins, as it normally did. When I heard it I awoke and found myself all in a sweat, and because of my dream I was most perplexed and astounded.)

Unable to dream dying, the Pilgrim is recalled to life by the religious commitment for which the bell stands. This event also figures his hoped-for passage into eternal life on that future morning when he will finally wake from the dream that is earthly existence. The passage thus doubly sidesteps the problem of personal extinction, highlighting an important limitation which affects many engagements with death. Christian thinking teaches that 'self-preservation leads to death, while self-oblation leads to eternal life', and secular modifications of this paradox are widespread within medieval culture:[3] death is a gateway to various other forms of life, while life wrongly lived incurs the death of some higher faculty. In this chapter I examine late medieval French uses of the *ubi sunt* topos, paying particular attention to their complex interweavings of death and life. The topos has a range of tones, from strictly ascetic and Christian variants, commonly supported by *contemptus mundi* and *vanitas* themes, to elegiac, classically rooted and secular modulations which lament the passing of youth, beauty and glory and urge either stoic resignation or seizing the day.[4] In this chapter I shall investigate the *ubi sunt* as one rhetorical strategy employed in the didactic project of persuading Christian subjects to confront their personal mortality and the world's impermanence. I look not at ecclesiastical or strictly spiritual contexts, where the message may be expected to be relatively consistent, but at the ambivalent multiple engagements of secular poetry in ballades (a fixed-form lyric fashionable in the late Middle Ages) by Deschamps and Villon.[5]

The *ubi sunt* topos invites layered responses. Overtly, its rhetorical questions – 'Where are they now?' or 'Where have they gone?' – encourage listeners to identify with a specific set of deceased people, reminding the former that they too will die. As the dead man interpellates the living through his epitaph, 'Itel cum es, itel jeo fu, E tel seras tel cum jo su' ('As you are, I was, and you shall be as I am').[6] However, because I instinctively recoil at the thought of my own death, evidence of the demise of others causes me to distance myself from them.[7] Even where the will to know death is present, the concept is elusive. 'I think, therefore I am' expresses an important truth independent of Descartes's historical moment: reflexive consciousness presents us with testimony of our own existence which it is difficult to refute. My ability to hear and read of and reflect upon the deaths of others proves my continued vitality. This can become a simple but effective syllogism: '*They* are dead, therefore *I* am.' This counter-movement appears to be inevitable; and texts which use the *ubi sunt* topos exploit it. The living reader's dissociation from the dead is diversely realized in different works. Both the soul's Christian immortality and secular renown through the ages are ways to prolong existence, while the embrace of momentary pleasures and glories is a means of intensifying it into another kind of transcendence. Situating its implied audiences between two deaths – their own and those of the recalled dead – the *ubi sunt* topos cannot but assert life present and lasting, the question then being in what relationship the text places this brand of life to the death that it primarily announces. Do *ubi sunt* works surreptitiously deny the transience that they ostensibly announce? Do they create a counter-counter-movement in order to deliver their message of mortality? The readings in this chapter will examine how two works of the Middle French period weave together the topos's effects.

I shall highlight two concepts in particular: the sovereign subject and memory. The sovereign subject is the subject of consciousness and especially of self-consciousness, a self which experiences, feels, desires, thinks, acts, reflects and remembers. (This is a phenomenological rather than a Lacanian notion of the subject, and I am here disregarding Lacanian distinctions between 'self' and 'subject'.) However, the sovereign is also 'subject to': that is, determined by rules, conventions and contracts, conscious of the will of others and of the collective as influencing its own potential for action. I am also interested in the relational and political dimensions of the self, and here 'sovereign' takes on the meaning of 'dominant' and sometimes specifically that of 'princely'. The subjects here considered have a will to dominate, hence to dominate someone else. It is commonplace to see women as the primary objects of domination; however, I am interested here mainly in the numerous masculine objects who also are posed to be dominated.[8] The position of 'sovereign subject' may be allotted exclusively to the speaker, the explicit addressee, the implied audience or the deceased of *ubi sunt* questions, but equally there may be co-operation within or competition for the role among the various masculine figures.

In the works I examine here the sovereign subject is defined not, as in much modern thinking, primarily as a speaker or writer, but as a listener; he is a cultural consumer, not a cultural mediator. This is the 'Prince' to whom the ballade envoy is addressed, retrospectively orienting the whole poem in his direction. In the court-poetry style as Deschamps and Villon use it, the writing poet and his speaking persona define themselves secondarily, through their relation to this sovereign listener, working to borrow his prestige or to moderate it. These efforts are not necessarily contradictory. Indeed, one of the themes of this chapter concerns the ways in which acceptance of one's own death or dominated position are linked positively to sovereignty and the ability to consign others to death. On the other hand, the convoluted interrelationships of life and death typical of the *ubi sunt* topos mean that another kind of power emerges, which enforces a certain way of life. For Foucault, archaic sovereignty is epitomized by the power to put to death, against modern biopolitics that instead manages life administratively.[9] The presence of both in these late medieval French works suggests (once again) the weakness of Foucault's periodizations, but it also bespeaks the prominent role in contemporary literary production of a certain bureaucratic class attached to the prince and hungry for influence within the court. In the ballades that I shall analyse, the late medieval sovereign reader and the more marginal poet figure have much in common: both are projected as shadowy figures *entre-deux-morts*. The different ways in which the various poems make them occupy that non-place will be discussed below.

Considering the interpersonal aspects of sovereign subjectivity leads us on to memory, essential to the self in society. Memory is both individual and collective, and although some instances are recognizably one rather than the other, there is substantial overlap. Collective memory is to a large degree experienced as personal, while individual memories exist against a shared background.[10] This overlap is necessary to produce socially mean-ingful activity, and the degree of overlap may be taken as an indicator of social integration. *Ubi sunt* questions call on the addressee to *remember* that he is mortal, grounding ethics in the difficult tasks of understanding what is already known and of connecting his personal experience of sovereign subjecthood to the universal fate of death. Memory relates both to the named or listed dead with whom listeners are repetitively encouraged both to identify and to disidentify, and also to the listener's own projected life to come. The spiritual afterlife of the soul stands in implicit or explicit contrast to secular renown, thus presupposing two, hierarchically orga-nized, collectives: temporal society and the divine universal. To the notion of spiritual second death or damnation, corresponds that of dishonour, a secular 'eternity of living death' (see p. 17, above). So it was alleged against the duke of Burgundy that his murder of the duke of Orleans was not his greatest crime: 'defaming the Duke of Orleans and destroying his reputation, he had in truth killed him "with second death" ["par seconde mort"]'.[11] Inasmuch as the *ubi sunt* topos presupposes and incites memory, oblivion is not contemplated within its system.

IMAGINING SOVEREIGNTY

My first text is by Eustache Deschamps (*c.* 1340(?)–1404), a prolific, mainly lyric French courtier poet of the minor nobility, attached at various times to the courts of Charles V, Louis d'Orléans and Charles VI, and known today for his celebrations of aristocratic love, for his moralizing, and for poems presenting recent public events and contemporary mores in a lively and 'personal' light.[12] His work has frequently been exploited as representative of its period by historians, notably Huizinga, for whom his being 'a super- ficial poet and a commonplace mind' had the virtue of making him 'so faithful a mirror of the general aspirations of his time'.[13] This view discounts the original and ambitious poetic programme developed in Deschamps's *Art poétique*; his formal developments and innovations, notably of the bal- lade, to which he may have introduced the envoy which will be central to my arguments below; and his opening up of courtly poetry to an extensive and unorthodox range of topics.[14] Critics have argued that Deschamps's 'mediocrity' has rhetorical, philosophical and political purpose, expressing his Aristotelian ideal of *mediocritas* and the 'estat moien' ('middle estate') on the one hand, gathering his society into a community purportedly speaking in unison through him on the other.[15] A further development consists in reading Deschamps's interest in the mediate as an exploration of difficult states of being uncomfortably caught between conditions that threaten the self's integrity – *entre-deux-morts* conceived as a precarious living-space between fatal whirlpools and monsters.[16] In this discussion I shall investigate how, in one of Deschamps's courtly ballades, the complex effects of the *ubi sunt* topos locate the sovereign subject *entre-deux-morts*, and how this leads to a special kind of social integration.

Deschamps uses the *ubi sunt* topos and related themes in a number of his works, including the interesting Ballade 1457:[17]

> Comment ce monde n'est riens quant à la vie
>
> Ou est Nembroth le grant jayant,
> Qui premiers obtint seigneurie
> Sur Babiloine? Ou est Priant,
> Hector et toute sa lignie?
> Achillès et sa compaingnie,
> Troye, Carthaige et Romulus,
> Athene, Alixandre, Remus,
> Jullius Cesar et li sien?
> Ilz sont tous cendre devenus:
> Souflez, nostre vie n'est rien.
>
> Ou est David le combatant,
> Judas Machabée et Urie?
> Ou est Charlemaine et Rolant,
> Godefroy qui fut en Surie,
> Baudouin, leur chevalerie,

Josué, Daires et Artus
Et ceuls qui conquirent le plus
Sarrazin, Juif et Crestien?
Ilz sont mis en pouldre et corrups:
Souflez, nostre vie n'est rien.

Ou est Atille le tyrant,
Caton plain de phillosophie,
Herculès, Jason conquerant,
Socratès et son estudie,
Augustin en theologie,
Le pouete Virgilius,
Es estoilles Tholomeus,
Ypocras le phisicien?
De mort n'est d'eulx eschapez nulz:
Souflez, nostre vie n'est rien.

L'Envoy

Prince, il n'y a que les vertus,
Bien faire et esjouir ça jus
Et departir pour Dieu du sien
Aux povres, pour regner la sus;
Nos eages est tantost conclus:
Souflez, nostre vie n'est rien.

(How this world is nothing where life is concerned

Where is the great giant Nimrod who first gained lordship over Babylon? Where is Priam, Hector and all his line? Achilles and his company, Troy, Carthage and Romulus, Athens, Alexander, Remus, Julius Caesar and his men? All are become ashes; a breath,[18] and our life is nothing.

Where is warlike David, Judas Maccabeus and Uriah? Where is Charlemagne and Roland, Godfrey who was in Syria, Baldwin, their knights, Joshua, Dares and Arthur and the greatest conquerors Saracen, Jew and Christian?[19] They are turned to dust and rotten; a breath, and our life is nothing.

Where is the despot Attila, philosophical Cato, Hercules, conquering Jason, Socrates and his learning, Augustine with his theology, the poet Virgil, Ptolemy with the stars, Hippocrates the physician? Not one of them has escaped death; a breath, and our life is nothing.

Envoy

Prince, only the virtues – doing good and spreading happiness here below, and distributing some of one's belongings to the poor for God's sake – will allow one to reign there above. Our time is so soon over; a breath, and our life is nothing.)

The poem calls on its audience to identify with the deceased as mortal, the refrain and last line of each stanza emphasizing the transience of 'nostre vie' and gathering speaker, audience and dead into a collective first-person plural. We are all effectively already dead, though in only some of us is that manifest. Deschamps's ballade also, however, incorporates a multi-level disavowal of death.[20] Most obviously, the envoy shifts the focus to the heavenly reward awaiting those Christian subjects who accept its message: Deschamps's reader may expect to 'regner la sus' (l. 34) in return for exercising 'les vertus' here below.[21] Deschamps regularly uses *regner* for temporal sovereigns and for God, and also to mean a stable, prosperous and independent existence at all social levels in accordance with his ideals of *franchise* ('freedom') and *médiocrité* ('sufficiency'), as in the refrain to Ballade 75 in praise of the religious life: 'Servir a Dieu est regner, si c'om dit' ('Serving God is living well, so they say'). Sovereignty is apparently available to all Christian subjects who obey these recommendations. Implicitly, however, other criteria are also at work in defining the sovereign subject of the poem.

A second aspect of *ubi sunt* disidentification is here associated with memory – as a faculty, and as a cultural construct inscribed in a communal store of references. Deschamps's list of famous men identifies and celebrates a tradition or *translatio* spanning hundreds of years and several countries; this early definition of what could today be called Western civilization writes a particular history.[22] The act of recognition that the *ubi sunt* text calls on its readers to perform confirms their individual participation in this collective structure, uniting them with the remembered heroes and with living, remembering beings in a greater whole which seems immune to death and which underwrites a form of immortality for its subjects.[23] A comforting sense of social integration and mastery of the cultural environment is the antithesis of death's trauma and flatly contradicts the explicit threat of dissolution. Huizinga quotes from a twelfth-century *ubi sunt* poem: 'Stat rosa pristine nomine, nomina nuda tenemus' ('The rose of yore is but a name, mere names are left to us').[24] Works like Deschamps's, however, celebrate the longevity of names liberated from corporeal corruption.

Deschamps's ballade, and each name in it, is what historian Pierre Nora calls a *lieu de mémoire*: 'any significant entity, whether material or non-material in nature, which by dint of human will or the work of time has become a symbolic element of the memorial heritage of any community'.[25] In the resonant phrases of Arthur Goldhammer, Nora's translator, *lieux de mémoire* 'emerge in two stages: moments of history are plucked out of the flow of history, then returned to it – no longer quite alive but not yet entirely dead, like shells left on the shore when the sea of living memory has receded'.[26] In Ballade 1457, the question 'Where are they now?' elicits both the Christian answer 'dead and gone into the afterlife', and the secular response 'here in us, their successors', as writing history works to efface the historical distance it also marks. Audience members themselves move towards a numinous domain of cultural legend. For this reason Deschamps's names must not be obscure, affirming only the individual poet's scholarship.[27] Audiences are invited to relish their own learning. Deschamps's reader experiences self-affirmation as subject of memory through this connection, where the individual response – 'I know that name!' – meets the collective imperative – 'These figures define this magnificent culture of ours; make yourself part of it by recognizing, admiring and emulating them.'

This interpersonal process can be understood from a phenomenological point of view in terms of what Ricoeur calls the dialectic between the complementary poles of reflexivity (*réflexivité*) and worldliness (*mondanéité*) which participate in any act of memory: 'One does not simply remember oneself, seeing, experiencing, learning [= reflexivity]; rather one recalls the situations in the world in which one has seen, experienced, learned [= worldliness].'[28] Thus the poem evokes the diverse circumstances in which audience members have encountered the names in question, harmonizing these by positing the notion of an education and a culture shared by all members of the elite. Death is thus, as so often said, a leveller; here, however, it levels (up and down) only within a single, dominant class whose cohesion the poem reinforces. Scope for not knowing the great names mentioned or for dissenting from their greatness is minimal. 'I' is here essentially part of a particular 'we' with claims which are at once normalizing and elitist.

The culture established in Deschamps's ballade provides a selective ancestry of fathers for the prince addressed in the envoy to ponder.[29] The first two stanzas offer him what initially appear to be exemplary forebears defining kingship ('seigneurie') as military activity, and more specifically as conquest. Deschamps celebrates paragons of conquering chivalry: pagan in his first stanza, Judaic and Christian in his second. No ideological barrier is drawn between deceased and audience, rather there is a rapprochement between 'them' and the implied cultural 'us' of the wider readership, whose extension is anticipated, thanks to the presence of an envoy, to an explicit princely 'you'. The inclusion of the Nine Worthies in these first two stanzas encourages readers to bridge epochs, and also to disregard the men's less admirable particularities in favour of their common status as great lords and conquerors. On the abstracted, exemplary life of all these, the prince may unproblematically model himself, striving to mimic the qualities which have made their names deathless.

Instead of continuing the progression from godless to godly warlike 'seigneurie' enacted in the first two stanzas, the third stanza suddenly shifts perspective to question conquest's value and might's right. Attila, the *flagellum dei* sometimes credited with the fall of the Roman empire, presents a different perspective on chivalric and political violence and challenges us to explain why the same actions are good in one context, bad in another. While Attila bears the name of 'tyrant' so feared by late medieval kings, Cato is an exemplary counsellor for having opposed the despotism of Rome's powerful. The focus moves, initially as if to a higher source of authority, onto figures of the most elevated learning, heroes of the liberal arts. The inclusion of such figures as Socrates and Virgil defines a specific role for scholarship in the prince's world. There is perhaps an implied threat, or at any rate a word of advice to the patron. If poets can make a prince's reputation, as Virgil made Augustus's, then they can also unmake it, bequeathing him to history as a despot. A wise prince cultivates his scholars. Rulers need thinkers also to help direct their warfare and government towards ends collectively useful and pleasing to God. Deschamps is often critical of courts and courtiers (sometimes by name), though in addressing patrons confines himself to exhortation and advice.[30] Throughout his œuvre he argues that all nobles from the knightly class upwards should be learned, a priori the king himself, for, in the proverbial refrain to Ballade 1244, 'roy sanz lettre est comme asne couronné' ('a king without learning is like a crowned ass').[31] Though this argument is not explicit in Ballade 1457, the list of historical names, as I argued above, merges the estates by implying a knowledgeable audience. The prince's education does not render the scholar obsolete. In Ballade 1244, Deschamps cites Alexander, Julius Caesar and Charlemagne as 'roys clers' (l. 21; 'learned kings' or 'clerk-kings') whose wisdom aided their conquests and government, whereas 'Princes non clers n'y ont voulu entendre [to advice], / Dont les pluseurs en sont desherité (ll. 27–8; 'Princes who were not learned [clerks] would not listen [to advice], wherefore the majority were disinherited'). His own learning, mediated by his erudite clerks, will bring the prince the discrimination and virtue he needs in order to rule, together with the humility which will allow him to appreciate their advice.

The names in the third and last stanza of 'Comment ce monde' therefore furnish both prince and poet with a genealogy, though the prince's is more admonitory. In one perspective learning surpasses chivalry; however, this stanza also works to limit clerical prestige by introducing into death's domain the scholar with his cultural, moral and even spiritual authority. Line 29, 'De mort n'est d'eulx eschapez nulz', pointedly puts the salvific knowledge of these sages on the same plane as that of the great lords of stanzas 1 and 2. If even Hippocrates, if even Augustine can die, then death is truly universal. *Clergie* is not allowed to escape *chevalerie*'s fate. Whereas in Ballade 1244, quoted above, Deschamps implies that a learned prince will have a durable reign, nothing here alleviates the foreshortening of the earthly lifespan. A further important point is that by associating clerks with tyrants, this stanza hints that learning may serve despotism; erudition, contrary to Deschamps's insistence elsewhere, is in this poem no guarantee of moral fibre or even of moral judgement. Although Augustine is cited as an intellectual rather than as a churchman, nevertheless notions of the clerk as a prime mediator of God's message are undercut. The answer to the prince's problem is not submission to churchmen. Nor is it submission to the learning of the intellectual, on which poets had been founding their capacity to advise the powerful for centuries before Deschamps.

Further doubt is cast on the authority of erudition by the heterogeneity of the names in this stanza and by the clumsily enacted internal shift of theme in the four-to-five-line opening section (the *ouvert*) in which the stanza lays out its theme; contrast the homogeneity of the previous stanzas' openings.[32] Professional scholars, the stanza demonstrates, may lack the discrimination correctly to interpret the material they study. The cosmic order will not come to earth from, or even through the poet; indeed, it seems that even the coherence of the poetic text does not originate with him. Instead of standing above terrestrial weaknesses, the speaking subject is demonstrably subject to corruption. Even if we choose to read the enactment of disintegration as reassuringly clever, the points remain valid ones. Cultural memory, genealogy and history writing are not self-sufficient; to yield their full educative potential, they require the practical wisdom that can be supplied only by an active, informed reader experienced in the ways of the world. The third stanza therefore raises materiality and corruption as threats to the prince who misuses his power, while highlighting their application to even exemplary clerks. The speaker is included by virtue of his office, the sovereign listener only where he abuses his.

The envoy which, like other envoys, 'manifests a certain detachment in relation to the poem's contents', fills the moral vacuum created by undermining the ideals of martial kingship and of scholarly insight with the figure of the virtuous prince, the poem's 'you'.[33] This conventional addressee of envoys has features of Everyman; the verb 'regner' (l. 34), as discussed above, allows for us all to be princes in heaven – provided that we fulfil certain stringent social and cultural conditions. The virtues recommended to this prince are distributing alms to the poor and good cheer to his fellows: 'Bien faire et esjouir ça jus / Et departir pour Dieu du sien / Aux povres' (ll. 32–4). The conduct urged here contrasts to the conquests that the opening stanzas associated with kingship, encouraging us to reread those conquerors as usual rather than ideal. Deschamps's ballade implies that conquest should be considered merely earthly acquisition, though he refrains from disparaging it. A modest, almost domestic model of exemplarity replaces the grand military undertakings referenced in the first two stanzas, thus redefining kingship as well as offering a pattern to those in other stations in life. Attention turns to the prince's spiritual and private self, implying a thoroughly revised idea of kingship. The new prince is to exercise the defining aristocratic virtues of largesse and patronage in personal piety, reorienting himself towards God. His acknowledgement that he will die impels him to works that will benefit both his soul and his people. Equally significantly, as a model subject (before death, before God) he is an exemplar for his own subjects.[34] He is, truly, a sovereign subject, and it is this novel combination which justifies his reign.

In a poem filled with familiar names it is, paradoxically, the prince's anonymity which marks his distinction. His non-inscription in his culture's historical genealogy expresses the humility which will allow him to inherit the consciously new and modern earth of the late Middle Ages. Spiritual immortality in God, not everlasting secular renown, is the reward promised for idealized princely behaviour; although secular immortality is not ruled out, for who will rein in the appreciation of the prince's beneficiaries and admirers? Better conquests are made by love and gratitude than by violence. The sovereign subject – here an actual ruler – unites in himself the secular and spiritual worlds, and the prince approaches simultaneously God and a redefined ideal of kingship. Deschamps's construction here would suit Charles V's commitment to learning, piety, diplomacy and political reform against martial tradition.[35] It contrasts with the poet's glorification of warfare in other works, for instance in the poems associated with the youth of Charles VI or in his repeated calls to retake Calais from the English. Over and above the occasional nature of his poetry, Deschamps espouses mainstream views heterogeneously, so that his works voice a range of often contradictory opinions. The compilers of the principal manuscript of his works, BN f.fr. 840 (whose order is followed in vols. I–IX of the *Œuvres complètes*), seem to have enjoyed pairing works with contradictory messages.[36] Thus Ballade 1458, 'Songeons à nous bien conduire en vue de la mort', undercuts the elevated moral and cultural tone of Ballade 1457 by comparing man's comportment in the face of death to the training of hounds. The envoy concludes:

> Princes, tout homme se soulace
> En vaine gloire ou il s'enlace
> Tant que vertus en pluseurs dort;
> N'aient plus les yeulx de lymace!
> Advisent que chascun trespace!
> Qui autrement fait, il a tort.
>
> (ll. 25–30)

(Princes, every man consoles himself in vainglory in which he becomes enmeshed, so that virtue lies drowsing in many; may they have snails' eyes no longer! Let them take notice that everyone dies! Whoever does otherwise is in the wrong.)

Are Ballade 1457's princely and poetic genealogies 'vaine gloire' distracting the subject from the universal truth of mortality? Ballade 1458's line 19, 'A congnoistre ont les oeulx derrier' (literally, 'for knowing they have their eyes backwards'), implies poor insight and perhaps encourages us to look back at the previous ballade and at its history lesson as instances of such delusional thinking. On the other hand, a further level of irony may be present intertextually, since this trope recalls the *Memoire* of Deguileville's *Pèlerinage*, whose eyes in the back of her head (ll. 4825–6) are explicitly connected with university clerks and their learning about the past, and with the message that these should be valued (ll. 4883–908). Although scholarly opinions vary over whether Deschamps himself oversaw the production of BN f.fr. 840, it may well be that he relished such juxtapositions; his single texts often encapsulate internal dialogues or shifts in contrary directions, verging on dialogue even when spoken by a seemingly single voice. Ballade 1457 manifests its own double movement when the prestige of the great warriors and clerks of the past is at once harnessed for and surpassed by the modern prince and poet. Modern monarchy and its servants claim both continuity with and discontinuity from their antecedents, portraying themselves as the modest representatives of a superior conception of duty, dwarfs on the shoulders of giants. By this means the demands of both secular and Christian traditions are satisfied.

The prince's glorious (because self-effacing!) rejection of older aggressive, self-aggrandizing values may, of course, be a way to recode his real-life failure to live up to those values. The early promise as a warrior that Charles VI manifested never came to mature fruition, and this fact, together with his other documented infirmities, altered monarchical ideology.[37] Deschamps provides the sovereign with a powerful cultural imaginary in the series of mighty forebears, then deals with the actual king's shortcomings by interpreting them as the inevitable shadow cast by the unattainable ideal on any living incumbent. Lacan argues in Seminar IV that inadequacy in face of the ultimate Father is itself a defining feature of the paternal position within the symbolic order; in the same way, it is Deschamps's prince's very insufficiency when measured against such strong paternal models as Charlemagne and Caesar that justifies his public position on earth as well as his personal place in heaven.[38] Ballade 1457's repeated invocations of the *nom-du-père* or death-defying name are therefore fulfilled and transcended at the same time as they are negated in the envoy's nameless prince, a *non-du-père*. This (non-)figure founds authority in lack and in a mortality that is not simple but reflexive: a self-effacing, virtuously humble rejection of the seigneurial claim to secular immortality. Anthropologist Max Gluckman observes that revelation of a leader's human frailty can bring his subordinates 'to question his authority . . . and ultimately to seek someone else who, they fondly imagine, will attain the ideals they desire'.[39] When Ballade 1457 exhibits the prince's weaknesses, it might therefore be understood to encourage rebellion. However, by including in his portrayal of the supermen their besetting frailties of pride, violence and tyranny, and by presenting his humanly weak prince as an ideally meek and virtuous subject of Christ as well as a community-minded fellow subject, Deschamps forestalls the impulse among audience members to 'seek someone else'. Charles VI's generosity and hospitality may have been often unwise, but they are well attested; and Deschamps highlights just these desirable virtues in the envoy. Finally, Poirion insists that ballade envoys mark 'a new connection to concrete, objective reality' after the stanzas' lyrical 'expedition into the domain of the ideal'.[40] What is designated 'reality' by inclusion in the envoy thus receives an ideological fillip. The envoy to Ballade 1457 signals that the idea of a strong and virtuous, perfectly kingly king is illusory. A prince who acknowledges both his personal failings and the ethical insufficiencies of the old, glorious, chivalric model of kingship – who acknowledges, in short, that the King is dead – is henceforth an excellent candidate for the throne and has an exemplary claim on the hereafter.

We may compare the end of the Oxford *Chanson de Roland*, where Charlemagne's authority flows from his weakened, mourning state (see Chapter 1, above). A position *entre-deux-morts* sponsors a political order which presents itself as bridging past and future: a revolution in ideas that yet relies on and strengthens the 'best' of existing institutions and ideologies. This vision of history incorporates a process of change into a transcendent eternity of spirit. Thus Deschamps's emphasis on innovation is not irrelevant. His new prince, like his new poet, must 'avoir a court un pié hors et l'autre ens' (Ballade 208, refrain; 'have at court one foot out and the other in'). Deschamps here articulates not a straightforward anti-curial message but an improved way of being courtly: to achieve the court's higher aspirations it is necessary to be partially outside it. Insight comes not from externality (which would be mere exclusion) but from a divided position, at once within and beyond.⁴¹ In Ballade 208, Deschamps establishes the subject's sovereignty in this space, arguing that its uncertainty is not incompatible with plenitude: 'vivre du sien' (l. 19; 'independent living') and 'demourer en paix de cuer' (ll. 19–20; 'dwelling in heart's peace'). This new courtliness presents a strange form of sovereignty, bounded by 'aucun meschief' (l. 15; 'some harm') on one side and 'aucun mal' (l. 17; 'some evil') on the other. To be between a rock and a hard place, it appears, permits effective social integration and domination for both poetic and princely subjects.⁴²

'JE SUIS MORT'

I turn now to explore this state of affairs via a long-running debate over the phrase 'je suis mort' between two great figures of modern criticism – a debate which throws light on the potential of 'between two deaths' as a trope. As a trope, the figure relates to the Lacanian imaginary or symbolic; I explore here the connections between those and the Real to which Lacan primarily links the notion.

At the famous symposium on *The Languages of Criticism and the Sciences of Man* held at the Johns Hopkins Humanities Center in October 1966, the critic Roland Barthes contributed a paper on the 'reflexive' relationship between writer and writing. Developing his theory of literature as a 'middle voice' neither active nor passive, Barthes drew on linguist Gustave Guillaume for the grammatical analogy of the French *passé composé* formed with the auxiliary *être*, giving the examples 'je suis sorti' and 'il est mort' ('I went out', 'he died') and adding parenthetically, 'for I can't say "je suis mort"' ('I am dead' / 'I have died').⁴³ In the following discussion, the philosopher Jacques Derrida disputes Barthes's rejection of the utterance as an invalid use of language and awards it instead a foundational value: 'You were reticent about saying "I am dead". I believe that the condition for a true act of language is my being able to say "I am dead"'.⁴⁴ For Derrida, the utterance 'Je suis mort' handily illustrates language's independence both of its user and of the referential world, key features in his philosophy. The necessary multiple repetitions and conventionality involved in using any symbolic system depersonalize and, in an important sense, de-animate every subject position, however intimate, which can be articulated within that system.

Derrida invokes Husserl's logical grammar to comment on 'I am dead' as a 'contre-sens' rather than 'nonsense'. That is, it is viable as an untruth, 'a possible proposition for one who is known to be living'.[45] The illegitimacy of untruths lies elsewhere. They break the 'pacte de la parole' or bond of trust that founds spoken language and emblematizes the metaphysics of presence central to Derrida's early thought. Writing, or *écriture*, contrastingly, is explicitly grounded in the possibility of lie, fiction, figuration or wish, hence in the subject's ability to articulate what it knows to be literally untrue. Derrida famously argues, against what he represents as Western tradition, that *écriture* and not *parole* is the primary form of language. Thus even where speech is concerned, the *pacte de la parole* is not 'living' but a 'phantasm', at once fantasy and ghost.[46] Language's 'power of meaning . . . independent of the possibility of its object' precludes any unmediated relation to the world – though such a relation haunts it. Hence the foundational nature of the disputed utterance, reiterated: 'the very condition for the living person to speak is for him to be able to say, significantly, "I am dead"'.[47]

Derrida, therefore, treats death as a figure for the alienation imposed on any subject who would use language. He attacks the fantasies of self-determination, straightforward interlocution, social integration and direct interaction with the non-linguistic environment that attend the spoken word, emblematized in the utterance 'Je suis' ('I am', but also the auxiliary in some cases of the perfect tense, hence 'Je suis mort' equates to 'I am dead' and to 'I have died'). 'Je suis mort' therefore encapsulates the death of a particular notion of the human subject, sometimes today called the humanist or Enlightenment subject: transcendental and authorial, atomistic and self-determining, present and self-present in language, entitled to and assured of a hearing. This figurative mortality is, for Derrida, a necessary condition of entry into human social life, reason and language. Our choice in relation to it is between clear-sighted acceptance and fantasmatic disavowal. Derrida's writing in his relatively early works renders the former option more attractive by emphasizing how it permits the emergence of a different subject, able to abandon itself to the proliferating, uncontrollable possibilities of meaning and to appreciate, even enjoy the play (in the senses of 'room for movement' and of 'game') within language.

In *Speech and Phenomena*, his discussion of the sign in Husserl, originally published in 1967, Derrida broadens the import of his analysis. In Husserl's thinking, according to Derrida, acceptance of our mortality is the price we pay for access to the universal which bestows all value: 'the possibility of my disappearance [/death] in general must somehow be experienced in order for a relationship with presence in general to be instituted'.[48] Derrida develops his critique of this stance by substituting for 'je suis mort' a new 'impossible proposition': 'I am immortal'.[49] He explains, in terms that extend the 1966 discussion, that the latter proposition's 'absurdity' and the 'truth' against which it is measured depend on culturally specific and challengeable methods of filtering and constructing knowledge which are themselves ultimately determined by a particular relation to death: 'as the classical idea of truth, which guides these distinctions, has itself issued from . . . a concealment of the relationship with death, this "falsity" ["I am immortal"] is the very truth of truth'.[50]

In spite of the similarities to his oral intervention a year earlier, Derrida's later argument is more disturbing. He here criticizes, not fantasies of personal immortality of the kind supposedly afforded by speech, but a notion of impersonal immortality which, he claims, illogically haunts Husserl's phenomenology specifically and Western metaphysics generally. Submitting myself to a greater symbolic structure (which I do when using or interpreting language) offers me immortality by proxy: the big Other will continue and I as part of it, although my specificity will pass. Those who renounce the transcendent ego are rewarded with another transcendence, creating an immortality that addresses what in Lacanian terms is the subject, not the self.

Derrida's point is no longer only that dying is the price we pay for a place in culture; instead he recognizes that this position may itself be the symptom of an overarching disavowal. He now alleges that Western thinking is ruled or driven by the unconscious need to deny what it consciously acknowledges and attempts to address, namely death. Even the philosophical subject who proclaims 'Je suis mort' seeks in that utterance a backdoor escape from extinction. We cannot understand the Western rational tradition unless we appreciate the significant role played in it by the attempt to rescue a transcendental subject from the reality of death, for this desire warps not only the conclusions reached but also the logic relied upon to verify or falsify, that is, the methodological basis. 'Je suis immortel' is treated as a lapsus, a return of the cultural structure's repressed indicating the secret imperatives that determine it: 'the very truth of truth'. In Derrida's 1967 argument, therefore, acceptance of personal mortality can actually sustain the possibility of transcendental meaning and of a transcendent existence for the subject, even though in some contexts transcendence may be deferred or partial.

Example may be taken from Deschamps's Ballade 1457, which shows how tropes of speech, voice and presence, as exemplified in the lists of great names, have no monopoly on fantasies of immortality in medieval texts; lacking earthly 'presence', the prince of the envoy and his attendant poet attain eternal life by means precisely of their absence, coded as transcendent Christian anonymity and humility. Thus the *ubi sunt* topos allows the subject a place within the universal dependent on the acknowledgement of personal as well as general mortality. 'La mort de soi' opens onto 'la vie de soi', not only in a Christian afterlife but on earth. It opens, moreover, onto secular authority. Renouncing the straightforwardly self-aggrandizing possibility of personal immortality on earth, the impersonal immortality of Deschamps's envoy in fact represents 'the height of narcissism', in Jean Starobinski's phrase.[51]

Supporting Derrida's 1966 intervention, Jean-Michel Rabaté affirms that 'For Derrida, the belief in a pure speech is a fantasy, a delusion under which Barthes is still working.'[52] Drawing on Derridean and Lacanian thinking, Barthes later defended his throwaway dismissal, developing the fantasmatic aspects of the utterance 'je suis mort' as 'pure speech'. In his 1973 close reading of parts of Poe's 'The Facts in the Case of M. Valdemar', Barthes took up Derrida's 1966 mention of 'that extraordinary story of Poe about M. Valdemar, who awakens at a certain moment and says, "I am dead"'.[53] Poe's short story relates a scientific experiment in which a man on the point of death is mesmerised. Interrogated as to his state, M. Valdemar replies on the first occasion that he is asleep, on the second that he is dying and on the third 'still asleep – dying'. When asked a fourth time, he dies before he can answer. Clinical death is verified, but then Valdemar's tongue writhes out the following words: 'Yes; – no; – I *have been* sleeping; – and now – now – *I am dead.*'

Like Derrida, Barthes highlights the impossibility at the heart of Valdemar's utterance and the challenge it poses to traditional notions of selfhood: 'In the ideal sum of all the possible utterances of language, the link of the first person [*Je*] and the attribute [*mort*] is precisely the one which is radically impossible.'[54] To highlight the distinctiveness of Poe's creation, however, Barthes notes that 'there exist numerous mythical narratives in which the dead person speaks, but only to say: "I am alive"'.[55] Barthes would presumably include under this rubric not only the epitaph quoted above (p. 104) but also the many medieval ghost stories in which the dead ask that their debts be paid – the persistence of debts implying the persistence of the dead person.[56] Thus in its normal fictional usage, the trope of the dead man talking sustains fantasies of the self's sovereignty and indestructibility against a background of general mortality.

Poe's Valdemar represents a different, more disturbing idea:

We have already extracted the theme of encroachment [*l'empiètement*] (of Life on Death). Encroachment is a paradigmatic disorder, a disorder of meaning. In the *Life / Death* paradigm the bar is normally read as 'against' (versus); it would suffice to read it as 'on' for encroachment to take place and the paradigm to be destroyed. That's what happens here: one of the spaces bites unwarrantedly into the other [*il y a morsure indue d'un espace sur l'autre*]. The interesting thing here is that the encroachment occurs at the level of language . . . Prior to the meaning 'I am dead', the voice conveys simply, 'I am speaking' – rather like a grammatical example which refers to nothing but language. The uselessness of what is proffered is part of the scandal: it is a matter of affirming an essence *which is not in its place* (the *displaced* is the very form of the symbolic).[57]

This encroachment is much less comforting than the mutual differential construction of a 'death'/'life' dyad or the erasure of death by the living voice in the epitaph.

For Barthes, the voice speaking through the deceased Valdemar is not that of any human subject. It is language itself, whose radically alien nature is revealed in the phallic, undead tongue – *la langue* – that inhabits the mortifying corpse of 'M. Valdemar'. Poe's story communicates the terrifying inhumanity of the symbolic order behind its familiar facade. The human subject's essential supports – language, the body, the voice, objective knowledgeable discourse, civic society – are defamiliarized together, exposed as inherently destructive of the accepted categories and habits of thought which perforce use them as their underpinning. This is 'death' as the truth of the symbolic, realized in something of its Real force and impossibility, thanks to literature's specific ability to engage the fantasmatic and the paradoxical. Writing as a literary critic (and himself employing considerable rhetorical colour), Barthes brings to the fore the rhetorical and narrative strategies by which Poe creates his scandalous text uncovering language's 'blind spot'.[58]

For both Barthes and Derrida, therefore, Poe's 'I am dead' indicates the constitutively contradictory position of the subject in language. Acknowledging this position represents for each an intellectual and ethical step towards a more accurate apprehension of human existence. Their differences may be illustrated via their contrasting notions of M. Valdemar's utterance, and thence of language and the human condition generally, as *entre-deux-morts*. Derrida argues that all active language users are figuratively dead due to their subordination to the symbolic order, indeed that they must first 'die' in order to 'live' within that order. Properly seen, therefore, human life is led in a deathly environment. This deathliness can, however, be negated by denial, leading to inauthenticity, or equally by an acceptance that purports to transcend. In reaction to what he construes as this banal vision, Barthes insists on the world-destroying horror which surges irrepressibly within the perilously thin fabric of everyday human existence – the symbolic order is for that existence at once its foundation, its generative principle and its nightmare. His impassioned, highly 'liter-ary' essay implies that Derrida's more measured and philosophical analysis serves to detract from the affective power of this frustrating and ghastly situation, and thereby to construct the same fantasmatic barrier against death's disruptiveness that Derrida criticizes in Husserl. 'La langue, c'est la parole':[59] with this gnomic utterance Barthes confronts the aberrancy of the forms within which we live. The phrase may be translated 'the tongue is speech' or 'the tongue is the word', thus grounding the subject's voice-consciousness in Valdemar's obscenely realized body whose materi-ality and drives defy human attempts at orderliness or transcendence.[60] It also indicates Barthes's rejection of the idealism and monism inherent in Saussure's identification of the primary focus of linguistic study; '*langue* is *parole*' implies that language, and hence culture itself, is composed out of multiple, conflicting forces incapable of totalization. These conflicts are suppressed in normal life; however, literary texts like Poe's, by emphasizing and exacerbating them, can open the door to an insistent and indestructible life-force. And this force figures the destruction drive working through the symbolic order better than does Nirvana (see Chapter 1, above). Barthes's concept of Valdemar's *entre-deux-morts* as a traumatic, perpetually unac-ceptable presentation of the alien and alienating nature of the symbolic is notably more Lacanian than Derrida's.

The disagreement under discussion is not reducible to strictly Laca-nian terms but, given the overall framework of this book, it is worthwhile attempting some rapprochement. In his reading of M. Valdemar's multiply inscribed utterance, Derrida gives ethical and ontological precedence to what we can call the symbolic order, conceived as the domain of formal structures independent of, estranged from and estranging the subject who lives in them. His analysis in *Speech and Phenomena* recognizes the power of the dreams of sovereignty which energize the human 'I' and criticizes the tendency to rework the symbolic into a ground of impersonal immor-tality, a stronghold of stability against change and decay. Barthes offers a different account of the symbolic order in which he stresses its conflicted plurality characterized by, and offering to the human subject, instability, confusion and discord: mortality, in short. His corresponding insistence on the aesthetic gives to the imaginary dimension a positive value that Derrida denies it. The horror inspired by the symbolic order's radically unassimilable nature can be felt only via the imaginary, which is therefore an indispensable heuristic tool – illusory in itself, but guiding us power-fully towards certain of life's truths. Voice is a key element, since it is only in *parole* – and not in *écriture* – that we hear the timbre of the alien; in Lacan's oft repeated phrase, 'le *ça* parle'. In contrast to Derrida's emphasis on writing as locus of figuration and absence, Barthes highlights the fact that 'I am dead' is inscribed in Poe's text as a spoken and literally true utterance, and shows that precisely for this reason, it bears the weight of a presence that it simultaneously renders unfeasible. In Barthes's presen-tation, symbolic and imaginary combine to produce a surging destructive force recalling Lacan's Real. For Barthes the literary critic, literature is val-ued not only for its ability to make us feel this destruction – as the work of art does for Heidegger, and for the Lacan of Seminar VII – but for the enormous aesthetic power and creative generativity which destruction calls into being. Derrida the philosopher demolishes logically the foundations of such a pretension; although his objection is not so much to imaginative art per se as to texts that purport to be objective, a target that Barthes too addresses in his insistence that the 'asymbolic' posture adopted by knowlegeable discourse is an imaginary, and indeed illusory one.[61] Thus in Deschamps's ballade, the fantasies of empowerment that are generated around the prince's and poet's acknowledgement of personal absence cir-cumscribe that acknowledgement's ethical and epistemological value. True to its author's 'non-literary', 'historical' reputation today, Deschamps's lyric may be taken to illustrate Derrida's analysis. In the remainder of this chap-ter I turn to a more 'artistic', and more troubling treatment of the *ubi sunt* topos.

DEAD MAN TALKING: VILLON'S 'BALLADES DU TEMPS JADIS'

The *Testament* of François Villon (1430/32 – mid-1460s?), a mock will writ-ten, according to its own testimony, in 1461, may be viewed as an extended exploration of the utterance 'Je suis mort', or of ways of imagining, know-ing and denying 'la mort de soi'.[62] The poem is placed insistently in relation to death, although precisely what relation is obscure; in the opening stan-zas Villon's persona is variously pronounced physically dying, symbolically dead, metaphorically resuscitated and still optimistic of spiritual redemp-tion. A death sentence hangs over the work, which shifts between gloomy or salty contemplation, revived hopefulness and studied defiance. Repetition, that manifestation of the death drive, impels the whole; it is not even Villon's first attempt at a will, a fact emphasized when he here rejects the intention that would name his 1456 *Lais* ('poems'/'legacy') a 'Petit Testament'.[63] The three ballades known collectively as the 'Ballades du temps jadis' are among a number of fixed-form lyrics contained within the *Testament*, some of which may have predated the larger frame poem or have circulated separately.[64] They form part of the meditation on death which occupies the first eight hundred lines or so of the poem, the remaining twelve hundred lines being dedicated to scurrilous and satirical legacies to Villon's contemporaries.[65]

Villon's *Testament* is characterized by its use of diverse registers and voices, though the dominant milieu is that of the bottom rungs of society, and there is a constant theme of social marginalization. The poem adopts a kaleidoscope of tones within the overarching frame of libellous satire and burlesque directed above all against those who enforce social rules.[66] Nevertheless, elements of the *Testament* approach court poetry in their style, and some may indeed have begun life in that context.[67] Bearing this in mind, I compare the treatment of the sovereign subject and of personal and cultural memory in the three 'Ballades du temps jadis' to that in Deschamps's undoubtedly courtly Ballade 1457.

Whatever the possible uses of some of the lyrics outside the *Testament*, their contexts within it orient interpretation in particular ways. It is important to bear this in mind when encountering the 'Ballade des dames du temps jadis', which has been widely read in isolation from the frame work; anthologized, quoted, translated and set to music. In the *Testament* it is followed and echoed by another string of *ubi sunt* questions in the 'Ballade des seigneurs du temps jadis'. In spite of their formal similarity, the poems have met with divergent critical judgements. Critics and readers have celebrated the 'Ballade des dames' not just as a high point of lyricism within the *Testament* but as one of the great lyrical moments in the European poetic tradition. The 'Ballade des seigneurs' is rarely examined in detail and commonly considered a prosaic and bathetic failure.[68] Closing the mini-sequence is the 'Ballade en vieil langage françois', also little discussed though less harshly judged, which abandons the *ubi sunt* question for a related theme reminiscent of that of the Dance of Death or *Danse macabre*.

Edgar Allan Poe's celebrated assertion that 'the death of a beautiful woman is, unquestionably, the most poetical topic in the world' envisages female death for a male writer and public as painful yet within the domain of aesthetic craft and pleasure, where it represents at once a limit case and a central theme.[69] This same topic contributes to the reputation of Villon's 'Ballade des dames' as a zenith of lyricism. The relationship between dead females and poetry will occupy much of the remainder of this book, pursued in discussions of *Pearl* and marguerite poetry (Chapter 4) and of Chaucer's *Book of the Duchess* and *Legend of Good Women* (Chapter 5). I embark on it here with a reading of the construction of femininity and masculinity in Villon's 'Ballade des dames' and its reception, arguing that the poem's celebrated 'most poetical' quality depends on its promotion of a particular masculine sovereign subject. Afterwards I consider in turn the 'Ballade des seigneurs' and 'Ballade en vieil langage', to show how reading the three 'Ballades du temps jadis' in sequence breaks down that sovereign subject. The relative obscurity and critical depreciation of the second and third ballades are no accident, for they work to spoil the 'poetry' of the 'Ballade des dames'.

THE 'BALLADE DES DAMES'

Dictes moy ou n'en quel pays
Est Flora la belle Romaine,
Archipïadés ne Thaÿs,
Qui fut sa cousine germaine,
Echo parlant quant bruyt on maine
Dessus riviere ou sur estan,
Qui beaulté ot trop plus qu'umaine.
Mais ou sont les neiges d'anten?

Ou est la tres saige Esloÿs,
Pour qui chastré fut et puis moyne
Pierre Esbaillart a Saint Denys?
Pour son amour eust ceste essoyne.
Semblablement, ou est la royne
Qui commanda que Buriden
Fust gecté en ung sac en Saine?
Mais ou sont les neiges d'anten?

La Royne Blanche comme liz
Qui chantoit a voix de seraine,
Berte au plat pié, Bietrix, Aliz,
Haranburgis qui tint le Maine,
Et Jehanne la bonne Lorraine
Qu'Engloys brulerent a Rouen,
Ou sont ilz, ou, Vierge souveraine?
Mais ou sont les neiges d'anten?

Prince, n'enquerrez de sepmaine
Ou elles sont ne de cest an
Qu'a ce reffraing ne vous remaine:
Mais ou sont les neiges d'anten?

(ll. 329–56)

(Tell me where, in what country is Flora the beautiful Roman, Archipïadés or Thaïs, who was first cousin to her once; Echo who speaks when one brings a sound over river or pond, who had much more than human beauty? But where are the snows of last winter?

Where is the very learned Heloïse for whom Peter Abelard was castrated and afterwards a monk at St Denis? For her love he suffered this outrage. Similarly, where is the queen who had Buridan thrown into the Seine, in a sack? But where are the snows of last winter?

The queen white as a lily who sang with a siren's voice, and flat-footed Berte, Beatrice, Alis, Haremburgis who held Maine, and Joan the good woman from Lorraine whom the English burned at Rouen; where are they, where, oh sovereign Virgin? But where are the snows of last winter?

Prince, you may not ask this week where they are nor this year, that I won't tell you back the refrain: But where are the snows of last winter?)[70]

I print the ballade here in order that it inform the following discussion; but I begin with the stanzas preceding the three 'Ballades du temps jadis'. These stanzas prepare the disidentification–identification sequence characteristic of the *ubi sunt* topos. After lamenting his poverty, Villon's poetic persona is advised by his heart:

Mieulx vaut vivre soubz groz bureau
Pouvre, qu'avoir esté seigneur
Et pourrir soubz riche tumbeau.

(ll. 286–8)

(Better to live under common cloth poor, than having once been a lord to rot under an expensive tomb.)

This short-lived triumph over the dead lord melts into identification as the poet reflects that he too will die. Future death orthodoxly swallows up present life. But there is no mention here of eternal glories merited by the humble – they get only an uncomfortable life in addition to the death which is the universal lot. The poet then dwells on the physical pains of dying and on the impossibility of finding another who will take one's place in the face of death. He turns abruptly to interrogate the female body:

> Corps femenin, qui tant est tendre,
> Poly, souëf, si precïeulx,
> Te fauldra il ces maulx attendre?
> Oy, ou tout vif aler es cieulx.
>
> (ll. 325–8)

(Body of woman so tender, so polished, so smooth, so dearly loved, must you too come to these agonies? Yes, or rise living up to the heavens.)

Feminine beauty is evoked with a sensuous emphasis on the tactile, transitively 'felt'. In one interpretation of this stanza, disturbed though he is by the thought of the female body's inevitable disintegration, the poet may nevertheless contemplate it with more equanimity because he does not fully identify with it. Eroticism in such a case objectifies the female physique and thereby distances its fate from the observing subject. The inevitable decay of every erotic object which temporarily plays the role of *objet a* can be mourned by the heterosexual male without necessarily impinging on his own sense of subjecthood. It may even produce a self-congratulatory sense of his own immunity to time so long as sexual desire or its counterpart, revulsion, spring anew in his breast to confirm his lustiness. A certain sadistic or narcissistic pleasure may therefore tinge representations of female decrepitude.

Consider this passage alongside that in which the Belle Hëaulmiere contemplates her ruined body in the *Testament*'s complementary exploitation of the *ubi sunt* theme (ll. 453–560) through the feminine voice. The former helmet-maker perceives that her body's ageing corresponds to a vertiginous collapse in her worth to others and to herself, and her experience of personal invalidity constitutes a fate worse than death: 'Car vielles n'ont ne cours ne estre / Ne que monnoye qu'on descrye' (ll. 539–40; 'For old women have neither currency nor being, any more than obsolete coin'). We may view this as symbolic death so long as we recognize that its pain stems from the combination of an invalid symbolic position with a living consciousness.[71] Villon joins that company of male writers who have expressed their most intense apprehensions of a supposed universal human condition through a representation of specifically feminine experience, with its restrictions and vulnerabilities – above all, in its privileged relation to the passive voice.[72] Contrastingly, the masculine subject of *Testament* lines 321–8 finds someone to suffer death in his place (compare Alceste, Chapter 5, below). The female body becomes his proxy (l. 320; 'son pleige') in corporeal extinction, allowing him to believe that he, at least, is something more than only flesh, and that masculine 'cours et estre' are assured.

However, lines 321–8 also suggest a reserve of disbelief in the possibility that the female body can suffer real disintegration. The constitution of that unblemished body in lines 325–6 against the torture of the previous lines, together with the notion of direct translation into heaven, gesture towards the notion of a feminine which is in essence unbreachably whole. This incorruptible female body is sought as a refuge against the horrors of physical dissolution. In a complicated way, the subject need not feel too guilty about sacrificing the female's body to save his own, since hers in any case cannot really die. This and the alternative reading sketched above, however logically contradictory, are not emotionally incompatible. Freud's paper on fetishism analyses complex responses in the masculine subject to the spectacle of the female genitals which, he claims, the boy reads as proof of castration.[73] The perception 'I see you castrated' leads to the gratifying 'And I, unlike you, have not been castrated' and thence to the anxious 'But I, like you, may be castrated.' 'Normal' resolution of the masculine castration complex occurs when the subject withdraws from Oedipal rivalry with the father, supposed agent of castration, in order to avoid the female's fate. A model of sexual difference is instantiated that leaves her in feminine inferiority and him within a masculinity which, while superior to femininity, is internally hierarchical, the boy submitting to paternal authority in the expectation of one day inheriting the father's prerogatives. The initial feminine 'you' becomes a third-person 'she', with interlocution limited to masculine subjects. However, where anxiety is overwhelming, the fetishist's response is to adopt gender difference while nevertheless disavowing female castration, finding evidence of the female phallus elsewhere – in a shoe, or a shiny nose. Freud extends himself in an exposition of the contradictory logic and self-splitting of the fetishist who both does and does not 'recognize' female castration; such dualities are a basic psychoanalytical tenet, discovered in numerous everyday and extraordinary stances.

Commentaries on the 'Ballade des dames' by two of its greatest male readers fall within the field of responses mapped by Freud. For Italo Siciliano, Villon has 'opened the doors of the infinite' with his cortège of dead ladies 'who live again for a moment, joyous and oblivious'.[74] Before this procession of female names conjuring up timeless immortality, the poet humbles himself: 'he is as if bewildered [*égaré*] before the grandeur of the thing, he makes himself ever smaller'.[75] Ultimately, however, it is the ladies who are effaced: 'the brilliant procession winds out, draws away and is lost in the night from which it emerged: dream and dust'.[76] In the face of this sublime vision, the poet remains in control, agent and beneficiary of his own temporary abjection. Siciliano locates the feminine at once 'above' and 'below' the masculine writing/reading subject, who is neither 'dream' nor 'dust' but acquires solidity and actuality from the contrast. Whereas Siciliano associates the transcendental quality he identifies in the lyric with the feminine, for Leo Spitzer it lies with the 'very gentle, paternal reprimand' of the refrain, among the elements of the poem 'alone . . . destined for immortality'.[77] The refrain's voice is distinct from that of the stanzas, answering its anguished *ubi sunt* questions with 'the assured, insistent and imperturbable tranquility of a parent much older and wiser than we'.[78] In Spitzer's account, the poem's poetic quality is due to the dialectical movement between masculine and feminine (both from a masculine viewpoint), the paternal wisdom of the refrain giving durable form and articulate meaning to evanescent maternal matter, which encompasses the subject matter of beauty, desire and loss as well as that materiality of language that Julia Kristeva calls the semiotic.[79] The poetic 'I' oscillates not, as for Siciliano, between two views of femininity, but between the maternal body and the paternal, super-egoic maxim – dialoguing, however, only with the latter. Although the feminine supplements the rationalist paternal proverb with an important poetic softening, the core masculine values of rationality and immortality remain central and the poetic voice's allegiance is clear. From a Freudian perspective, Spitzer's position, which is more explicit about consigning the feminine to death in place of the masculine and about the need to accept, with reservations, paternal Law, exhibits a more 'normal' dramatization of the castration complex, while Siciliano's position, which construes femininity as simultaneously deathless and extinct, constructs the feminine as a fetish object which disavows while it represents male castration. Neither position confers subjecthood on women; instead these constructions work together to characterize an other which defines and shores up the universality, exclusivity and sovereignty of (internally differentiated) masculine subjectivity.

I am not arguing that either critic is mistaken, rather that the 'Ballade des dames' encourages gendered readings that, in turn, invite analysis. Feminist philosophers have analysed at length the apparently contradictory ways in which constructions of the feminine other strengthen the masculine self's claim to represent neutral universality and the only genuine form of selfhood. In her awe-inspiring aspect, woman mediates between men and the divinity – witness the Virgin Mary's appearance in stanza 3 of the 'Ballade des dames'. Her superhuman assimilation into the transcendent realm answers in mortal man a striving towards transcendence. But woman is also the material ground of man's more-than-material being, his superior spiritual and cultural potential. 'Dream and dust', she provides the inhuman support for that consciousness which in him is half angelic, and which typifies the highest 'human' aspirations. Read in these terms, the 'Ballade des dames' and the stanzas leading up to it allow simultaneously a consignment of woman to annihilation in man's place and an assertion of her elemental wholeness in his service.

Comparing the 'Ballade des dames' with Deschamps's Ballade 1457 throws light on the former's peculiarities. Villon's lyric opens with a question which, in spite of following *ubi sunt* conventions, leads towards an unusual response. Instead of eliciting the usual range of responses – 'in the grave', 'damned in hell' or 'reborn in our own culture' – the query 'Dictes moy ou n'en quel pays' (l. 329) suggests an elsewhere in which these figures may still exist, thus enhancing the topos's death-denying tendency. This space is supplemented in the first stanza by classicizing-orientalizing connotations and by watery landscapes that recall the Celtic *merveilleux*. The *dames'* association with such natural-supernatural phenomena distances them from the world of human society, erudition and ethics. These women's 'place' is in legend, not in the virile history outlined by Deschamps. Although masculine learning put them there, moreover, their names are not presented in a way that evokes the world of clerical scholarship any more than its political application by princes and their advisers. The names are evocative but mainly indeterminate, with minimum social structuring and barely sketched reference points.[80] Editions note that Flora and Thaïs were courtesans (and 'la belle Romaine' sounds like a prostitute's cognomen), but Flora was also known as a goddess, Thaïs as a saint.[81] Similarly, it is commonplace to remark that 'Archipïadés' may originally have been the Greek general Alcibiades, famed for his beauty, but this, like other historical knowledge considered to contravene the spirit of the ballade, is swept aside on the tide of gendered lyricism.[82] Both Spitzer and Siciliano declare that there are things they do not want to know about the 'Ballade des dames', an arresting pronouncement in view of the weight of historical scholarship that the *Testament* generates.[83] Against the frame poem's notable tendency to elicit epistemophilia, the 'Ballade des dames' calls on us to suspend detailed knowledge. The names of the first stanza constitute *lieux de mémoire* in a cultural tradition, but the *lieux* with which they are associated are unlocatable in a 'real world' frame, contributing to the sense of a mysterious, feminine 'other place' outside historical time and profoundly unlike the manly, public world conjured up by Deschamps's lists. The masculine readers and writers implied in these two poems indulge in quite different fantasies and desires.

The refrain may be interpreted either to counter or to confirm the construction of femininity encountered in the first stanza. It is difficult for English speakers today to read the 'Ballade des dames' without hearing in its refrain, 'Mais ou sont les neiges d'anten?', the resonant phrasing of Dante Gabriel Rossetti. His celebrated 'Where are the snows of yesteryear?', according to Spitzer, brings to mind virgin wastes of eternal snow, an otherwhere in which time has no relevance. Complementing Rossetti's lyrical rendering, Robert Lowell's prosaic translation 'Where is last year's snow?' to my mind underlines how thoroughly the passage of time obliterates the past.[84] If Rossetti's romantic rendering emphasizes the Eternal Feminine in the poem, Lowell's rationalist version suggests a feminine as insubstantial and transient as meltwater. This version too gestures towards eternity, albeit in a different mode, for last year's snow will return as next year's, essentially no different. In the same way, individual women's deaths seem as irrelevant as the particularities of their individual lives. What matters is that femininity endures, not the demise of its incarnations (this idea will be explored further in Chapter 5). 'Poetic' and 'prosaic' renderings of the refrain are therefore more congruent than they may appear.[85] As Martineau-Génieys comments, 'at the end of the day, there is no difference between going "living up to the heavens" and evaporating like snow in the spring thaw!'.[86]

In the second stanza of the ballade, the focus moves to women exercising sexual power over men. Against the background of the first stanza and refrain, in which the women are at once eternalized and consigned to existlessness, vulnerable corporeality enters for the first time, recalling that evoked in the stanzas preceding the lyric. It is not, however, feminine: woman is castration's agent, not its victim. *Femmes fatales* literally castrate and dishonour Abelard and humiliate Buridan. Castration reinforces the gender divide, opposing male and female in a traditional misogynistic configuration around heterosexual desire. At the same time it particularizes masculinity, since it is the clerical body that is sacrificed. This has two important effects. According to the Lacanian account, castration attends subjects' inscription in the symbolic order and thus enables them to write, speak, generate and desire; in the 'Ballade des dames', it transforms its victims into cultural champions, great writers and martyrs to love, the poet's forebears. Castration institutes literature and genealogy – two meanings of the term 'culture'. In the second place, the clerk's mutilation does not entail that of the princely reader conventionally addressed in the envoy. On the contrary: the cultural mediator takes castration upon himself in order to relieve the cultural consumer of that vulnerability. A prince may smile at these scholarly fools, comfortably reassured by his inferiors' foibles. As in Deschamps's lyric, clerks, however learned, lack both the self-governance and the practical political insight that are the preserve of a ruler. Any ethical reflection, any science issuing from their scholarship benefits less themselves than the princely consumer and those he governs. Its sacrificial assumption of castration makes clerical masculinity tragic, comic and heroic, all at once.

In *Over Her Dead Body*, the major study that she grounds in Poe's pronouncement, Elisabeth Bronfen argues that dead female figures express a lack in the masculine. In this instance, that lack founds a cultural authority that may be appropriated by a prince exempted from the concretely realized disgrace foisted onto his clerical proxies. Thus in the second stanza of the 'Ballade des dames' the abject clerical body, instead of denying feminine castration, represents while circumscribing the negative effects of masculine castration, inviting the princely reader at once to reap castration's patriarchal benefits and to discount the possibility of his own castration. Some part of the benefits acquired will, by way of patronage, be graciously passed on to the poet. The feminine's fetishistic representation therefore serves the splitting of the masculine subject into two essences: intact sovereign reader and abject, castrato writer. However, the ambivalence of that fetishized femininity, with its combination of corporeal death and eternal, inhuman life, also sustains, through the binary gender opposition that the poem encourages, masculine 'cours et estre': man's pragmatic mastery of the material world and management of the sublime, which is thus clawed back from the edge of the Real for the symbolic (within which it is further tamed for the prince by the clerk's sacrifice). The feminine triangulates a co-operative relationship between prince and clerk-poet. Only in the following ballades will this relationship be revealed as competitive.

In the 'Royne Blanche comme liz' (l. 345) who opens the third stanza of the 'Ballade des dames', the natural and supernatural references of stanza 1 are gathered together with the predatory female sexuality of stanza 2.[87] Whereas the siren-like 'lily-white queen' recalls the world of legend, 'Blanche', a not uncommon name among the late medieval aristocracy, carries us into a framework of political, collective activity involving dynasties, land and battle, where female sexuality is important in property transfer and kinship relations. This sets the tone for the stanza. Reference remains imprecise, however, keeping us at a remove from the historical world. Bietrix and Aliz are names evocative of *chansons de geste* without being attributable to any particular song or cycle, while Berte 'au plat pié' is perhaps significantly not quite Berte 'au grant pié', daughter of Floire and Blancheflor, mother of Charlemagne, and heroine of the eponymous poem by Adenet le Roi.[88] None of these names supplies its own context, nor is one provided for us (unlike those of Abelard and Buridan in stanza 2); this is neither history writing nor princely advice as Deschamps presented them. Instead of concrete evocation, the third stanza returns us to the legends and fantasies that provide the world of men with a glamorous 'bordering of reverie and infinitude'.[89]

Whereas the stanzas of the ballade focus on femininity, the envoy directly addresses masculinity. Suddenly we turn to a history familiar from earlier parts of the *Testament*, in which time, shaped into weeks and years, carries with it a sense of practical, moral urgency pressing on the present moment: 'Prince, n'enquerrez de sepmaine / Ou elles sont ne de cest an' (ll. 353–4). This kind of time, unlike that of the stanzas, can be wasted. Space similarly shifts mode, as the Prince is warned not to seek some really locatable place in which the women may be found. Sovereign masculinity's proper dimension is not the timeless otherwhere assigned to the feminine. Whereas the great men named by Deschamps are presented as, among other things, subjects with whom the princely reader may – up to a point – identify, the women of the 'Ballade des dames' remain objects in the field of collective, masculine cultural memory. Villon heightens the disidentification effect of the *ubi sunt* topos. Being neither the reader's forebears nor active makers of the culture that he is invited to join, the famous ladies constitute no genealogy on Deschamps's model. The collective memory of which their poetry is guardian holds little practical utility for the patron. Dallying with it could at best make him an 'asne couronné', at worst castrate him: this learning makes a man ineffectual within the lordly sphere. In other respects, the imaginary that this lyric offers to lordship is not so distinct from Deschamps's. To be a prince is, in the 'Ballade des dames', to move in the historical world, with a real-life public role and political function, very different from the fairytale nymphs and queens in their eternal present which is also essentially past and gone. It is different also from the clerk's dangerous and circular tarrying with the feminine and the legendary, with unruly bodily and textual urges, and with alluring deceptions. The envoy suggests that the *ubi sunt* question which the poem has so insistently posed represents an appropriate quest only for the poets and clerks who fantasize in the prince's place – and suffer the penalty. Again the clerk, rendered helpless by his pursuit of the dreamily impractical and unanswerable, takes on impotence and frees the prince to appropriate in the real world the executive power that submission to the paternal Law bestows. Unique princely authority over the natural, clerical and political worlds is constructed over the clerk's mutilated body as well as over the lady's numinous one. Lordly power is grounded in its distance from the unearthly immortality granted to ladies and from the poetic impotence of clerks.

As I shall argue in the remaining sections of this chapter, the organization of ethical, social, political and cultural spaces in the 'Ballade des dames' lays a trap for the reader. Although this trap will be sprung in the following lyrics, disturbing elements are already detectable within the 'Ballade des dames'. The compelling lyricism makes these easy to ignore, especially when, as so often, the lyric is read outside its textual context. The envoy's 'n'enquerrez' (l. 353; 'do not inquire' or 'you will/shall not inquire') confirms the stanzas' push away from cognitive knowledge and suggests that the reader does not want to know the truth about women. That knowledge might require confronting the reality of his own death like theirs, in fulfilment of the moralizing *ubi sunt* function. The text implies that what the princely reader desires is reassurance of his own sovereign subjecthood – his life and power – and this the poet, a dutiful prince-pleaser, supplies through feminine and clerical proxies.

The poet thus adopts the stance of Echo, 'parlant quant bruyt on maine' (l. 333) to create an illusory other that merely reflects his own words back to the initiating subject. This relationship interprets and comments upon the mechanisms by which Deschamps served his prince. In the 'Ballade des dames', the process of constructing a mythologized cultural tradition is shown to involve the suppression of detailed, factual, worldly knowledge; the sovereign subject of collective memory relies on a certain forgetting. Read in the context of the *Testament* as a whole, with its manifold historical details, its focus on marginalized and marginalizing social groups, and its deliberate eschewing of lyricism, this revelation calls attention to those whose exclusion from the public sphere of power and history both sustains the princely subject and exposes his dependence on their willing or forced submission. Furthermore, it disconnects the prince from the actual, historical world, thus undermining the princely authority grounded in its allegedly superior grasp of that world. Only wilful obliviousness can allow Joan of Arc to take her place among the long-dead, legendary females evoked in the rest of the ballade. Executed in 1431, Joan had been formally rehabilitated only a few years before the writing of the *Testament*: on 7 July 1456 (coincidentally, the year ascribed to Villon's *Lais*), her 'trial and sentence . . . together with the abjuration, the execution and all their consequences' were pronounced 'null, invalid, without effect or value'.[90] Her

resulting undeath can stand alongside Antigone's, a reproach to the political order and 'eternal irony of the community'. 'Jehanne la bonne Lorraine
/ Qu'Engloys brulerent a Rouen' (ll. 349–50) is an anomalous figure. Her
official rehabilitation testifies to the challenge that she always presented to
princely activity in the fields it here claims as its own: real-world political
immediacy.[91] Her transgression of the ballade's gender rules is clear but difficult to respond to; it is easier to fit her into the overarching poetry. From a
feminist standpoint, other historical and legendary women invoked within
the 'Ballade des dames' have been similarly reduced by gendered stereotype,
Heloise being a case in point. Instead of near-immaterialization, we ought
perhaps to see in the ladies' liquefaction the disagreeable bodily viscosity
that Irigaray associates with feminine resistance to patriarchy.[92] Thus, while
the treatment of most of the ladies may not have appeared discordant to
Villon or his contemporaries, certain cases do, at the margins, question
the structure as a whole and raise the spectre of a quite different understanding. By drawing attention to the limitations of the prince's inquiry
and to the self-interested nature of its results, the 'Ballade des dames' hints
at the tenuous nature of a sovereignty based in the imaginary rather than
the symbolic. The following ballades will exploit and bring to fruition the
potential for anxiety that the 'Ballade des dames' discreetly plants within
the prince's position. Joan the undead cross-dresser anticipates features that
will typify the prince of the following ballade – though cultural evidence
shows that she had a contemporary grandeur beyond what the 'Ballade des
seigneurs' will impute to its lords.

THE 'BALLADE DES SEIGNEURS'

Qui plus, ou est ly tiers Calixte,
Derrenier decedé de ce nom,
Quy quatre ans tint le papalixte,
Alfonce, le roy d'Arragon,
Le graci̇eux duc de Bourbon,
Et Artus le duc de Bretaigne,
Et Charles septiesme le bon?
Mais ou est le preux Charlemaigne?

Semblablement, le roy scotiste
Qui demy face ot, ce dit on,
Vermaille comme une emastiste
Depuis le front jusqu'au menton,
Le roy de Chippre de renom,

Helas! et le bon roy d'Espaigne
Duquel je ne sçay pas le nom?
Mais ou est le preux Charlemaigne?

D'en plus parler je me desiste,
Le monde n'est qu'abusïon;
Il n'est qui contre mort resiste
Ne qui treuve provisïon.
Encore faiz une questïon:
Lancellot, le roy de Behaygne,
Ou est il? ou est son tayon?
Mais ou est le preux Charlemaigne?

Ou est Clacquin le bon Breton,
Ou le comte daulphin d'Auvergne,
Et le bon feu duc d'Alençon?
Mais ou est le preux Charlemaigne?
(ll. 357–84)

(Moreover, where is the third Calixtus, last of his name to die, who for four years held the papacy; Alphonso king of Aragon, His grace the duke of Bourbon, Arthur duke of Brittany, and Charles the seventh, the good? But where is the worthy Charlemagne?

Similarly, the Scottish king, half of whose face, it's said, was crimson as an amethyst from forehead to chin; and the well-known king of Cyprus, alas, and that good king of Spain whose name I don't know? But where is the worthy Charlemagne?

Let me say no more. This world is only a cheat. No one can fight off death or lay up store against it. But let me ask one more question: Lancelot, king of Bohemia, where is he? Where is his grandfather? But where is the worthy Charlemagne?

Where is Claquin [Du Guesclin] the good Breton, or the count dauphin of Auvergne, and the late, good duke of Alençon? But where is the worthy Charlemagne?)

In apparent reaction to the disidentification between implied audience and deceased subjects in the 'Ballade des dames', the immediately following 'Ballade des seigneurs du temps jadis' imposes identification. This is achieved by making the deceased according to the same parameters which in the envoy to the 'Ballade des dames' constructed the reader's self-representation as masculine, sovereign and efficient. Locating the subject in terms of chronological time and public office, the details of lines 357–9 create an impression of precision, an *effet de réel* which instantiates a certain notion of what counts as 'real'.[93] Chronology is here closely related to genealogy, Callixtus being specified as third to have taken that name on accession to the 'papalixte', literally the 'papal list'. Cultural patriliny – the *nom-du-père* – provides an important reference point for the authority referred to in this stanza (compare Deschamps's Ballade 1457). In the next lines, place is similarly interpreted in terms of public power, function and title (ll. 360–3). Thus the opening stanza of the 'Ballade des seigneurs' foregrounds the historical and public dimensions of sovereign identity.

Its position immediately after the 'Ballade des dames' encourages us to read the 'Ballade des seigneurs' as half of a gendered diptych. As Marot's titles suggest, one major theme emerging from this contrast is the difference between feminine and masculine modes of power and effectiveness, which are ultimately also modes of being. The 'Ballade des seigneurs' reserves for men a mode of 'cours et estre' that I shall call 'lordship', which operates in a historical dimension unlike the legendary non-time and other-place in which the ladies are situated, and differently efficacious from their nebulous, mythical, but hardly executive power over male life and death (even the attempt on Buridan's life failed). The real-life influence and authority that many medieval women exercised is erased by this gendered model, while lordship is extended to all men who participate in the world here delineated. Not every man can consider himself a prince in his own domain, but many can feel, as the 'Ballade des seigneurs' presents it, that they exercise a certain active, practical masculine authority, presentist in the double sense of 'here' and 'now'.

By its opening lines, therefore, the 'Ballade des seigneurs' announces that its illustrious dead represent the same lordly masculinity that was sketched in the envoy to the 'Ballade des dames'.[94] Continuity between the princely reader of the envoy and the subjects of the 'Ballade des seigneurs' is reinforced by the initial 'Qui plus', which implies both an afterthought and a shift to the really important subject matter: the sovereign subject himself. In thus blocking the reader's ability to dissociate himself from the deceased, the identification imposed by the 'Ballade des seigneurs' frustrates a tendency vital to the affirmative effect associated with the *ubi sunt* topos. Taken together, the two ballades manoeuvre the sovereign subject into a situation of risk.

Almost all the titles and given names mentioned in the 'Ballade des seigneurs' are dynastic and had, by Villon's time, a lengthy history. This has led to modern scholarly dispute when pinpointing the individuals involved (note that we return here to the desire for exact, historical knowledge elicited by the bulk of the *Testament* and suspended in the 'Ballade des dames'). For example, Rychner and Henry discuss the candidacy of Béraud

II and Béraud III to be the relevant 'comte daulphin d'Auvergne' (l. 382), while Brittany had had three dukes called Arthur before 1461. It has become conventional to identify each name (excepting those in the final four lines) with the 'Derrenier decedé de ce nom' (l. 358). If these identifications are accepted as reflecting an impetus within the text, then it is noteworthy that the majority died after the presumed composition of Villon's *Lais* in 1456; more recently too than Joan of Arc's rehabilitation trial. This period of history is therefore already positioned *entre-deux-morts* by important references contained within the *Testament* itself. The 'Ballade des seigneurs' points to men who had in recent memory played active roles on the European political stage, their names if not their persons a presence in readers' own social and political lives. In the 'now' imposed by this lyric, they are yesterday's men, pointing the transience of worldly influence and status in a less celebratory, more anguished mode than does the deathless fame of Deschamps's great men. Lordship's short lifespan is further stressed when, for instance, all previous kings of Cyprus are obliterated in favour of the most recently deceased (even where, as Rychner and Henry note, John II was considerably less well known in Western Europe than Peter I),[95] who has himself been displaced by the present incumbent. Genealogy's very success as a cultural strategy threatens those it benefits. These barely dead men stand on the verge of life, if 'verge' can refer to a succeeding as well as a preceding state. They are not in those Elysian Fields of the physically departed but culturally vital implied in the 'Ballade des dames' or by Deschamps; indeed, the 'Ballade des seigneurs' raises the important problem of access to that realm from the kind of existence its lords have embraced. Will today's notables be remembered or forgotten? The text is concerned with their oblivion, here not the neutral act of time but actively hastened by the text. These seigneurs therefore illustrate one interpretation of what it means to be between two deaths.

For the reader, recalling these men to mind is a very different operation from the instant though somewhat nebulous recognition inspired by the ladies in the 'Ballade des dames', where even names we may not actually know, such as the otherwise unattested 'Haranburgis', are made to seem familiar by the rhythm, rhymes and easy reference of the verse. Turning again to Ricoeur's distinction between reflexivity and worldliness, we may say that the 'Ballade des dames' works to make the reader overlook not only the particularity of the remembered objects themselves but also the 'situations in the world in which one has seen, experienced, learned' the names. It introduces instead a familiarity effect composed of a general sense of acquaintance and a broad background knowledge, whose value lies in part in its resistance to specific recall. Unlike the exclusivity seemingly imposed by many of the *Testament*'s obscure references, the 'Ballade des dames' works to define as wide a community as possible, and the (implicitly masculine) reader's consciousness of sharing in an interpersonal cultural space is an important component of its celebrated lyricism; its continuing popularity is witness to its success. Contrastingly, the 'Ballade des seigneurs' draws significantly on worldliness, both because the masculinity it embraces is worldly (of the social world, and especially that of movers and shakers) and because bringing to mind named, recently deceased individuals who have been influential in one's own social existence recalls the circumstances in which one encountered their names, persons or influence. One noteworthy corollary is that where the ballade's lords are concerned, readers must rely on individual knowledge and powers of remembrance, whose limitations the second stanza highlights: 'Helas! et le bon roy d'Espaigne / Duquel je ne sçay pas le nom' (ll. 370–1). The lament seems to refer less to the king's corporeal death than to the oblivion already swallowing up both his earthly existence and the remembering subject's reminiscences. 'Living' memory is seen to decay in an almost burlesque representation of forgetfulness. The anonymous kings of Cyprus and Spain are qualified by the vapid epithets 'de renom' and 'bon', while the only fact retained about the Scottish king is his disfigurement (ll. 365–8). Although some argue that his birthmark expresses the king's fierce nature and is therefore of public import, 'ce dit on' (l. 366) evokes the register of gossip, the shadowy, half-secretive publication of a perhaps shameful private condition. The princes are actively de-faced and defaced, defamed and de-famed by the text which belittles them. Like Jean of Burgundy slandering Louis of Orleans (p. 106, above), the ballade aims at second death in its attack on the lords' memories. To be remembered awry is more shaming than merely to be neglected. In the second stanza of the 'Ballade des seigneurs', therefore, we see a disintegration of the public space and of the sovereign subject's place in it. Given the close identification established with the reader via the 'Ballade des dames', this affects the sovereign or lordly reading subject as well as the particular princes referred to.

Decay here afflicts the masculine. This is particularly evident from the contrast with the 'Ballade des dames'. Unlike feminine names, masculine ones slip from recollection. Whereas the ladies seem disembodied and almost volatilized, the lords live with physical imperfection, encumbered with bodies that refuse to reflect their owners' noble nature or, like the poet's own in the *Testament*'s frame, to obey their will. The 'Ballade des seigneurs' forces a rift between the mortal bodies of individual sovereigns and the immortal body of sovereignty, imposing particularity on the lords while detaching them from the universal that is the source of their authority.[96] This is quite different from the anonymity that inscribed Deschamps's prince in the big Other, or from the impersonal immortality via the universal that Derrida criticizes in Husserl. The option of castration as a means of inscription into the symbolic has been foreclosed for the prince since the 'Ballade des dames'. Memory's interpersonal worldliness works in the 'Ballade des seigneurs' against the subject's sense of participating in an enabling concrete or abstract collective. Masculine society becomes only an accretion of individuals in their singular places, times and relationships, incapable of connecting to the communal identity which should properly cement the group and ground individual identities.

The lack of lasting impact imputed to the figures by the 'Ballade des seigneurs' could be taken to suggest that they are individually poor examples of lordship. It is, of course, difficult to determine what their contemporaries thought of them, but worth mentioning that most were prominent in defending French, European or Christian interests. There is also an emphasis on the long-standing struggle against the English; however, this does not stand alone. A theme of rebellion against the Crown and of tightening absolutism, albeit neither approved nor condemned, also runs through the French names. Thus, in the first stanza, Arthur duke of Brittany, as Constable of France (the 'connétable de Richemont') and a favourite of Charles VII, was a principal object of the Praguerie or noble rebellion of 1440, in which Charles I, duke of Bourbon, participated (as did Charles VII's son, Louis XI, the king flatteringly addressed by Villon early in the *Testament*). Alençon and Brittany were among the great nobles lately subdued by the Crown. A third strand consists in connections to Joan of Arc; within the same first stanza, Callixtus III ordered her retrial, Bourbon and Brittany fought on her side, Charles VII was her dauphin.[97] One could certainly construct several politically partial interpretations of the list of lords in the 'Ballade des seigneurs,' although these associations would be normal for major nobles involved in events of moment during the years preceding the *Testament*'s composition. Villon's selection strategically avoids affirming unambiguously any single theme. As elsewhere, his poetry is flexible in application, offering, if not all things to all men, certainly points of interest to many potential patrons.

In sum, there is, as far as I know, no partisan explanation for the bathos that Villon's rhetoric here bestows on these names. The selection of titles and the associated activities, indeed, provide one definition of the European political theatre of the mid to late fifteenth century, seen from a French centre with extended interests in southern, central and eastern Europe and further afield. Glynnis M. Cropp's judgement that these names 'must have resonated with particular force in the fifteenth century', if correct, heightens the rhetorical effect of their effacement in the ballade.[98] Rather than exposing individual departures from the norm, the 'Ballade des seigneurs' destabilizes the norm itself via what the preceding 'Ballade des dames' construed as a centrally defining quality and strength of princely identity. Just because they are embedded in their own moment by their historical and public agency, these princes are subject to time in a way the ladies of the 'Ballade des dames' are not. By its very constitution, the princely subject is anchored in transience, in what Nora calls 'the thin film of current events', and its fame occupies only the present moment, cut off from the dimension of near-immortal legend that here defines collective memory and group vitality.[99]

Turning to a quite different cultural context can clarify an unfamiliar way of thinking. Annette Weiner's analyses of Trobriand society (Papua New Guinea) provide an interesting comparison.[100] Weiner poses the problem of cultural longevity in relation to the 'complementary and confounding' Trobriand gender roles, and especially to difference between masculine and feminine 'cours et estre'. Weiner argues that where the distinction between individual and collective is organized by gender, women may be entrusted with the enduring, symbolic and transpersonal aspect. Thus in Trobriand society, wealth produced and controlled by women symbolizes the group (in the event, a descent group), its long-term existence over time and its political status, in distinction to men's wealth, which remains strictly individual in import:

In the contrast between women's and men's wealth we find exposed the human condition of how one expands outward into the lives of others descended from different ancestors while keeping one's own ancestral identity intact. Loss, decay, and death continually attack the cultural semblance of wholeness and the vision of immortality. For these reasons, the loss of things and the death of people translate into political action – because such losses are a threat to all that went before – expressed in the creation and regeneration of identities, ancestors, and rank. Without a past that is given a concrete existence in time and space, it is difficult to control the future.[101]

Today's prince is justified while he lives and reigns, but what will happen when he dies? The wholeness and immortality in question are secular, implying not only individual renown but the fate of dynasty and regime, ultimately of society. The masculine real-world political present and future need the feminine legendary past.

This argument is helpful in approaching the first two ballades in Villon's mini-sequence. The 'Ballade des dames' sustains lordship in the here and now through a contrast with a feminine otherworldliness seemingly extraneous to the political realm. Only during the 'Ballade des seigneurs' does the reader discover that by assenting to the terms of the first ballade, he has ceded his claim on the politically meaningful past and with it the future, thus querying the legitimacy of lordly activity in the present. Does the name of Charlemagne, which occupies the refrain of the 'Ballade des seigneurs', reconnect masculine lordship to the legendary domain? Of all names, that of Charlemagne – emperor of Europe, defender of the pope and conqueror of the pagan – defines the ideal self-image of French princes. In order to justify their own occupancy of the French throne, kings over the centuries turned repeatedly to a perceived continuity with this iconic figure, whence the Valois Charleses of Villon's own day.[102] Some critics understand Charlemagne's name as transferring lordship's imaginary support into the legendary, communal realm, in which case a sharp discontinuity becomes apparent between the recently dead lords and the illustrious father figure. There is here no legendary seigneurial ancestry such as Deschamps created for his prince but a series of failed attempts to constitute a genealogy, expressed peremptorily in the 'Ou est il? ou est son tayon?' of line 379. Names such as that of Arthur duke of Brittany or Lancelot king of Bohemia fail in this environment to convey the charisma and effectiveness of their more famous legendary and historical forebears, emphasizing the gap which separates the ancestral from the recent past. The princes of the 'Ballade des seigneurs' seem incapable of exercising the paternal function either by begetting their own ancestors or by founding a genealogy of their own. Instead of standing as guarantor to these men, the paternal figure of Charlemagne would thus become a source of anxiety and reproach. He would represent the *nom-du-père* with emphasis on the *nom*, his disabling excess of nomination inverting the empowering anonymity of Deschamps's prince.

I am inclined, however, to include Charlemagne's name in the destitution of lordship and of the sovereign reader operating in the stanzas. Deschamps's lyric made ideological profit both from magnificent genealogy and from its final anonymous rejection. Villon's poem operates the negation of both; refusing to install the seigneurs in the second life of glorious memory, it inscribes their anonymity only as genealogy's failure and as the defacing of historical record, opening no door onto the universal. The seigneurs are merely undead, without the *éclat* attaching to Antigone or to Joan; though *entre-deux-morts* like the prince in Deschamps's envoy, they have nothing like his high-minded, high-deserving humility. Even Charlemagne's name rings hollow in this company. The point would therefore be more subtle than a straightforward contrast between past plenitude and modern insufficiency. Du Guesclin, a chivalric paragon from a much more recent period than Charlemagne, and the still less recently deceased Count-Dauphin of Auvergne and 'late good Duke of Alençon' in the final lines, could perhaps bridge the gap between yesterday's men and Charlemagne – but their names are not singled out. All these lords are in the same boat. Nor, however, can the impact of the 'Ballade des seigneurs' be reduced to the idea that Charlemagne and other icons of lordship are simply illusory, vanities to be disregarded in the face of death.[103] Even within the earthly realm where it has staked out its authentic efficacy over lives such as Villon's (see especially the *Testament*'s opening), lordship rests on a foundation of quicksand, and the poem's strength is the way in which it makes us feel that constitutive instability. The legendary dimension needed to underpin any effort at ancestral legitimacy remains with the feminine alone.

Relatedly, some critics consider that the clerical subject fares better than the princely in the 'Ballade des seigneurs'.[104] However, the second stanza shows that neither has access to that source of authority that is collective memory, the prince due to his inability to be memorable, the poet due to the reduction of his powers of recall to the merely personal. This is a professional shortcoming, since it is the scholar's job to provide the names which will be woven into the prince's legendary history, or, in a different phrasing, to imbue present-day princes with the glories of the collective past with an eye to future generations. Formally, too, the poem enacts the failure of the poet's powers. Notably, there is no proper envoy. It has been suggested that the lines which begin the third stanza (ll. 373–6) fulfil that function, for they contain the sort of generalizing, moralizing conclusions that are normally found in an envoy.[105] These ideas about the poem's formal arrangement are attractive for the questions and observations they raise about the loss of control which the poet represents himself as experiencing. He can neither put the envoy in the correct place nor compose the poem correctly around it. After the pseudo-envoy he returns apparently compulsively to the *ubi sunt* theme – 'Encore faiz une questïon' (l. 377) – as if the banal, irrefutable answer (or sage advice) just sketched were no answer. The wisdom of the super-egoic, 'gentle, paternal' voice that Spitzer detected in the 'Ballade des dames' refrain is ineffective. In the ballade's final lines the questioning continues relentlessly, tediously, beyond its own closure (ll. 381–4). The formal *ubi sunt* frame rolls pointlessly on, overriding the quest for meaning. No coherent system has been convincingly identified for the selection and ordering of the seigneurs in the ballade, although a nebulous intentionality is everywhere signalled. This is a very different vision of the poetic situation from that proposed in 'Ballade des dames'. Like the lords, the poet is caught within formal systems stripped of their necessary imaginary supports. The ballade contains no address to an implied reader and no patron, hence no interlocution between masculine first and second persons; the relationship which links poet and prince in other ballades has broken down. Ironically fallen from the precedence they enjoyed in the 'Ballade des dames', the lords here join the poet as abject masculine 'others'. If the ballade's princes cannot beget ancestors, their impotence is inseparable from the poet's failure to produce the poem of collective memory which would establish that ancestry in culture. Yet the categories of men form no company in misery. Where Deschamps's third stanza offers poetic disorientation as a compliment to the Prince as bringer of order, Villon's poem apparently lacks any central ordering authority that might endow it with sense and purpose, and exhibits its own lack of mastery with more conviction and less elegance. Neither *chevalerie* nor *clergie* emerges unscathed. By these manoeuvres the deathly message of the *ubi sunt* theme is delivered, as the lordly reader has to confront his own death without the reassurance afforded by Deschamps. There is no affirmation of a sovereign subject in the 'Ballade des seigneurs'; no wonder it has been so unpopular.

We need, nevertheless, to recognize a constructive dimension to the ballade's negativity. This point may be illustrated via Nora's influential delineation of modernity, at times conspicuously reminiscent of the masculine, historical universe of the 'Ballade des seigneurs' and of the sense of loss which separates that universe from the 'past' of tradition and collective memory represented by the 'Ballade des dames':

Acceleration of history: the metaphor needs to be unpacked. [In modern times] Things tumble with increasing rapidity into an irretrievable past. They vanish from sight, or so it is generally believed. The equilibrium between the present and the past [which once existed] is disrupted. What was left of experience, still lived in the warmth of tradition, in the silence of custom, in the repetition of the ancestral, has been swept away by a surge of deeply historical sensibility. Our consciousness is shaped by a sense that everything is over and done with, that something long since begun is now complete. Memory is constantly on our lips because it no longer exists.[106]

Modernity's melancholia is not crippling; on the contrary, it grounds modernity's own creative practices. A similar note has recently been introduced by thinkers seeking to return to Huizinga's autumnal vision of the later Middle Ages while revising his emphasis on the period as a geriatric one: excessive, devitalized and decadent. Jacqueline Cerquiglini-Toulet and Michael Camille, to name only two, argue for the vitality inherent in the period's fascination with death, commemoration, mourning and melancholy.[107] A writing position grounded in loss will characterize the late medieval texts discussed in the remaining chapters of this book.

When Derrida insists that 'the very condition for the living person to speak is for him to be able to say, significantly, "Je suis mort"', he accentuates the utterance's productive as well as its disruptive aspects. The new subject to which this utterance may give birth, with its reformed relation to truth and reality, is deployed in the late Middle Ages to imply superior ethical and spiritual potential and to augur an improved social and cultural future for the collective. This is, in Derrida's terms, to live the possibility of one's own death and disappearance in order to institute a relation to presence. It is this constitutive role borne by the sense of inadequacy, loss and rupture in relation to a more vital, self-assured past that Barthes interprets in Derrida, and Derrida in Husserl, as an evasion of death. Villon's text, however, by showing in full measure how painful it is to instantiate death as the speaking subject's foundational position within the symbolic order, indicates a possible defence of Derrida, and perhaps of Husserl. The pairing of the 'Ballade des dames' and 'Ballade des seigneurs' leads the reader along a path that communicates the alien nature of the symbolic order and the discomfort of inhabiting the 'impossible' situations to which it obliges us, so keenly that '[le] réel pâtit du signifiant' ('the [R]eal . . . suffers from the signifier'):[108] the pressure of the Real makes itself felt. Whereas Derrida criticizes Husserl for a transcendental security which negates earthly uncertainty, Villon emphasizes how the subject 'at home' within the big Other is tormented by placelessness. The 'Ballade des seigneurs' thus contrasts with Deschamps's Ballade 1457, whose final address to the princely reader and sovereign subject was more reassuring in tone. Villon's poem focuses on a bleak, processual extinction which leaves no authoritative figure or institution untouched. It threatens precisely the sovereign aspects of the masculine subject: those in which it invests in the big Other by imposing on others and on its environment (lordship), and those it achieves through self-consciousness leading to a belief in its own immortality. More searchingly than Deschamps's poem, therefore, both Derrida's and Villon's discourses point towards an ethical critique of the privilege that would say 'Je suis immortel' – though no doubt the particular lessons to be drawn diverge. While the philosopher objects to what in Lacanian terms may be glossed as the comforting use of the imaginary, the poet demonstrates the discomfort of the symbolic by exploiting the imaginary, in the shape of the lords' disintegration in body and memory and his own dissolution in poetry.

THE 'BALLADE EN VIEIL LANGAGE FRANÇOIS'

> Car ou soit ly sains appostolles,
> D'aubes vestuz, d'amys coeffez,
> Qui ne seint fors saintes estolles
> Dont par le col prent ly mauffez
> De mal talant tous eschauffez,
> Aussi bien meurt que cilz servans,
> De ceste vie cy buffez:
> Autant en emporte ly vens!
>
> Voire, ou soit de Constantinobles
> L'emperieres au poing dorez,
> Ou de France le roy tres nobles,
> Sur tous autres roys decorez,
> Qui pour ly grant Dieux adorez
> Batist esglises et couvens,
> S'en son temps il fut honnorez,
> Autant en emporte ly vens!
>
> Ou soit de Vïenne et Grenobles
> Ly daulphin, ly preux, ly senez,
> Ou de Dijon, Salins et Dolles
> Ly sires filz le plus esnez,
> Ou autant de leurs gens prenez,
> Heraux, trompectes, poursuivans,
> Ont ilz bien boutez soubz le nez,
> Autant en emporte ly vens!
>
> Princes a mort sont destinez
> Et tous autres qui sont vivans;
> S'ilz en sont courcez n'atinez,
> Autant en emporte ly vens!
>
> (ll. 385–412)

(For be it his holiness the Pope wearing his alb and amice, who puts on his holy stole with which to strangle the devil all flaming with evil power, he dies exactly as his servant swept off from this life. It all goes with the wind.

Yes, or be it the emperor of Constantinople, with the golden fist, or that most noble king of France, singled out above all kings to build churches and monasteries to the greater glory of God; even if he was honoured in his day, it all goes with the wind.

Or be it the brave and wise dauphin of Vienne or of Grenoble, or the great men and their eldest sons of Dijon, Salins and Dole, or the same number of their servants – heralds, trumpeters, men-at-arms, didn't they happily stuff their faces? It all goes with the wind.

Princes are destined to die and so are all others who live, whether they rage against it or tremble, it all goes with the wind.)

The last ballade in the mini-sequence addresses memory and the sovereign subject differently from the other texts reviewed in this chapter. There is no attempt to create a communal memorial tradition; the lyric presents only unnamed personages, not even contrasting these to durable famous names. The content displays no obvious interest in times past; there are no *ubi sunt* questions, and the subjects referred to are living. Unlike the just-dead lords of the 'Ballade des seigneurs', suspended in inactivity, here great ecclesiastical and secular magnates are presented in the vigorous exercise of their executive functions. Strikingly after the previous ballade, all are here anonymous, abstracted into their functions. The final ballade is preoccupied with and absorbed in the symbolic order and the present moment. Both men and Death are busy doing their jobs.

Its archaizing language earned the 'Ballade en vieil langage françois' its common title. Late medieval French rewritings of earlier romances sometimes justify their proceeding by alleging the incomprehensibility to modern readers of the older language.[109] A similar sense drives Villon's ballade, albeit with significant differences. In the first place, it is written in the supposedly incomprehensible and irreproducible idiom of olden times. Its linguistic desuetude is signified by the use of the obsolete case system for nouns, and also by the errors which mark that language as non-current, notably the confusion over the final –*s* which in Old French marks the masculine singular subject case. (Compare the modern English 'Ye Olde Tea Shoppe'.) It is debatable whether Villon or his audience would have been aware of such errors, though I shall argue for their effective significance. In the second place, neither archaisms nor errors affect the ballade's intelligibility to a modern reader (although they do place details into debate) and it seems likely that a fifteenth-century reader would have been similarly situated. Indeed, the poem creates a parallel between these two audiences. The ballade projects its contemporary reader into the position of a hypothetical future one, encouraging the former to experience and imagine himself into the latter's linguistic frustration. It thus raises questions of posterity, at once decrying and creating (difficult, obscure, partial) communication between distant future and distant past. A *mise en abyme* of the twenty-first-century reader's relation to the *Testament* is planted in its text for its contemporaries, partially depriving their present of the support afforded by cultural longevity – the imagined future that complements the imagined past. The poem therefore is written in a 'dead' language which, because and not in spite of that death, 'speaks' to its audience, then and now, in a present which has no place in temporal sequence. Its poetic position is, in Barthes's phrase, 'radically impossible'.

The 'Ballade en vieil langage' is often compared to a *Danse macabre* or Dance of Death, that stereotypically late medieval mixed-media genre in which Death leads away members of various estates.[110] Like a Dance of Death, the poem respects hierarchy in the arrangement of social station within stanzas and in the register of comment, dignified for the masters, bumptious for the men. In spite of a breathless *dégringolade* through the social and linguistic hierarchy, it follows convention in beginning with ecclesiastics before proceeding to secular powers. A certain clerical ideology would approve the elevation of the meanest cleric over the greatest prince, and this is not a performance of rootless disorderliness akin to the 'Ballade des seigneurs' or to Deschamps's third stanza.[111] The overall impression given by the 'Ballade en vieil langage' is one of order, purpose and achievement. There is no nostalgia, no sense of loss, and nothing to regret. The tone is upbeat, lively and brisk, sometimes jaunty. The up-and-down rhythm reinforces the sense of hustle and activity, punctuated by the irreverent and somehow always abrupt refrain, 'Autant en emporte ly vens'.[112] The rhetoric of the 'Ballade en vieil langage' is a resurgence of life in a dead language, and after the death notice served on lordly authority by the 'Ballade des seigneurs'.

This represents no natural rebirth or renewal of the life cycle, but an occasion when, in Barthes's vivid terms, 'one of the spaces [of life and death] bites unwarrantedly into the other' (p. 120, above). Vitality is expressed in a language visibly decaying.[113] Between the distant past of the first ballade and the projection into a near future of the second, the third presents the over-inhabited present as the site of living death. Instead of mourning an inevitable rupture with the past (or even celebrating such a rupture), it represents the poetic voice as unstoppable while impossible. This final ballade declares 'Je suis mort', but not as Derrida analyses the utterance. We must turn to Barthes to throw light on Villon's inaccurate use of obsolete syntactical markers: 'grammatical example[s]' referring to 'nothing but language', of scandalous inutility. Speaking in a tongue marked as extinct, the voice of the 'Ballade en vieil langage' affirms 'an essence *which is not in its place*'. Its displacement accords with the *Testament*'s dramatization of a poetic persona consistently in the wrong place, stuck inside peering out at the action or locked out and looking in, subject to secular and religious powers that constrain his and others' bodies and social spaces in frustrating and sometimes violent ways.[114] Authority to determine who shall occupy these spaces and in what ways belongs to princes like Thibaut d'Aussigny, bishop of Orleans (l. 6), and Louis XI, 'le bon roy de France' (l. 56; 'the good king of France'). But Villon 'son lieu ne congnoistra jamais' (l. 292; 'will never know his place').[115]

In the 'Ballade en vieil langage', the effect is not – as in Deschamps's ballade – to assert the poet's centrality to the politico-cultural project of sovereignty. Nor is it to avenge him on those lords who have persecuted or patronized him and on their agents, for the socially low as well as the high figures identified within the ballade are members of the establishment. Privilege and marginality are equally vulnerable to the passage of time and vagaries of collective memory, concretely presented here in language's mutation. The final ballade gathers first, second and third persons into a common fragility. Most truly when in their places within the symbolic order, no one is 'in their place', and yet they have no other. The escapism of the 'Ballade des dames', the anxieties of the 'Ballade des seigneurs' are rejected. So, by implication, is the pious transcendence voiced in the envoy of Deschamps's Ballade 1457, for in the 'Ballade en vieil langage' there is no prospect of a beyond.

And here the poem becomes Barthesian in the use it makes of the symbolic (which Bowie compares to a *Danse macabre*).[116] It embraces as a poetic topic the present moment, empty of past and future, and the unquenchable vitality with which it bites into death's space. The ballade corresponds to the *Testament*'s overall strategy of presenting a highly per-sonally invested, hostile and ostentatiously realistic late fifteenth-century Paris in its impact upon the perpetually displaced poet dictating his second living will. This is not an art that separates itself from life; poet and poem reject transcendence to immerse themselves in an immanence which has already passed beyond the culturally sanctioned boundaries of life, and is distinct from 'the thin film of current events' on which lordship floats. Reading the *Testament* we experience Villon's vibrantly realized present as past, and labour to revitalize that past, hence the fascination for recover-ing the facts of Villon's and his subjects' biographies. This is not a work of memory. The ephemeral yet paradoxically solid now-ness that he cre-ates ensures his poetry a longevity to rival the immortality of the dead ladies, though of a quite different sort. The vulnerability of language, the poet's medium, joins other forms of obscurity foregrounded in the *Testament* as means of tantalizing and inciting in readers an epistemophilia which is – not necrophilia, but whatever term would be appropriate for love of the fully realized, grinningly vital undead.[117] By presenting us with a language and a poetry speaking insistently in its own death, the final ballade in Villon's inset sequence troubles paradigmatic distinctions between life and death and the normative functions those distinctions often carry, examples of which are provided by the other texts discussed in this chapter.

Perhaps the most subjectively invasive instance of this encroachment occurs in the envoy (ll. 409–12). As edited by Rychner and Henry, these lines may be translated as given above. However, ballade envoys generally begin with an address to a 'Prince' or 'Princes'. 'Prince' indicates a singular reader, 'Princes' generally plural though sometimes, especially in earlier instances, singular.[118] An alternative translation of lines 409–10 is therefore: 'Prince [or 'princes'], also all others who are living are destined to death.' Whereas Rychner and Henry's translation includes princes in the common fate, this alternative rendering places them outside it, allowing them to transcend it through knowledge and consciousness, and over others' dead bodies. The sovereign subject demolished by version one (the overt *ubi sunt* message) is instated by version two (the secondary denial). The choice between versions is undecidable because of the syntactical confusion that the ballade has worked to create through its chaotic use of archaisms. It is this confusion that places a question mark over the interpretation of 'Princes', and thence over the envoy. Each reading gnaws into and inhabits the other. The ballade is as irreducible and as resistant to totalizing meaning as is death itself – or life. To summarize: in the 'Ballade des dames', Villon builds up the sovereign self over the dead and castrated bodies of imaginary others; his 'Ballade des seigneurs' then submits this self to the symbolic imperative to utter 'Je suis mort', while depriving it of the expected recompense, namely the support afforded by the notion of its own immortality within the big Other (a notion that in Deschamps's ballade grounded the anonymous prince's sovereignty). Finally the 'Ballade en vieil langage' creates a dynamic overlap between life and death in the spectacle of old language reanimated though not restored, of life seething after death has been pronounced, in a symbolic whose decay proceeds visibly. The final ballade in the sequence thus exemplifies and draws attention to what Barthes calls language's 'blind spot', its contradictory, impossible and horrific situation, encouraging and expressive of life as well as of death.

Thus Villon's intense engagement with existence, extinction and the literary pre-empts Barthes's. His text incorporates similar ironic critiques of the sovereign subject, which dominates even in its escapist and its elegantly resigned modes, and of the processes of reading as and writing for a sovereign. Villon is less ready to assert the artist's independence of the princely reader, hardly surprisingly given his situation. Allowing for historical specificities, Barthes's description of Valdemar could sum up Villon's poetic voice in the 'Ballade en vieil langage': 'the chthonic voice, the voice from beyond the grave'.[119] This, in a particularly visceral inflection, is the voice of the *Testament*. I leave the last word to Barthes, whose comments on Poe may be adapted to describe the quality of Villon's poetic voice in the work:

It is, then, visceral life, the life of the depths, which is assimilated to the spoken word [*la parole*], and this itself is fetishized in the form of a phallic organ which begins to vibrate, in a sort of pre-orgasm. The momentary vibration is the desire for [/of] jouissance and the desire for [/of] language [*le désir de parole*]: it is Desire's movement *to arrive at something*.[120]

CHAPTER 4

Ceci n'est pas une marguerite: anamorphosis in Pearl

The Pearl-Maiden is dead.[1] Cutting through the Jeweller's elaborate, indeterminate metaphors (ll. 9–10), she insists on the fact by repeated references to the rotting of her corpse (ll. 857, 958). Jean-Claude Schmitt notes that revenants (returned spirits of the departed) often materialize in medieval texts in response to some irregularity in the dying process which hampers their progress within the afterlife, typically an unconfessed sin, a wrong left unrighted or an unpaid debt.[2] This, as the Pearl-Maiden explains to the Jeweller, is not her case. The notion that her death, untimely to him, represents an acme of Christian aspiration is one of many shifts of perspective that he has to confront in the course of the poem. She died innocent and is therefore 'saf by ry3t' (l. 684; 'saved by right'), having incurred no debts. Her spirit has been incorporated properly – indeed, ideally – into the society of the afterlife. As a Christian she has, in leaving the flesh, been subtracted from death; for, as baptism replaces birth as the commencement of life in the spirit, so bodily death is superseded by 'þe deth secounde' (l. 652; 'the second death') of damnation or spiritual death, from which Christ's sacrifice releases the baptized. For the first time in this book, we encounter the extremist Christian opposition between corporeal and spiritual life. For the elect there is no spiritual death. The pearls with which the Maiden is encrusted and identified recall the dry, clean bones that many cultures view as the support of eternity; the conventional comparisons of her skin to ivory and whalebone point the contrast with corruptible, impermanent flesh. There is nothing unquiet about her death and when she returns it is not as a disturbed spirit. The Jeweller, in contrast, is a ghostly figure; unable to leave his lost pearl, he haunts her. In this poem problematic, placeless figures are recruited from among the living, not the dead. The bereft Jeweller's existence before his dream is one of aimless drifting through a world devoid, for him, of meaning and substance, a living death.

Thus *Pearl* offers us two distinct ways of being 'between two deaths'. On the one hand, the Pearl-Maiden presents the spirit liberated from the obscurities of the flesh into a truer, transcendent existence achieved by ritual rebirth. Not all Christians will be granted her elevated condition, however; she explains that grace is given at God's pleasure. The high heaven that she occupies is and will remain accessible to the common adult Christian reader only as a witness, through visions such as that granted the Jeweller. The Pearl-Maiden therefore is not only inaccessible in herself but, like the mirror in Lacan's analysis, presents an impassable boundary that organizes the inaccessibility of God's love as ultimate object of desire.[3] Her deathly existence structures the reader's but is no model for it.

Chastising and consoling the Jeweller with the aim of improving his spiritual fate, the Pearl-Maiden is, like many another revenant, the bearer of a demand or imperative. In this case, however, the demand has nothing to do with her personally. There is nothing in her address to the Jeweller of a child's claims on its parent. One effect of presenting the Maiden as a transmuted toddler is to make clear that the knowledge and demand she supports do not issue from her. She forms a screen onto which are projected the knowledge and the demand that she articulates, but which also hides, and thereby generates as an enigma, the source of that knowledge and that demand somewhere beyond the screen, in a Real *au-delà* which is here identified with God. Less obviously, the screen also generates a Real *en-deçà*, a space not transcendent but falling short, and which the poem's ideological thrust aims to overlook. The self-possessed, independent Pearl-Maiden's apparition makes it plain that the infant of less than two years, with the neediness, affection and babbling which are part of its charm for adults, has been suppressed in the process of sublation into the Maiden. This double loss is not to be mourned within the poem which, in fact, produces it.[4] Pearls appear in both medieval bestiaries and lapidaries. If a sensuous but inarticulate pearl, more animal than stone, is an appropriate image for the toddler, the incorruptible gleam of the Pearl-Maiden, God's own signifier, conjures up a pearl that is more stone than animal. Since pearls are crystallized out of dew, she proceeds in the opposite direction from Villon's equally white and disembodied ladies.[5]

On the other hand, the Jeweller, a human being mourning a traumatic loss, is potentially Everyman. Contrasting with the Pearl-Maiden, who is 'neither dead nor alive, but *beat[a]*', the Jeweller exists in a melancholy state in which death circumscribes the possibility of living – without, however, extinguishing life itself.[6] Life, indeed, proliferates around him:

Þat spot of spyseȝ mot nedeȝ sprede,
Þer such rycheȝ to rot is runne;
Blomeȝ blayke and blwe and rede
Þer schyneȝ ful schyr agayn þe sunne.
Flor and fryte may not be fede
Þer hit doun drof in moldeȝ dunne;
For vch gresse mot grow of grayneȝ dede;
No whete were elleȝ to woneȝ wonne.

                                                 (ll. 25–32)

(That spot where such a rich thing has run to rot must necessarily overspread with spices; blooms yellow, blue and red shine brightly there in the sunshine. Flowers and fruit may not be decayed there where it drove down into the dull clods. For each grass must grow from dead seeds; otherwise no home would have wheat.)[7]

The narrator attempts to make death meaningful by giving it a function in producing life. The 'cycle of corruption and regeneration' (to borrow Sade's phrase, discussed in Chapter 1, above), however, fails to console, its bleakness only enhanced by the acknowledgement of its utility to people. This reductive perspective is insufficient to sustain human life: man cannot live by bread alone. The comparison with Sade shows what is lacking in this first section of *Pearl*, namely a dimension to life beyond the material and earthly cycle – that dimension which Lacan associates with 'creationist sublimation'.[8]

As well as registering death's omnipresence, these lines seem to protest against an oppressively irrepressible quality in life.[9] The vision is reminiscent of Žižek's discussion of Leni Riefenstahl's deep-sea films, whose 'fascinating crawling of primitive life-forms' he interprets as an image of 'the ultimate life-substance' which is also 'the indestructible palpitation of life beyond death'.[10] This substance gestures towards the Real, naked confrontation with which is unsustainable for human consciousness. Žižek notes: 'the barrier separating the [R]eal from reality is therefore the very condition of a minimum of "normalcy"; "madness" (psychosis) sets in when this barrier is torn down, when the [R]eal overflows reality (as in autistic breakdown)'.[11] Similarly, the Jeweller fails to maintain the barrier between life and death which is essential to an engagement with earthly existence. Everyday life can be lived only within convenient fictions, which the Jeweller now sees through to the proliferating, indestructible life-substance palpitating beneath. His melancholy condition calls forth the Pearl-Maiden – 'life beyond death'. His dream of her is, of course, the vehicle of a beneficent Truth reinstalling stable divisions and counterbalancing the impure, death-directed vision of mourning; yet it also partakes of the Real in its continual alienations, in the carefully constructed outrages it presents to implied common sense, and in the insistent auditory repetitions which link the poem's different sections. These Real qualities ground the religious vision's claim to be more than merely symbolic or imaginary. I have looked in earlier chapters at texts exploiting the *entre-deux-morts* to political ends; however, in *Pearl* ideological value becomes both more complex and more critical, for at stake is Christian Truth. This Truth has ancient, learned resources for justification, but I have been concentrating on its modish presentation in the forms of late fourteenth-century court poetry: *Pearl* makes age-old Truth novel and fashionable. Moreover, many would argue that Christianity is Real. Arguing that Christianity has an important Real dimension does not imply accepting or denying the revealed Truth, but it does raise the question, as in Terry Eagleton's ambiguously rhetorical poser: 'What is the desire of the Real but what Augustine and Kierkegaard knew as faith?'[12] There is an important perceptual antagonism between those for whom God is Real and those for whom he is not. I shall examine in this chapter how that antagonism is at issue within *Pearl* itself, where the argument is not that God is an instance of the Real but that the Real is an instance of God. In my analysis I accept intellectually the first position, but not the second, that turns all instances of the Real into proofs of God's existence. I am interested rather in the ideological possibilities opened up by such a view and by the consequent ethics of the Real staged by the poem, which asks how humans do, should or can relate to a God whose Reality overflows human reality.

After an introductory plot summary, I shall analyse in the first part of this chapter how the Real serves the Truths that the poem promotes: its political and cultural messages. I concentrate on Lacan's discussion of the visual art technique of anamorphosis in Seminar VII. Lacan's extended exploration of the 'looking awry' by which psychoanalysis purports to reconstruct unconscious truths has much to offer readings of medieval dream visions, with their traditional interrogation of the relationship between *songe* and *mensonge*, 'dream' and 'lie'. Both psychoanalysis and dream visions insist that truth cannot be read directly from the surface or manifest content, but that dreams, like anamorphoses, in their distortions yield truths which require a different, and further distorting perspective if they are to be interpreted correctly. My analysis bears both on these heuristic processes and on their potential for ideological exploitation.

The Jeweller's *entre-deux-morts* draws on a courtly melancholia elaborated in numerous fourteenth- and fifteenth-century poems, notably in French. In the second part of this chapter I shall turn to aspects of *Pearl*'s contemporary literary context in this French-language tradition. I do not attempt a comprehensive overview nor to identify particular sources, but to trace certain poetic dialogues and discursive fields which illuminate the poem. In my opinion, *Pearl* represents courtly writing of the sort produced by Machaut, Froissart and Deschamps, and practised by such contemporary insular writers as Chaucer, Gower and Usk. *Pearl*'s provenance has been a puzzle; my argument may support those scholars who assign it to the court of Richard II, with its international, francophile culture and noteworthy Cheshire presence.[13] Through its themes and its frames, *Pearl* forms part of a series of international and interlingual literary dialogues, in which the various texts inflect the concerns of the discussion differently, draw on distinct sources, and gesture in divergent directions.

One of the most famous focal points today is that of the *marguerite*, a term translatable into English by 'daisy', 'pearl' or the saintly and courtly name of 'Margaret'. Marguerite literature has been widely written on in connection with Chaucer's Prologue to the *Legend of Good Women* (to which I shall turn in the final chapter), but it is rarer to explore the implications of the fact that *Pearl* is also a marguerite poem.[14] Although Chaucer criticism has perhaps overstated its distinctness and importance, the marguerite, in its polyvalence and equivocation, is a significant motif in a small number of fourteenth-century French-language works – notably by Froissart, for whom it may be considered a signature.[15] It is one among a number of tropes through which the roles of courtly poetry and of the courtly and/or court poet are interrogated. More widespread and influential are the discourses of the *dit* and the dream vision, which may overlap with that of the marguerite; *Pearl* belongs to all three.[16] The non-exclusive relationship is evident from the classification; marguerite works are defined by their central image, *dits* by their formal and thematic discontinuity and first-person clerical enunciation, dream visions by the frame within which they construct their fictions. The discursive field associated with the marguerite – its engagement with poetry and history, with loss, the beloved and her sponsor, with the courtly and the religious, with the court poet and his patron, with formal sophistication and poetic innovation – informs the artistic, philosophical and ideological practices of the *Pearl*-poet. I am concerned here both with how these practices serve the poem's religious message and with their earthly contexts.

THE NARRATIVE

Pearl presents a narrator who laments the loss of his favourite pearl, which he refers to as either 'it' or 'her', describing it in womanly terms – 'So smal, so smoþe her sydeȝ were' (l. 6; 'so small, so smooth her sides were') – as well as in terms of a precious stone. Unable to recover from his loss, he 'slode vpon a slepyng-sla3te' (l. 59; 'slid into a sudden, deathly sleep') in the garden where 'hit fro me sprange' (l. 13; 'it sprang away from me') and has what he declares to be an out-of-body vision (ll. 61–4). He finds himself walking through a glittering aureate landscape alongside a light-filled river, on the other side of which he eventually spies 'a faunt, / A mayden of menske, ful debonere' (ll. 161–2; 'an infant, a noble maiden, very gracious'), dazzling white and pearl-encrusted. He addresses her as his lost pearl and identifies himself as a jeweller. During the ensuing exchanges we learn that she is a dead human being, not yet two years old at the time of her death, and that, in the Jeweller's words, 'Ho wat3 me nerre þen aunte or nece' (l. 233; 'she was nearer to me than aunt or niece'). In answer to his hailing her the Maiden rebukes him, first for describing her as lost, then for believing all and only what he sees and finally for imputing to himself the power to cross the water which separates them and to stay with her forever. She advises him rather to seek reconciliation with the Lord whom he has offended by his rebelliousness. Taken aback, he asks about her present state and she explains that she is a queen in heaven and Bride of the Lamb. As he challenges her abrupt elevation in rank, she describes heaven's social organization, where the elect become kings and queens, and its economy, which values innocence and purity above everything and which permits each individual to enjoy absolutely sufficient good without encroaching on any other's similarly absolute enjoyment. The Maiden relates and glosses at length the parable of the labourers in the vineyard to emphasize how different earthly and heavenly orders are and to stress the importance of God's grace. She explains the significance of the New Jerusalem as divine not historical city. In culmination, she has arranged for the Jeweller to have a vision of the New Jerusalem, which is conveyed with repeated reference to the vision of St John in the Apocalypse. 'Rauyste with glymme pure' (l. 1088; 'ravished with sheer radiance'), the narrator tries to swim the river separating him from the holy city and his 'lyttel quene' (l. 1147; 'little queen'), who has now joined the procession of the one hundred and forty-four thousand Brides of the Lamb witnessed by St John. Foundering, he wakes to regret the rash act that has deprived him of insight into still greater mysteries and concludes the poem with expressions of submission to divine will and a commendation of the Eucharist as divine presence in the everyday.

ANAMORPHOSIS

Lacan discusses anamorphosis at length in Seminar VII and again in Seminar XI of 1964 (*The Four Fundamental Concepts of Psychoanalysis*). As I have done elsewhere in this book, I shall refer primarily to the former for its contextual association with discussions of courtly love, death and the sublime; although I do not follow strictly the terms of the latter, more developed account, I do have them in mind.[17] In the earlier account, Lacan draws heavily though selectively on Jurgis Baltrušaitis's 1955 popular art historical work, *Anamorphoses*.[18] The most famous example exploited by Lacan is Hans Holbein's 1533 portrait of two French ambassadors to the court of Henry VIII. As is well known, the foreground of this richly detailed, mimetic painting is disturbed by a spot or stain – a peculiarly distorted image which is in fact a skull painted at an angle steeply oblique to the picture plane, hence from a perspective much at odds with that of the main representation.[19] Once a viewer is standing at the appropriate angle to perceive this death's head, the remainder of the picture itself fades into the background and eventually suffers distortion, even disappearing from view (according to Lacan, at least). Other, less celebrated anamorphoses are also of interest. Lacan mentions several times the case of a panel painted with 'quelque chose d'assez dissous et dégueulasse' ('something decomposed [or shapeless] and disgusting');[20] when one stands a cylindrical mirror upright in a specified place on the picture there appears, projected in the mirror, an image of the Crucifixion based on a Rubens painting. Works of this sort illustrate Lacan's point that anamorphosis presents us with an unreadable image which becomes intelligible as we change the point of view from which we look at it.[21] A secular counterpart to the Crucifixion anamorphosis is provided by a double-sided canvas. One side presents a portrait of Charles II in royal regalia, on the other a small central skull is surrounded by a distorted image that Ariès describes as 'the severed head' of the English King Charles I. When the cylindrical mirror is placed over the skull, obscuring that image but grounded in it, it reveals what Ariès in a parallel discussion calls the 'bust of the king when alive'.[22] The function of such anamorphoses is fundamentally ambivalent. On the one hand, they prevent the dominant regime of reality from constituting itself as all-inclusive and all-explanatory. On the other hand, they provide a productive absence around which dominant reality has the opportunity to (re-)organize itself; the support thus afforded can, and often does, work to authorize that reality.

This ambivalence gives anamorphosis as a figure complex ideological value, predicated on three terms: 'normal', everyday reality; the illegible stain that lies across reality; and the image which that stain makes intelligible. All three are present in Holbein's work, where the ambassadors themselves by the grandeur, content and representational manner of their painting represent the regime portrayed as normatively real. This vision is interrupted by the strange foreground blob, which, when 'properly' viewed, becomes a death's head commenting ironically on the mastery of cosmic and earthly knowledge implied by the various objects on the shelves at the centre of the painting. The message is that death's Reality shatters earthly life and human pretensions to control that life (compare the sovereign subject of Chapter 3). Strictly speaking, the death's head itself does not instance the Real (that is done by the unintelligible, distracting stain), for it refers to the important sixteenth-century *memento mori* tradition. The void of death is created in order to be filled by what Lacan calls a *sublimation créationniste* ('creationist sublimation' – see p. 42, above), represented by the crucifix in the upper left-hand corner which, though not in anamorphosis, is only marginally visible and intelligible. Present in the dominant field but not belonging within its worldly vision, the crucifix complements the death's head. The painting rebukes the ordinary piety which leaves religion a subsidiary or banal concern; Christianity should ideally be as extraordinary, exacting, uncompromising as death. It nevertheless seems to acknowledge that for the Real to overflow reality in this way risks making life unliveable. Thus the crucifix, notably less alienated and alienating than the death's head, bridges the gap between 'everyday' and 'psychotic' perspectives. Adopting a Christian viewpoint does not here require total dislocation from the standard view, though it will demand a certain shift of focus. Invoking the Real thus serves a propagandistic purpose – not so much via the anamorphotic skull itself as by the cachet that the anamorphosis confers on the (supposedly) overlooked crucifix. This familiar artefact acquires the aura of another world while also providing a coherent answer to the problem of death. Thus the Real is converted to serve specific Truths (Christian and courtly), with the two structurally *entre-deux* elements – anamorphosis and crucifix – positioned as respectively untenable and reassuring (though still strange) alternative points of view on the fissure running through earthly normality. Importantly, however, that 'normality' is itself an artwork. The high worldly concern of international diplomacy, figured by the extremely skilful painting, is drained of the Real support that its symbolic and imaginary aspects require, only for this to be restored in a trickle-down of transcendence.

Holbein's painting thus points to an essential feature of anamorphosis as a trope. By layering different visual fields it suggests that all such fields, and indeed all concrete representations, are symptoms or screens projecting beyond themselves a further and transcendent truth which they both indicate and obscure. This structure is itself polemical, working to limit alternatives to acceptance of the projected truth. It is easy to reject that truth wholesale – if one is prepared to condemn oneself to meaninglessness; difficult to critique it constructively, to consent only in part, or to find substitutes. Anamorphosis therefore tends towards either mysticism or nihilism as its final destination. The ideologically constructive aspect becomes clearer on examining the simpler Crucifixion or Charles I anamorphoses. Here ordinary reality is represented by the surrounding world itself rather than by a depiction of it, as in the realistic field of the 'Ambassadors'. The resulting structure is therefore simpler – the 'real world' plays itself, and the distorted image is the stain unsettling normality and urging viewers to inquire into a different dimension. When the secondary image springs into sight, a superior reality or truth is made accessible to those who know how to interpret it; what was initially perceived as an accidental, contingent disturbance of the regular visual field is transformed into a symbol of revelation or initiation. Implied in this concrete metaphor is another audience, undiscriminating and superficial, which lacks the ability to appreciate the higher truth projected via the secondary image. For this audience the stain (or nasty canvas) will remain a stain. In a secondary move, therefore, in the eyes of the enlightened audience the stain as figure symbolizes the hollowness of inferior, common, workaday reality and also the distorted understanding of those who are limited to that dimension.

The kinds of anamorphosis and the historical period of the Reformation and Counter-Reformation on which Lacan focuses lend themselves both to promoting transcendent over limited world-views and to associating truths with secrets, intrigues and initiation. The examples I have been discussing, like numerous others, take the relationships between life and death, immortality and mortality, as central themes. Holbein's painting makes mortality the secret truth behind worldly existence but hints at a revealed countertruth through the liminal crucifix indicating Christ's triumph over death. Death disrupts human consciousness only to encourage its reorganization around different and transcendent grounds. In the anamorphoses that require a cylindrical mirror, the secret truth corresponds to that eternal, authentic life which is accessed only through fleshly death and especially through sacrifice. For a Christian, Christ's divine nature is consummated in his Crucifixion and Resurrection. Royalist politics borrows the Christian archetype to instate Charles as divine victim, and kingship as beneficiary of that sacrifice. The King never really dies, and beheading an individual monarch only makes manifest the indestructible symbolic body of monarchy: 'The king is dead, long live the king!' This point is hammered home by the double-sided canvas with its complementary images of Charles II triumphant and Charles I in defeat; the death's head, on which the father's anamorphosis centres, corresponds to the son's royal orb. In these instances, viewing corporeal death as an end in itself is presented as simultaneously ordinary, false and distorting; rightly regarded, death is a screen hiding and generating the sublime life which contradicts and complements the earthly. Note that such anamorphoses also generate an idealized image of their audience. The Royalist work, with its air of a secret portrait preserving clandestine loyalties from Cromwellian eyes, projects for its owner the story of a fidelity maintained in secret during the interregnum and meriting reward after the Restoration that it celebrates. This construct works equally well prospectively and retrospectively, testifying that its owner kept the faith against the dominant political tenor and rejected historical contingency in the name of a supreme value, here divinely ordained monarchical right. Ahistorical transcendence can thus serve highly political and historically specific ends.

Lawrence Besserman in a classic essay likened the double plot of *Sir Gawain and the Green Knight* to double images of the duck/rabbit variety as analysed by Gombrich. According to Gombrich, the brain can know cognitively that both images are present in such a work and 'we can switch from one reading to another with increasing rapidity; we will also "remember" the rabbit while we see the duck, but the more closely we watch ourselves, the more certainly will we discover that we cannot experience alternative readings at the same time'.[23] An analogous situation prevails with anamorphosis, except that anamorphosis does not present two equally weighted alternatives but a hierarchy, demanding that the viewer pass through the primary image to the secondary. 'Demanding' means that such a change is both necessary if the painting is to be viewed in full and is firmly imposed on the viewer as a desire and a duty. Perception of the anamorphosis in its correct perspective thus comes to resemble progress in knowledge, which in turn lends conviction to any particular ideological content for which the image may be a vehicle. Anamorphoses are in this sense lures: ideological, epistemological and ethical bait. Moreover, it is very difficult to forget the presence of the hidden image when seen. Once over the perceptual hurdle, even when viewing the unintelligibly messy or grotesque image or the ambassadors in their full-frontal glory, one adds to the image dominating the visual field one's knowledge of the other, secret image, positioned not only as the key making sense of the visual whole but also as morally and ontologically superior. After the primary field, however imposing, has been identified as the inferior term in a determinate binary, it becomes difficult to sustain at any level other than the merely physical. It comes instead to signify materiality's status as a signifier or symptom, at once useful and inadequate; the critical question then being how to reconnect, by some modification, with the Real support needed for meaning. The rhetoric of anamorphosis leads viewers towards the hidden, transcendent, ideologically determined 'truth' that it projects *au-delà* the image – any image. Anamorphosis is a particular and little-used artistic technique; however, for Lacan it clarifies how all artworks project a transcendent entity while casting doubt on pre-existing understandings of the world. This is a Heideggerian notion of art, though for Heidegger the new and universally valid truths made accessible by the work of art are multiple, particular insights into human 'world'. Lacan, warned by Heidegger's ideological captation, emphasizes instead the monotonous truths of the Real (which are 'nothing for us') while dissecting how art can seemingly elevate propaganda to the status of Truth.

PEARL AS ANAMORPHOSIS

Looking awry: heaven versus earth

Pearl works much in this way when inducting audience and Jeweller into the truths of the Kingdom of Heaven. His mourning detaches the Jeweller from his surroundings and society, stains them for him and him for them – and for us. He has become one of those who, according to Julian the Apostate, 'grovel among tombs . . . for the sake of dream visions' – equally horrifying impurities in the eyes of the pagan emperor.[24] His grief makes him look awry on the world, and his anamorphotic point of view leads him to the higher truths presented by the Pearl-Maiden; though it is arguable whether he grasps them, they are made available to the audience. It also serves to reveal the emptiness and falsity of a certain view of earthly society when the Jeweller within the vision voices an everyday perspective according to which the Maiden's account is nonsensical. The heaven she projects is jarringly counter-intuitive yet it is the earthly view that is designated inaccurate and senseless, as the Maiden relentlessly informs us that the Jeweller sees things from the wrong angle.[25] The pearl which he believes lost is revealed to be where it truly belongs, the child whom he considers dead turns out to be alive in a superior sense, and her value is far beyond what he imagines. The notions of stain and stainlessness are key here, the poem's terminology resonating with Lacan's. Over and over, what the Jeweller sees as blemish – in her, in heavenly society, in the Lamb – is reinterpreted as being in truth the price, passage or mark of a superior purity.[26] The erstwhile 'blot' (l. 782) in sublunary vision – life and death beneath the 'spotty' (l. 1070) moon – must be transformed into a lens permitting proper vision. Here the Jeweller's function is to register by his repeated objections the discrepancies between heaven and a common earthly sense. It appears that the heavenly Father's demand for an altered perspective exceeds the conceptual abilities of the earthly father and, by extension, of the culture he epitomizes. This is not identical to the audience's culture, for the Jeweller's position and experience are not entirely those of the poem's implied audience; his role is to misread. Nevertheless, the repeated astonishment that he expresses prevents the audience from becoming acclimatized to the divine regime, whose power to disorient, even scandalize, is one of the poem's achievements.

Speaking for the inferior understanding, the Jeweller questions divine values:

> Þou lyfed not two ȝer in oure þede;
> Þou cowþeȝ neuer God nauþer plese ne pray,
> Ne neuer nawþer Pater ne Crede;
> And quen mad on þe fyrst day!
> I may not traw, so God me spede,
> Þat God wolde wryþe so wrange away.
>
> (ll. 483–8)

(You lived not two years in our land, you never knew how to please or pray to God, nor either the Our Father or the Creed; and yet you were made a queen on your first day! I cannot believe, so help me God, that God would distort things so awry.)

In response the Pearl-Maiden relates the parable of the labourers in the vineyard (Matthew 20: 1–16). Demonstrating that God is not bound by earthly notions of fairness, this parable undermines ideas of desert measured in terms of time, effort or product. (So, at least from a modern perspective, does courtly life; however, this parable concerns spiritual reward.) According to Stephen Wailes, commentaries frequently use the vineyard tale to rebuke stalwart Christians, in particular those in religious orders, for their expectation of heavenly reward. Several commentators interpret the parable's day as the span of a life, with the groups of workers representing persons converted to God's service at different ages. Those who arrive in the vineyard at the eleventh hour symbolize deathbed converts; thus the parable interpreted allegorically demonstrates 'the full validity of late conversion'. In Gregory the Great's influential interpretation, 'The householder first gave the denarius to the last because he gathered the thief to the peace of paradise before Peter.'[27] This parable was therefore commonly invoked to address a more than ordinarily devout, orthodox and obedient audience and raises, in order to settle, the spectre of rebellious incomprehension within even that audience. This conventional use to signify an important sticking-point for Christian understanding explains its function in *Pearl* as a pivot between orders, where choices must be made, distinctions cannot be fudged, and God's will must be accepted regardless of human sensibilities. The parable expresses the imperative to submit to the heavenly perspective even when it seems distorted to us. Given the common identification of the latecomers as in extreme old age, *Pearl*'s application of this category to the infant may contribute to its emphasis on defamiliarization.

Heavenly reason: heaven plus earth

In spite of this imperative, and to some extent undermining it, *Pearl*'s heaven is anything but irrational; on the contrary, the poem justifies the divine order at length through a kind of ethnographic exposition of alternative cultural values. Thus the Maiden carefully explicates the vineyard parable as an analogy for the Kingdom of Heaven. One explanation concerns the heavenly valuation of innocence and purity, a long life inevitably accumulating more sins as well as more good works such that the value lost outweighs the value added. Another turns on linked conceptions of sovereignty, contractual obligation and property rights which reserve to the lord the right and the virtue of distributing gifts as he sees fit, so long as he does not fall below the contracted amount in any individual case. Such a principle elevates monarchical rights and places the aristocratic ideology of largesse and gift-giving above an ethics relating to labour economics (ll. 565–6).[28] A third rationalization argues for an egalitarian interpretation of the labourers' reward, disregarding economic criteria to award each the same pay. This last interpretation makes a heavenly virtue out of homogenizing what on earth are different categories of people. However, it addresses only imperfectly *Pearl*'s Kingdom of Heaven, where an insistent rhetoric of sameness combines paradoxically with a presentation of hierarchy, to baffle human understanding. The egalitarian message seems rather to address the earthly realm. John Bowers has been the principal proponent of the argument that *Pearl* engages with the historical conditions of post-Black Death England with its scarce labour and discontented labourers.[29] He contends that the labourers' demand for a penny a day was also that of real-life wage-earners, and that God's practice in distributing spiritual rewards is cited in order to reject a similar practice on earth. This elitist urge in the poem can alternatively be described through the three terms of anamorphosis: by including in its field both a stain across ordinary reality (the Jeweller's grief) and the intelligible heavenly Truth which that stain eventually reveals, *Pearl* renders the everyday, earthly objections to divine practice of the insubordinate lower ranks as the chaotic product of inferior understanding. The labourers' condition thus becomes an intellectual failing to be addressed by a change of perspective, not of material circumstance.

Elicited in response to his protests against the heavenly order, the field of rebellion rejoins that of the Jeweller and is associated with his personal objections to the Maiden's revelations:

> Me þynk þy tale vnresounable.
> Godde3 ry3t is redy and euermore rert,
> Oþer Holy Wryt is bot a fable.
>
> (ll. 590–2)

(I think that your account is irrational. God's justice is prompt and ever supreme, or else Holy Scripture is only a fable.)

We should perhaps say that the Jeweller here speaks not from his grief-stricken point of view but from that of the ordinary human world which that grief drains of meaning for him. But the human shortcomings – grief, envy, jealousy – that blinker the Jeweller appear to meld with those colouring the labourers' response, compounding the rejection of what is already presented as an order of being inferior to that of heaven.[30] At the very moment when they are articulated in the poem, the lower-class economic-ethical demands are made to seem almost the antithesis of articulation itself, an unenlightened distortion of the true order. Earthly reality is so empty that it is deformed. It has the same heuristic value as the Jeweller's mournful gaze, which calls forth divine truth wherein the egalitarian appeal to justice merges into the lord's right to dispose of his own as he wills. In line with the logic of anamorphosis, we can observe that the consistency of the heavenly vision, and therefore its effectiveness as a model for earthly labour and class relations, is maintained by insisting on its distance from earthly perceptions and practices, measured in the repeated surprises it provokes in the Jeweller and in the recourse to rhetorical tropes which conjure up a further dimension beyond the highly realized vision. Here, as with the Charles I anamorphosis, we see the historical masquerading as history's transcendent negation.

However, we should be wary of equating the vision of earthly reality that is generated within *Pearl* with the poem's own historical context, even allowing for the presence of political bias in the representations. An earlier generation of scholars sought evidence for the poet's real-life loss of a daughter on essentially the same rhetorical basis. Whatever the referential status of the labourers, *Pearl* is not alone among medieval courtly dream visions in producing a 'realistic' version of contemporary social life at the height – or depth – of its fiction; indeed, this had already become a tradition. Jean de Meun's *Roman de la Rose*, notably, having layered mediation upon mediation, short-circuits to recent Parisian university politics when Faux-Semblant, the personification of misleading appearances, turns to discuss the long-running conflict between the fraternal orders and lay clergy for the control of academic chairs at the Sorbonne (a topic familiar from Rutebeuf's poetry and hence also a literary reference). Analogously, the prophecy made by the God of Love naming the *Rose*'s authors at the mid-point of poem and dream provides the main evidence for the existence of the first author, Guillaume de Lorris.[31] The appearance of 'history' in *Pearl* in a highly mediated context – a parable concerning biblical labourers (thus coloured by established uses of Scripture), related by a semi-allegorical figure in the vision within the dream – should be approached with comparable caution. This is not to deny them political relevance. Fourteenth-century French and English courtly dream visions, to different extents and in distinct ways, aim to include both poetry and politics within an englobing ethical framework and an overarching discourse, while at the same time drawing attention to the processes involved and displaying their workings. This they do by exaggerating the dislocations of perspective needed to shift from one to the other, as Holbein includes the world of the French ambassadors, the crucifix and the anamorphotic skull in his painting. Dream, vision, fable, allegory and the traditions of courtly love writing are all deployed within late medieval literary texts alongside meticulous discussions of the statecraft, patronage and spiritual and professional duties that mark the poet's and audience's lived realities. When these works switch between private and public, love and war, or fictional dream vision and historical dispute, they emphasize the interdependence of these dimensions precisely through their dissonance. They teach that literature, including the fantastical, provides examples of and reflections on order or disorder through models of ordering and cases of order's disarrangement and institution, which are indispensable to an intelligent approach to the complex, heterogeneous political and social situations of the fourteenth century; and that major shifts of perspective are necessary when measuring each one's pertinence to another. *Pearl* amplifies the strain by rejecting the historical, legendary and biblical examples with which late medieval literature is stuffed, in favour of the Gospels and especially of the Apocalypse, least overtly realistic and historical of biblical sources. The effect is to pose, not the particular vision that the dream articulates, but the reference implied beyond that fictional vision, as transcendent, eternal and ultimately true. Like its contemporary works, though, the poem does not seek to obscure the political concerns which lie behind its seemingly disinterested philosophical discussions, but rather highlights an ideological agenda.

Thus in *Pearl*, heaven is the domain in which sense is made. Similar in this to the images projected by the anamorphoses of Charles I and of the Crucifixion, the heaven of the dream vision is the text's principal symbolically differentiated field. Significantly, heaven produces not only the poem's ideal, properly otherworldly systems, but also the earthly systems that are contrasted to them. The earthly becomes intelligible as lacking only in heaven's representations of it, which also tell us exactly what it lacks. Thus the unheavenly labourers have their genesis as well as their refutation within the bounds of the vision. Contrast the Jeweller's mourning account before his dream, in which his relation to the pearl is free-floating and amorphous, and where she or it is variously lost, trapped, dead and metamorphosed into vegetable life. Within the vision, that relation becomes richly polyvalent, subject to a variety of interpretations in terms of human relations. He calls her his near relative, his child, his courtly beloved, his social superior, and longs for her in all these roles. An instance of the Thing (see Chapter 2, above), the Maiden throws into relief not only the Real but also, and here more strikingly, the symbolic.[32] Although she insists that the heavenly reality of her relation to the Jeweller is to be understood as *not* any of the above structures, nevertheless it is within the vision that those earthly relations and structures become manifest. Thus he is introduced into the structures of desire and exchange. He becomes a subject in the sense of one whose unruly longings can be trained, negotiated with, 'subjected' to a guiding influence. Order and its complement, intelligible disorder, are equally heaven's creations. Thus do dream poems, like anamorphosis, make the 'ordinary' world seem intrinsically chaotic and unreal, a *mensonge* awaiting the truth that the anamorphotic *songe* will somehow impart; this may be called the medieval dream-work. *Pearl* utilizes the Real of anamorphosis not only to differentiate strictly and hierarchically between the particular symbolic and imaginary regimes of heaven and earth but also, paradoxically, to operate a rapprochement between those regimes such that heaven's courtly, monarchist ideology, counter-intuitive to earthly sense and the product of 'creationist sublimation', persuades as the best system also for us below. Rendering unto Caesar the things that are Caesar's comes to be part of the greater project of rendering unto God the things that are

God's (Matthew 22: 21). It can be argued even in modern secular times that God imparts the Real to anamorphosis and not, as Lacan claims, vice versa; but few today would defend the view that a king is similarly Real in his own right, though kings may have seemed so at moments.

PEARLS AND DAISIES

From the above theoretical exploration of the complex relations between earth and heaven in *Pearl*, I turn now to explore those same relations through a selective literary history. I take fourteenth-century courtly fran-cophone literature to be an important cultural context of *Pearl*, and there-fore examine some of the poetic dialogues in which the text participated, with an eye above all to the marguerite, a figure in which courtly, religious and poetic ideas interact. According to the standard Old French dictionar-ies (Tobler-Lommatzsch, Godefroy), the principal meaning of *marguerite* was 'pearl'. The dictionaries record only one use of the meaning 'daisy': in *Aucassin et Nicolette*, generally dated to the early thirteenth century. Nicolette's whiteness is described: 'et les flors des margerites qu'ele ronpoit as ortex de ses piés . . . estoient droites noires avers ses piés et ses ganbes, tant par estoit blance la mescinete' ('and the marguerite flowers that she crushed with the toes of her feet . . . were quite black next to her feet and legs, so white was the girl').[33] The Robert *Dictionnaire historique de la langue française* ('marguerite') notes that in *Aucassin*'s locution the precise meaning is 'fleur de perle' ('pearl flower').[34] Dictionaries date the abso-lute use of *marguerite* meaning a flower to 1364, with Machaut's 'Dit de la marguerite' (hereafter 'Marguerite').[35] All the earliest examples in the *Anglo-Norman Dictionary*, *Französisches etymologisches Wörterbuch* and *Dictionary of Medieval Latin from British Sources* date from the fourteenth-century vogue for marguerite poetry. It seems likely, therefore, that when the mar-guerite came into fashion, pearly connotations bore heavily on the flower. Daisies are, as far as I can discover, something of a *tabula rasa* symbolically, but when called *marguerites* they assume some of the pearl's emblematic associations without being limited to those. They acquire instant gravitas, symbolic weight and polyvalent, even ambivalent density while remaining relatively underdetermined, thus becoming highly flexible figures.

It is crucial to grasp the marguerite's novelty and flexibility in order to appreciate the innovations it enabled within courtly poetry. The fourteenth-century French-language poets who write of marguerites give the impression of investing a new courtly symbol. Written perhaps some months after Machaut's opening sally, Froissart's 'Dit de la marguerite' (hereafter 'Flor') lingers over the naming process to emphasize its unfamiliarity:

> Je ne me doi retraire de loer
> La flour des flours, prisier et honnourer,
> Car elle fait moult a recommender:
> C'est la consaude, ensi le voel noumer,
> Et qui li voelt son propre nom donner,
> On ne li puet ne tollir ne embler,
> Car en françois a a nom, c'est tout cler,
> La margerite.[36]

(I must not draw back from praising, extolling and honouring the flower of flowers, for it is greatly to be recommended: it is the daisy, thus I wish to name it; and whoever wishes to give it its proper name, one cannot take that from it nor steal it away, for in French it has the name, quite clearly, of marguerite.)[37]

Naming the marguerite is staged as revelation and investiture of the patrician status of the seemingly humble *consaude*; the poet leads his community in awarding it its 'propre nom' of 'marguerite'. This sense that marguerites invite revision clings. Marguerite poems in French repeatedly stage a defence of the flower against what are presented as more obvious or established courtly choices, thus redefining what courtliness might consist in and suggesting really or purportedly new aspirations to guide the court.[38] Most notably, the newly elevated daisy supersedes the rose, marking for late medieval writers at once a genealogy and a change of orientation within courtly writing in relation to the thirteenth-century *Roman de la Rose*.

Sublation is, therefore, an attribute of the marguerite. The same process is enacted in the English translation into 'pearl' – which is also, given the pearly connotations borne by the signifier *marguerite*, a back-translation. Much has been written on pearls in connection with *Pearl*. In spite of the gem's associations with purity and revelation, it is ambiguous, adorning the Whore of Bablyon as well as the gates of the New Jerusalem.[39] Pearls' ambivalence is one expression of the traditionally equivocal and variable relationship in courtly writing between the earthly court and its heavenly prototype. It may be that translating *marguerite* as 'pearl' renders this relationship tenser. My aim here, however, is to explore the poetic field not of the pearl but of the marguerite, to which field *Pearl* also belongs. I stress the poem's French-language connections, and defer on questions of its Englishness to other scholars.

Arts of mourning

The marguerite is linked to a debate relating the complex of life, death and life beyond death to that of desire, love and poetry. The *Pearl*-poet enters into this debate, revising its terms in different directions; note that participating in the debate ideally requires a poet to differ in this way. Thus Machaut, apparently founding the marguerite discourse, states that 'Sa grant douçour garist les mauls d'amer, / Sa grainne puet les mors ressusciter' ('Its great sweetness cures the ills of love; its seed can resuscitate the dead').[40] It enables the poet to write in defiance of his woes, and indeed of his triumphs; the life-beyond-death that it figures is above temporal concerns. Against Machaut's assertion of life-giving power, Froissart associates the marguerite with pain, wounding and death. In the version of his invented origin myth found in the *Joli Buisson de Jonece*, marguerites spring from the tears shed by Herès over the dead body of her lover Cepheüs.[41] This latter's 'ardant folie' (l. 3208; 'burning madness') and 'grant merancolie' (l. 3209; 'great melancholy') are related to those of Pygmalion, Narcissus, Orpheus and many other tragic lovers current in court poetry. Marguerites memorialize those dead of passion but can never bring them back. Flowering even when 'toutes flours sont mortes pour l'ivier' ('all flowers are dead because of winter'), they symbolize the perpetual rebirth of desire, with its characteristic, tantalizing semi-pleasure, and consequently of poetic inspiration or compulsion.[42] Unlike Machaut's, Froissart's marguerite renews desire and its pains ('en cascun floron, je vous creant, / Porte la flour un droit dart a taillant'; 'in each petal, I assure you, the flower bears a keenly cutting dart').[43] Returning to the subject in the 'Dit de la fleur de lis et de la marguerite', thought to be one of his final works, the older poet rejects this conception, emphasizing again how the flower calms the pangs of desire ('Froide est et seche et restreintive'; 'she is cold and dry and extinguishing') and heals 'maus amoureus' ('ills of love').[44] Machaut hymns the marguerite for transcending the life cycle with its joys and pains, Froissart for material renewal progressing through loss to memorialization, mourning and – perhaps – rebirth, though without transcendence: his lover returns essentially to the same place, more repetition than renascence.

The Jeweller's condition as a lover who has lost his beloved is familiar to readers of medieval courtly literature. It is tempting to summarize in Lamartine's memorable phrase: 'Un seul être vous manque, et tout est dépeuplé' ('You lack a single being – and the whole is depeopled'). However, in medieval *dits* the lack of the beloved typically leads the poet not to solitude but to an over-peopled world. One has to sympathize with the Man in Black of Chaucer's *Book of the Duchess* who, seeking to lament alone, is joined by the inquisitive Dreamer (himself in search of seclusion), though the latter is no doubt less officious than the narrator of Machaut's *Jugement du roy de Behaigne*, who thrusts himself into a thorn bush to overhear the courtly mourners whom he will eventually drag back to the court like an Arthurian knight sending outlanders and renegades to his king. The beloved need not even be dead to be thus missing. The dreamscape of the *Roman de la Rose* is crowded with personae with whom the lover has to negotiate willy-nilly in his quest for the silent, vegetable Rose. In courtly love lyrics, similarly, the poet-lover of the unattainable lady finds himself interacting primarily with *lauzengiers* and other, to his sense, superfluous figures. Social life is apparently something conducted on the margins of the principal preoccupation. This is one way in which we can interpret Lacan's claim that *amour courtois* emphasizes the vacuole, the empty space at the heart of the symbolic order (see Chapter 2, above). The Jeweller's experience is thus a typically courtly one in that he will move from lovelorn isolation to a highly peopled social environment. In this case that environment is explicitly Christian, comprising both the courtly afterlife described by the Maiden, culminating in the vision of the heavenly Jerusalem, and the lowlier milieu of labouring and trading that she invokes through parables. Like other late fourteenth-century poet-narrators, the Jeweller will remain marginal to the poem's court, a partial outsider who serves without fully understanding or belonging. Like others, he is nevertheless a lover, for the Maiden's parable of the pearl of great price situates him socially as a tradesman but also elevates him as a true desirer of one prize.[45] We leave him conventionally lonely among society, for the poem's closing lines show that he is finally conscious of a structure which surrounds him though inaccessible to his (grief-stricken? lower-status? worldly? fleshly?) understanding.

It has become commonplace to observe that melancholy is fundamental to the literary process in much fourteenth-century francophone literature.[46] Writers portrayed themselves suffering from collective as well as individual mourning and melancholia (subgroups of the sin of *acedia* or sloth), overwhelmed by the cultural weight of a past tradition which had said all there was to say and which they could never hope to equal; in this very situation they found the wellspring of their own innovative literary practice. This model influenced English writers at least during the Ricardian period. Chaucer phrases it with characteristic skill in making well-worn themes seem novel, in his own marguerite poem:[47]

For wel I wot that folk han here-beforn
Of making ropen, and lad awey the corn;
And I come after, glenynge here and there,
And am ful glad if I may fynde an ere
Of any goodly word that they han left.[48]

(For well I know that people have reaped the field of poetry before now, and taken away the corn; and I come after, gleaning here and there, and am very glad if I can find an ear of any good word that they have left behind.)

In this context we must distinguish between the role of the clerkly narrator and that of the courtly patron, as found, for instance, in the *Book of the Duchess* and in *dits* by Machaut and Froissart. Although both narrator and patron may figure as bereaved or unrequited lovers locked into their fixation, this state has a distinct value for each. *Acedia* is a potentially productive condition for the writer, whose semi-conscious and segregated state leads him to compose, even if it is often not his own fixation that inspires him. Other unhappy lovers generally occupy the main body of the work, whether as patrons, consolees or legendary examples.[49] For the patron, even if he is also secondarily a poet, *acedia* is destructive inasmuch as it diverts him from his public function and saps resources asserted to be vital to the larger community. Thus in the *Book of the Duchess* it is inappropriate for the Man in Black to adopt the same model of lovesickness within which the narrator can and even must operate as a writer. Although the Man's desires are shown to be conditioned by the courtly ethic which dictates that the lover's own death or eternal mourning are the proper responses to the loss of the beloved, he must, willingly or not, eventually conform to what Georges Duby called the 'aristocratic' model of marriage, which subordinates choice to dynastic strategy.[50] The alternative model of love as election, compatibility and uniqueness, which Duby terms 'clerical', is in this late fourteenth-century work shown to be an appropriate pattern for living not for the knight but for the clerk who, seemingly lacking another centrally important role, 'works' for the community by acting out this model as a proxy for his patron while simultaneously gesturing to the superior performance that his betters would naturally deliver, were it not inappropriate for them. Thus the nobles of the court are enabled to espouse the ethically superior affective model while practising pragmatic marital politics.[51]

Within a substantial corpus of works representing the relation between writer and his subject or patron in this way, the ambiguous situation of *Pearl*'s Jeweller is conventional. He is one, socially not of the first rank, who works for the pleasure of his betters. These aristocratic patrons constitute important sources of creativity, to whom the specialist craftsman lends his professional knowledge and skill; although some poems present the nominal producer as a dignified co-author and the patron's brother-in-art, others depict him as a mere ghost writer or even a courtly idiot savant. By portraying the Jeweller's melancholy, isolation and marginality, the *Pearl*-poet situates and authorizes him as an artist-narrator within an internationally fashionable, courtly literary tradition. Poets working in this rhetorical mode frequently represent their own positions within the tradition as an oppressive source of anxiety and alienation. The common position therefore has anti-communal tendencies, and its ability to ground an artistic community or identity is precarious. Attempts to construct these tend to take the form of negation, undermining what they also function positively to sustain. On the other hand, while the writer's conventional claim to alienation can in fact reflect or produce real alienation from dominant literary practice, at the same time it also awards authority within the terms of that practice. Thus Christine de Pizan's representation and performance of her own marginality in relation to masculinist cultural institutions is one strong variant on the typical poetic position of her time. In *Pearl*, analogously, the Jeweller, although conventional as a bereaved lover, is unusual among courtly narrators in being portrayed as neither a writer nor a reader of secular material. This narratorial presentation isolates him from any putative courtly-literary network. In situating his narrator outside such networks, the *Pearl*-poet (in this respect like Christine) pursues the rationale of a conventional poetic position to one logical extreme. Paradoxically, he thus claims for that narrator a privileged position in relation to those networks. The Jeweller's distinction from other courtly *dit* narrators constitutes his distinction within that company.

Marguerites

Thus far, then, the *Pearl*-poet's persona and practice are only conventionally unconventional, their narrow divergence from the common model part of a shared poetic programme and conferring merit within that programme. Most significant is the Jeweller's non-literary presentation. This is surely linked to the fact that *Pearl* omits the explicit flaunting of classical erudition that characterizes other writers working within the same broad cultural milieu, including Chaucer, Gower and Usk, not to mention the French writers. Such writers generally exploit biblical material in the same antiquarian, scholarly spirit (compare the poems by Deschamps discussed in Chapter 3, above). Contrastingly, the Jeweller is not justified by arcane historical learning. Instead his experience emphasizes, as the sources of moral, spiritual and intellectual reflection, the New Testament and those parts of the Old Testament that can be read as types of the New, with special attention being paid to St John's Apocalypse or Book of Revelations. The implied claim appears to be that poetic authority rests not at all on the poet's erudition or on secular knowledge, but directly on God's word and especially on personal revelation of that word. *Pearl* here effects a definite reorientation of reading and writing practices in relation to other marguerite texts; nevertheless, that reorientation remains within the discourse's possible extension, the groundwork for it having been laid elsewhere. We may compare and contrast the middle-aged and uninspired writer-narrator of Froissart's *Joli Buisson de Jonece*, who is in the habit of praying every morning to St Margaret before Venus interrupts him, transporting him to a second youthfulness of love which will rescue his poetic 'frois . . . art' ('cold art'). This illusory youth, treated with considerable irony, forms the basis for significant ethical reflection and for the body of the poem; finally the dreamer awakes to turn again to sacred poetry, addressing his art to the 'Flour d'onneur tres souverainne' ('Flower of most sovereign honour') that is the Virgin Mary.[52] Turning rather to holy subjects as the matter for a poem whose sophistication and dexterity of form, language and thought match that of his great contemporaries, the *Pearl*-poet both claims descent from such a stance and re-targets it towards other concerns.

Both aspects of this bilateral presentation are crucial. Unlike those French and English writers who adore daisies, the Jeweller is concerned with pearls, the more durable kind of marguerite. So too is the *Pearl*-poet. He, however, is a reader and writer of courtly literature, and his poem takes its place in literary networks of which the Jeweller seems oblivious. Thus, for instance, the 'gleaning' topos, quoted above in Chaucer's version, surfaces in the first section of *Pearl* as part of the Jeweller's sense of unstoppable, death-saturated life. The Jeweller enters the garden 'In Auguste in a hy3 seysoun, / Quen corne is coruen wyth croke3 kene' (ll. 39–40; 'in August, at the height of the season, when corn is cut with keen scythes'). The poet advertises his courtly-literary qualifications subtly and with consummate skill by naturalizing them within an apparently non-'literary' account. These lines must themselves be read in the light of the previous stanza's evocation of the lost pearl's fertile rotting, 'For vch gresse mot grow of grayne3 dede; / No whete were elle3 to wone3 wonne' (ll. 31–2; 'for each grass must grow from dead seeds; otherwise no home would have wheat').[53] This bleak evocation recalls the Ovidian metamorphoses so beloved of courtly writers throughout the medieval period. Compare the learned, classicizing tenor of Froissart's marguerite origin myth of Herès and Cepheüs; in *Pearl*, the metamorphosis is at once utilitarian and biblical in tone. However, refusal to be governed by tradition is an essential part of the courtly literary tradition, in which novelty is an important aesthetic criterion. Courtly *dits* typically raise through the poem as an artefact philosophical questions that are only begged within the narrative. Thus the *Pearl*-poet's cultural experience exceeds the Jeweller's: the pearl-seed will go on to produce not flowers and wheat but marguerites, the stuff of courtly cultural exploitation. Displaying an awareness of contemporary literary fashions and a wide cultural and theological learning denied to the Jeweller, the *Pearl*-poet distances his humble intratextual I-persona from his own poetic role as a scholar and counsellor without whose advice and knowledge his earthly prince is no more than an 'asne couronné', and whose principal function is now to remind of the greater Prince who rules them both, in their spheres.[54] Distancing of this sort is standard, but not to this degree; the Jeweller's position outside courtly-literary and scholarly networks constitutes a material intervention in the debates conducted through the marguerite, among others. The Jeweller's knowledge is not undermined by the poet's courtly supplementation of it. We can go further: just as other works suggest that the noble patron and audience may appreciate the value of the bookish narrator's learning more correctly than he himself does, so the Jeweller's sincere piety and revelation may here be the rarer and more valuable commodity that the poem offers up to a courtly audience, its pearl of price.

The relation between the secular and the religious is a recurring problem within fourteenth- and fifteenth-century courtly poetry, with its turn to moral seriousness and spiritual worth. Marguerite discourse, with its endless glossing, typically replaces the common-or-garden daisy with its higher avatar, 'the *margarita preciosa*, the Biblical pearl of great price (Matthew 13: 45–6): an image of absolute desire, of absolute perfection, by definition unattainable in this life, and nameable only metaphorically'.[55] It is a central part of courtly discourse to reject older courts in the name of some superior manifestation of the courtly ideal. Machaut notably argues that true courtliness shares many of the values of Christianity, in particular its piety and its purity. The alliance of 'clannes' and 'cortaysye', as *Sir Gawain and the Green Knight* has it, is in Machaut's ideal system a tautology. Courtliness complements Christianity as an *art de vivre* rendering its ideals more humanly accessible. In the fullest statement of his marguerite conception, in the 'Dit de la fleur de lis et de la marguerite', Machaut contrasts the austere theological virtues of the embattled, martyred lily to the gentler

qualities of the marguerite. The two flowers share several qualities such as
a strong green stalk, white petals and golden seeds, but the significations
ascribed to each are different. Whiteness, for example:

> La fueille dou lis, qui est blanche,
> Autant ou plus com noif sus branche,
> Signefie, je n'en doubt mie,
> Purté, chasté et nette vie,
> Sans pechié, sans tache et sans vice
> Et sans penser mauvais malice.
>
> (ll. 137–42)

(The lily's petal, which is as white as or whiter than snow on a branch, signifies,
I have no doubt, purity, chastity and a clean life, without sin, without stain and
without vice and without thinking any wicked malice.)

The same colour is resignified in the elaboration of the marguerite:

> De fueilles a une ceinture
> Si blanche, qu'il n'est creature,
> S'il la voit, qu'il ne s'en resjoie,
> Car le blanc signefie joie.
>
> (ll. 213–16)

(It has a belt of petals so white that there is no creature who does not rejoice on
seeing her, for white signifies joy.)

Machaut asserts that the marguerite's more pleasurable virtues are no less
admirable than the lily's glacial merits. He emphasizes the former's usefulness to others, hence the long passage on its medicinal qualities.[56] Much
of the imagery and language applied to the marguerite is Marian or Incarnational, the parallel authorizing its convivial attractions as rendering it
at once closer to ordinary mortals and, because it forms a bridge between
earth and heaven, in a sense nearer to the divine. Evaluating the merits of
what appear to be distinct forms of the *via activa*, Machaut concludes:

> Raison, justice et equité:
> Tant ont loange et grace et pris
> Et si ay d'elles tant apris
> Qu'assez loer ne les porroie
> Ne leurs biens dire ne saroie,
> Tant en y a, tant en y truis,
> Et mieus vorroie estre destruis
> Que d'elles vous deïsse rien
> Que tout ne fust honneur et bien.
> Toutevoie tant en diray

> Et puis mon ouevre fineray:
> Tout veü, tout consideré,
> Vertu, grace, douceur, biauté,
> Pour chose que d'elles soit ditte
> Ne lairay qu'a la marguerite
> Ne me teingne tant com vivray,
> Car mis en ses las mon vivre ay.
> Or vueille Dieus qu'elle soit moie,
> Qu'en ce monde plus ne vorroie
> Que li pour avoir esperence,
> Joie, pais, merci, souffissance,
> Pris, et honneur, loange et gloire
> En la fin, et tresbon memoire.
>
> (ll. 394–416)

(Reason, justice and equity have so much praise, grace and worth, and I have learned so much of them that I could never praise them sufficiently, nor tell all their good, for there is so much in them and I find so much in them; and I had rather be destroyed than say anything to you on their subject which was other than completely honourable and good. Nevertheless I will say this much on the topic and then finish my work: whatever may be said about virtue, grace, gentleness and beauty, all things seen and considered, I shall not refrain from cleaving to the marguerite while I live, for I have placed my life in its net. Now would to God that she were mine, for in this world I would want no other thing than her in order to have hope, joy, peace, mercy, sufficiency, renown, and honour, praise and glory at the end, and an excellent memory.)

The lily remains isolated and inaccessible, surrounded by thorns from which God will ultimately rescue it in triumph (ll. 160–7) but which also endow it with a certain rebarbative quality compared with the marguerite, which in semi-mystical fashion gives enjoyment even without sexual possession. While the lily guards itself from the sexual dishonour which would constitute spiritual death (an Old Testament reference; ll. 51–8), the marguerite confers itself generously and chastely, resuscitating the dead (ll. 275–9). Although both are proposed as metaphorical dresses for the poet's lady (ll. 381–8), the lily is said to be a masculine flower, the marguerite feminine (ll. 171–2), perhaps recalling the sense in which the Incarnation is also gendered feminine.[57] Flexible, accommodating, gentle and serviceable, the marguerite defines a notion of femininity quite different from that exemplified by the lily (compare White and Alceste in Chapter 5, below).

There is a moment of surprise when the lily shifts from the femininity previously constructed for it to the masculinity its grammatical gender implies – an example of the shifting interpretative grounds which characterize courtly *dits* so consistently that we may consider them to sub-scribe to a hermeneutics of surprise or of 'looking awry' (*Pearl*'s inversions being another example). Fourteenth-century dream poems, similarly, play with references to or illusions of extra-poetic reality, delighting in unsettling the perspective from which the reader has become accustomed to view the poem. Machaut's re-gendering of the flowers may be interpreted as block-ing the lily as an aspirational object of erotic desire for heterosexual male readers and of identificatory desire for females, directing both towards the more acceptable and, though equally pure, somehow more accessi-ble and certainly more utilizable marguerite. This would be, however, an anachronistically narrow conclusion. Both male and female virgin saints were available for a variety of identificatory and desirous appropriations by audiences of both sexes, while the confusions of gender and sexuality in the *Roman de la Rose* set the terms for later medieval courtly expectations as well as following on from the mixed gender of the earlier lyric Lady.[58] The fact that the marguerite is posited as the preferable norm should not blind us to the fact that the lily is elevated above the norm and recalls the models of the Christian virago and of the unattainable courtly Lady. Moreover, both flowers are commended as inhibiting lust, or at any rate its direct expression, in the beholder who desires them. Either can therefore be loved only in sublimated modes. Thus Machaut's poem at once tempts the reader to *jouissance* and bars her or him from it by the standard Lacanian obstructions of beauty and virtue.

Of the two flowers in Machaut's *dit*, the Pearl-Maiden is closer in presen-tation to the lily. Authoritative, severe and otherworldly, she recalls such other great visionary guides as Boethius's Lady Philosophy, the *Roman de la Rose*'s Reason and Deguileville's Grâce Dieu, all spokesmaidens for transcendent against secular realms and for the ultimate impossibility of compromise between the two. Lapidary, the Pearl-Maiden is distanced from compliant feminine objects of male heterosexual desire, and desire such as the Jeweller's to enjoy her takes sodomitical forms, at once incestu-ous and excessively exogamous.[59] It is all the more significant therefore that the Maiden, and indeed *Pearl* itself, occupy the same structural position as does Machaut's marguerite (and not his lily), poised between prized material beauty and hagiography, the courtly and the religious, at once connecting these realms and organizing them hierarchically:

> Chascuns scet c'une marguerite,
> En France, en Ynde et en Egypte,
> C'est une pierre precieuse

> Qu'est mout digne et mout vertueuse,
> Et dames et signeurs s'en perent
> Pour ce que plus cointe en apperent.
> Sainte Marguerite jadis
> Fu sainte et est en paradis.
>
> (ll. 261–8)

(Everyone knows that in France, India and Egypt a marguerite is a precious stone most worthy and with many virtues, and ladies and lords adorn themselves with it in order to appear more elegant. Saint Margaret was once a saint and is now in Paradise.)

Whereas Machaut's marguerite emphasizes the continuum between these domains, the Pearl-Maiden represents a pivotal point between fundamentally incommensurate perspectives, distinguishing them stably and hierarchically for the reader. She specifically does not cross the river separating the world occupied by living humans even out of body from that of the blessed who, having passed through fleshly death, live forever in Christ. Yet she is clearly a mediator, meeting the Jeweller as near to that barrier as is possible in order to channel his desire towards the Christian truth that she also marks as ultimately irreconcilable with earthly perspectives. In this duality she parallels the poem itself, whose effect is to yoke together in hierarchy what it also establishes as incompatible: the highest manifestations of courtliness with an elite spirituality.[60] The vision's main function is not to supply cognitive knowledge (the Jeweller identifies the New Jerusalem from John's description, showing that he is already familiar with it) but to orient and train longing in the direction of revelation.[61] Against ideally inexhaustible satisfaction, the inflationary nature of human desires appears greedy. This rhetorical contrast can evidently be used in various contexts, and can emphasize conveniently either mode or object of desire. No doubt this trope is relevant to Bowers's social reading of *Pearl's* demanding labourers: in the late Middle Ages, inflation is the curse of the modern world as well as its condition of possibility.[62] One political answer to inflation is just to say no. With the help of a king (or his poet) acting as a therapist, his subjects may realize that *jouissance* is not withheld by a tyrant but is simply impossible, and thus accept their lack. With an essential proviso, however: *Pearl's* final section draws out the moral that submissiveness on earth to God's will earns its reward in the hereafter. 'Now al be to þat Prynce3 paye' (l. 1176; 'Now let everything be at that Prince's pleasure'), sighs the Jeweller after his exile, in contrast to the folly of desiring which impelled him across the stream. Unlike Lacanian psychoanalysis, *Pearl* promotes a transcendent figure capable of withholding and bestowing *jouissance*.

Heavenly fulfilment underwrites deferral of satisfaction on earth, justify-
ing the labourers' and Jeweller's willingness to suffer denial in the here
and now. Civilization's discontents will be answered by God; meanwhile,
resigned contentment is the practical solution.

In spite of the advice to give up on our earthly desire, however, human
desire's inflationary demand for more than its allotted share is not in *Pearl*
really a cause of disorder. Contrariwise, it sustains heaven's prestige as an
object of desire and authority in the poem, as the Jeweller seeks ever more
and closer contact with the divine. This desire is evidently necessary if
humans are to progress towards the goal that God has set them. Who
could not desire heaven, and what would be the consequences of such a
position? One answer is rebellion, as Bowers suggests; another is proposed
in the poem's mournful opening section. Heaven intervenes to reinstall the
symbolic order that the Jeweller has lost. He must learn again to desire in
relation to 'the barrier separating the [R]eal from reality'. Human desire
will be transfigured in heaven, but on earth its proper form is inflationary.
What needs readjustment is therefore the object and not the mode of desire;
real-life labourers are urged to focus not on the dross of their earthly wages
but to read those as a metaphor and their paltry nature as an anamorphosis,
raising their eyes to the true prize that is their afterlife reward.

My analysis of the 'more and more' form of desire in the poem – which
is, in my view, also the poem's analysis – coincides with Lacan's account
of courtly love. To recap briefly on material covered at length in Chapter
2, above: according to Lacan, desire is torn between an impulse towards
a fulfilment which would be the death of desire, hence the destitution of
the subject, and an inertia impelling us towards a frustration that enables
desire to spring anew, and therefore subjective life to continue. The former
impulse, in Lacanian terminology, represents desire's 'goal', the latter its
'aim'. Humans move within this field, now nearer, now more distant, and
our constant circling round the goal allows anything that stands within the
field to masquerade as the ultimately fulfilling object of desire. Approaching
the goal provokes anxiety, and it is with relief as well as disappointment
that we fall back under the sway of the (un)pleasure principle, whose job
is to allow us to enjoy as little as possible. Courtly desire, for Lacan, is
distinguished by its attention to maintaining this circuit over reaching
the final object, and by its consequent emphasis on the 'vacuole': the
unbearably stimulating, terrifying black hole that all this circling generates
at the centre of the structure of desire. In *Pearl*, the Jeweller's trajectory is
one of mounting excitement and impatience, realized as increasing visual
proximity to his apparent goal and ending with a frenzied attempt to cross

the final boundary. This returns him to the circuit of frustration, thus satisfying desire's aim. Filling out the central vacuole with the Christian God, the vision in *Pearl* gratifies its earthly subjects by reassuring them that an ultimately fulfilling object of desire exists and will one day be achievable, while at the same time postponing the approach to it until after death. By making that approach contingent on moral and spiritual behaviour in life, it displaces but does not avoid the anxiety that such an approach must provoke. The Jeweller's failure is therefore a necessary part of the vision's consolation as well as of its ideological functioning, the courtly analysis supporting an ethics of deferral which applies both to late fourteenth-century English politics and to the good Christian's relation to God. This accords to the Lacanian vision of human life in which, as observed earlier, we are reconciled to temporary suspension of our wishes and submit realistically to the dominant order. When *Pearl* appears to expose courtly love's shortcomings in the face of eternity, it serves courtly hegemony.

Desiring marguerites

The shift from the Pearl-Maiden to the Lamb as object of desire is anticipated in other marguerite works but develops significantly on those precedents. Both Machaut and Froissart make their marguerite belong to the sun, its lord and beloved, superior to the writer. The poet of Machaut's 'Dit de la marguerite' may fantasize about plucking his marguerite and 'li porter a ma bouche, a mon oueil, / Et a loisir / Baisier, touchier, odourer et sentir' (ll. 39–41; 'bear her to my mouth, to my eye, and at leisure kiss, touch, smell and feel her'); his intimacy is limited by the poem's opening lines:

> J'aim une fleur, qui s'uevre et qui s'encline
> Vers le soleil de jours quant il chemine,
> Et, quant il est couchiez sous sa courtine
> Par nuit obscure,
> Elle se clot, einsois que li jours fine.
>
> (ll. 1–5)

(I love a flower that opens and that inclines towards the sun by day when he is out and about, and when he has retired behind his curtain in the dark night, she closes herself up before the day ends.)

'Rien plus ne vueil' (l. 44; 'Nothing more I want'): as in same poet's later 'Dit de la fleur de lis et de la marguerite', the marguerite satiates, liberating the subject from desire's 'more and more' nature. In the course of the 'Dit de la marguerite' the marguerite's physical presence recedes while its emotional presence to the poet increases, and he declares himself satisfied with increasingly distant mediations. 'Dous Pensers' (l. 83; 'Sweet Thought'), a wind blowing from her country and his single-minded devotion to her service are sufficient to sustain him in life, health and honour (ll. 96, 118–19). His love overwhelms and inhabits him so intensely that it may even survive him, for he envisages 'mon ame, moy mort' (l. 170; 'my soul, me being dead') continuing to love and serve the marguerite. Ultimately the flower is absorbed into the sun figure of the opening lines:

> C'est li solaus qui esclaire et qui luit,
> C'est la lune qui fait la clere nuit,
> C'est l'estoile qui par mer me conduit.
> (ll. 178–80)

(It is the sun which gives light and shines, it is the moon which makes the bright night, it is the star guiding me at sea.)

The marguerite dissolves in a chain of metaphors of guidance, inspiration and maintenance that runs through the whole sixteen-line stanza. There is no shift of allegiance but a suavely realized continuum, his commitment to her elegantly expressing the poet's dependence on and affectionate esteem for his patron.[63] 'Lys' maintains the same pattern in a more religious orientation, as the sun adored by the chaste marguerite 'fleurs, fruit et tous biens meüre / Par l'ordenance de Nature' (ll. 257–8; 'brings flowers, fruit and all good things to ripeness by the disposition of Nature'). She emanates from the sun, a privileged signifier of his goodness and might.

Froissart's 'Dit de la marguerite' ('Flor') develops different positions for poet, marguerite and patron and substantially complicates the networks of desire between them. 'Flor' initially establishes the marguerite as beloved. The poet cannot get his fill of looking at her (ll. 10–11) and finds her unmatched in virtue and beauty. He hopes for further joy in reward for his devotion, and comments that he has lived in hope for a long while (ll. 39–40). It is clear early on that this peerless creature is abstracted from multiple individual flowers, since it can be found in all seasons (l. 9) and in all green places, growing equally in 'le praiiel d'un hermitte' (l. 19; 'a hermit's meadow') and in 'les biaus gardins d'Egipte (l. 21; 'the beautiful gardens of Egypt'). The marguerite next becomes the figure for female desire in bereavement, through the origin myth of Herès and Cepheüs; daisies sprang from the earth seedlessly, a metamorphosis of her tears after his death (ll. 65–82). Mercury then enters, lovelorn discoverer of Cepheüs' tomb and of the surrounding daisies. He marvels:

> Car en jenvier,
> Que toutes flours sont mortes pour l'ivier,
> Celle perchut blancir et vermillier
> Et sa coulour viveté tesmongnier.
> Lors dist en soi: 'Or ai mon desirier!'
>
> (ll. 96–100)

(For in January, when all flowers are dead because of winter, he saw this one white and crimson, its colour testifying to liveliness. Then he said to himself, 'Now I have my desiring!')

He makes a garland which he sends via Iris to Ceres, his love, who returns the message that 'jamais jour n'amera sans partie' (l. 116; 'he [Mercury] will never love unrequitedly'). The poet laments that his own fate is not so, though he still has high hopes. He declares again his devotion to the marguerite and compares his love with that of Mercury, whom the poet claims to emulate in his devotion to the marguerite and whose happy standing with his lady he would like to enjoy. From jealousy of Mercury the poet turns to fears of losing the marguerite, spoiled by the touch of a human hand 'ne rudes ne villains' (l. 140; 'rough or ignoble'), and fantasizes about the possibility of enclosing the flower for himself alone – a far cry from the egalitarian ubiquity celebrated in the opening. The poem turns to a competition between lovers:

> S'en ce parti vivoie, nul millour
> Ne doit querir
> Homs, ce m'est vis, qui tant aimme et desir
> La flour que fai, car n'ai aultre desir
> Que del avoir, pour veoir a loisir
> Au vespre clore et au matin ouvrir
> Et le solel de tout le jour sieuir
> Et ses florons contre lui espanir.
> Tele vertu doit on bien conjoïr
> A mon semblant;
> Si fai je, voir: la gist tout mon plaisir.
>
> (ll. 159–69)

(If I lived in this condition, no one ought to seek for a better, it seems to me, who loves and desires the flower as I do, for I have no other desire than to have it so as to watch, at my leisure, it closing in the evening and opening in the morning, and following the sun all day long and spreading its flowerets for him. Such virtue should be celebrated, in my view. And indeed I do so: therein lies all my pleasure.)

The poet's pre-eminence thus lies in his toleration of his beloved's prefer-ence for another, the sun which both displays and shields the marguerite, forming a barrier between her and other lovers which renders her more desirable (ll. 49–63). Although he begins by lauding the marguerite's gen-erous spreading of itself across social and cultural conditions, the poet ends by coveting the flower, fearing for it and enclosing it within a limiting, conventionally courtly model. In the course of the poem he therefore loses the flower, for he loses what he prizes in it. Not enjoying exclusive posses-sion of the flower is painful, but aspiring to own it in this way is evidently a worse option. Froissart's marguerite is finally to be enjoyed only vicariously, as the object of a sovereign's pleasure.

This is not the end, though; the poet goes on:

> Il m'est avis, le jour que le remir,
> Qu'i ne me puet que tous biens avenir.
> Et pour l'amour d'une seule a cui tir,
> Dont je ne puis que de regars joïr
> (C'est assés peu, mais ce me faut souffrir),
> Toutes les voel honnourer et servir
> D'or en avant,
> Et si proumech a la flourette, quant
> Es lieus vendrai la ou il en croist tant,
> Tout pour l'amour de la ditte devant
> J'en quoellerai une ou .II. en riant,
> Et si dirai, son grant bien recordant:
> 'Vechi la flour qui me tient tout joiant'.
>   (ll. 170–82)

(It seems to me, in the day when I look on it, that only all good things can come to me from it. And for the love of one alone to whom I aspire and whom I can enjoy only by sight (which is little enough, but I must put up with it), I wish to honour and serve them [feminine plural] all henceforward. And I promise the little flower that when I come into a place where many of them grow, all for the love of the aforementioned one I shall laughingly gather one or two, and then I shall say, recalling her great worth, 'Here is the flower which keeps me all joyful.')

His devotion to the singular, unpossessable marguerite will impel him to pluck flowers whenever possible. The relation between the universal and the particular allows the poet to promise himself amorous satisfactions, the marguerite's proxies compensating for her own inaccessibility, as Ceres promises Mercury love always requited but not necessarily by her. Each individual petal of every flower found by the poet bears one of Love's darts to inflame him; the unattainable object of desire is the very fount of particular, plural desires, these latter presumably corporeal and satisfiable. Constancy is maintained by promiscuity, so long as each individual flower is approached as an avatar of the marguerite, sole object of the poet's constant affection.

Thus Froissart turns Machaut's single-minded devotion awry. The positions are superficially similar but the effects are opposed. In the 'Dit de la marguerite', Machaut's flower is unique and irreplaceable, the mere thought of her more rewarding than possession of all other flowers could be.[64] The erotic substitutions instigated by Froissart's marguerite are quenched by Machaut's, as it also extinguishes inflationary desire directed towards the flower itself. For Froissart, however, the marguerite initiates and supports a series of substitutions which allow the subject to maintain his satisfactions at a tolerable, manageable level according to the pleasure principle – neither too much nor too little. Becoming through her a handler of the chains of signification that make up the symbolic order, he also becomes a poet. Whereas Froissart celebrates dissemination, plurality and substitution, Machaut in 'Lys' presents 'marguerite' as the original and exemplary signifier:

> Et aussi chascuns aperçoit
> Que c'est li plus biaus nons qui soit,
> Et je croy tout certeinnement
> Que cils nons fu premierement
> Que ne furent les autres nons:
> Pour c'en est si grans li renons.
>
> (ll. 269–74)

(And also everyone perceives that it is the most beautiful name there is; and I believe quite firmly that this name existed first, before other names: and for this reason is its renown so great.)

The idea of poetic as well as of erotic activity implied here is very different from Froissart's revision.

The French texts I have been analysing emphasize the shift from a relatively socially humble setting, whose occupiers take direct and straightforward pleasure in the marguerite, to an elevated context in which both desiring subject and desired object are mysterious to the narrator. They accept and acclaim the marguerite as the possession of a higher authority while asserting that it can for that very reason be enjoyed by the poet in his own, lesser pursuit of pleasure. *Pearl* follows this pattern but develops it differently. It similarly emphasizes the overlord's pleasure; indeed, this dominates the final section of the poem, where the link-word 'paye' ('pleasure') is on almost every occasion joined to the alliterating 'Prince'.

However, the Jeweller initially positions himself not as another legitimate though secondary enjoyer of the marguerite, but as one who must realign his own desire because this otherwise competes with that of the prince; and while no effective rivalry is possible, his desire is nevertheless significant for its rebelliousness. His new primary goal must be to interpret and satisfy the prince's desire, itself focused on his submission; this is to be achieved by identifying with the marguerite, learning to desire and possess her in a different way.

Faced with the impossibility of possessing his marguerite, *Pearl*'s Jeweller turns not to substitute objects but to emulation, aiming to become like her an object for the delectation of a mighty overlord: 'He gef vus to be his homly hyne / And precious perle3 vnto his pay (ll. 1211–12; 'May he grant us to be workers of his own household, and precious pearls to his pleasure'). The potential which the chain of substitutions and significations opens up for the Jeweller, therefore, is not that of which Froissart's persona takes advantage – the not inconsiderable pleasures to be gleaned from consciously allowing one's desire to enter into that chain and from its dexterous manipulation (these pleasures are available to the *Pearl*-poet, in distinction to his unwriterly first-person narrator, but are not dramatized within the poem). Nor is it that construed by Machaut's later *dit*, of the Incarnational bridge redeeming earthly desires in heavenly ones. In *Pearl*, the chain as it presents itself to the Jeweller offers not only the possibility of taking pleasure in an object whose value is enhanced because it is also the object of the Other's desire, but also the possibility, by submitting to the Other's desire, of becoming oneself an object of the Other's pleasure. For Lacan, influenced by Kojève's interpretation of Hegel, desire is always 'le désir de l'Autre', a complex notion which includes desire for the Other, desire of the Other's object of desire, and desire to be the object of the Other's desire. The Jeweller's final fantasy of becoming another marguerite and thus the Prince's (l. 1212) therefore represents a logical though surprising extension of the French court poets' desire; neither identifies with the feminine, aristocratic marguerite, and thus *Pearl*'s vision is significantly more humanly levelling and homogenizing – a thrust associated both with the rebellious vineyard labourers and with heaven itself. It also expresses a central human tendency according to Lacanian thinking.[65] Not that the Other here is found wanting; the various arguments relating to heaven's sufficiency, where the rule is 'more and neuer þe lesse', allow the heavenly Prince to desire without lacking.

When considering the moral lesson that in order to please the Other one ought to try to desire no more than is granted to one, it is important to remember that the Jeweller attracts the Prince's notice by his act of attempted transgression. He insists on this in the poem's final section:

> When I schulde start in þe strem astraye,
> Out of þat caste I watȝ bycalt:
> Hit watȝ not at my Prynceȝ paye.
> Hit payed hym not þat I so flonc
> Ouer meruelous mereȝ, so mad arayde.
> Of raas þaȝ I were rasch and ronk,
> ȝet rapely þerinne I watȝ restayed.
>
> (ll. 1162–8)

(When I was about to plunge wrongly into the stream, I was summoned out of that purpose: it was not my Prince's pleasure. It did not please him that I in such frenzy flung myself over marvellous waters. However eager and impetuous I was in my headlong course, I was smartly restrained in that.)

The inflationary and transgressive logic earlier shown to characterize human desire also has its part to play in the Jeweller's submission:

> To þat Prynceȝ paye hade I ay bente,
> And ȝerned no more þen watȝ me gyuen,
> And halden me þer in trwe entent,
> As þe perle me prayed þat watȝ so þryuen,
> As helde, drawen to Goddeȝ present,
> To mo of his mysterys I hade ben dryuen;
> Bot ay wolde man of happe more hente
> Þen moȝte by ryȝt vpon hem clyuen.
> Þerfore my ioye watȝ sone toriuen,
> And I kaste of kytheȝ þat lasteȝ aye.
>
> (ll. 1189–98)

(If I had always bent to that Prince's pleasure, and longed for no more than was given to me, and had stopped myself there, in faithful intent, as the pearl who was so fair requested, most likely I would have been guided to more of God's mysteries, drawn to God's presence; but always man wants to seize more happiness than falls to him by right. For this reason was my joy soon torn apart, and I cast out of lands that last forever.)

In concluding that he would have seen more had his excessive desire not prevented him, the Jeweller points the difficulties of freeing oneself from this earthly form of desire and of adopting heaven's. He also, however, demonstrates the value of this inherently extremist desire in leading us towards, and not only away from, the true, final object. Inflationary 'courtly love' is here awarded a place within the economy of Christian desiring as a temporary perceptual aberration which brings the Jeweller the special favours of the Pearl-Maiden's visitation and the vision of the New Jerusalem, melding his vision with the apostle's.[66] This is in line with the ideological exploitation of anamorphosis discussed in the first part of this chapter. However, as I have argued above, 'courtly love' is induced in the Jeweller by the vision. In *Pearl*, queer desires and identifications 'stand for' sublimation and for piety. The Jeweller's initial difficulties over the lost pearl are something else, and it is with a return to this unformed something that I close this chapter.

FULL CIRCLE?

Famously, *Pearl*'s final line links back to its first. This circular structure recalls that of some late medieval fixed lyric forms, such as the rondeau, where the opening strophe acts as a refrain to each of the remaining strophes, resulting in a series of returns to the beginning. Part of the art of working with such a form lies in making the return or refrain seem different at each reprise; the final repetition in particular may mark a significant realignment of the poem as a whole. This is so with *Pearl*, which returns us to the Jeweller's heartache and confusion. Christopher Cannon has recently argued that the formally realized theme of circularity emphasizes how grief remains intractable in the face of consolation, and God's ways incomprehensible to the human mind.[67] I end this chapter by considering the role in *Pearl* of the return of the inconsolable, linking that to two distinct ways of understanding the function of anamorphosis within the poem.

Read from beginning to end once only, the later parts of the poem seem to answer the problems of melancholy, mourning and lethargy posed in the early section. A recognizably courtly experience is given new and personal meaning not, as in many other poets' work, by the intervention of secular scholarship (classics, science, history) but by the revivifying return to and reworking of sacred text. The question of what to write about, which faces so many late medieval writers, is here answered resoundingly with Christian material, itself revivified by being filtered through the courtly discourses of the dream vision poem, *dit amoureux* and marguerite. Within *Pearl*'s visionary space, heaven dominates earth by imposing its own construction of the latter as a distortion, ethically inferior though heuristically useful, of the former. From a different perspective, earth dominates heaven, for the latter is conceived within the courtly framework as the courtly topos of the 'improved' court; even the biblical labourers with their uncouth demands are portrayed as embryonic courtly lovers. Thus the court and the courtly link heaven and earth and determine the limits of the poem's strictly discursive universe. Even where earthly subjects are urged to give up desiring 'more and more', that desire is shown to be a route, via transgression, to immortality in the Christian afterlife for those who are less innocent and more sophisticated than the dead infant. The urgency and demand generated by the Maiden as a figure 'between two deaths' is put to the service of a courtly ideology which is also a Christian one: make a sacrifice to the Other of your desire, for only so can you achieve the desire of the Other, which is the real object of your quest. Anamorphosis is absorbed into, indeed a key element of, the poem's ideological functioning.

This is not, however, the end of the matter. The 'constant dialectic' between 'pattern and resistance to pattern' that A. C. Spearing noted in *Pearl* powers both ideological pattern and its unstructured remainder.[68] If we resist the pressure to look exclusively from the combined viewpoints of the revealed Truth and of the court, we see a different perspective in the formless world glimpsed before the vision begins; and this is more evident when a rondeau-style reading returns us to the opening section to repeat our early experience of the poem. This procedure emphasizes not 'more and more' desire, shown to be inferior yet also recuperable into and indeed supportive of heavenly desire. Instead it highlights the loss suffered by the I-persona (not yet a Jeweller?) and his attempts to come to terms with it by assuring himself of its utility within a notion of the greater good. We see repeated his inability fully to accept this argument. The sense persists of a loss that resists compensation, rationalization or symbolization, and that is materialized in the unredeemed, palpitating life-substance and in the contaminated vision spoiling human reality for the mourner.[69] This loss, associated in Lacanian psychoanalysis not with desire but with drive, is present in the poem as both life's base substance and as unliveable. Thus the dream vision purports to transform that loss into a lack which can act as the black hole at the centre of the symbolic order, undermining and grounding that order by means of the inflationary logic of desire. Substitution is no doubt the way for life to continue; in the end the poem itself is commended to the prince as the pearl that the Jeweller (at last a poet?) has brought to birth around his tears. *Pearl* thus foregrounds something more or less directly addressed in the poems I have discussed in this chapter, namely that the marguerite can be enjoyed only where loss is converted into lack, drive into desire. One must 'give up on one's desire' in order to occupy a coherent, valued place within the symbolic order.[70] This is justified in *Pearl* through the notion of redemptive sacrifice. But the poem also foregrounds a human wanting which resists both the dialectic of desire and the discourse of sacrifice, and this resistance in a way pays the lost pearl closer and deeper attention than does its sublation into the Pearl-Maiden. Nor is it lacking in artistry, even though it rejects what the poem advances as the conditions for the symbolic. On the contrary, it is the distinctive work of art, for Lacan as for Heidegger, to induct the Real into the human world (if an artwork fails to do so then it is mere formal experiment or pastiche). Thus *Pearl* allows us a glimpse, a temporary intuition, of a non-ideological Real before and after the vision. It seems, from the way the poem backs away from and marginalizes it, that this is not a poetic position to be occupied long-term; nevertheless, it does show us an art of loss unconverted into lack, thus moving from desire to drive. Anamorphosis, in this understanding, presents us with a Real which escapes the poem's courtly, Christian ideology.

Identifying hallmarks of the Real ought not to blind us to the fact that the poem's opening section sketches a coherent, though hardly fully expressed, ethics. The individual's loss feeds the collective – literally, as the seed-pearl is imagined to grow into wheat. Those who do not share my pain and about whom I do not specially care nevertheless benefit from my loss. This account appears only as a metaphor, but, after all, the whole poem is metaphorical; neither its figurative nature nor its failure to console the Jeweller diminishes this early account's ethical status. Here loss is not negated by being reinterpreted as sacrifice, sublation or recompense; only its material usefulness to others is affirmed, and that remains vague, as generalization or hypothesis – certainly it does not amount to a coherent symbolic system of exchange and substitution. The Jeweller's *entre-deux-morts*, although converted in the course of the poem into a Christian understanding of that state as one of submission to the Lord, at the poem's beginning and possible repetitive end makes an acceptance of subjective destitution the basis for another ethics of the Real, which could push both the court and Christianity in a significantly different direction from that elaborated within the dream vision. There is potential for a new order here, however marginally; one that might conceivably permit the labourers to move from rebellion to revolution.

On the other hand – and this constitutes my final argumentative turn – the persistence of loss within the poem is also its strongest argument for Christianity. Religion would be of little worth if it did not address the very gravest human problems, while to pretend that faith simply cures or obliterates grief would be trivial. The challenge gives the measure of the response. Exactly by escaping and even countering the poem's ideology, the non-ideological Real provides the supplement or constitutive exception which grounds that ideology, thus it is in the Jeweller's unaccounted-for pain that God is most manifest. The Reality that overflows human reality is His – He is the life-substance persisting beyond death, scandalizing our norms and nullifying our knowledge. Our second understanding of anamorphosis therefore folds back into the first. The stain remains across the artwork's foreground, to become a lure addressing the reader: you may not know God but you do have contact with the Real. Make your experience meaningful by accepting the doctrine here presented as His, though you know it to be factitious. Through its final repetition, *Pearl* calls upon its readers to confront themselves in their most meaningless and painful experience as shapeless oysters – the parallel with Riefenstahl's sea-life is suggestive – for out of that confrontation a pearl 'perfected in [its] incompleteness' may come to birth.[71]

We thus find in *Pearl* Christianity interwoven between the three Lacanian registers, evident from the various critiques above. Whereas Christianity's imaginary aspect in the poem makes it seem 'clubbish' in the insistent homophilia and satisfaction of the heavenly horde, the symbolic shows it to be 'thin-blooded' and calculating in its proposal to overlook the death of a fleshly child in favour of her formal exaltation, while the Real emphasizes its 'unsociable' quality through the isolation of the bereft Jeweller. These shortcomings are even highlighted in the text. Following a logic that is at once characteristically Christian and typically courtly, the poem's ideology 'finds a redemptive truth precisely in th[e] most unpropitious of places'.[72] As in earlier chapters the king's inadequacies raised him above rational challenge and the courtly beloved's failings guaranteed his desirability, so in *Pearl* the vision invading and overwhelming human life is ultimately authenticated by its alien, unreal and illogical quality.

CHAPTER 5

Becoming woman in Chaucer: on ne naît pas femme, on le devient en mourant

This final chapter considers the various relations between female characters, ideals of femininity and death in two poems by Chaucer: the early *Book of the Duchess* and later *Legend of Good Women*, principally the Prologue.[1] Both poems foreground figures between two deaths. The *Legend* is dominated by Alceste who, herself returned from the dead, colours the heroines of the legends, while the *Book* throngs with undead. I explore the explanatory value for these poems of an anthropological account relating to funerary rites of passage by which a deceased person is detached from the community of the living and, after a threatening liminal stage, is integrated into the community of the dead. I find that this model accentuates the normative and socially constructive uses of the 'between two deaths', thus it enhances understanding of how the dead lady central to the *Book* is elevated as a feminine exemplar. The absence in the *Legend* of such a close fit between theory and text is itself productive, enabling us at once to refine the anthropological model and to argue that the *Legend* works against certain normative constructions of femininity exemplified in the *Book*. I return to a Lacanian model in analysing the more disturbing figures in both poems.

My subtitle derives from the famous opening line of volume II of Beauvoir's *Le Deuxième Sexe*: 'On ne naît pas femme: on le devient', in Parshley's translation: 'One is not born, but rather becomes, a woman' – a rendering of Beauvoir's insistence on the subject's existentialist freedom and becoming. Contrastingly, the recent translation by Borde and Malovany-Chevallier reads: 'One is not born, but rather becomes, woman', foregrounding the feminine archetype.[2] Beauvoir's text examines the interactions between female subjects and essentializing myths, and I follow her lead in investigating the role of death in producing either woman or a woman – an archetype or a subject capable of interacting creatively with the givens of gender. In the *Book of the Duchess* the lady's elevation depends on her laudable willingness to leave the land of the living for that of the dead, whereas the virtuous women of the *Legend of Good Women* take their stand in a zone between earthly and heavenly life, resisting both passage into the afterlife and the rites designed to facilitate it. This resistance is an act of political, ethical and poetic significance, and the idealized representation of these ladies is consequently of a very different order from that found in the earlier poem.

DOUBLE OBSEQUIES

French anthropologist Robert Hertz, a student of Durkheim's, published in 1905–6 his 'Contribution to the Study of the Collective Representation of Death'. Hertz focuses on societies in which the funerary process has two phases: death is followed initially by the temporary disposal of the body and by a period of mourning, which ends with a secondary burial involving the permanent disposal of the body and the memorialization of the deceased, these last elements sometimes separated in time but in essence parts of a single process through which the death will be 'fully consummated'.[3] The period between death and the final obsequies permits a process of social disaggregation, gradually detaching the dead person from the collectivity to which he or she belonged in life. During this period the dead person is placeless, belonging fully to neither the land of the living nor the land of the dead. 'Pitiful and dangerous', it exerts a continued claim on its mourners' solicitude (which must ensure its successful passage to the afterlife) while threatening them: 'It finds the solitude into which it has been thrust hard to bear and tries to drag the living with it.'[4] The mourners themselves mirror the deceased's 'illegitimate and clandestine' existence beyond the bounds of the community.[5] Considered impure, they must remain isolated, distinguished by their dress, diet and activities: 'They live in darkness, dead themselves from a social point of view, because any active participation on their part in collective life would only spread abroad the curse they carry in them.'[6] Hertz uses paradoxical and sometimes poetic expressions to articulate the strange existence in which both deceased and mourners are trapped during this intermediary or liminal period. Secondary burial ends this temporary suspension of everyday life and social cohesion, and brings about a dual restoration. It liberates the living and returns them to earthly society while marking the soul's rebirth as a full member of the invisible community of the dead. Regenerating the survivors and revitalizing earthly society, secondary burial also causes the deceased definitively to cast aside its polluting mortal remains to emerge in a purified, idealized form, 'reborn transfigured and raised to a superior power and dignity' consonant with the status of the afterworld.[7] Only once the deceased is cleanly separated from the world of the living can a lasting memorial be constructed marking the absence of what it commemorates. In its new incarnation the soul may become a benign guardian spirit protecting and guiding the living. The purpose of the intermediary period between physical death and final burial is to perform this metamorphosis of 'a familiar person ... like ourselves' into 'an ancestor', 'sometimes worshipped and always distant'.[8]

Hertz describes the function of this metamorphosis as psychological and psychosocial. The belief that the soul 'only gradually severs the ties binding it to this world' expresses the emotional challenge facing the survivors who must let the dead person go. Similarly society confronts the loss of 'the social being grafted upon the physical individual', a being which the collective has carefully formed over a long period.[9] The notion of death's finality threatens to annihilate society, and thus the very terms on which life can be lived, and must be deflected into the idea of regeneration and rebirth. Secondary burial aims to transform a traumatic perception of loss into an orderly, healing apprehension of a greater pattern in which death is necessary to and a source of life.[10]

A crucial point which remains tangential to Hertz's work though developed by some other thinkers is that this final reconciliation, a function of the living's deliverance from the disorientation of grief, makes the deceased available for political exploitation.[11] The definitively dead and gone are henceforth conjured as spirits to serve the interests of the dominant survivors, though constrained significantly by the degree to which social conventions defy manipulation. The dead, in short, enter the transcendent world only on terms set by the living. Recent anthropological thinking emphasizes the performative and competitive aspects of ritual, against the Durkheimian (and Hertzian) view that ritual represents and perpetuates existing social structures. Rituals 'are not productions from cultural templates or "expressions" of structure, but instead are acts of power in the fashioning of structures: acts that make gods, kings, presidents, and property-rights by declaring that the authority of the priest, judge or police officer resides in a higher source, a *mana*, *dharma* or constitution'.[12] Chaucer's *Book of the Duchess* illustrates such a use of ritual in the service of one powerful player in late fourteenth-century English politics.

BOOK OF THE DUCHESS

Told in the first person, the *Book* recounts how after prolonged insomnia the narrator reads the story of Ceyx and Alcyone, in which a mourning queen is informed of her husband's death by his temporarily reanimated corpse, and eventually falls asleep.[13] Waking into his dream he follows a courtly party hunting a hart and meets a knight in deep mourning. His uncomprehending questioning prompts the knight to recall in lengthy detail his beloved lady. Her fate is initially referred to through the mediation of courtly forms, but because the narrator fails to understand the fact of her untimely death, the knight finally states it in a blunt form which the narrator immediately acknowledges, bringing both dream and poem to a rapid close.

The Man in Black's lady has been brutally torn out of her own and others' lives. It is clear from her lover's emotional state that this loss is unresolved; outcast from society, 'Always deyinge and . . . not ded' (l. 588; 'always dying and . . . not dead'), his deathly life is closely reminiscent of Hertz's description of the mourner.[14] Unable even to contemplate engaging with life, the Man in Black feels excluded from and yearns for death (ll. 679–90). If, as Hertz has it, 'mourning is merely the direct consequence in the living of the actual state of the deceased', then the Man's condition implies that his lady's death remains unconsummated.[15] Expelled from the community of the living, she has yet to be incorporated into that of the dead. It is not so much that she is an unquiet spirit, as that her mourner cannot resolve his loss. The former role is borne for her by the narrator who has 'felynge in nothyng' (l. 11; 'no feeling'), and who appears at the swooning Man's 'fet' (l. 502) just as the body of Ceyx returned earlier to the 'fet' of Alcyone's bed (l. 199): half-life messengers bringing news of a loved one's demise. Like Ceyx's, the lady's treatment to date has only functioned as a partial ritual which cries out to be made whole – though not with the same outcome.[16] The *Book of the Duchess* represents itself as responding to this need in a way which corresponds to the lady's secondary burial. The narrator elicits from the Man in Black an elegiac portrait and narrative which conjure his lady and their love in idealized form. This process involves a forgetting which becomes increasingly evident, for instance when the knight does not record the actual words by which the lady initially rejected him, only their import for himself (ll. 1236–44). The narrator's scepticism driving the Man on (ll. 1042–53), his experiences and emotions come into focus while hers remain indistinct; she is generalized as he is particularized. Knight and lady act out the purgative process which is the *raison d'être* of Hertz's intermediary period, ending with their tranquil departure in opposite directions. Memorialized as the perfect woman, 'goode faire White' (l. 948) enters the transcendent beyond and passes out of her former lover's life, her death consummated by his performative admission that 'she ys ded' (l. 1309) – this time without the deathly swoon that accompanied his earlier efforts at articulation.

The poem draws out the public implications of these private rites. Because his mourning is demoralizing and slowly killing the magnate, it is damaging the society in which he ought to hold a prominent place and which cannot function properly without him. His return to the living community at the end of the poem is represented poetically by an abrupt shift into a different mode of signification:

> With that me thoghte that this kyng
> Gan homwarde for to ryde
> Unto a place, was there besyde,
> Which was from us but a lyte –
> A long castel with walles white,
> Be Seynt Johan, on a ryche hil,
> As me mette; but thus hyt fil.
>
> (ll. 1314–20)

(At that I thought that this king rode homeward to a place nearby, only a little way from us – a long castle with white walls, by Saint John, on a noble hill, as I dreamt; but thus it occurred.)[17]

The Man is identified as John of Gaunt by the references to the saint, the 'ryche hil' – Richmond, of which Gaunt was earl for part of his life – and the 'long castel' – Lancaster, which he acquired through his wife Blanche (d. 1368), the real-life prototype of the lady in the poem. As the Man in Black moves towards historical specificity and agency, Blanche the duchess moves in the opposite direction. The Christian ideology which in *Pearl* transforms the toddler into a living stone in the New Jerusalem is here answered by a secular ideology. Initially translated into 'goode faire White' in the poem's intermediary fiction, Blanche is now further metamorphosed. Petrified into the 'walles white' of Lancaster, she is become a 'whit wal' (l. 780) or blank canvas receptive to reinscription.[18] Thus, through secondary burial, she is installed as protectress of the building and of her House, the social group that constructs its identity around it, first and foremost her former husband. Her final separation from the everyday world guarantees her symbolic authority but deprives her of human identity, form and autonomy. The poem's funeral effigy in language operates within the narrative not as a lasting memorial but as a temporary construction easing the lady's disappearance.[19] Blanche and White are gradually erased from figuration, commemorated by incorporation into the substance of Blanche's own former castle (not White's, note), which thus becomes their non-figurative monument. Leaving the here and now altogether, the lady moves simultaneously into the fully abstract and the fully material domains. However, she is not evicted from history; rather she is given (a fixed) historical meaning. On the other side, Gaunt and the Man in Black leave the poem with enhanced prestige too, thanks not only to the lady but also to the legendary companions the Man invokes when describing his love. Initially seen in the company of contemporary males and females like (although inferior to) themselves, the lady and her lover are afterwards surrounded only by ancestors, legends of Western culture. At the same time the knight records his own adoption of the idealizing mode of lyric, itself given an ancient pedigree (ll. 1159–70). Gaunt benefits from this even more than the Man, since the dream's closing move between worlds allows the prestigious otherness of the ancestral realm(s) to be conflated with Gaunt's real life which, as here represented, acquires the air of legend (compare Deschamps's Ballade 1457, Chapter 3, above). Here as everywhere, the eternal and the transcendent as well as the private and domestic serve specific political ends.[20]

Key to the lady's idealization is the opposition between her and Fortune.[21] As the Man in Black evokes it, Fortune is not simply a force within which all human beings exist under God's law, but stands for an unbearable vision of life without the comfort of transcendence. Ruled by Fortune, earthly life is characterized by meaningless and traumatic accident and mutability (compare Lacan's Real). Pendant to this is a vision of death as a process of bodily decay and incapacitating grief which eats away at deceased and survivor, threatening to annihilate both, a death conceived without the secondary burial which transforms it into a meaningful part of the greater life cycle. According to her mourner, however, White's virtues of 'trouthe', constancy and moderation freed her from Fortune's whims and made her the living proof of a transcendent sphere. Although the Man does not appear to grasp them fully, the logical implications are clear: because even in her earthly life she made manifest the existence of God, White is the Man's means of redemption, his path to faith when he is in danger of despair because of her bodily death.

The vision of White as Beatrice-like mediator between earthly life and Christian transcendence proceeds from the secondary burial which her lover's reminiscence gives her.[22] In the Man's portrait of her, White is puri-fied of Blanche's lived (and her own fictional) singularity; those aspects of the lady's biography and character which would suggest that she lived under Fortune's sway or within time's flow are discarded and forgotten, coded thereby as inessentials and imperfections. This is not per se a denial of death, but its working through in a process comparable to the physical transformation which Hertz insists must be undergone before secondary burial can take place. The soft parts of the corpse must disappear, leaving only those considered immune to time: bones, ashes or a mummy.[23] Reduction to 'immutable elements' represents purification from life's corruption but also corresponds to the construction of a new, incorruptible body fit for the soul in the afterlife.[24] Similarly, White/Blanche's newly pure self emerges phoenix-like (ll. 982–3) from the ruins of the old mortal being. This new self is available for ideological remodelling and exploitation by her survivors. Not, of course, that the male and female members of great families were not already subject to such a process; but the lady's value and malleability are evidently augmented by her secondary burial.

Ancestral patrons may be male or female, but in the *Book of the Duchess*, transfiguration into the Lancastrians' tutelary spirit is a highly gendered process. The opposition between the lady and Fortune delimits the kind of woman she can be. Fortune, 'the trayteresse fals and ful of gyle' (l. 620; 'the false traitoress, full of guile'), epitomizes a familiar negative idealization of femininity as fickle, dangerous and sexually uncontrolled.[25] Against this stereotype stands what we may call, following Beauvoir (herself drawing on Goethe), that of the Eternal Feminine. The content of this positive type changes culturally while retaining a supposed changelessness essential to its meaning. In the incarnation in question, beauty, chastity, good sense, modesty and a kind heart are necessary but not sufficient qualities of perfected womanhood. Her fundamental attribute is her location beyond the world of change and contingency. The Eternal Feminine, unchanging and incorruptible, inhabits that timeless 'death beyond death' achieved by secondary burial, outside material existence but with symbolic authority for the life continuing on earth.[26] Secondary burial thus construes life as safe and meaningful, under the protection of a higher power which orders its events for the best in accordance with a greater plan. Earthly life and eternal life bridge the temporary state of death to minimize its destructive aspect. And in the *Book of the Duchess* the spirit embodying this transcendent vision is uncompromisingly feminized.

For living women, accessing the authority granted to the Eternal Feminine poses problems. Already in Hertz's account it is evident that entry into the company of ancestors requires the dead person to accept the necessity of his or her own death, bowing to the general interest and gracefully exiting the mortal scene. By accepting individual fate the deceased allows society to renew itself and earthly life to continue in others. The small opportunity for dissent is decreased when gendered pressures are added in.

It seems from the *Book of the Duchess* that individual women participate in the Eternal Feminine only by adopting its lofty indifference to incident and time as well as its other virtues. This further discourages women from behaving with singularity. It is true that White is elevated to universality by the rhetorical construction of her uniqueness; according to the Man she was in every way superlative, a hapax in femininity. But these qualities are not abnormalities; on the contrary they are highly normative. Insofar as they are validated by their virtues, women appear to be all the same, avatars of the Eternal Feminine. Any peculiarities which might distance them from the ideal must be forgotten, as Blanche's are; to insist on them would be perverse and invalidating and might even suggest a disastrous identification with Fortune.[27] Hence the symbolic authority granted to the Eternal Feminine is limited to activities and uses which demonstrably accord with that ideal. Furthermore, the woman who wishes to exercise this authority must recognize that she is merely a conduit for power. White is represented as authoritative only in proportion to her usefulness for those who promote her memory. As she becomes Woman, the lady ceases to be an independent agent; she must either be dead or, being alive, behave as if her autonomous or idiosyncratic self were dead. The *Book of the Duchess* thus gives exemplary form to a specific connection for women between power, death and a particular paradigm of femininity.

Blanche's absorption into the castle, material symbol of a clan's political power and longevity, makes her patron and protector of that clan and therefore available to sponsor whatever policies its prime representative chooses to follow. She becomes a potentially important piece in a strategy which aims both to bring about a desired political state and to extend it into the future. Remarriage may very well play a part in this strategy. The interpretation I have been outlining might therefore have some bearing on the question of the *Book*'s date in relation to Gaunt's remarriage in 1371. It is obvious that the secondary burial which the *Book* performs on its duchess is symbolic and suggestive, not legal and formal. There was no official prohibition to prevent Gaunt remarrying before Chaucer's poem was written, nor did its composition alter his position in law. However, the anthropological material presented here does suggest that memorializing Blanche is not incompatible with urging Gaunt to remarry, or even with retrospectively endorsing such a project.[28] Assimilation into the Eternal Feminine, the outcome of White's secondary burial, increases the possibilities contained in Blanche's fruitful absence. For the Man in Black to marry another good woman will be tantamount to having White returned to him, for all good women are in a sense avatars of the type she is brought to represent. Marrying another version of his dead lady is a way to express performatively not only his continuing love for her but also hers for him. The Man's extreme mourning, recorded in the poem, also plays its part in this construction. He is discreetly reminded of the effects of love, which once before made him 'as blyve / Reysed as fro deth to lyve' (ll. 1277–8; 'as glad as if raised from death to life'). These rites of mourning and sec-ondary burial allow the deceased to be enlisted as an advocate of her former husband's remarriage, as she joins the community of guiding spirits which preside over social renewal. Not that the poem presumes to instruct the lordly widower. The contingent and dependent nature of White's authority is demonstrated by its pliability in the service of various potential strategies on Gaunt's part.

Hertz stresses the dead person's progression through the troubling period, during which it is uncontrolled by and even hostile to society, to a final resting-place in which it is socially integrated once more. He emphasizes how survivors move correspondingly through unliveable grief towards a comfort which accommodates the altered aspects of their lives. He analyses the ways in which death is worked into a stage on the path to regenera-tion, allowing potentially traumatic changes in social and individual lives to be recuperated as part of a cycle by which life endlessly renews itself. Such a model permits variations in the social order so long as they can be anchored in a framework of continuity and tradition. Although change itself is acceptable, the potentially disruptive forces which may bring it about cannot be tolerated while they appear as such.[29] This traditionalist process is illustrated by the passing of both White and Blanche. However, a different account might emphasize the 'intermediary' period as a possible site from which opposition to the dominant order and its renewal could be elaborated. Lacan's *entre-deux-morts* provides such an account. What in many, especially older anthropological accounts is a liminal or transitional space, a description emphasizing the solidity of the 'states' between which passage must be achieved, becomes in Lacan's version a queer, uncanny site challenging the integrity of those 'states'. Lacan thus brings out the extent to which such descriptions reiterate and reinforce the desired polit-ical effect of rites of passage: the presentation of historically contingent ideological orders as coherent and durable, phenomena as natural as life and death themselves. The *entre-deux-morts*, in contrast, draws attention to the necessary incompleteness and hence incoherence of any particular order; it is, strictly speaking, revolutionary. Hence Lacan's formulation allows us to focus on ethical and political resistance to the dominant order, whereas Hertz emphasizes society's tendency to assimilate and adapt.[30]

With this alternative vision in mind, we can turn to the *Legend of Good Women*. In a poem which focuses on women true in loving all their lives, we might expect to encounter a series of Whites. However, the notion of dual obsequies allows us to appreciate the deep-seated differences which separate Alceste and her cohorts from White, and still more strikingly from Blanche.

LEGEND OF GOOD WOMEN

The *Legend of Good Women* consists of nine short narratives, with a Prologue surviving in two versions, F and G. In the Prologue the poet declares that his devotion to books is interrupted only by his preference for going out to the fields in spring to worship the daisy flower (on marguerites, see Chapter 4, above). He falls asleep and dreams that he sees a regal god of Love leading by the hand a lady whose dress recalls the daisy. They are accompanied by a host of other women, all true in love. The daisy-lady is named as Alceste (early in G, towards the end of F). The god of Love reproaches the poet-narrator for having produced in English the *Romaunt of the Rose* and *Troilus and Criseyde*, which attack him and his devotees.[31] In particular, the poet is accused of choosing to retell only women's 'wikednesse' even though wicked women are rare exceptions to the general rule of female 'goodnesse' (G.268–9, 277).[32] Alceste intervenes to disarm the god's threats by discoursing on tyranny and on the responsibility of a ruler to uphold justice and exercise mercy, at the same time advancing a series of arguments absolving the author of responsibility for the content of the works under dispute. She lists works by Chaucer, some of which, like the *Book of the Duchess*, are positively friendly to love, and others Christian in theme. The lady then suggests that the poet be required to repair the damage he has caused, and sets what she calls his 'penaunce':

> Thow shalt, whil that thow livest, yer by yere,
> The moste partye of thy tyme spende
> In makynge of a gloryous legende
> Of goode women, maydenes and wyves,
> That were trewe in lovynge al here lyves;
> And telle of false men that hem betrayen,
> That al here lyf ne don nat but assayen
> How manye wemen they may don a shame;
> For in youre world that is now holden game.
>
> (G.471–9)

(You shall while you live, year on year, spend the greatest part of your time in making a glorious legend of good women, maidens and wives, who were true in loving all their lives; and tell of false men who betray them, who all their life do nothing but try to see how many women they may disgrace; for in your world that is now considered fun.)

The poet begins his legend but the text is incomplete. The life of Alceste with which the god instructs the poet to conclude is lacking. The lives that survive are those of Cleopatra, Thisbe, Dido, Hypsipyle and Medea, Lucrece, Ariadne, Philomela, Phyllis, and Hypermnestra, this last lacking an ending.

The *Legend* has not been popular in modern times.[33] Commentators have found it repetitive and limited in range, while its insistence on a particular idea of female virtue and the way it reshapes its source material to fit that idea have caused unease. It is strange to modern eyes, for example, to see Medea rub shoulders with Lucrece as virtuous victims of male betrayal. In the *Book of the Duchess* Medea is said to have killed her children in response to her abandonment by Jason (ll. 726–7), but in the *Legend* she confines herself to writing him a letter.[34] Some critics argue that the *Legend*'s true subject is poetic activity, while others focus on the poem's relevance to issues of kingship, government and statecraft, linking this to the contemporary political situation. Critics who engage with the poem's treatment of women generally argue either that the poem endorses medieval ideas and practices relating to female virtue and understood to be unacceptable today, or that it ironizes such ideas; some impute to Chaucer an antifeminist position, others an anti-antifeminist one. In spite of this, the poem remains largely unpalatable. Moreover, arguments constructed around it often seem to leave the text behind or even to obscure it; it is almost traditional to appeal to the poem's 'obvious' qualities while contending that this surface conceals a deeper meaning requiring additional interpretation or information which must be supplied from outside the text. The *Legend* today is at once unappealing and obscure, difficult to enjoy and difficult to capture. I do not apologize for these qualities but interpret them as essential to the radical aesthetic of the Prologue. I shall argue that the *Legend* is difficult to enjoy not because it is overly conventional or because it enshrines long-dead cultural practices but because it pays insufficient regard to conventions which still today govern our lives as readers and as social beings. It is difficult to capture because its own partialities of vision produce blind spots in its readers, so that what tends to evade our attention is not what the poem omits but, surprisingly, that which it highlights. Drawing on Lacanian insights as well as on the anthropological material presented above, my analysis will focus on three central features of the poetic programme laid out in the *Legend*'s Prologue which have proven resistant to critical analysis. These relate respectively to Alceste as revenant, to repetition and to the proper topic of poetry. Comparison with the *Book of the Duchess* in each case emphasizes the significance of certain characteristics of the *Legend of Good Women*.

The revenant

The *Legend of Good Women* is placed under the aegis of someone who has returned from the grave. When the poet fails to recognize the classical figure of Alceste in the daisy-lady before him, the god of Love reminds him of her story:

> . . . and that thow knowest wel, parde,
> Yif it be so that thow avise the.
> Hast thow nat in a bok, lyth in thy cheste,
> The grete goodnesse of the queene Alceste,
> That turned was into a dayesye;
> She that for hire husbonde ches to dye,
> And ek to gon to helle rather than he,
> And Ercules rescued hire, parde,
> And broughte hyre out of helle ageyn to blys?
>
> (G.496–504)

(. . . and that you know well, indeed, if you reflect. Don't you have in a book lying in your chest the great goodness of the queen Alceste, who was turned into a daisy; she who chose to die for her husband and also to go to hell sooner than he; and Hercules rescued her, indeed, and brought her out of hell back to bliss?)

The emphasis on Alceste's return is the more evident if we compare the brief summary of her story in *Troilus and Criseyde*. Troilus objects to Cassandra when she announces Criseyde's infidelity with Diomede:

> As wel thow myghtest lien on Alceste,
> That was of creatures, but men lye,
> That evere weren, kyndest and the beste!
> For whan hire housbonde was in jupertye
> To dye hymself but if she wolde dye,
> She ches for hym to dye and gon to helle,
> And starf anon, as us the bokes telle.
>
> (V.1527–33)

(You might as well slander Alceste who, unless men lie, was of all creatures that ever were the kindest and the best! For when her husband was in danger of dying unless she would agree to die, she chose to die for him and go to hell, and perished soon, as the books tell us.)

Troilus ends Alceste's story with her dying in her husband's place, the act which makes her the paragon both of 'fyn lovynge' and 'of wifhod the lyvynge' (G.534–5; 'pure, courtly loving' and 'the behaviour expected in a wife'). In the *Legend*, however, this death has a sequel, as Alceste is rescued and returned to 'blys' by Hercules. In the mythographic works from which Chaucer is thought to have drawn her story, Alceste is restored to wedded bliss in an idealized human marriage. However, the echo of the Harrowing of Hell in Chaucer's text confers overtones of a life beyond the human, as also does the reference to metamorphosis into a daisy and the subsequent mention of stellification (G.513–14).[35]

Figuring Alceste's situation in Hertz's terms, we may say that the narrator and the god of Love discuss Alceste as if she were not only dead but had undergone secondary burial. Buried in a book which is itself entombed in a coffin-like chest, she is said to lie dormant within the poet's memory, at once familiar and comfortably forgotten.[36] She is presented in the aspect of an artefact, as submissive and adapted to the natural cycle as the heliotropic daisy (compare pp. 180–4, above):

> In remembraunce of hire and in honour
> Cibella made the dayesye and the flour
> Ycoroned al with whit, as men may se;
> And Mars yaf to hire corone red, parde,
> In stede of rubies, set among the white.
>
> (G.518–22)

(In memory and in honour of her, Cybele made the daisy and the flower crowned all with white, as men may see; and Mars gave to her crown red, indeed, for rubies, set among the white.)

By speaking as if Alceste had already undergone secondary burial, the male characters attempt to perform that rite. The image they conjure aligns Alceste with the idealized female who is the final product of the *Book of the Duchess*: a figure of authority who dispenses solace to living men and serves the interests of her male sponsors.

Even here, however, there are signals that this transformation may be more difficult than that of White. Cybele and Mars, unusual champions of the marguerite, set a combative note. Alceste's actual manifestation in the Prologue suggests a curious relationship with Hertz's intermediary period. The returned Alceste does not seem to be in an identifiable afterlife, Christian or pagan; but if she is not exactly in the land of the dead, nor is she in the land of the living. Her condition is, though, not identical to that of the *Book*'s undead duchess, which cries out for secondary burial. After her physical death, that lady's image is a construct manifested only in her lover, at first in his physical and psychic deterioration and latterly in his memorial to her; Alceste has a positive presence of her own, surging beyond death and appropriation. Whereas Lady White exemplifies Hertz's model in her initially destructive effect on the living and in her progressive enhancement, as an artefact (ironically recalling Pygmalion's Galatea), into a wholly benevolent patron spirit, Alceste is consistently creative and independent, saving the poet from the god's wrath and furnishing him with material and occasion for future productions. She nevertheless remains an ambiguous figure, restricting and domineering, never in this text safely dispatched into the symbolic land of the benignly dead. While White's authority over the living is derived from her status as a legitimized member of the eternal, spiritual community, Alceste's is associated with her survival of both physical death and attempted secondary burial. Her experience affords her knowledge designated in the Prologue's opening lines as inaccessible to mortals.[37] Insofar as the human condition necessitates mediation between earthly and transcendent, it excludes Alceste. With Alceste, the intermediary period *entre-deux-morts* becomes another scene, beyond the concrete sequence of life–death–afterlife proposed by Hertz. This placeless, undead quality is far from being associated with weakness.

The problematic authority of this resilient revenant manifests itself throughout the Prologue, although F, which concentrates on the daisy-muse, gives greater prominence to a transformed, benevolent, useful Alceste, whereas the uncompromising Alceste, resistant to glossing, on whom I am concentrating is stronger in G, as is the contrast between this figure and the product of secondary burial.[38] In each version, Alceste shows little of White's malleability. Unlike White's, her authority actually finds expression within the poem, in a direct command to the narrator and in assertion of her own wishes against those of her male companion and patron. Her decrees are not negotiable. After she has won forgiveness for the narrator by arguing that he cannot be considered responsible for those works to which the god of Love objects, the narrator himself intervenes to claim rather more authorial status. Alceste silences him sternly:

> And she answerde, 'Lat be thyn arguynge,
> For Love ne wol nat counterpletyd be
> In ryght ne wrong; and lerne this at me!'
> (G.465–7)

(And she answered, 'Cease your arguing, for Love will not be disputed with rightly or wrongly; and learn that from me!)

These lines are sometimes held to show how reasonable Alceste is by comparison with the tyrannical god of Love. Yet it is she who, in winning the argument, refuses to countenance any point of view other than her own.[39] This uncompromising absolutism also characterizes her attitude towards her husband. Her inflexible fidelity could be interpreted as tantamount to a demand for death, but death finds itself marginalized where Alceste is concerned. She dismisses its power over her not only when she dies for her husband but much more spectacularly when she returns to his side. If there was ever a love that 'wol nat countrepleted be', surely this is it ('and lerne this at me!' posits Alceste herself as the exemplar). It may seem ironic that it should be Alceste's utter refusal to accept separation from her husband which results in her final independence of that husband, himself nowhere present in the Prologue, and in her ability to bend to her own wishes the god of Love, a character often of dubious benefit to women.[40] However, Alceste's appearance in the Prologue without her husband but with her story suggests that the fact of her love has primacy over its object and that her unparalleled 'trouthe' should be understood above all as truth to her own desire, partially coincident with but not reducible to fidelity to her husband.[41] Antigone-like, Alceste exceeds the framework within which the god of Love wishes to contain her.

Repetition

It is Alceste's demand which generates the repetitive scenario which is so prominent a feature of the legends. Their repetitiveness has been a major cause of the low critical esteem in which the *Legend of Good Women* is held and defences have generally been on the grounds of hitherto neglected variety, but it is evident from Alceste's prescription that the project is conceived as a repetitive one. Variations between the individual legends are irrelevant to what is identified at their inception as their primary characteristic: the single scenario to be played out again and again and again. This scenario defines the male role as serial betrayal, and the male characters do indeed repeat themselves as well as repeating each other. Similarly, the heroines each follow Alceste's example, replicating her and each other. Within the text itself there is repetition of word and imagery. Some of these features can be evaluated as developing patterns of similarity and difference which organize meaning and literary effect, as one usually expects of literary texts, but repetition here far outruns any such justification. It becomes wearisome repetitiousness, a negation of the aesthetic. The existence of two redactions of the Prologue and also their standard printing strengthens the sense that repetition is central to the *Legend of Good Women*'s impact.[42] The text gives the impression of proceeding not from an artistry of which the poet is fully in control, but from irrational compulsion generated by the need to resolve an insoluble but unavoidable problem.[43] Rather than trying to free the legends of Alceste's prescriptive constraint by emphasizing their individuality, I want here to keep in sight the poem's monotonous, monologic and obsessive qualities. Moreover, I interpret these qualities as central to the text's resistance to dominant norms.[44]

This 'perpetual recurrence of the same thing' (to borrow a phrase from Freud)[45] originates with Alceste. She demands of the narrator that he spend the rest of his days repeating a single, extremely limited, rigid and essentializing version of gender roles and relations. Her version is not, however, that recommended by the god of Love; he again echoes the *Book of the Duchess*, and again Alceste dissents. Both *Book* and *Legend* present pre-emptive variations on Poe's assertion that 'the death... of a beautiful woman is, unquestionably, the most poetical topic in the world'.[46] Poe continues, 'and equally is it beyond doubt that the lips best suited for such topic [sic] are those of a bereaved lover'. In the *Book*, the Man in Black is inspired to lyric composition by the death of a woman who, as recreated by him, has inner as well as outer beauty, while his dream motivates the narrator, also an unhappy lover, to write. In the *Legend* Prologue, the god of Love urges the poet to write the stories of women of the following sort:

> . . . to hyre love were they so trewe
> That, rathere than they wolde take a newe,
> They chose to be ded in sondry wyse,
> And deiden, as the story wol devyse;
> And some were brend, and some were cut the hals,
> And some dreynt for they wolden not be fals;
> For alle keped they here maydenhede,
> Or elles wedlok, or here widewehede.
>
> (G.288–95)

(They were so true to their love that rather than consent to take a new they chose to die in various ways, and died, as the story shall relate; and some were burned, and some had their throats cut, and some drowned because they would not be false; for they all preserved their maidenhood, or wedlock, or their widowhood.)

One way to understand the god of Love's formulation is as a prescription for suicide. A 'trewe' woman will recognize that severance from her man, even involuntary or undeserved, is equivalent to death; her actual suicide seems thus to be only a belated acting out, an obedient translation into the physical world of patriarchally determined symbolic rules. In the poem's pagan setting suicide may be considered the ultimate good death for a woman, granting her instant passage into the Eternal Feminine. By this act she declares her superiority to Fortune. To do otherwise would threaten her social identity in ways spelled out above.[47]

On the other hand, the god seems here to envisage a series of martyrdoms in which women are tortured by third parties but remain true to him, their Love.[48] This interpretation, as Fradenburg points out, is reminiscent of Lacan's insistence on the indestructible beauty of Sade's female victims:[49]

La victime survit à tous les mauvais traitements, elle ne se dégrade même pas dans son caractère d'attrait voluptueux... elle a toujours les yeux les plus jolis du monde, l'air le plus pathétique et le plus touchant. L'insistance de l'auteur à mettre toujours ses sujets sous une rubrique aussi stéréotypée pose en elle-même un problème.[50]

(The victim survives all the ill-treatment, she does not even lose any of her voluptuous attraction... she still has the loveliest eyes in the world, the most pathetic and touching air. The author's insistence on always placing his subjects under such a stereotyped heading is itself a problem.)

The last sentence could stand as an epigraph for the legends. Lacan posits that Sade seeks in these women evidence of 'le caractère indestructible de l'Autre' ('the indestructible character of the Other'),[51] in other words of the existence of a metaphysical ground to being which makes death strictly impossible and guarantees the limits and structures necessary to produce such human phenomena as society, ethics, meaning and the person. And he links this fantasy to Christianity, 'apothéose du sadisme' ('apotheosis of sadism') for its emphasis on the passion of Christ, echoed in those of the martyrs.[52] Tormented and humiliated beyond tolerance, the *Legend*'s women become sublimely beautiful. Their superhuman endurance points to a divine entity – in this case the god of Love – who underwrites the immortality of the male viewer, torturer or writer. From a more feminist standpoint, Simon Gaunt argues that female characters who die for love in Old French literature enact a specifically feminine *jouissance* (following Lacan's Seminar xx) which constitutes a subversive relation to the universal. According to Gaunt, for all that it is a male fantasy, feminine *jouissance* may nevertheless trouble patriarchal social organization.[53]

These are productive ways of understanding the *Legend of Good Women*, but I would go further: the feminine voice in the Prologue positively exploits the sublimation which male fantasies impose upon it to stake out a potentially more independent territory beyond male sponsorship and torment. To adopt for a moment the Lacanian terms used in Chapter 2 above, analysing the courtly Lady Alceste as also inhuman Thing would be insufficient since she introduces into the poem a position not caught within the dialectic of sublimity and abjection.[54] Alceste proclaims the proper topic of poetry to be the single scenario in which women *were* faithful 'al here lyves' (G.475; 'all their lives') while men *spend* 'al here lyf' (G.477; 'all their life') betraying women. Her prescription constructs gender difference around dissimilar modes of living and of representing lives, not around the distinction between life and death. Men are lumped together in a perpetual present having only one story, but for women she stipulates the detail of their historical particularities. This leads to the repetitiousness of the *Legend*, which rehearses the women's individual stories and the 'sondry wyse' of their deaths within an overarching insistence on one unvarying interpretation. Some are tortured, some commit suicide, some die, others remain alive; these distinctions are less significant than the issue of whether the god's or Alceste's interpretative framework triumphs.

Death is an important element in Alceste's vision, which insists on lifelong fidelity. In the legends themselves, some of the heroines die immediately, others after a lifetime which is presented as a sort of long-drawn-out death, as in Hypsipyle's case:

> And trewe to Jason was she al hire lyf,
> And evere kepte hire chast, as for his wif;
> Ne nevere hadde she joye at hire herte,
> But deyede for his love, of sorwes smerte.
> (ll. 1576–9)

(And she was true to Jason all her life, and kept herself chaste forever, as his wife; nor did she ever experience joy in her heart, but died for his love out of sorrow's pain.)

Hypsipyle's loyalty prevents her from living in any social role other than that of Jason's wife. From the moment of their abandonment the heroines' futures are foreclosed; they are set apart from everyday life even before their physical death. Their refusal to participate further in life nevertheless does

not make them the acquiescent suicides which the god of Love may envisage. Nor is it merely the turning upon themselves of a violence impotent to
harm its true object.[55] It is an act which 'almost parodies the death which is
the ultimate manifestation of altruistic self-abnegation'.[56] The decision of
those heroines who choose to follow their lovers into death is coloured by
Alceste's return from the grave. For it is not in fact her severance from her
man which seals each heroine's fate but her wilful refusal to be detached
from her former partner. Nor does her decision imply submission to male
desires; we can rather say that each heroine refuses to allow her partner to
detach himself from her. There are no liberating secondary burials in the
Legend. On the contrary, its good women go to extraordinary lengths to
ensure that their men will never be free of them nor licensed to remodel the
women's personae to suit their own agendas. Thus the emphasis in Alceste's
prescription of the most poetical topic lies on women's rejection of normal
existence and the patriarchal authority decreeing it. Physical death does
not bring this rejection to an end but instead preserves it. Choosing to
exist suspended beyond the masculinist cycle of normal life and consummated death, the *Legend*'s heroines withhold the regenerating power which
their deaths ought normally to contribute to the social order. In place
of the exemplary bearers of patriarchal meaning proposed by the god of
Love, Alceste links the making of poetry to the presentation of a group
of women who defy the 'boundes' that they 'oughte kepe' (G.536; 'boundaries', 'should observe'), the confines of social life and of the socialized
death that is an integral part of that life. It is Alceste's totalizing, monologic project that ensures for these women a spectral presence which outrages recognized forms but is nonetheless immovable, defying conventional
aestheticization.

The legends themselves are sometimes considered to undermine Alceste's
prescription and sometimes to disappoint the expectations it arouses. However, in certain respects Alceste's command is precisely realized in the
legends. Each heroine repeats the intransigent position that Alceste articulates in the Prologue. *Pace* those critics who see them as dying for love,
monogamy or their menfolk, these women die for nothing but to uphold
the desire which inhabits them, exemplifying Lacan's description of psychoanalytic ethics.[57] 'Fiercely monogamous', these women can, of course,
be reclaimed for the marital ideology proposed by the god of Love.[58] However, the poem warns with remarkable consistency and obviousness against
such appropriation. Monogamy in this poem appears not as a manifestation of masculine authority but as a mode of feminine resistance to that
authority. Unlike the ladies of the *Book of the Duchess*, the heroines of

the legends could never be transformed into patrons of remarriage. In declining to be replaced they repudiate the idea of women's essential inter-changeability and combat the endless recycling of ideal types associated with the Eternal Feminine. Paradoxical though it may appear, the poem's repetitive quality is key to its heroines' uniqueness. They embody that com-bination of 'concrete singularity' and 'concrete collectivity' which Irigaray attributes to Antigone (see pp. 23–5, above). The ladies' re-enactment of Alceste's adamant resolution preserves their personal couplings perpetu-ally in human memory, a ploy whose success is borne out by the *Legend's* own reproduction of their stories. The repetitiousness that originates with Alceste must therefore be distinguished from the repetition which char-acterizes the supposedly eternal cycle of life and death; whereas the latter erases and discourages particularity and promotes conformity in favour of a socially useful norm, the former is here allied with an unassimilable singularity which is all the balder for being independent of accidental bio-graphical details, pared down to the bare facts of desire and its assertion. Central to the discomfort that the poem inspires is the *Legend's* insistence on its ladies' undying protest.[59]

Alceste's heroines refuse to be passed along into the transcendent realm from which Blanche and White preside puppet-like over their own replace-ment, and by this means they resist conscription as patrons of social renewal. Female resistance to a patriarchal order could easily be coded as misogyny, but in the *Legend* it is couched in positive moral terms. Alceste is no less a paragon than White, and the quality she and her hero-ines exemplify is once again *trouthe*. I can hardly overstate the difference between the *Legend* and the *Book* where this value is concerned. Whereas Lady White's *trouthe* is the prime mechanism inducting her into the polit-ically manipulated symbolic realm beyond time and change which is the land of the dead, Alceste's *trouthe*, realized in the poem as her unshakeable demand, removes her from that realm without integrating her into every-day life. *Trouthe* makes White doubly socially useful, easing her through ideal normativity into the universal and thus back into substitution on earth, but it fixes Alceste and her ladies in the *entre-deux-morts* outside society's living and deathly manifestations. Their *trouthe* represents the women's rejection of the customary identification of femininity with lack: their reason for preserving their prior states of maidenhood and so on is 'nat kept for holynesse, / But al for verray vertu and clennesse, / And for men schulde sette on hem no lak' (G.296–8; 'not maintained out of holiness, but entirely out of true virtue and purity, and so that men should accuse them of no lack').[60] The *Legend* provides its heroines with a positive ethical position which gives them the power to engage seriously in debate with other views. It creates out of traditionally feminine virtue a place distinct from the Eternal Feminine ideal and from the hegemonic ideological order, and critical of both.

The *Legend* emphasizes that insistence and lack of orthodox aesthetic appeal are poetically generative. Since the narrator is to have no other subject until he dies, 'yer by yere' (G.471; 'year on year') his life is as foreclosed and dominated by a single repetitive model as those of the ladies he is to write about. His poetry is henceforward to occupy a domain if not analogous to that of the ladies' lives, then bearing testimony to it. This is a 'perverse poetic' to counter the tradition of 'hylomorphic poetics' in which a male author paternally imposes form on inchoate feminine material; it contradicts the 'Father of English Poetry' myth, frustrating desires and identifications tenacious in Chaucer criticism.[61] The Lady who imposes her non-negotiable bidding upon him exemplifies the desire that inhabits us against what would ordinarily be considered our better judgement. Alceste's unrefusable gift to the narrator's poetic production is expressed in the ballade in her honour inserted into the Prologue. This ballade lists paragons of 'trouthe in love' (G.221; 'fidelity in love'), all feminine except for two masculine names in the first stanza, naming each only to surpass it with the refrain 'Alceste is here, that al that may desteyne.' The *MED* gives three principal glosses for *disteinen*:

1 To color or stain (sth.); (b) fig. to disguise (one's purpose).
2 To deprive (sth.) of color, brightness, or beauty; (b) fig. to dim or obscure (sth.), put in the shade; (c) fig. to fade away, vanish.
3 to sully (someone's reputation); desecrate (the name of God); ~ **tonge**, speak vilely; (b) to dishonor or defame (sb.); defile.

The ballade's refrain is commonly understood to suggest that Alceste's pre-eminence is such that she extinguishes all other claims, a reading which relies on sense 2.[62] Attention to the other glosses alters our appreciation. Alceste's effect is to cast a particular colour or stain over – or even, given the connotations of sense 3, to discolour – any woman she stands next to.[63] The heroines of the *Legend* all acquire Alceste's livery, turning a corpse-like pale or taking on a bloody flush as they manifest the uncompromising *trouthe* that projects them into the zone beyond life and death and opposes them to the life cycle. '[P]hysical loss of control' here represents a step beyond the order of everyday life.[64] Its involuntary nature reflects the essential, instinctive impulse to resist that order. These are the colours of the marguerite reinterpreted by Cybele and Mars. Seen in the light Alceste casts, the ladies appear quite different from their realizations in other texts.

Testifying to the revenant's effect, each resists being appropriated to the reproduction of the established order. This explains the peculiar treatment of source material in the *Legend*; to tell a story under Alceste's aegis is to distort its natural, which is to say its usual ideological purposes.[65] As Žižek, discussing anamorphosis, puts it: 'If we look at a thing straight on, i.e., matter-of-factly, disinterestedly, objectively, we see nothing but a formless spot; the object assumes clear and distinctive features only if we look at it "at an angle", i.e., with an "interested" view, supported, permeated, and "distorted" by *desire*.'[66] The formless spot of the boring and conformist *Legend of Good Women* comes into focus when the desire of Alceste and her heroines is made the basis for the critical gaze. Small wonder that the ballade urges its pantheon of conventional exemplars of true love to hide and be silent. If these names represent figures who, like Blanche and White, have undergone secondary burial, Alceste comes to disinter them. The warning signalled by the ballade's insistent refrain is a real one, for through Alceste the lyrical, symbolic domain to which Blanche and White are dispatched will be dismantled in the name of a different, awkward and particular femininity.

The Prologue suggests that distortion is not so much a valid as an inevitable interpretative principle, for desire intervenes in even the most supposedly disinterested of accounts. Its achievement is to grant to Alceste's refractory desire an effective authority usually reserved for the representatives of the established order. The secondary burial and translation into the Eternal Feminine professedly achieved in the *Book of the Duchess* contrast with the inflexible revenant, obsessive repetition in form and content, and assertiveness of female *trouthe* which give the *Legend of Good Women* its unpalatable, ungraspable quality. These attributes of the later poem are, in a sense, blindingly obvious; simultaneously impossible to ignore and impossible to confront directly, they invite us to 'desteyne' the literary material if we are to see what it really sets before us.[67] The *Legend* opposes the possibility that we may assimilate it comfortably into an existing system, thereby challenging our potential appropriation of it as much as it does that of the god of Love in the Prologue. Taking their stand in the intermediary zone through which their system's rites are designed to hurry them, the legends' heroines contest the social and poetic vision consecrated by those rites. As woman after woman ceremonially upholds her singularity she not only protests against the sacrifice of women to a male-dominated order but also conjures new ethical and political possibilities. Insistent poetic repetition elevates behaviour into ritual, and the cumulative effect of Alceste's and her heroines' actions is to replace the ritual they challenge with one of their own: a 'ritual of resistance'.[68] Although Hertz does not discuss the possibility, an altered rite can be an engine of change. Alceste's exemplarity is of a new and radical kind. Refusing the satisfaction of sublimation, it remains resolutely demanding, geared not to ideological reproduction but to critique, not to the normative but to the alternative.

From one perspective, the uncompromising aesthetic of the Prologue fails to impose itself on the legends and on Chaucer's later compositions. It may be that it can never found a workable poetics, since by definition we cannot remain long in the *entre-deux-morts*. Chaucer re-enacts the male role of abandoning the heroines, thus both fulfilling and denying Alceste's prescription. If we take a different point of view, however, we can open up the question of the *Legend's* possible success. *Entre-deux-morts*, the revolutionary position on the far side of blind folly or human ruin – to phrase it in Lacanian terms discussed earlier in this book – may be invoked as a trope with the aim of challenging the existing order and of making it past, placing its norms into suspension or abeyance for critical reconsideration. We should, therefore, judge the success of the *Legend of Good Women* not only by whether it actually provided a workable model for Chaucer's future productions but by how *passéiste* it makes some other productions appear. Against the courtly and scholarly melancholia that characterizes modernity in much fourteenth-century writing, the *Legend's* Prologue presents a poetry that engages fully with death but refuses equally to mourn, to declare it 'nothing for us', or to Christianize it; and thus gestures towards quite other cultural possibilities. Of all the figures in this book, Chaucer's dreamt Alceste bears closest comparison with the Antigones portrayed by Irigaray and by Butler. She acts not out of a self-destructive drive but from urgent desire to have things done differently. Both Irigaray and Butler envisage a future shaped by Antigone: Irigaray, an order which includes Antigone as a coherent feminine principle to balance the hitherto dominant masculine; Butler, the possibility of recognizing far more forms of desire and attachment than those restricted few privileged by patriarchy. For all the moral distance separating the exemplar of wifehood from Oedipus' child, Alceste's ambivalence for Chaucer's poetry balances on precisely the knife-edge that Butler identifies for Antigone: 'what she draws into crisis is the representative function itself, the very horizon of intelligibility within which she operates and according to which she remains somewhat unthinkable'.[69] Alceste is not sacrificed by her text to normality and to the death drive, as Lacan has Antigone; nor is she a

Žižekian constitutive exception, foundational for an order that she also negates and that must necessarily reject her. More pessimistically than in Irigaray's vision, Alceste's authority rests on her death; more optimistically than in Butler's, Alceste in living death stands at the admired centre of an entire court with its symbolic and social order, and actively engages the living court poet.

Conclusion: living dead or dead-in-life?

Previous chapters have, I hope, established both the recurrence of the 'between two deaths' in medieval literature and the variety of meanings and uses to which it bends. A question which it has not been possible to pose earlier is: are the formally dead but apparently alive significantly and systematically different from the technically alive but effectively dead? The evidence surveyed here suggests that the former (the Pearl-Maiden, Alceste) are more associated with the idea of demand or obligation which it is the living addressee's duty to fulfil, the latter (Roland, Galehot) with that of sacrifice or willingness to die for a person or cause, thus creating an obligation. However, these categories are not stable. Whereas the Pearl-Maiden bases the authority for her advice to the Jeweller on Christ's death for humankind, Galehot's death for Lancelot's sake is also a petition to Lancelot, although it remains a question whether the latter's failure to reciprocate frustrates or answers Galehot's desire. Roland's death is not originally a sacrifice for Charlemagne, though the later parts of the assonanced *Chansons de Roland* and the rhymed redactions *in toto* make it one retrospectively. Blanche/White's consummated death too is rewritten as a sacrifice that she and her mourner make, albeit involuntary on her part and painful on his, for the benefit of surviving members and future generations of their House. This interpretation extracts her from the *entre-deux-morts* and lays her to rest.

In the works analysed in this book, the living dead are female, the dead-in-life male. This observation has suggestive correspondences with the distinction elaborated by Simon Gaunt between men who 'talk the talk' of death, in that their deaths for love are subordinated to their own deployment of the symbolic order of discourse, and women who 'walk the walk'; their deaths are much less mediated by language, at any rate by language over which they exercise direct control, and therefore have a potentially closer connection with the Real.[1] Male-authored texts, perhaps unsurprisingly, tend to represent the masculine melancholy as subjectively and ethically the more serious, whereas female death, however gratifying in one respect to the male ego, retains a troublesome aspect insofar as it represents an independent female desire. This Gaunt characterizes as feminine *jouissance*, drawing on Lacan's Seminar xx. In the schema based on Seminar vii that I have used in this book, there is no distinction made either between masculine and feminine characters *entre-deux-morts*, on the one hand, or between the living dead and the dead-in-life, on the other. I have presented upholding desire unto death as essentially genderless though malleable into different gendered frameworks, and have treated the different inflections in its realizations as cultural, social or political phenomena stemming from and impacting on the texts' ideological positioning. While accepting the Real antagonism of sexual difference and of other differences not limited to gender, I adopt the methodological principle that it is better to proceed as if the terms in which such antagonisms are couched were human-made and variable. Such a procedure is preferable analytically and politically. I accept Butler's reiterated objection to Lacanian psycho-social analysis, namely that the empty ontological or formal categories it posits are easily confused with particular social structures and arrangements. Her point is, indeed, illustrated by Žižek, whose political insights often depend on a creative conflation of the two. Literary criticism is an ethical and political practice. Even though the fundamental alienation of sexual difference can never be finally overcome, it is, in my opinion, not only excusable but necessary to believe in the possibility of a less unjust and inhumane social order. This reflects my view (Chapter 2, above) that Lacan's account of actual gender differences is historically determined (which I imagine he would accept) and inadequate in its restrictive nature (where he would retort that I am nostalgic or utopian, in any case unrealistic). Alceste and the Pearl-Maiden, the dead females who speak in this book, do so through named or presumed male authors, respectively Chaucer and the *Pearl*-poet, though God may also be considered the Maiden's Author. Their opposition to the established earthly order does not in my view represent a transhistorical and irreducible female otherness; neither is it accidental or insignificant. Gaunt's distinction is important, but both these feisty dead females and the Lacanian gendered explanation of them need to be related to available cultural codes of femininity. Male characters can also play the role of demanding living dead, as they do in many visionary exempla of the sort studied by Schmitt. My corpus is, after all, selective and no doubt reflects at some level my own preconceptions about gender roles. I nevertheless offer the distribution of fully realized male and female figures within my sample as a fact to be noted.

Žižek offers a further way of thinking about the difference between living dead and dead-in-life. After noting an antagonism between the ordinarily living and dead on the one hand and the awkwardly unliving and undead on the other, he further divides up the problematic category: 'For a human being to be 'dead while alive' is to be colonized by the 'dead' symbolic order; to be 'alive while dead' is to give body to the remainder of Life-Substance which has escaped the symbolic colonization.'[2] Huot has shown how fruitful this distinction can be in the context of madness in medieval literature. Among my texts, the correlation cannot be sustained, though it remains stimulating. *Pearl*, for instance, inverts the relationships that Žižek proposes. The Pearl-Maiden, who is 'alive while dead', is the creature of the symbolic order, while the Jeweller in his 'dead while alive' condition in the poem's first section is overwhelmed by a meaningless life-force, a 'remainder' as well as a 'reminder' of his infant's death. Throughout the text he is construed as excessive in relation to the poem's symbolic order and, I argue, remains so at the end in spite of the Maiden's overwhelmingly normative integration. This reversal of Žižek's pattern could, however, be ascribed to *Pearl*'s Christian/courtly strategy of inverting perspectives and tropes. The *Chanson de Roland* provides further ground for exploring the distinction. In the assonanced *Roland*s, the various ethical discussions over behavioural norms of, for instance, masculinity, leadership and baronial or Christian conduct, happen around Roland without containing him. Although 'dead while alive', Roland, precisely by embodying the 'remainder of Life-Substance which has escaped symbolic colonization', provides an initially free-floating energy which those norms that fasten onto him, whether as exemplar or counter-exemplar, compete to harness in order to impose themselves more widely. Roland's empty demand, realized in his destruction drive, elicits various responses from different ideologically constituted bodies, all of which construe Roland's actions as a question to which they have the answer, thus ascribing retrospectively a specific content to his demand.[3] In the Oxford and Venice 4 texts Roland is colonized by the symbolic order, that is, recuperated for meaning – regardless of which particular one – only after his corporeal death. To phrase it in the Hertzian terms of Chapter 5, the Baligant, Aude and Ganelon episodes constitute the hero's 'secondary burial' as he is integrated into the community's afterlife and recycled into social use as a symbol. This second life is energized by his own focus on second death. In the rhymed *remaniements*, however, we see a situation more like that which Žižek proposes; Roland, 'dead while alive', from the start emblematizes the texts' (imaginary) symbolic order, the site of meaning and social contract, accounting for the mysterious fascination he exercises over every other character as well as for the need to distance him from the textual world.

The tension that Žižek identifies between excessive remainder and symbolic colonization has run throughout this book, although it does not correlate neatly with the distinction between 'dead while alive' or 'alive while dead'. *Entre-deux-morts* – to return to a phrase which places the two conditions on a par – generates psychic and aesthetic energy by its position beyond the symbolic order; precisely this energy is valuable to ethical, poetic, political and ideological regimes, which therefore hasten to bind it, in Freud's term, to a specific meaning serving particular interests. Žižek's various developments of Lacan's notion of the *point de capiton* ('quilting point', 'anchoring point') suggest too many directions for inquiry to follow up here.[4] I shall refer briefly to only two such. In *For They Know Not What They Do*, Žižek reads the *point de capiton* as an ideological operation in which a particular signifier is attached to a particular signified. He emphasizes how this in practice produces a '"magical inversion" of defeat into triumph': 'Here one is dealing with the act of "creation" *stricto sensu*: the act which turns chaos into a "new harmony" and suddenly makes "comprehensible" what was up to then a meaningless and even terrifying disturbance' (and Žižek continues, 'It is impossible not to recall Christianity').[5] Such inversions are put to political use in the assonanced *Roland*s, in *Pearl* and in the *Book of the Duchess*, and supply one way of reading the figure of Galehot as well as the Prologue and legends of the *Legend of Good Women*. In my second citation, from *Tarrying with the Negative*, Žižek treats the *point de capiton* in a way that recalls Barthes's definition of myths, stressing that although the highly invested signifier expresses fears associated with real material circumstances, it is a proxy figure deployed so as to shield those circumstances and their exploitation by particular forces from effective analysis and engagement. His privileged examples here are the Jew in anti-semitism and the shark in *Jaws*:

> To say that the murderous shark 'symbolizes' the above-mentioned series of fears [e.g. big business manipulations] is to say too much and not enough at the same time. It does not symbolize them, since it literally annuls them by itself occupying the place of the object of fear. It is therefore 'more' than a symbol: it becomes the feared 'thing itself'. Yet, the shark is decidedly less than a symbol, since it does not point toward the symbolized content, but rather blocks access to it, renders it invisible.[6]

Žižek concentrates on feared figures, but Lacan's analysis of *le beau* in Seminar VII argues that beauty can also be used at once to body forth the Real for us and to bar us from it. Such figures as the Pearl-Maiden, Alceste and her cohorts of indestructibly beautiful women or Galehot with his extraordinary self-abnegation both indicate and conceal hinterlands of economic, material and psychic disturbance. The art object itself performs a similar dual function.

Some instances are more productive than others. Blanche/White never has much disruptive energy, her effect on her mourner being closely contained by courtly paradigms which determine that he will not, in fact, die of his love. As Machaut's Reason affirms before the king of Bohemia, love cannot survive the death of the beloved; Love and Youth will bring forgetfulness and thereafter, presumably, a new attachment. Whereas an unfaithful beloved effectively kills love itself for the lover, a faultless and dead one actually enables future loves.[7] Losing one's perfect beloved to death in fact favours the probability that the survivor will fall in love with another, and live that love happily. It is perhaps cynical to suggest that the Man in Black's lady was partially disinterred in order that some political or marital capital might be wrung out of her. Blanche/White is certainly an etiolated specimen of the 'between two deaths', dispatched with a grace, convenience and coherence that arouse suspicion. The Nirvana drive is too strong in her portrayal, the destruction drive too feeble. Symbolic colonization dominates the primary narrative of the *Book of the Duchess* (the minor narrative of Ceyx and Alcyone may tell a different story), and the dead woman's weak disruptive force generates correspondingly little ideological fuel. Contrast the Pearl-Maiden, with whom Christian ideology smashes through everyday life. Alceste, however, fits Žižek's model of the 'alive while dead' so well that she carries it further than Žižek envisages. So strong is she that she remodels the symbolic order in accordance with her will, at least for the space of the *Legend*; she colonizes the Poet-Dreamer to be the foreclosed instrument of that order, repeating her instructions year by year for the rest of his life. (Can this recolonization of the living poet for the reordered symbolic succeed? The examples of Alceste and the Pearl-Maiden – who attempts the same thing – suggest doubt but not certain disbelief.) The transparency of the meaning borne by figures *entre-deux-morts* is therefore not an indicator of their colonization by the symbolic order; Alceste invests a specific message – the injustice of females' treatment under patriarchy – with all the energy of an indestructible life-substance. Galehot, for his part, rather than being defeated by the symbolic order represented by Lancelot, enthusiastically and painfully submits himself to it, becoming its abject, undead creature, hence its symptom. He remains excessive; Lancelot does not want his overgenerous adhesion or his sacrifice-demand, which therefore become themselves acts of protest against knighthood and per-haps, beyond that, against the symbolic order per se. Contrast the prince of Deschamps's Ballade 1457, called upon to sacrifice earthly glory and to become the symbolic order's anonymous subject on earth in order to access eternal life. In the texts foregrounded in Chapter 3, the *ubi sunt* topos implants a constant toing and froing between 'alive' and 'dead' that deliberately confuses efforts to separate the terms. Of the ladies of Villon's 'Ballade des dames', only Joan of Arc could be said to be 'alive while dead', all the others being properly dead in their sublime otherwise. Or so they seem at first. The lords, coming after, appear dead in a different mode, not eternal but ephemeral. For these latter we are pushed to ask whether they were ever really 'alive' in the sense of embodying the life-substance; and the symbolic order falters with them. Their unsettling clears the ground for the writing subject and the speaking *vieil langage* of the third ballade, 'dead while alive' in a promisingly disturbing way, refusing either to lie down quietly or to be generative within normal forms, proliferating without changing except to rot.

The evidence of this book, therefore, suggests that symbolic colonization and escape are related dialectically. Rather than a formal taxonomy tying the living living dead to one set of tropes or meanings and the dead living dead to another, their distribution varies within this dialectical field. They may be related within particular texts and textual networks in assorted ways, these relations being the primary generators of meaning. The major antag-onism, therefore, lies between the normative and the disturbing, in living as in dying; and even this produces in many cases a mutually reinforcing dynamic, witness *Pearl* and *Roland*. In the strange overlap between death and life – when, in Barthes's phrase, 'one of the spaces bites unwarrant-edly into the other' – cultural laws are suspended along with natural ones. Established norms are temporarily deracinated, leading ultimately to one of three outcomes: restoration, modification or revolution. The practical outcome in terms of the regime is an important topic; equally interesting are the philosophical, existential explorations which centre on the figure caught in the overlap or interstice between life and death. 'Between two deaths' is itself 'good to think with'. The most fundamental challenges to their and our cultures' ways of thinking are posed by those figures whose desires lead to an impasse. Galehot, Villon's testator and Alceste found no tradition in their own time and therefore finally appear merely (grandly, tragically, foolishly) idiosyncratic. The demands they articulate not only are not met by the individuals to whom they are nominally addressed but also fizzle out as movements of the collective: for Lacan the hero, as opposed to the common man, is one who may be betrayed with impunity.[8] It is therefore important for us to register that those demands point towards a profound dissent from the aesthetic, social or subjective regime. This dissent, of course, also makes them available for appropriation by particular interests such as my own. I asked in the Introduction whether there was a medieval Antigone commensurate with Sophocles. Perhaps not; but I consider these other figures at the cusp of representability to be Antigone's kin.

Notes

INTRODUCTION: LIVING DEATH

1. Epicurus, 'Letter to Menoeceus', p. 29.
2. Inwood, *Hegel Dictionary*, 'Death and Immortality', pp. 71–4, and *Heidegger Dictionary*, 'Death and Dying', pp. 45–6.
3. Inwood, *Heidegger Dictionary*, p. 45.
4. Geary, *Living with the Dead*, p. 1. The relationships linking the living and the dead are central to Binski, *Medieval Death*.
5. See also Davis's characterization of the medieval dead as 'a kind of "age group" to put alongside the children, the youth, the married, and the old' ('Ghosts, Kin, and Progeny', p. 92). I owe this reference to Prof. Elizabeth Edwards.
6. Geary, *Living with the Dead*, pp. 119–20.
7. Schmitt, 'Les revenants', pp. 300–1 (quotation on p. 301).
8. Julian, 'Against the Galilaeans', p. 415. I am grateful to Prof. Robert Bartlett for this reference.
9. Dei Segni, *De miseria condicionis humane*, 1.22, p. 130, 'Of the Proximity of Death'.
10. *New Catholic Encyclopedia*, 'Death (in the Bible)' and 'Death (Theology of)'.
11. Saward, *Perfect Fools*, pp. 6–7. On the approach to death of those who are sure of salvation, see Leclercq, 'La joie de mourir'.
12. Saward, *Perfect Fools*, p. 3. Saward notes that Sophocles uses *mōros* to describe the madness of Antigone (*Antigone*, l. 469): 'The tragedian, like the apostle, also acknowledges the relativity of insanity and madness; he perceives that what looks like folly to one may be true wisdom to another' (p. 5). In the *Phoenician Women*, Euripides' Creon also uses the term *mōría* of Antigone, who there moderates her demands to cleaning Polyneices' corpse but insists on being allowed to leave Thebes with her exiled father.
13. See the trials recounted by the *Artes moriendi* which circulate widely with the advent of printing; for instance, Caxton, *Here begynneth a lityll treatise*.
14. Ariès, *Images*, p. 147; on earlier notions, see p. 143. For a different view on the earlier period, see McLaughlin, *Consorting with Saints*, especially chapter 5.
15. Le Goff could write in 1980 that 'la mort est à la mode' (preface to Chiffoleau, *La Comptabilité de l'au-delà*, p. v). Of a very large bibliography not referenced elsewhere in these notes, see especially Huizinga, *Waning*; Ariès, *Western*

Attitudes toward Death and *Hour of Our Death*; Boase, *Death in the Middle Ages*; Brown, *Cult of the Saints*; Vovelle, *La Mort et l'Occident*; Camille, *Master of Death*; Alexandre-Bidon, *La Mort au Moyen Âge*; and Schmitt, *Ghosts in the Middle Ages*. Also the following collections: *La Mort au Moyen Âge*; Braet and Verbeke (eds.), *Death in the Middle Ages*; Jane H. M. Taylor (ed.), *Dies illa*; and DuBruck and Gusick (eds.), *Death and Dying in the Middle Ages*. Mention must also be made of the substantial historical literature on medieval death published in German, which I regret I have been unable to consult first-hand.

16. Lefay-Toury, *La Tentation du suicide*; and (as Toury), *Mort et fin'amor*; Fradenburg, *Sacrifice Your Love*; Greene, *Le Sujet et la mort*; McCracken, *Curse of Eve*; and Gaunt, *Martyrs to Love*. Older works include Martineau-Génieys's literary-historical study, *Le Thème de la mort*; and DuBruck, *Theme of Death*.

17. Lochrie argues convincingly in *Heterosyncrasies* that modern concepts of statistical normativity cannot be read back into earlier periods; however, medieval literary texts constantly engage with various kinds of norm, which invite discussion.

18. The shared discursive field (not based on a model of influence and imitation) is emphasized especially in Salter, *English and International*; and by Butterfield, 'Froissart, Machaut, Chaucer', 'French Culture and the Ricardian Court', 'Chaucer's French Inheritance', 'England and France', and *Familiar Enemy*. Calin, *French Tradition*, though not widely referred to by scholars of Middle English, shows authoritatively how interconnected were French- and English-language literatures throughout the medieval period.

19. Kay, *Courtly Contradictions*; Huot, *Madness*.

20. Lacan, *L'Éthique*, p. 291 (compare the translation in *Ethics*, p. 248).

21. Bloch, *Etymologies and Genealogies*, pp. 1–29; Kay, *Political Fictions*, pp. 16–18 (p. 18).

22. *Entre-deux* is also a French noun in common use, defined as 'espace délimité par deux choses', 'espace de temps entre deux dates, deux événements' or 'état intermédiaire entre deux extrêmes' (*Trésor de la langue française*, 'entre-deux': 'space delimited by two things', 'expanse of time between two dates, two events' or 'state intermediary between two extremes').

23. Though Lacan does not always do so, I capitalize the Real to distinguish it from reality as the world of human constructions within which we live our lives.

24. Evans, *Introductory Dictionary*, p. 82; a clear account of Lacan's three registers, and of their relation to truth, is given in Bowie, *Lacan*, pp. 88–121.

25. On the development of Purgatory as a specific place, see especially Le Goff, *Birth of Purgatory*; and Vovelle, *Les Âmes du purgatoire*. The notion of purgatorial spaces and times within the Christian afterlife was widespread before the official doctrine was declared; see McLaughlin, *Consorting with Saints*. Le Goff's influential book needs to be read with reference to the controversy it provoked; McLaughlin gives a brief, helpful overview and bibliography, *Consorting with Saints*, pp. 17–19. On late medieval views, see especially Chiffoleau, *La Comptabilité de l'au-delà*.

26. See, for example, the discussions of cloistered 'career virgins' in Wogan-Browne, *Saints' Lives*. It is commonplace to note that an unworldly lifestyle was an important component in clerical authority after the very early Christian period.
27. Heidegger: 'When we fill the jug, the pouring that fills it flows into the empty jug. The emptiness, the void, is what does the vessel's holding. The empty space, this nothing of the jug, is what the jug is as the holding vessel . . . The vessel's thingness does not lie at all in the material of which it consists, but in the void that holds' ('The Thing', p. 169). The pot and potter are an ancient image, used notably in the Bible (e.g., Isaiah 45:9; Romans 9:20–1).
28. Lacan, *L'Éthique*, p. 150 (*Ethics*, p. 125).
29. *Ibid.*, p. 170 (p. 141).
30. *Ibid.*, p. 161 (p. 135).
31. *Ibid.*, p. 163 (compare the translation in *Ethics*, p. 136).
32. Lacan's discussions of art in Seminar VII dialogue with Heidegger's influential essay, 'The Origin of the Work of Art'; and his combination of ethics and aesthetics throughout the seminar is closely linked to Heidegger. See especially Lacoue-Labarthe, 'On Ethics'.
33. Lacan, *L'Éthique*, p. 290 (compare the translation in *Ethics*, p. 248).
34. Freud, *Civilization and Its Discontents*, p. 134.
35. Crowell, 'Existentialism'.
36. Aristotle, *Nicomachean Ethics*, II.3, p. 32: 'moral excellence is concerned with pleasures and pains; it is on account of the pleasure that we do bad things, and on account of the pain that we abstain from noble ones. Hence we ought to have been brought up in a particular way from our very youth, as Plato says, so as both to delight in and to be pained by the things that we ought; this is the right education.'
37. Thus Lacan interprets *Civilization and Its Discontents* in the light of speculations which Freud advances and immediately withdraws in *Beyond the Pleasure Principle*, p. 38: 'If we are to take it as a truth that knows no exception that everything living dies for *internal reasons* – becomes inorganic once again – then we shall be compelled to say that "*the aim of all life is death*" and, looking backwards, that "*inanimate things existed before living ones*"' (emphases original). 'Seen in this light, the theoretical importance of the instincts of self-preservation, of self-assertion and of mastery greatly diminishes. They are component instincts whose function it is to assure that the organism shall follow its own path to death, and to ward off any possible ways of returning to inorganic existence other than those which are immanent in the organism itself . . . the organism wishes to die only in its own fashion. Thus these guardians of life, too, were originally the myrmidons of death. Hence arises the paradoxical situation that the living organism struggles most energetically against events (dangers, in fact) which might help it to attain its life's aim rapidly – by a kind of short-circuit. Such behaviour is, however, precisely what characterizes purely instinctual as contrasted with intelligent efforts' (p. 39). According to Strachey, in editions before 1925 a footnote appeared

affirming that 'A correction of this extreme view of the self-preservative instincts follows' (*ibid.*). Freud then theorizes about the relations between the sexual instincts and self-preservation before closing with a 'critical reflection' in which he both distances himself from and reasserts his prior conclusions (pp. 59–61).

38. 'Tant qu'il s'agit du bien, il n'y a pas de problème – le nôtre et celui de l'autre sont de la même étoffe. Saint Martin partage son manteau, et on en a fait une grande affaire, mais enfin, c'est une simple question d'approvisionnement, l'étoffe est faite de sa nature pour être écoulée, elle appartient à l'autre autant qu'à moi. Sans doute touchons-nous là un terme primitif, le besoin qu'il y a à satisfaire, car le mendiant est nu. Mais peut-être, au-delà du besoin de se vêtir, mendiait-il autre chose, que saint Martin le tue ou le baise' (Lacan, *L'Éthique*, p. 219). Note the play on ethical, material and economic senses of *le bien*. ('As long as it's a question of the good, there's no problem; our own and our neighbor's are of the same material. Saint Martin shares his cloak, and a great deal is made of it. Yet it is after all a simple question of training; material is by its very nature made to be disposed of – it belongs to the other as much as it belongs to me. We are no doubt touching a primitive requirement in the need to be satisfied there, for the beggar is naked. But perhaps over and above that need to be clothed, he was begging for something else, namely, that Saint Martin either kill him or fuck him', *Ethics*, p. 186.)

39. Lacan, *L'Éthique*, p. 359 (*Ethics*, p. 311).

40. *Ibid.*, p. 370 (p. 321).

41. *Ibid.*, p. 305 (p. 263).

42. *Ibid.*, p. 362 (compare the translation in *Ethics*, p. 314).

43. *Ibid.*, p. 328 (p. 282).

44. *Ibid.*, pp. 369–70 (pp. 320–1).

45. Eagleton, *Trouble with Strangers*, p. 147.

46. Quoted by Fraisse, *Le Mythe d'Antigone*, p. 153; ellipses are Fraisse's. The lines derive from 'Toujours de la grippe', an imaginary dialogue with a doctor on the place of death in Christianity. Péguy compares the living death of damnation to Antigone's entombment.

47. Leonard, *Athens in Paris*.

48. For Žižek, Lacan permits a distinction between 'historicism' and 'historicity'. The former is ideological and 'always "false", a narrative of the victor who legitimizes his victory by presenting the previous development as the linear continuum leading to his own final triumph'. The latter, attending to repetition, reveals this supposed linear development to be in fact 'a series of ultimately failed attempts to deal with the same "unhistorical" traumatic kernel' – in Marxism, class antagonism, which for Žižek lies in the Real (*Enjoy Your Symptom*, pp. 80–1).

49. This is the message of the final section of Lacan, *L'Éthique*, 'La dimension tragique de l'expérience psychanalytique' (*Ethics*, 'The Tragic Dimension of Analytic Experience'). On 'beyond the second death' as the central stance of the modern subject, see Žižek, 'Eclipse of Meaning', pp. 226–8.

50. Butler, *Antigone's Claim*, p. 30.
51. My discussion is indebted throughout to three major works on philosophical and political thought about Antigone: Steiner, *Antigones*; Fraisse, *Le Mythe d'Antigone*; Leonard, *Athens in Paris*. There is a substantial bibliography on Antigone. For those interested in her role in psychoanalysis, the following stand out: Guyomard, *La Jouissance du tragique*; Sjöholm, *Antigone Complex*; and Zajko and Leonard (eds.), *Laughing with Medusa*. Also valuable are the five essays in the section, 'De *L'Éthique*: à propos d'Antigone', in Avtonomova *et al.*, *Lacan avec les philosophes*, pp. 19–66; these include Lacoue-Labarthe's 'On Ethics'.
52. Leonard, *Athens in Paris*, pp. 96–156.
53. Fraisse, *Le Mythe d'Antigone*, p. 93, my translation. Emphasis original.
54. Sophocles, *Antigone*, ll. 905–12. A brief account of the controversy over these lines is given by Leonard, *Athens in Paris*, pp. 117–18.
55. A contentious interpretation, given that she invokes a 'law' in the lines preceding and following the above quotation; see further below.
56. Hegel, *Phenomenology of Spirit*, §594, p. 362. Compare Lacan's ascription to Antigone of 'le désir pur, le pur et simple désir de mort comme tel' (*L'Éthique*, p. 329; 'pure desire, the pure and simple desire of death as such', *Ethics*, p. 282).
57. Sophocles, *Antigone*, ll. 891–928.
58. In *Glas*, Derrida relates Antigone's fascination and *éclat* to her essential unrepresentability.
59. Žižek, *Looking Awry*, p. 172, n. 1 (emphasis original).
60. References to Antigone are scattered throughout Žižek's substantial oeuvre; some will be given below. However, I am here attempting to summarize a doctrine which explicitly resists systematization.
61. A very short introduction to the inheritances and revisions of Revolutionary history is Doyle, *French Revolution*, pp. 81–108.
62. Fraisse, *Le Mythe d'Antigone*, pp. 94–5. She quotes Georges Renard, *Le Droit, l'ordre et la raison*.
63. Lacan, *L'Éthique*, p. 293 (*Ethics*, p. 250). On the reception of Anouilh's *Antigone*, see Fleming, 'Fascism on Stage', in the interesting Zajko and Leonard (eds.), *Laughing with Medusa*.
64. Žižek, 'Introduction', *Virtue and Terror*, p. xi.
65. *Ibid.*, pp. xiv–xv.
66. Steiner, *Antigones*, pp. 297, 231–2.
67. *Ibid.*, p. 231.
68. Butler, *Antigone's Claim*, p. 43.
69. Irigaray, 'The Eternal Irony of the Community', in *Speculum*, pp. 214–26.
70. Irigaray, 'She before the King', in *To Be Two*, pp. 77–84 (p. 77).
71. On the Enlightenment ethics of the imaginary represented by such as Hume and Adam Smith, see Eagleton, *Trouble with Strangers*, Part I.
72. Butler, *Antigone's Claim*, pp. 1–4. Butler's dissociation of Antigone from the maternal (e.g., pp. 22, 71–2) works less against Irigaray's position than in

support of the latter's objection to the traditional blaming of all the play's troubles on the mother's desire.

73. *Ibid.*, p. 66.
74. *Ibid.*, p. 68. On pp. 67–9, Butler criticizes the brief discussion of Antigone on p. 46 of Žižek's *Enjoy Your Symptom*. Žižek's critique of Butler's Foucauldian model of change invokes Antigone (*Ticklish Subject*, pp. 263–4).
75. Butler, *Antigone's Claim*, p. 58.
76. *Ibid.*, p. 72.
77. Compare Derrida's exploration of Antigone's absolute resistance to representation, in *Glas*.
78. Fraisse associates the Antigone of this tradition, which dominates until the German Hellenist movement, with respect for hierarchy and gentle feminine virtues (*Le Mythe d'Antigone*, p. 50). This figure's excessively zealous conception of her familial duties at times causes her to confront earthly authorities.
79. Lacan, *Le Séminaire, livre XI*, p. 49 (*Four Fundamental Concepts*, p. 49).

1. ROLAND AND THE SECOND DEATH

1. Among Christian readers, see Calin, *Epic Quest*; and Brault, most influentially in his edition, *Song of Roland*. Important warrior readings include Jones, *Ethos*; and Cook, *Sense*. Recent discussions of moral and strategic criticism, which also discuss whether or not the poem can be considered a tragedy, include van Emden, *La Chanson de Roland*; and Ailes, *Absolutes and Relative Values*.
2. Kay, 'Life of the Dead Body', p. 94.
3. This view of the genre is criticized by Kay, 'Introduction', in *Political Fictions*. Other significant critiques of *chanson de geste* ideology include Auerbach, *Mimesis*, chapter 5; Bloch, *Etymologies and Genealogies*; Haidu, *Subject Medieval/Modern*, and *Subject of Violence*; Keller, *Autour de Roland*; Kellogg, *Medieval Artistry*, chapter 1; and Alter, 'L'esprit antibourgeois'.
4. Information about texts and manuscripts is drawn from the indispensable *La Chanson de Roland: The French Corpus*, gen. ed. Duggan. Further references will be given in the form: Duggan vol. no., part and page number. I quote Duggan for all versions except Oxford, where I follow the classic *La Chanson de Roland*, ed. Segre, rev. edn, trans. Tyssens.
5. Duggan's edition localizes and dates the manuscripts as follows: Oxford (O), 1125–50, Anglo-Norman; Venice 4 (V4), early fourteenth century, Franco-Venetian; Venice 7 (V7) and Châteauroux (C) (a closely related pair), end of the thirteenth century, Franco-Venetian; Paris (P), 1265–90, Picard or Ardennais; Cambridge (T) shows traces of an older text in a western French dialect, greatly modernized by the scribe who copied it not much after 1431; Lyon (L), late thirteenth or early fourteenth century, Burgundian. Three fragments of rhymed *Roland*s also survive, with assonanced fragments within some rhymed texts.
6. Freud, *Beyond the Pleasure Principle*, p. 38 (emphasis original). For a fuller discussion, see p. 224 below, n. 37.

7. Lacan, *L'Éthique*, pp. 249–50 (*Ethics*, pp. 210–11).
8. *Ibid.*, pp. 250–1 (pp. 211–13).
9. Freud, *Beyond the Pleasure Principle*, pp. 55–6.
10. Delpech-Ramey, 'Interview with Slavoj Žižek', p. 33.
11. On the omnipresence of death in the poem, see Brault, 'Le thème de la Mort'; and Hemming, 'La mort dans la *Chanson de Roland*'. Also relevant is Le Gentil, 'Réflexions sur le thème de la mort'.
12. In translating, I have consulted and often followed *Song of Roland*, trans. Glyn Burgess.
13. As Bédier observes of Roland: 'On comprend . . . que sa défaite à Roncevaux n'est que la rançon de ses victoires passées; que la condition de ses exploits fut toujours son "orgueil" et sa "folie"' (*Les Légendes épiques*, vol. iii, pp. 440–1).
14. Lacan, *L'Éthique*, p. 305 (*Ethics*, pp. 262–3).
15. *Ibid.*, p. 315 (p. 270).
16. Žižek, *Sublime Object*, p. 117.
17. Vitz comments that Roland in the course of the narrative gets everything that he wants, assuming that 'he had no desire to live a long life . . . One complication is that he died from sorrow at getting just what he thought he wanted' ('Desire and Causality', p. 186).
18. The literature on Roland's *démesure* is substantial. I treat it here as an example of Lacanian ethics, in contrast to what Lacan epitomizes as the Aristotelian virtue ethics of moderation, well-being and liveable norms.
19. Lacan, *L'Éthique*, p. 249 (*Ethics*, p. 211). According to Bloch, '[Roland] remains a terminal figure. Childless, a hero so thoroughly defined by the past that both he and his sword are excluded from the future, Roland embodies the fear that haunted France's feudal aristocracy – that is to say, the prospect of interruption'; 'Nor is *La Chanson de Roland* unique in the impossibility of its own future. The *chanson de geste* is a virtual home for the aged childless, just as the novel will become a school for orphans' (*Etymologies and Genealogies*, pp. 105, 107).
20. Butler, *Antigone's Claim*, p. 22. See Introduction, above, pp. 23–5.
21. Lacan, *L'Éthique*, p. 326 (*Ethics*, p. 280).
22. *Ibid.*
23. Kay considers the explosion of energy emanating from the dying both prospectively, in relation to a (not necessarily Christian) life to come, and retrospectively, death focusing 'the vigor and energy' of the biography rehearsed at the point of death ('Life of the Dead Body', p. 97).
24. Starobinski, 'L'immortalité mélancolique', p. 247.
25. Lacan, *L'Éthique*, p. 251 (*Ethics*, p. 212).
26. *Ibid.*, p. 250 (p. 211).
27. *Ibid.*, pp. 252–3 (pp. 213–24).
28. Huet, *Mourning Glory*. See also Robespierre's selected writings and Žižek's commentary on them, in *Virtue and Terror*.
29. Duggan, 'L'épisode d'Aude'; Kay, *Political Fictions*, pp. 209–11; Matlock, '"Clear Visions"'.

30. On Ganelon in the rhymed *Roland*, see Brook, 'Ganelon's Path to Treachery', and 'La traîtrise et la vengeance'; and Simpson, *Fantasy, Identity and Misrecognition*, chapter 1. On the legal background, see Mickel, *Ganelon, Treason*.

31. Kinoshita's analysis of these problematic similarities is stimulating, in '"Pagans are wrong"' (rev. in *Medieval Boundaries*, chapter 1). For Vance, contrastingly, 'the poet and his audience are so ideologically sure of themselves that the former can lavish feudal terms of praise on the Saracens to magnify their evil and not be misunderstood' (*Reading 'The Song of Roland'*, p. 36).

32. Gaunt, *Gender and Genre*, chapter 1, and *Re-Telling the Tale*, pp. 118–26.

33. Rychner, *La Chanson de geste*, pp. 74–93.

34. Brook, 'Expressions of Faith'.

35. Compare, for the quoted passages, O, *laisse* 242.

36. Freud, *Beyond the Pleasure Principle*, pp. 12–17.

37. Kellogg, *Medieval Artistry*, p. 19. Though disagreeing with Kellogg here, I am indebted to her economic and political analysis.

38. Segre, 'La première "scène du cor"'.

39. Kay analyses romance and *chanson de geste* as each other's 'political unconscious', in *Political Fictions*. Manuscript L provides its *Roland* with a romance introduction.

40. Duggan, vol. III, 5.25–6.

41. On prequels and literary responses to the *Roland*, see especially James R. Simpson, 'Gifts of the *Roland*'. Many more examples are discussed by van Emden, 'Reception of Roland', and 'La réception du personnage de Roland'.

42. I borrow my subheading from Žižek's corresponding title.

43. Kay, *Courtly Contradictions*, pp. 216–31.

44. Cohn, *Pursuit of the Millennium*, and McGinn's corrective, *Visions of the End*. McGinn in my view underplays the urgency to change and the violence of vision inherent in apocalyptic rhetoric.

45. Thus in the cathartic, tragic action of Sophocles' *Antigone*, 'nous sommes purgés, purifiés de tout ce qui est de cet ordre-là. Cet ordre-là, nous pouvons d'ores et déjà le reconnaître – c'est, à proprement parler, la série de l'imaginaire. Et nous en sommes purgés par l'intermédiaire d'une image entre autres' (Lacan, *L'Éthique*, p. 290; 'we are purged, purified of everything of that order. And that order, we can now immediately recognize, is properly speaking the order of the imaginary. And we are purged of it through the intervention of one image among others', *Ethics*, p. 248).

46. Huet, *Mourning Glory*, especially chapters 2 and 3.

47. For Macey, contrastingly, 'Lacan displays no enthusiasm for being articulated with Marxism and has little of interest to say on that subject' (*Lacan in Contexts*, especially pp. 15–21, quotation on p. 16).

48. Compare the invocation of 'La Douce France' by Sarkozy's government in the grand debate on French national identity launched on 25 October 2009. The phrase recalls both the *Roland* and Charles Trenet's 1943 song.

49. William of Malmesbury, *Gesta regum Anglorum*, para. 242 (vol. 1, pp. 454–5). On Gaston Paris and Raoul Mortier, see Duggan, 'Franco-German Conflict'.

On the search for a national epic, see Andrew Taylor, 'Was There a Song of Roland?' (revised in *Textual Situations*, chapter 2).

50. D. C. Douglas, 'Norman Conquest'. The Normans sailed under a papal banner. Mandach argues for sponsorship of *Roland* material throughout the Norman and Angevin empire, in *Naissance et développement*, vol. I: *La Geste de Charlemagne et de Roland* (1961), and vol. VI: *Chanson de Roland: Transferts de mythe dans le monde occidental et oriental*, especially 'Le commonwealth normand et le mythe de Charlemagne et de Roland' (pp. 123–37).

51. Bartlett distinguishes the common use of the label 'Frank' (*Making of Europe*, pp. 101–5) from more specific uses; see also Kinoshita, '"Pagans are wrong"'.

52. Mandach, *Naissance et développement*, vol. I, pp. 57–8.

53. Cook discusses V4's language in the introduction to his edition in Duggan, vol. I, 2.17–25. On the diffusion of *chansons de geste* in Northern Italy, see Vitullo, *Chivalric Epic*. I owe this reference and the observations relating to Occitan lyric tradition to Prof. Simon Gaunt.

54. See especially Kinoshita, '"Pagans are wrong"'. Kinoshita's argument that we see in O the solidification of religious and cultural opposition between Christians and pagans is challenged by the observation that later *chansons de geste* commonly show Christian–Saracen alliances, often against an internal Christian threat; see Kay, 'Le problème de l'ennemi'; and Jubb, 'Enemies in the Holy War'.

55. My analysis of the ideological currents of the later parts of O is indebted to Haidu, *Subject Medieval/Modern*, and *Subject of Violence*.

56. Žižek, *Sublime Object*, p. 116.

57. Haidu, *Subject of Violence*, p. 192.

58. I refer to Freud's myth of 'the beginning of so many things – of social organization, of moral restrictions and of religion', *Totem and Taboo*, vol. IV (5), p. 142.

59. Recent debates over St Paul's writings explore the relevance for modern secular societies of Christian revolutionism; see especially Agamben, *Time That Remains*; Badiou, *Saint Paul*; Žižek, *Puppet and Dwarf*; and Odell-Scott (ed.), *Reading Romans*.

60. Morrissey, *Charlemagne and France*. Krynen writes on the importance of *imperium* to later medieval French kings' moves towards absolutism, with an introductory chapter covering earlier Capetians (*L'Empire du roi*). Kermode highlights the connections between *imperium* and apocalypse (*Sense of an Ending*).

61. Haidu, *Subject Medieval/Modern*, pp. 60–5. Haidu offers a corrective to his earlier *Subject of Violence*, where he argued that the battle of Roncevaux represents the self-destruction of the barony and of feudalism as a regime (incarnated in Roland), to be replaced with a monarchism that he there had difficulty grounding in the contemporary ideological context.

62. 'It is knighthood, that social complex of strengths and weaknesses, that spells out the annihilation of the flower of knighthood in the Frankish rear guard' (Haidu, *Subject of Violence*, p. 84).

63. See especially Suard, 'Les épopées de la révolte'.
64. On the cycle of *chansons de geste* into which the Paris manuscript inserts the *Chanson de Roland*, see Andrew Taylor, *Textual Situations*; Gaunt, *Gender and Genre*; James R. Simpson, *Fantasy, Identity and Misrecognition*; and Reejhon in Duggan, vol. III, 2.40–76. L is included with orthodox religious texts, emphasizing the Christian dimension. T was copied with the letter from Prester John (a fictional Christian monarch of the Indies) to the Roman emperor Frederick Barbarossa. Uebel, 'Imperial Fetishism', analyses imperialist investments in this popular text.

2. THE KNIGHT AS THING: COURTLY LOVE IN THE NON-CYCLIC PROSE *LANCELOT*

1. *La Mort le roi Artu*, chapter 71, ll. 26–8.
2. 'Dead or alive, Lancelot and Galehot lack Galahad's ontological integration: they are men of the border, men covered with seams' (Warren, *History on the Edge*, p. 201).
3. Kennedy, *Lancelot and the Grail*, especially chapter 3; and *Lancelot do Lac*, vol. II.
4. The full cycle comprises the *Estoire del Graal*, the prose *Merlin*, the prose *Lancelot* proper, and the much shorter *Queste del saint Graal* and *Mort le roi Artu*. It is usually considered to have been composed *c.* 1215–35, the *Estoire* and the *Merlin* being the latest compositions. Both textual and publishing histories are fiendishly complicated. Sommer's edition of the short version, *Vulgate Version of the Arthurian Romances*, has recently been superseded by the Bibliothèque de la Pléiade edition with modern French translation: the *Livre du Graal*, ed. Poirion. Although critical editions of the long versions of most branches exist, there is as yet no edition of the whole. The English translation of the French Vulgate and Post-Vulgate, *Lancelot-Grail*, ed. Lacy, is based on the long version. Alison Stones maintains an online list of editions within the Lancelot-Grail project ('The Lancelot-Grail Project: Text Editions').
5. I refer the reader to the summary of the non-cyclic *Lancelot* in Kennedy, *Lancelot and the Grail*, pp. 5–9; for the cyclic version, to the summaries provided in vol. V of *Lancelot-Grail*, ed. Lacy. I use Kennedy's edition of the non-cyclic version, *Lancelot do Lac*, vol. I; references in my chapter to *Lancelot* (unless qualified) are to this text. For the cyclic (Vulgate) prose *Lancelot*, I use *Lancelot*, ed. Micha.
6. Kennedy's comparative reading of the versions from the point where they diverge until the death of Galehot remains authoritative (*Lancelot and the Grail*, pp. 253–72).
7. Micha argues that the non-cyclic version is later ('Les épisodes'); and see Kennedy's responses in 'Two Versions', and *Lancelot and the Grail*.
8. Kennedy summarizes the complicated manuscript tradition, in *Lancelot do Lac*, vol. II, pp. 37–41.

9. Žižek, *Looking Awry*, p. 28.
10. Schultz's *Courtly Love* extensively defends the term against such modern alternatives as 'desire' or 'heterosexuality'.
11. Cohen, 'Masoch/Lancelotism'; Krueger, *Women Readers*; (Lefay-)Toury, *Mort et fin'amor*, concentrates on troubadour and trouvère lyrics; on romances, see her *La Tentation du suicide*. Fradenburg, *Sacrifice Your Love*; Gaunt, *Martyrs to Love*; Huot, *Madness*; Kay, *Courtly Contradictions*. Kay's analysis is further developed in a series of important articles, notably 'Contradictions of Courtly Love', 'Desire and Subjectivity', and 'Courts, Clerks, and Courtly Love'. See also Jaeger, *Ennobling Love*.
12. Greene, 'The Knight, the Woman, and the Historian', p. 51.
13. The association between artistic realism and bourgeois milieu is persistent though repeatedly discredited. On the complexities of the thirteenth-century *roman réaliste*, see Lejeune, 'Jean Renart et le roman réaliste'. On moral rewritings, see especially Brown-Grant, *Gender, Morality and Desire*.
14. Paris, 'Études', p. 521.
15. Jaeger, *Ennobling Love*, p. 186; and see pp. 109–54.
16. Thomas, *Tristan*, Sneyd 1, 317–36.
17. Paris, 'Études', pp. 518–19.
18. Krueger, 'Questions of Gender', provides an overview of recent thinking in relation to gender.
19. Lacan, *L'Éthique*, p. 218 (*Ethics*, p. 185). See Evans, *Introductory Dictionary*, 'pleasure principle'.
20. Lacan, *L'Éthique*, p. 83 (*Ethics*, p. 68).
21. Žižek, '"No Sexual Relationship"', pp. 209–10.
22. Lacan, *L'Éthique*, p. 182 (*Ethics*, p. 152).
23. Spitzer, *L'Amour lointain*, pp. 1–2.
24. 'Lacan argues that the purpose of the drive (*Triebziel*) is not to reach a *goal* (a final destination) but to follow its *aim* (the way itself), which is to circle round the object (S11, 168)' (Evans, *Introductory Dictionary*, p. 46).
25. Lacan, *L'Éthique*, p. 175 (*Ethics*, p. 146).
26. Gaunt analyses male personae and characters talking about dying as a form of subject-assertion that generally replaces actual death (*Martyrs to Love*, chapter 5).
27. Spitzer, *L'Amour lointain*, p. 9.
28. Lacan, *L'Éthique*, p. 182 (*Ethics*, p. 152).
29. *Ibid.*, p. 175 (p. 146).
30. *Ibid.*, p. 150 (p. 125).
31. Lewis, *Allegory of Love*, p. 12.
32. *Ibid.*, p. 18.
33. *Ibid.*, p. 29.
34. *Ibid.*, pp. 16–17.
35. See especially Lacan, *L'Éthique*, pp. 191–4 (*Ethics*, pp. 161–4).
36. Lewis, *Allegory of Love*, p. 2.
37. Lacan, *L'Éthique*, p. 208 (*Ethics*, p. 177).

38. *Ibid.*, p. 223 (p. 189).
39. *Ibid.*, especially pp. 211–23, 257–70 (pp. 179–90, 218–30).
40. *Ibid.*, p. 223 (p. 190).
41. *Ibid.*, p. 219 (p. 186).
42. Žižek, 'Real of Sexual Difference', p. 347.
43. Kay, 'Desire and Subjectivity', pp. 218–19.
44. All translations of *Lancelot* represent my adaptation of the translation of parts of the non-cyclic version: *Lancelot of the Lake*, trans. Corley.
45. Writing from a different critical perspective, Lazar analyses how, in *Le Chevalier de la Charrette*, Guinevere is the 'desired mediatrix' between Lancelot as self-seeker and Lancelot as self-realizer, 'between the project of his being and the plenitude of his existence' ('Lancelot et la "mulier mediatrix"', p. 244). Lazar reserves for Love the title of 'absolute mediator' (*ibid.*).
46. Lacan, *L'Éthique*, pp. 107–8 (*Ethics*, p. 89).
47. 'Masochism . . . is made to the measure of the victim: it is the victim (the servant in the masochistic relationship) who initiates a contract with the Master (woman), authorizing her to humiliate him in any way she considers appropriate (within the terms defined by the contract) . . . It is the servant, therefore, who writes the screenplay – that is, who actually pulls the strings and dictates the activity of the woman (*dominatrix*): he stages his own servitude' (Žižek, 'Courtly Love', pp. 91–2). See also Deleuze, *Coldness and Cruelty*.
48. Numerous critics consider Lancelot's chivalry in the cyclic prose romance to differ from Round Table norms because authentically marked by the Other's desire. See Suard, 'Lancelot et le chevalier enferré'; Plummer, 'Frenzy and Females'; and Longley, 'Guinevere as Lord', and 'Lady of the Lake'.
49. Paris, 'Études', p. 518.
50. Žižek, 'Courtly Love', p. 90.
51. Chrétien de Troyes, *Le Chevalier de la Charrette*, l. 5654.
52. Paris, 'Études', p. 518.
53. Guinevere's presentation is analysed by Krueger, 'Desire, Meaning, and the Female Reader'; Noble, 'Character of Guinevere'; and Bruckner, 'Interpreter's Dilemma'.
54. Žižek, 'Courtly Love', p. 90.
55. Hanning, *Individual*, especially pp. 53–60.
56. Mary Douglas, *Purity and Danger*. Carroll, 'Savage Bind', contextualizes Douglas's work as a response to Lévi-Strauss's celebrated essay on myth.
57. Kay, *Courtly Contradictions*, chapter 2.
58. Saward, *Perfect Fools*, notes repeatedly that Catholic tradition distinguishes between laudable folly for God's sake and sinful folly in other contexts.
59. Kay, *Courtly Contradictions*, pp. 81–8; Gaunt, *Martyrs to Love*, chapter 4. Kay allows both a 'high' and a 'low' reading of Lancelot.
60. Bruckner, 'Interpreter's Dilemma', p. 73.
61. Kennedy, 'Failure'. See also Rockwell, '"Je ne suiz mi soffisanz"'.
62. Spitzer, *L'Amour lointain*, p. 27.

63. Cohen, 'Masoch/Lancelotism'. Contrast Žižek, for whom courtly masochism reinforces patriarchal power structures ('Courtly Love', pp. 108–9).
64. Jaeger's judgement on the *Charrette* in my view fits the non-cyclic prose romance better: 'Lancelot overcome[s] shame, but not by the double operation of exalting/debasing – but rather a progress from debasement to exaltation' (*Ennobling Love*, p. 138).
65. Longley, 'Lady of the Lake'; Flori, 'L'épée de Lancelot'.
66. On the shifting value of Lancelot's name, see especially Kennedy, 'Re-Writing and Re-Reading'. On the re-troping of Lancelot's love in different versions, see Dover, 'From Non-Cyclic to Cyclic *Lancelot*'.
67. Elizabeth Edwards, 'Place of Women', p. 48.
68. Kay, 'Adultery and Killing'. On the ethical value of death in the *Mort Artu*, see especially Greene, *Le Sujet et la mort*.
69. Kennedy, *Lancelot and the Grail*, especially pp. 10–48. She considers (p. 256) that the equivalent episodes in the cyclic version place less emphasis on the identity theme.
70. Žižek, '"No Sexual Relationship"', p. 243.
71. Hence the insistence on the mirror's role as limit, 'ce que l'on ne peut franchir' (Lacan, *L'Éthique*, p. 181; 'that which cannot be crossed' [alternatively, 'that through which one cannot go'], *Ethics*, p. 151), organizing the inaccessibility of the object.
72. Kennedy, 'Figure of Lancelot'. If, however, Tristan is construed as an ethical hero (Gaunt, *Martyrs to Love*, pp. 104–18), then such references or their absence take on a different significance.
73. Paris, 'Études', p. 519.
74. Frappier, 'Le personnage de Galehaut', pp. 553–4. Ménard discusses Galehot's name, origins and titles ('Galehaut, prince conquérant', pp. 263–5).
75. On giants in medieval literature, see especially Baumgartner, 'Géants et chevaliers'; and Cohen, *Of Giants*.
76. On the *chanson de geste* giant Fierabras, see Ailes, 'Faith in *Fierabras*'. On the desires of Palamedes, the gigantic Saracen knight in the prose *Tristan*, see Huot, *Madness*, chapter 4.
77. Huot provides a post-colonial analysis of Galehot's half-human, half-giant character ('Love, Race, and Gender'). See also Warren, *History on the Edge*, pp. 171–221. On giant appetites, see Crofts, 'Perverse and Contrary Deeds'. According to Hyatte, Galehot illustrates the ethical paradox in which, virtue being represented by the mean, to excel is also to transgress (*Arts of Friendship*, p. 106).
78. As Guinevere comments, 'mais il ne me requiert nule rien' (p. 347; 'but he does not ask me for anything'). 'This "nothing", of course, is the unmistakable index of true love: [the lover] is not to be satisfied with any positive content or act (going to bed with him, for example) by means of which [the beloved] could reciprocate his love. What he wants her to offer in return is the very "nothingness" in her, what is "in her more than herself" – not something she possesses but precisely what she does *not* have, the return of love itself' (Žižek,

'"No Sexual Relationship"', p. 239). Much the same may be said of Galehot's modest requests of Lancelot.

79. Stäblein, 'L'art de la métamorphose'.
80. Huot argues that Galehot in both the prose *Lancelot* and the prose *Tristan* splits the eponymous heroes into chivalric paradigm and adulterer ('Love, Race, and Gender', p. 384). It could also be argued that he connects and even reconciles, though in tension, the two identities.
81. Zeikowitz, *Homoeroticism and Chivalry*, chapter 4, especially pp. 72–7; Schultz, *Courtly Love*, p. 80.
82. A series of pieces by Hyatte considers these parallels in detail: 'Recoding Ideal Male Friendship', *Arts of Friendship*, especially pp. 102–21, 'Praise and Subversion', 'Dream-Engendering Dreams', and 'Reading Affective Companionship'. See also Dover, 'Galehot and Lancelot'; and Mieszkowski, 'Queering of Late Medieval Literature'.
83. 'Plus vos ai ge anmé que terriene anor' (p. 329; 'I have loved you more than worldly honour'). Both Galehot (p. 325) and Guinevere (p. 609) reject shame in loving Lancelot. Note also p. 324 (Lancelot will never be shamed by Galehot). Hyatte discusses the logic of inversion, folly to wisdom, in relation to Galehot (*Arts of Friendship*, pp. 118–20).
84. Paris and Lacan offer equally plausible explanations: Galehot's fear for his beloved's safety combines with fear of attaining his desire. This distinguishes Galehot's situation from that of those male characters in medieval texts who cement a friendship with another male by the gift of a female; Chaucer's Pandarus being perhaps the most famous example. The fundamental similarity between these instances and cases where two men struggle over a woman, as in Chaucer's *Knight's Tale*, is advanced by Girard, *Deceit, Desire, and the Novel*, chapter 1. For queer developments, see Sedgwick's ground-breaking *Between Men*. Medievalist appropriations are too numerous to detail.
85. According to Lacan, 'C'est pour autant qu'est soutenu le plaisir de désirer, c'est-à-dire, en toute rigueur, le plaisir d'éprouver un déplaisir, que nous pouvons parler de la valorisation sexuelle des états préliminaires de l'acte de l'amour' (Lacan, *L'Éthique*, p. 182; 'It is only insofar as the pleasure of desiring, or, more precisely, the pleasure of experiencing unpleasure, is sustained that we can speak of the sexual valorization of the preliminary stages of the act of love', *Ethics*, p. 152). Compare Spitzer's view of the troubadour *paradoxe amoureux* (*L'Amour lointain*).
86. Roubaud, 'Galehaut et l'éros mélancolique'.
87. Ménard, 'Galehaut, prince conquérant', shows in detail how Galehot's career is overshadowed by death, a point emphasized by Roubaud.
88. In the cyclic versions Galehot is not finally expelled but buried in Lancelot's fortress of Joyous Guard, where Lancelot will ultimately join him.
89. Klosowska (Roberts), *Queer Love*, p. 144. On chivalry, friendship and homoeroticism, see notably Gaunt, *Gender and Genre*, chapters 1 and 2; Burgwinkle, *Sodomy, Masculinity, and Law*; Huot, *Madness*, chapter 4; the works by Hyatte referred to in note 82, above; Zeikowitz, *Homoeroticism and Chivalry*; Bray,

Friend; Jaeger, *Ennobling Love*; and Burns, *Courtly Love Undressed*, chapters 4
and 5. The oft-cited conclusion to Marchello-Nizia, 'Amour courtois', namely
that courtly heterosexual relations express the suppressed homosexual love
between husband and lover, simplifies her subtler exploration of the theme.

90. The notion of monologic masculinity is related to the *chanson de geste* by
Gaunt, *Gender and Genre*, chapter 1.

91. The most influential expositors of courtly love as an expression of male–male
social and political relations are Duby, *Mâle Moyen Âge*; Köhler, *L'Aventure
chevaleresque*; and Frappier, *Amour courtois et Table Ronde*. Though they
remain influential, these scholars' minimizing of female agency has been
overturned in recent years by, for instance, Greene, 'The Knight, the Woman,
and the Historian'; Evergates (ed.), *Aristocratic Women in Medieval France*;
Cheyette, *Ermengard of Narbonne*; and Bouchard, *Those of my Blood*.

92. Rubin, 'Thinking Sex', pp. 307, 308. Schultz renews Rubin's plea and documents how critics have confused the two (*Courtly Love*, chapter 4, especially
p. 60).

93. Warner, 'Thoreau's Bottom', p. 65 (quoted by Bersani, *Homos*, p. 4). See also
Warner, 'Homo-Narcissism'.

94. On this notion of 'antagonism', which derives from the work of Laclau and
Mouffe, see Žižek, 'Spectre of Ideology'.

95. Butler, 'Arguing with the Real', in *Bodies That Matter*, pp. 187–222; and
her contributions to Butler, Laclau and Žižek, *Contingency, Hegemony, Universality*. Copjec defends the utility of Lacan's formulations on gender and
sexuality to a feminist cultural critique (*Read My Desire*).

96. There is nevertheless queer potential in feminizing either or both of the
heroes. Burns draws out the feminizing effect of Lancelot's dress, in 'Refashioning Courtly Love', and *Courtly Love Undressed*, especially chapter 4.
Gaunt develops a Lacanian reading of Galehot's role as troubling third in
the Lancelot–Guinevere relationship (*Martyrs to Love*, pp. 191–204).

97. See the condensed analysis of critical treatments of Galehot's sexuality in
Gaunt, *Martyrs to Love*, p. 192, n. 28. I use 'gay' here for its political valency.

98. Schultz, 'Heterosexuality as a Threat', and *Courtly Love*, especially chapters
4, 5 and 6. Further possibilities are opened up by Lochrie, *Heterosyncrasies*;
and Burger, *Chaucer's Queer Nation*. See also Burgwinkle, 'Queer Theory
and the Middle Ages'.

99. Bersani, *Homos*, p. 1.

100. Žižek, 'Between Symbolic Fiction and Fantasmatic Spectre'.

101. Bersani, *Homos*; Edelman, *No Future*; Butler, *Antigone's Claim*. However,
MacCannell, *Regime of the Brother*, offers a dystopian reading of relations
under the banner of equality and fraternity.

102. Huot discusses the colonial aspects of Galehot's treatment ('Love, Race, and
Gender').

103. Lacan developed the concept of the *objet (petit) a*, 'any object which sets
desire in motion' (Evans, *Introductory Dictionary*, p. 125), during the early
1960s. For a discussion of courtly romance in terms of *objet a*, see Griffin,

Object and Cause. The *objet a* has clear links with the Thing, a term which almost disappears from Lacan's work after Seminar VII (Evans, *Introductory Dictionary*, p. 205). I have preferred the analytical concept of the Thing as foregrounding the abject dimension, crucial to Lancelot's *vilains/vaillanz* (worst/best) characterization, and to my interests in this book generally.

104. 'L'une e l'altre pur mei se dolt, / E jo m'en duil pur duble Ysolt' (Thomas, *Tristan*, Sneyd 1, 471–2; 'Both the one and the other suffer because of me, and I suffer from double Ysolt').

105. Sunderland explores how the production of a *Lancelot* cycle, with its need for Lancelot to remain alive, affects heroic ethics (*Old French Narrative Cycles*, pp. 78–88). Greene analyses subjectivity (for characters and reader) as a function of the fear of death in the *Mort Artu* (*Le Sujet et la mort*, especially pp. 139–82). For Greene, the *Mort Artu*, 'being a romance of death still to come or having already come, teaches its characters and listeners what anxiety is rather than what death is. It tells them not, "Think on Death", but "Think on Thinking"' (p. 147).

106. Guinevere is also described as Lancelot's 'compaigne' by the Lady of the Lake after the consummation (p. 557). Hyatte notes that Arthur, Guinevere and Galehot compete less for Lancelot's affection than for his companionship or company (*Arts of Friendship*, p. 105).

107. In reference to Galehot's dream of Lancelot as a leopard, see the following comment: 'In a celebrated passage, the author of the *Song of Lewes* compared Edward [I] to a leopard. On the one hand, he was a *leo*, a brave lion, proud and fierce. On the other hand, he was a *pard*, inconstant and unreliable, making promises when he was in a tight corner, and then forgetting them' (Prestwich, *Edward I*, p. 25). I owe this reference to Dr Shelagh Sneddon.

108. Žižek, 'Eclipse of Meaning', p. 209.

109. Lacan, *L'Éthique*, p. 170 (*Ethics*, p. 141).

110. Kennedy considers that the cyclic *Lancelot* enhances Galehot's prominence, but subordinates it to the central tragedy (*Lancelot and the Grail*, pp. 257–8). Her discussion suggests that the cyclic Galehot becomes a double as much of Arthur as of Lancelot.

111. Gauvain's vision of an exclusive relationship here does not correspond to his famously free amorous behaviour and to his many close male friendships in this and other French texts. It could perhaps explain that behaviour.

112. Baumgartner discusses the epitaph on Galehot and Lancelot's joint grave, which combines their names with Galahad's, in 'Lancelot et la Joyeuse Garde'.

113. See Žižek's commentary on the lady in courtly love as an 'exemplary case' of the 'male logic of exception' (the 'not-all'): 'In the figure of the lady, this inaccessible absolute other, woman as sexual object, reaches existence. There woman exists, yet at the price of being posited as an inaccessible thing. Sexualized, she is transformed into an object that precisely insofar as it gives body to sexuality as such renders the masculine subject impotent' ('Connections of the Freudian Field', p. 74). The wounded Gauvain's adoption of this figure as fantasy position suggests, in my view, a more complex rendering of the

'not-all' within the masculine domain than Žižek posits, with correspondingly more complicated configurations of gender and sexuality.

114. Chênerie, 'L'aventure du chevalier enferré', analyses the interrelated themes of wounding and of giants.

115. A different reading of the gender indeterminacies of this scene is given by Burns, 'Which Queen?'. See also Greene, *Le Sujet et la mort*, on Gauvain, Arthur and Lancelot in the *Mort Artu* as respectively ego, id and superego; she summarizes each's differently mediated desire on p. 160.

116. Plummer, 'Frenzy and Females'.

117. Evans, *Introductory Dictionary*, p. 181.

3. THE *UBI SUNT* TOPOS IN MIDDLE FRENCH: SAD STORIES OF THE DEATH OF KINGS

1. Ariès summarizes his cultural history in *Hour of Our Death*, pp. 602–14.

2. Deguileville, *Le Pèlerinage de vie humaine*, ll. 13491–502. On the different redactions, see the entry on Deguileville in the *Dictionnaire des lettres françaises: Le moyen âge*.

3. Saward, *Perfect Fools*, pp. 6–7.

4. Liborio, 'Contributi'; Gilson, 'De la Bible à François Villon'. My considerations on death and subjectivity in this chapter are indebted to Greene's study of the *Mort Artu* (*Le Sujet et la mort*).

5. Heger, 'La Ballade et le Chant Royal'.

6. *Le Chastoiement d'un père à son fils*, Appendix C, ll. 2080–1.

7. Bronfen explains: 'Horror at the sight of death turns into satisfaction, since the survivor is not himself dead' (*Over Her Dead Body*, p. 65). For Bronfen, 'the corpse is feminine, the survivor masculine' (*ibid.*), a view which will become significant later in the present chapter.

8. On the gender of subject and object, the *locus classicus* is of course Beauvoir, *Second Sex*, and the argument is influentially developed in a phenomenological context by Irigaray (see especially *Ethics*).

9. See especially Foucault, 'Right of Death and Power over Life', in *The History of Sexuality*, vol. I, pp. 133–59. Mills discusses sovereignty in Villon's work in the light of Agamben's writings ('Sovereignty and Bare Life'). Agamben's model combines sovereignty with biopolitics, to which Foucault contrasted it. For a critique, see Prozorov, *Foucault, Freedom and Sovereignty*, chapter 5.

10. On collective memory, see especially Connerton's classic essay, *How Societies Remember*. On individual memory, I refer especially to the phenomenological accounts by Casey, *Remembering*; and Ricoeur, *Memory, History, Forgetting*.

11. Guenée, *Un Meurtre*, p. 206.

12. Laurie, 'Eustache Deschamps'. Historical contextualization of Deschamps's major themes is provided in Boudet and Millet (eds.), *Eustache Deschamps en son temps*. Becker, *Eustache Deschamps*, provides an overview of recent criticism.

13. Huizinga, *Waning*, p. 169.

14. See especially Laidlaw, 'L'innovation métrique'.
15. Kendrick, 'La poésie pastorale'; Lacassagne, 'Rhétorique et politique'.
16. Sobczyk, 'La place du Moi'.
17. Deschamps, *Œuvres complètes*, vol. VIII. Laurie ('Eustache Deschamps', pp. 51–2, n. 80) dismisses Raynaud's suggestion (*Œuvres complètes*, vol. XI, pp. 43–4) that Ballade 1457 reflects on the death of the duke of Anjou in September 1384, without assigning it another date.
18. *Sofler* as an intransitive verb can mean 'gust', as of wind; 'breathe deeply, pant'; or 'whisper'.
19. Under the heading 'Saracen', Deschamps elsewhere includes Muslims such as Saladin or the Turks, as in the 'Miroir de Mariage' (*Œuvres complètes*, vol. IX, ll. 11,339–71), and also classical antique figures, as when he refers to the distribution of the Nine Worthies as 'Trois Sarrasin, trois Juif, trois Crestien' (Ballade 93).
20. Martineau-Génieys, among others, considers that resistance to death characterizes Deschamps's poetic character (*Le Thème de la mort*, pp. 142–3).
21. Deschamps frequently puns on Vertus in Champagne, his home.
22. Davies compares various definitions of Western civilization, in *Europe*, pp. 19–31.
23. Corresponding to Kermode's account of the *aevum*, a 'kind of eternity within a non-eternal world', in *Sense of an Ending*, pp. 67–89 (p. 74).
24. Huizinga, *Waning*, p. 135.
25. Nora, 'From *Lieux de mémoire* to *Realms of Memory*', p. xvii.
26. Nora, 'Between Memory and History', p. 7.
27. Poirion, *Le Poète et le Prince*, p. 587.
28. Ricoeur, *Memory, History, Forgetting*, p. 36.
29. As Deschamps's chanson royale 368, another *ubi sunt* poem, puts it: 'Bienfait s'en va o l'ame, et le renom / Si demourra exemple a la lignée' (ll. 33–4; 'Good deeds go with the soul, and the renown stays as an example to the line').
30. Changing views of the court in late medieval France are discussed in Lemaire, *Les Visions de la vie de cour*.
31. Krynen details the increasing professionalization of the kingly role in the late Middle Ages (*Idéal du prince*).
32. The structure of argument in late medieval ballades and the internal structure of the stanzas are analysed by Poirion, *Le Poète et le Prince*, pp. 374–91.
33. *Ibid.*, p. 368.
34. On the late medieval political subject, see Guenée, *Un Meurtre*, pp. 42–5. See also the analyses in Haidu, *Subject Medieval/Modern*, and *Subject of Violence*.
35. See Krynen, *Idéal du prince*; Quillet, *Charles V, le roi lettre'*; Guenée, 'Le vœu de Charles VI'; and Delisle's classic study, *Recherches sur la librairie de Charles V*. Lemaire, *Les Visions de la vie de cour*, outlines the changing ideas of the court under late medieval French kings.
36. Interesting light is thrown on the copyist's workshop by Tesnière, 'Les manuscrits copiés par Raoul Tainguy'.

37. The crisis of authority in France under Charles VI has been widely analysed, for instance by Guenée, *Un Meurtre*. On ideological changes, see especially his *La Folie de Charles VI*.
38. Lacan, *Le Séminaire, livre IV*, pp. 209–14.
39. Gluckman, 'Frailty in Authority', pp. 27–8.
40. Poirion, *Le Poète et le Prince*, pp. 373–4.
41. Mühletahler analyses the equivocally critical and ludic positioning of Deschamps's ballades ('Aux limites de la satire').
42. Sobczyk, 'La place du Moi', notes the assertive as well as hesitant aspects of Deschamps's self-presentation.
43. Barthes, 'To Write: An Intransitive Verb?', p. 143. I have not found the discussion following the paper (pp. 145–56) published in French. I do not have space to go into the ramifications of the different English renderings of 'Je suis mort', nor of the tenses in French.
44. *Ibid.*, pp. 155–6.
45. *Ibid.*, p. 156.
46. In the 1966 debate, Derrida draws on Hyppolite's earlier intervention: 'I wonder if the *pacte de la parole*, a "complicity of speech", that you mention at the end of your talk, is wholly maintained in writing. Or, when one writes, doesn't interlocution undergo a sort of transformation, so that writing often becomes a phantasm of interlocution?' (*ibid.*, p. 146). Hyppolite focuses on how speech and writing imply different interpersonal situations between originator and addressee, even where these are superficially similar. It should be noted that Barthes's text refers to a 'pacte de parole' (*ibid.*, p. 144) or 'pact of language' and not only of 'speech'.
47. *Ibid.*, p. 156.
48. Derrida, *Speech*, p. 54.
49. *Ibid.*
50. *Ibid.*, p. 54, n. 4.
51. Starobinski is discussing the haunting of modern literary activity by notions of immortality: 'This manner of dying to oneself is at the same time a way to seek refuge from death by passing over to its side. The desired immortality is concealed beneath mourning weeds' ('L'immortalité mélancolique', p. 248).
52. Rabaté, *Future of Theory*, p. 44.
53. Derrida, in Barthes, 'To Write: An Intransitive Verb?', p. 155. Barthes's essay is 'Textual Analysis'; I have occasionally silently emended Bennington's text to give a more literal rendition of the original. Derrida and Barthes refer to Baudelaire's translation of Poe; Barthes cites the edition *Histoires extraordinaires* (Paris: Poche, 1969), pp. 329–45. I quote Poe's text as given in Bennington's translation of Barthes.
54. Barthes, 'Textual Analysis', p. 153.
55. *Ibid.*
56. Joynes's scholarly and entertaining collection, *Medieval Ghost Stories*, contains numerous examples.

57. Barthes, 'Textual Analysis', p. 153 (translation adapted). The reference to grammatical examples sketches a link to Barthes's own 1966 use of 'je suis mort'. Much of this debate takes place under the aegis of the lapsus or the aside.
58. *Ibid.*
59. Barthes, 'Analyse textuelle', p. 45.
60. Barthes, 'Textual Analysis', p. 150.
61. *Ibid.*, p. 142.
62. Dates are taken from Freeman, *Villain's Tale*. On mock wills, see Cerquiglini-Toulet, *L'Écriture testamentaire*; Rossman, *François Villon*; and Regalado, 'Villon's Legacy'. For an extensive study of real wills and the associated mentality of the late Middle Ages, see Chiffoleau, *La Comptabilité de l'au-delà*.
63. Villon, *Le Testament Villon*, vol. 1, ll. 753–60. All references to the *Testament* are to this edition unless otherwise specified.
64. The titles, of course, originate in Marot's 1533 edition. On the technique of lyric insertion in the *Testament*, see Huot, 'From Life to Art'.
65. On death as a contemporary poetic theme, see especially Siciliano, 'La Mort', pp. 227–79 of *François Villon*. Martineau-Génieys argues, against Siciliano, that the theme of death was in decline, that of mourning on the rise when Villon was writing (*Le Thème de la mort*, pp. 157–89).
66. Geremek, *Margins of Society*.
67. Some unexceptionably courtly lyrics survive from Villon's approaches to great nobles in the late 1450s; see *Le Lais Villon et les poèmes variés*.
68. A representative assessment is Siciliano's, in *François Villon*, p. 274.
69. Poe, 'Philosophy of Composition' (1846), p. 19.
70. Translations of Villon are adapted from *Poems*, (ed. and) trans. Kinnell.
71. Old age for Villon represents the 'présence de la mort dans la vie', the old person being 'incapable de susciter l'attention et *a fortiori* l'amour', according to Dufournet in 'Deux poètes du moyen âge', p. 164.
72. On the transformations to be wrought by adopting active-voice theories in sociological study, and more widely on associated notions of agency, see Mary Douglas, 'Passive Voice Theories'.
73. Freud, 'Fetishism' (1927). My analysis is indebted to Bronfen, *Over Her Dead Body*, especially pp. 95–109.
74. Siciliano, *François Villon*, p. 273.
75. *Ibid.*, p. 272.
76. *Ibid.*, p. 273.
77. Spitzer, 'Étude ahistorique', pp. 10, 9.
78. *Ibid.*, p. 10.
79. Kristeva, *Desire in Language*, especially 'From One Identity to an Other', pp. 124–47, and 'The Novel as Polylogue', pp. 159–209.
80. On time, see Kada-Benoïst, 'Le phénomène de désagrégation'.
81. Jane H. M. Taylor, 'La poétique de l'incohérence', p. 45; see also her *Poetry of François Villon*.

82. On Archipïadés, see the still valuable notes in Thuasne's edition of Villon, *Œuvres*.
83. For instance, Siciliano, *François Villon*, p. 272. On naming strategies in the *Testament*, see especially Cholakian, '(Un)naming Process'.
84. Draskau, *Quest for Equivalence*, especially pp. 246–66. Readings of the refrain focus on controversy over the prosaic or poetic connotations of *antan*; for a recent review, see Freeman, 'Snows of Yester-Year'.
85. I am indebted to Johnson's deconstruction of the verse/prose binary in 'Poetry and Its Double'.
86. Martineau-Génieys, *Le Thème de la mort*, p. 169.
87. Kuhn (Mus) links the natural themes to fertility and to an idealized femininity, in *La Poétique de François Villon*, chapter 4. On sirens, see Elizabeth Eva Leach, '"The Little Pipe Sings Sweetly"'.
88. Rychner and Henry discuss the variant 'Berte au grant pié', in *Testament*, vol. II, s.v. l. 347 (p. 55). See also Ménard, '"Berthe au grant pié"'.
89. Spitzer, 'Étude ahistorique', p. 13.
90. Craig Taylor (trans. and annotated), *Joan of Arc*, p. 349. On Joan and Antigone, see Žižek, 'Interlude: The Feminine Excess'; and Fraisse, *Le Mythe d'Antigone*, pp. 47–50.
91. See the discussion of secondary burial in Chapter 5, below.
92. Irigaray, 'The Mechanics of Fluids', in *This Sex*, pp. 106–18, and 'Volume-Fluidity', in *Speculum*, pp. 227–40. Martineau-Génieys, however, refers the ladies to a dry, white, symbolically useful and ornamental form of the macabre; compare Chaucer's *Book of the Duchess*, Chapter 5, below. Martineau-Génieys notes that Villon, like Deschamps, does not follow the contemporary literary fashion for decomposition (*Le Thème de la mort*, pp. 168–70).
93. Regalado, '*Effet de réel, effet du réel*'.
94. Fox, 'Note'.
95. Rychner and Henry give Jean III, in error.
96. Kantorowicz's familiar theory of the king's two bodies can be refined on. Jean Gerson theorized that the king has three lives. As described by Guenée, *Un Meurtre*, p. 25: 'His spiritual life is that of his soul. Like any man, he lives with a natural or corporal life when his soul and his body are united in a single person. But he has, as king, a third life, that Gerson calls "public" or "civil and universal" or "civil and political" or "civil and mystical". That life is "everlasting", it will have no end; it "endures in this kingdom by legitimate succession through the royal line, without a definite term or as if eternally".'
97. Other than sources mentioned elsewhere in these notes, my information derives from the *Dictionnaire de biographie française*.
98. Cropp, 'La "Ballade des seigneurs"', p. 236. Cropp's reading is contested. For Freeman, the lords are like the ladies, haloed 'stuff of fable' (*Villain's Tale*, p. 162). Contrastingly, Frappier is dismissive of the lords' reputation ('Les trois Ballades du temps jadis').
99. Nora, 'Between Memory and History', p. 2.

100. Weiner, *Trobrianders*, p. 164.
101. *Ibid.*, p. 163.
102. Morrissey, *Charlemagne and France*; Spiegel, *Romancing the Past* and '*Reditus Regni*'; Beaune, *Birth of an Ideology*.
103. Dufournet, 'Une ballade méconnue de Villon', pp. 42–3.
104. Notably Frappier, 'Les trois Ballades du temps jadis'.
105. Kada-Benoïst, 'Le phénomène de désagrégation'; Jane H. M. Taylor, 'La poétique de l'incohérence'.
106. Nora, 'Between Memory and History', p. 1.
107. See especially Cerquiglini-Toulet, *Color of Melancholy*; and Camille, *Master of Death*. On Huizinga's complex legacy, see Gumbrecht, 'Intertextuality and Autumn'; and Shaw, 'Huizinga's Timelessness'.
108. Lacan, *L'Éthique*, p. 150 (*Ethics*, p. 125).
109. This generally accompanied a move to prose, and often also to print. For instance, Philippe de Vigneulles's prosification of *Garin le Loherain*, published in Metz in 1515 and no longer extant, began: 'L'histoire est de grant excellence et merveilleux faitz d'armes, laquelle se lisoit du tout au livre et n'estoit pas quasi plus memoire d'icelle par ce que moult de gens n'entendoient plus bien le langage' ('The story, which was there to be read in full in the book, relates great excellence and marvellous feats of arms. There was almost no more memory of it, because many people could not well understand the language'). Quoted by Ménard, '"Berthe au grant pié"', pp. 123–4.
110. The most extensive exploration is Varty, 'Villon's Three *Ballades*'. Jane Taylor relates the illustrations at the Cimetière des Innocents to Villon's interweaving of real and fictional worlds ('Metonymy, Montage, and Death'). Her wide-ranging 'Un miroer salutaire' argues that cultural ideas about mirrors would have predisposed medieval audiences to accept the *Danse macabre* message of 'la mort de soi' over affirmative disidentification. On the *Danse macabre* in medieval culture, see Delumeau, *Le Péché et la peur*, especially pp. 44–97; and Clark, *Dance of Death*.
111. Batany argues for the social conservatism of the *Danse macabre* ('Les "Danses Macabres"').
112. For Frappier, it is 'the same insolent, disaggregating rhythm' that we find elsewhere in Villon's work ('Les trois Ballades du temps jadis', p. 341).
113. Varty, 'Villon's Three *Ballades*', p. 91.
114. On this effect, see Vitz, *Crossroad of Intentions*. I would explain in similar terms and as a rhetorical effect the phenomena of audience inclusion and exclusion ingeniously analysed by Fein, *François Villon and His Reader*. Compare the rhetorical analysis of Occitan lyric in Gaunt, *Troubadours and Irony*.
115. See Hunt's discussion of this line, in *Villon's Last Will*, pp. 20–1.
116. Bowie, *Lacan*, p. 120.
117. Contrastingly, Huot argues that the *Testament* subtracts the poetic persona from life and death to give him immortality in the symbolic ('From Life to Art', p. 36), a position that I associate with Deschamps.

118. For an example of the plural, see Deschamps, Ballade 93; of the singular, Deschamps, Ballade 94 (both in *Œuvres complètes*, vol. 1).
119. Barthes, 'Textual Analysis', p. 152. The same phrase – unsurprisingly, given its echoes of Chateaubriand – is used by Méla, '"Je, Françoys Villon . . . "', p. 777. Méla's reading emphasizes the persistence of the symbolic.
120. Barthes, 'Textual Analysis', p. 150 (adapted).

4. CECI N'EST PAS UNE MARGUERITE: ANAMORPHOSIS
IN *PEARL*

1. *Pearl*, ed. Gordon. Further references are to this edition unless otherwise specified.
2. Schmitt, *Ghosts in the Middle Ages*, and 'Les revenants'. As Žižek puts it: 'The return of the living dead . . . materializes a certain symbolic debt persisting beyond physical expiration' (*Looking Awry*, p. 23).
3. Lacan, *L'Éthique*, p. 181 (*Ethics*, p. 151).
4. However, Kline argues that the Jeweller comes to appreciate the Maiden as a real child ('Female Childhoods', p. 15).
5. For a selection of relevant material, see Appendix 1 in Usk, *Testament of Love*, pp. 415–22. In hagiography, saints' bodies are commonly compared to jewels.
6. Ariès, *Images*, p. 37. The Pearl-Maiden's physical appearance corresponds to the 'resurrection body' as distinct from the mortal, corrupt flesh or earthly body (Bynum, *Resurrection of the Body*).
7. I adopt the interpretation of 'fede' in line 29 from *Pearl*, ed. Stanbury.
8. *Pearl's* images of seed and jewel have attracted the attention of numerous critics. Bynum compares their histories as images of resurrection ('Introduction: Seed Images, Ancient and Modern', in *Resurrection of the Body*, pp. 1–17).
9. Bogdanos, *Image of the Ineffable*, pp. 19–30.
10. Žižek, '"No Sexual Relationship"', p. 230.
11. Žižek, *Looking Awry*, p. 20.
12. Eagleton, *Trouble with Strangers*, p. 153. On the relations between Christianity and the Real, see also *ibid.*, pp. 287–94 and Conclusion.
13. Cargill and Schlauch give a detailed account of the court's cultural interchanges, in '*The Pearl* and Its Jeweler'. The Cheshire connection is argued in several places by Bennett: see especially 'Court of Richard II', and 'Historical Background'. For an overview, see Andrew, 'Theories of Authorship'.
14. But see Wimsatt, *Allegory and Mirror*, pp. 124–5.
15. My discussion is indebted especially to Nouvet, 'Distinctive Signature'; Huot, 'Daisy and Laurel'; and Travis, 'Chaucer's Heliotropes'. See also Lowes's seminal articles on the Prologue to the *Legend of Good Women*: 'French *Marguerite* Poems', and 'Chronological Relations'. More generally, and among very many articles, the classic references to Chaucer's relation to French-language works are Muscatine, *Chaucer and the French Tradition*; Palmer (ed.), *Chaucer's French Contemporaries*; and three books by Wimsatt, *French Contemporaries*, *French Love-Poets* and *Marguerite Poetry*.

16. Cerquiglini(-Toulet), 'Le Dit'; Spearing, *Medieval Dream-Poetry*; Phillips, 'Dream Poems', and 'Chaucer and Dream Poetry'; Lynch, *High Medieval Dream Vision*; Russell, *English Dream Vision*, especially pp. 159–74. For further links with debate and dialogue, see Kruger, 'Dialogue, Debate, and Dream Vision'.

17. Notions of the stain and the screen, for instance, are elaborated in the later work. The relevant section is 'Du regard comme *objet petit a*', in *Le Séminaire, livre XI*, pp. 63–109 (*Four Fundamental Concepts*, pp. 65–119).

18. The book has since been reissued several times in expanded and revised forms. I use the edition available to Lacan. On Holbein's 'Ambassadors', see especially pp. 56–70.

19. Lacan, in *Le Séminaire, livre XI*, develops the idea of the anamorphotic stain to express the paradoxically dependent and exclusionary relation of the subject to the field of collectively constituted reality. Žižek glosses in relation to the subject, notably in *Tarrying with the Negative*, pp. 65–71. See also Feldstein, Fink and Jaanus (eds.), *Reading Seminar XI*.

20. Lacan, *L'Éthique*, p. 318 (*Ethics*, p. 273).

21. *Ibid.*, p. 161 (p. 135). See p. 11, above.

22. Ariès, *Images*, p. 193 (Figure 288). The double-sided painting, in Gripsholm Castle, Sweden, is illustrated (and the Charles I side demonstrated with a cylindrical mirror) in Philippovich, *Kuriositäten/Antiquitäten*, Figures 6–8 (pp. 9–11). It can be seen online, without the mirror correction: http://commons.wikimedia.org/wiki/File:Charles_I._Anamorphosis.jpg, and http://commons.wikimedia.org/wiki/File:Charles_II._Anamorphosis.jpg (accessed 21 December 2009).

23. Gombrich, *Art and Illusion*, p. 5; quoted by Besserman, 'Idea of the Green Knight', p. 228.

24. Julian, 'Against the Galilaeans', p. 417.

25. The classic account of defamiliarization is Spearing, *'Gawain'-Poet*, pp. 96–170.

26. 'The power represented by the pearl is not one which can triumph only through the exclusion and denial of ugliness and death but one which contains and transforms them' (Field, 'Heavenly Jerusalem', p. 15). The image of the wounded yet spotless Lamb brings this theme to a climax.

27. Wailes, *Medieval Allegories*, pp. 137–44; Wailes's own words and those of Gregory are quoted from p. 143.

28. See Chapter 1, above.

29. I follow Bowers, who relates the vineyard parable to labour concerns ('Politics of *Pearl*', expanded in *Politics of Pearl*). I am not concerned with Bowers's argument that the Maiden figures Queen Anne. Fletcher in his recent critique of Bowers makes valuable points about the poem's universalizing theological reach but, in arguing against ideology in poetry, overlooks Christianity's ideological and historical aspects ('Limits of History'). I am indebted also to Watkins's discussion of individualism, '"Sengeley in Synglere"'.

30. On earthly and heavenly notions of justice, see Horgan, 'Justice in the *Pearl*'.

31. Guillaume de Lorris and Jean de Meun, *Roman de la Rose*, vol. II, ll. 10496–648.

32. *Pearl* actualizes the mystical dimensions of the Thing, on which Lacan insists, for instance in *L'Éthique*, pp. 77–8 (*Ethics*, pp. 62–3).

33. *Aucassin et Nicolette*, XII.25–8.

34. The technical word for *daisy* in botanical and medical manuals was '(petite) consaude', a term having a specialist, technical register.

35. Machaut, 'Dit de la marguerite', dated by Fourrier to 1363–4.

36. Froissart, 'Le Dit de la marguerite', in *'Dits' et 'Débats'*, pp. 147–53 (ll. 1–8). Fourrier dates the poem to 1364. To distinguish it from Machaut's *dit*, I use 'Flor' for Froissart's poem as a short form of its older title, 'Le Dittié de la flour de la margherite', as found in *Œuvres de Froissart: Poésies*, vol. II, pp. 209–15.

37. 'It' referring to the daisy could in each case be translated by 'her', emphasizing the gynomorphic connotations borne by the flower in all the French works. This ambiguity can be rendered in English by shifting between neuter/nonhuman and feminine/human pronouns and terms, as the *Pearl*-poet does. His English thereby loses the smooth sliding across an ambiguous field that the French texts perfect, instead intensifying the abrupt hermeneutic, shifting characteristic of these and other courtly works; these aesthetics are equally, though differently effective. I have varied my translations according as I feel the texts shifting emphasis, but the unchosen term should ideally also be borne in mind.

38. See, for instance, Froissart's Pastourelle XVII, in *Lyric Poems*, pp. 185–7. Among marguerite poems, the most directly challenging to court values is Deschamps's 'Lai de Franchise' (or Fourth Lay, *Œuvres complètes*, vol. II, pp. 203–14), which restrictions of space compel me to omit.

39. On the connotations and circulation of pearls in the fourteenth century, see Riddy, 'Jewels in *Pearl*'; and Barr, '"The Jeweller's Tale"'.

40. Machaut, 'Marguerite', ll. 25–6. The same claim is made in the ballade by Egidius quoted by Wilkins in his 'Review of Wimsatt, *Marguerite Poetry*'. Wilkins gives four examples of marguerites in short lyrics.

41. Froissart, *Le Joli Buisson de Jonece* (hereafter *Joli Buisson*), ll. 3208–41. The *Joli Buisson*, where Cepheüs is mentioned by Venus, does not include the coda relating the genesis of the marguerite, which is found in Froissart's Pastourelle XVII, ll. 57–66, and in 'Flor', ll. 68–82. On the probability that this myth is invented by Froissart, see Kelly, 'Les inventions ovidiennes'.

42. Froissart, 'Flor', l. 97.

43. *Ibid.*, ll. 187–8.

44. Machaut, 'Le Dit de la fleur de lis et de la marguerite', hereafter 'Lys', ll. 291, 322. Wimsatt argues for a date of 1369 (*Marguerite Poetry*, pp. 54–7).

45. On different interpretations of this parable, in particular the question of whether the wares sold by the parable's jeweller are to be interpreted as lesser goods or as evils, see Wailes, *Medieval Allegories*.

46. See especially Cerquiglini-Toulet, *Color of Melancholy*.

47. On the novelty effect of Chaucer's use of English, see Cannon, *Making of Chaucer's English*. A less pithy rendering of the gleaning topos occurs in the

Prologue to Usk, *Testament of Love*, ll. 60–90. On the topos, see Martin, 'Chaucer's Ruth'; and Cerquiglini-Toulet, *Color of Melancholy*, chapter 4.

48. Chaucer, *Legend of Good Women*, G.61–5.
49. Zeeman, 'Lover-Poet'.
50. Duby, *Knight, Lady and Priest*. On the courtly ethic of dying for love, see the works cited in Chapter 2, note 11, above.
51. See Chapter 5, below, for further discussion of mourning and marital politics in the *Book of the Duchess*.
52. Froissart, *Joli Buisson*, l. 5198. The prayers to St Margaret are mentioned at lines 1106–12. Venus explains the narrator's lack of inspiration by the assertion that, in his case, 'Frois a esté li ars maint an / De mon chier fil, dont moult le carge' (ll. 931–2; 'My dear son's art has been cold many a year, for which I blame him'). On *Pearl* and the saint, see Earl, 'Saint Margaret'.
53. Usk too uses the 'dissemination' topos (*Testament of Love*, Prologue, ll. 5–7).
54. See Chapter 3, above, p. 111.
55. Huot, 'Daisy and Laurel', p. 251.
56. Machaut, 'Lys', ll. 275–304.
57. Bynum, *Holy Feast*, and *Fragmentation and Redemption*. Bynum's rejection of the likelihood of queer desires and acts in medieval representations is critiqued by Mills, *Suspended Animation*, pp. 178–80.
58. There is a large literature on saintly gender and sexuality; see in particular Gaunt, *Gender and Genre*, chapter 4; Wogan-Browne, *Saints' Lives*; Salih, *Versions of Virginity*; and Mills, *Suspended Animation*. On queer desire in the *Rose*, see especially Gaunt, 'Improper Allegory'; Raskolnikov, 'Between Men, Mourning'; and Klosowska (Roberts), *Queer Love*, chapter 2.
59. On sodomy as desire for one who is, categorically, simultaneously too similar and too different, see Gilbert, 'Gender and Sexual Transgression'; and Spearing, '*Purity* and Danger', in *Readings*, pp. 173–94. On difference and desire in *Pearl*, see Stanbury, 'Feminist Masterplots'; Bullon-Fernandez, 'Byʒonde þe Water'; and Cox, '*Pearl*'s "Precios Pere"'.
60. On *Pearl*'s 'aristocratized theology', see Watson, 'Vernacular Theologian'.
61. Field, 'Heavenly Jerusalem'.
62. Whatever its causes, the late medieval turn to quantification was a phenomenon on a European scale, whose influence in the domain of piety is analysed notably by Chiffoleau, *La Comptabilité de l'au-delà*.
63. Nouvet, 'Distinctive Signature', views the sun in these poems as a figure for the poet. I follow Huot, 'Daisy and Laurel', in reading it as the patron.
64. Machaut, 'Marguerite', ll. 44–8.
65. On likeness as a trope of the divine, see Javelet, *Image et ressemblance*.
66. Field, 'Heavenly Jerusalem'.
67. Cannon, 'Form', pp. 187–9.
68. Spearing, 'The *Gawain*-Poet's Sense of an Ending', in *Readings*, pp. 195–215 (p. 208).
69. On literary treatments of unsymbolizable loss, see Watts, 'Inexpressibility'; Aers, 'Self Mourning'; and Stanbury 'Feminist Masterplots'.

70. Note the slippage here between 'drive' and 'desire'; see Introduction, above, p. 21.
71. Eagleton, *Trouble with Strangers*, p. 182.
72. *Ibid.*, pp. 322, 323–4.

5. BECOMING WOMAN IN CHAUCER: ON NE NAÎT PAS FEMME, ON LE DEVIENT EN MOURANT

1. All references to works by Chaucer are to *The Riverside Chaucer*. The *Book* is generally dated between 1368 and 1376. Of the two versions of the *Legend*'s Prologue, F is at present generally accepted to be earlier, although there remains disagreement. *Riverside* dates F to 1386–8, G (which appears only in the earliest surviving manuscript) to 1394–6; some of the legends may have been written earlier.
2. Beauvoir, *Le Deuxième Sexe*, vol. II, p. 13 (*Second Sex*, trans. Parshley, p. 295; trans. Borde and Malovany-Chevallier, p. 293). The difference between the translations is trenchantly explained by Moi, 'Adulteress Wife', para 25 of 43.
3. Hertz, 'Contribution', p. 52.
4. *Ibid.*, pp. 37, 36.
5. *Ibid.*, p. 36.
6. *Ibid.*, p. 52.
7. *Ibid.*, pp. 79–80.
8. *Ibid.*, p. 82.
9. *Ibid.*, p. 77.
10. Hertz's essay just predates van Gennep's today better-known general theory of transitional rituals, *Rites of Passage*, which appeared in 1908. For a different discussion of female death in relation to rites of passage, liminality and second death, see Bronfen, *Over Her Dead Body*, pp. 197–201.
11. For instance, in the introduction to their edited volume, Bloch and Parry understand ritual to serve the dominant authority (*Death and the Regeneration of Life*, pp. 1–44).
12. Kelly and Kaplan, 'History, Structure, and Ritual', p. 140.
13. My reading is indebted to Butterfield, 'Lyric and Elegy'; Ellmann, 'Blanche'; Fradenburg, '"Voice Memorial"', and '"My Worldes Blisse"'; Hardman, 'Memorial Monument'; Margherita, 'Originary Fantasies'; and Schibanoff, 'Courtliness and Heterosexual Poetics in the *Book of the Duchess*', in *Chaucer's Queer Poetics*, pp. 65–97.
14. Hertz, 'Contribution', pp. 37–53.
15. *Ibid.*, p. 51.
16. Gaunt, *Martyrs to Love*, chapter 5, observes that women die for love while men talk of dying as a means of finding a place within the symbolic. Alcyone and the Man are further differentiated by their respective legendary/distant past and 'real-life'/modern status.
17. Disputes over the role of the 'king' are irrelevant for my purposes.
18. Ellmann, 'Blanche'; Travis, 'White'.

19. On commemoration and forgetting, see Forty's introduction to Forty and Küchler (eds.), *Art of Forgetting*, pp. 1–19. An example of the commemoration by obliteration described by Forty is the destruction of the palace of Sheene ordered by Richard II after Anne's death – replicated (if the G Prologue is later than the F) by the elision from the *Legend*'s text of Sheene and of Anne, as noted by Wallace, *Chaucerian Polity*, p. 373.

20. Compare Kantorowicz's account of royal funerary effigies in the late Middle Ages (*King's Two Bodies*, pp. 419–37). On elite funerals, see especially Binski, *Medieval Death*. Stanford, 'Held in "Perpetual" Memory', introduces the processes involved.

21. Hardman, 'Memorial Monument', p. 209; Phillips, 'Fortune and the Lady'.

22. Hardman, 'Memorial Monument', p. 209.

23. Hertz, 'Contribution', pp. 41–8.

24. *Ibid.*, p. 43.

25. '[S]exuality is . . . opposed to fertility. It is associated with flesh, decomposition and women, while true ancestral fertility is a mystical process symbolized by the tomb and the (male) bones' (Bloch and Parry, *Death and the Regeneration of Life*, p. 21).

26. Hertz, 'Contribution', pp. 78–80.

27. '[A]s against the dispersed, contingent, and multiple existences of actual women, mythical thought opposes the Eternal Feminine, unique and change-less. If the definition provided for this concept is contradicted by the behaviour of flesh-and-blood women, it is the latter who are wrong: we are told not that Femininity is a false entity, but that the women concerned are not femi-nine' (Beauvoir, *Second Sex*, trans. Parshley, vol. I, part III, chapter 3, p. 283). Beauvoir insists that the Eternal Feminine, like all idealizations of women, is twinned with a feared and loathed alternative.

28. Referring to the anniversary services which Gaunt ordered for Blanche, Ellmann suggests that the act of burial 'demanded repetition every year' ('Blanche', p. 103). Compare the double tomb which Gaunt had built for himself and Blanche in 1374–5 (Hardman, 'Memorial Monument', p. 206).

29. Compare the different treatments of Roland's death, Chapter 1, above.

30. More recent anthropologists insist on the contestatory and transformative potential within ritual; see Kelly and Kaplan, 'History, Structure, and Ritual'.

31. On the *Legend* as palinode, see Percival, *Legendary Good Women*, especially pp. 151–70; and as marguerite poem, pp. 23–42. Apart from the sources men-tioned in Chapter 4, n. 15, above, an important discussion of Chaucer's rela-tion to marguerite writing is Rowe, *Through Nature to Eternity*, especially pp. 15–46.

32. Against the common view that the sources cited in G by the god of Love are antifeminist, see Phillips, 'Register, Politics', p. 114.

33. Spurgeon's evidence suggests that the *Legend* was never one of Chaucer's more popular works (*Chaucer Criticism and Allusion*, vol. I, especially the table on p. lxxix). Collette summarizes some interesting recent attempts to recuperate the work, in Collette (ed.), *Context and Reception*, pp. vii–xii.

34. On Medea in the *Legend*, see Minnis, *Shorter Poems*, pp. 371–8; Percival, *Legendary Good Women*, pp. 203–20; and McDonald, 'Doubts about Medea'. See also the much broader study by Morse, *Medieval Medea*; Chaucer is discussed on pp. 224–30.

35. On the mythographic tradition, see Wetherbee, *Chaucer and the Poets*, pp. 141–3; and Kolve, 'From Cleopatra to Alceste', pp. 171–4. Chance uses mythographic material to argue for Alceste's strength as a descender into hell ("'A Wonder Thing"').

36. Cerquiglini-Toulet discusses the coffer used by late medieval poets to express the painful sense that 'they followed after more illustrious predecessors' (*Color of Melancholy*, pp. 58–64, quotation p. 54). She links it to the presentation of the patron actively co-operating in the text: 'Storing poems in a coffer plays on the notions of deferral and delegation; poetry operates at a distance rather than directly, in the poet's presence' (p. 59). Boitani discusses Chaucer's 'dream-books and book-dreams', in 'Old Books' (p. 60).

37. Sanok, 'Reading Hagiographically', p. 332, n. 25.

38. Robert R. Edwards analyses the differences between the treatments of Alceste in F and in G in the light of contemporary politics ('Ricardian Dreamwork'). Coleman returns to the argument about women's importance in the literary culture surrounding Richard's court ('"A bok for king Richardes sake"', and 'The Flower, the Leaf, and Philippa of Lancaster').

39. The tendency of Chaucer critics to downplay female cultural authority in order to save the poet's virile dignity is critiqued by Andrew Taylor, 'Anne of Bohemia'.

40. For James (W.) Simpson, 'Ethics and Interpretation', the god is a figure for exploitative male desire; however, a long literary history establishes the god as an ambiguous patron for either sex.

41. Green links the legends to Chaucer's wider interest in the gendering of *trouth* ('Chaucer's Victimized Women').

42. Other of Chaucer's poems extant in substantially different versions are not generally printed as separate texts. See, for example, *Troilus and Criseyde*, ed. Windeatt, pp. 36–54. I owe this point to Prof. Ardis Butterfield. For a creative critical exploitation of the difficulties of establishing a text, see Quinn, 'Performance, Performativity, and Presentation'.

43. Compulsion and loss of self-control are differently figured in the abdication of authorial authority to the legends' commissioners. I stress that I am not concerned with whether Chaucer was fully in control of the processes I am analysing, or with his conscious political and ethical position.

44. In *Master of Death*, Camille undertakes a comparable project in relation to the work of the illuminator Pierre Remiet but in fact emphasizes small but significant variations, resulting in – in this respect – a more traditional analysis. Quinn points out that the *Legend* would seem much less monologic 'and therefore monotonous' in its original medieval manuscript and reading-performance contexts ('Performance, Performativity, and Presentation', p. 13). Aside from Quinn's, interesting recent articles on court debate context include

McDonald, 'Games Medieval Women Play'; and Boffey, '"Twenty Thousand More"'. Note also that some manuscripts produce their own patterned effects, such as the sequence of female complaints into which mansucript Ff, the Findern Anthology, inserts the legend of Thisbe; see McDonald, 'Ladies at Court', pp. 36–9.

45. Freud, *Beyond the Pleasure Principle*, p. 22.

46. Dinshaw relates the phrase to the *Legend* (*Chaucer's Sexual Poetics*, p. 77). For further discussion of Poe's dictum, gender and lyricism, see Chapter 3, above.

47. On the philosophical and ethical problems of suicide in Old French romance, see Lefay-Toury, *La Tentation du suicide*, especially pp. 35–57 on Dido. Schmitt, 'Le suicide au Moyen Âge', analyses suicide as social disintegration and as withdrawal into private isolation.

48. The *Legend* borrows the framework of martyrology to produce actively resistant and politically radical deaths but removes the Christian content, thus doubly exploiting the pagan setting. These aspects of the text have attracted considerable attention, notably from Kiser, *Telling Classical Tales*; and Percival, *Legendary Good Women*.

49. The rapprochement is made as part of a different argument by Fradenburg, 'Loving Thy Neighbor: *The Legend of Good Women*', in *Sacrifice Your Love*, pp. 176–98 (pp. 195–6).

50. Lacan, *L'Éthique*, p. 238 (*Ethics*, p. 202, adapted).

51. *Ibid.*

52. *Ibid.*, p. 304 (p. 262).

53. Gaunt, *Martyrs to Love*, chapter 5. See my Chapter 2, above, for further discussion.

54. I disagree with Fradenburg's analysis (*Sacrifice Your Love*) of Alceste as partially sublime, although I share her view of the figure's aggression.

55. Mann, *Geoffrey Chaucer*, p. 44.

56. Bloch and Parry, *Death and the Regeneration of Life*, p. 17.

57. Numerous critics note the text's departures from the apparent ideological message. For instance, some of the heroines 'are primarily or partly victims of themselves' (Cowen, 'Structure and Tone', p. 433); 'Lucrece dies for her high principles of wifely fidelity rather than for her actual husband' (Minnis, *Shorter Poems*, p. 436).

58. Minnis, *Shorter Poems*, p. 406.

59. Dinshaw refers to readerly boredom with the *Legend* as a form of defence against it but aligns that boredom with the poem's 'soothing and re-assuring' use of repetition (*Chaucer's Sexual Poetics*, p. 86). In Chapter 1 above, pp. 48–51, I distinguish between soothing and disturbing forms of repetition.

60. Phyllis 'warns Demophon that she will make of her dead body a sign of her "trouthe" to him' (Dinshaw, *Chaucer's Sexual Poetics*, p. 83).

61. I borrow my terms from Schibanoff, *Chaucer's Queer Poetics*, pp. 15–23. Schibanoff's interpretation of Aristotle should be read with the critique by Schultz, *Courtly Love*, pp. 53–4.

62. The *Middle English Dictionary* gives the refrain as an example of sense 2 (b). The lines following the ballade in F (272–5), which support this reading, are absent from G.

63. See Fradenburg's brilliant analysis of the aggression of *disteinen* (*Sacrifice Your Love*, especially pp. 192–3).

64. Dinshaw, *Chaucer's Sexual Poetics*, p. 75.

65. '[P]oetically disfigured' by their single scenario, the legends distort notions of narrative and *trouthe* (Eleanor W. Leach, 'Morwe of May', p. 305).

66. Žižek, *Looking Awry*, p. 12 (emphasis original). I discuss anamorphosis in relation to dream vision literature in Chapter 4.

67. Žižek defends and reworks de Man's thesis of interpretation as 'a violent act of disfiguring the interpreted text' based on close reading but opposed to 'historical archaeology': 'it is through the very "pullback" from direct experience of "reality" to the textual mechanisms that we are brought closer to the traumatic kernel of some Real "repressed" in a constitutive way by so-called "reality" itself' (*Plague of Fantasies*, pp. 95–6).

68. Kelly and Kaplan, 'History, Structure, and Ritual', p. 135.

69. Butler, *Antigone's Claim*, p. 22.

CONCLUSION: LIVING DEAD OR DEAD-IN-LIFE?

1. Gaunt, *Martyrs to Love*, chapter 5. See also the extended discussion in Machaut's *Jugement du roy de Navarre*.

2. Žižek, *Plague of Fantasies*, p. 89, cited in Huot, *Madness*, p. 137.

3. On norms of masculinity in the *Chanson de Roland* and in *Roland* criticism, see Kay, *Political Fictions*, especially pp. 25–30. Kay's book revises the marginalized position that criticism has awarded to women in the *chanson de geste* genre.

4. On the *point de capiton* ('quilting point', 'anchoring point'), see Lacan, *Le Séminaire, livre III*, pp. 293–306 (*Seminar, Book III*, pp. 258–70), and 'Subversion du sujet'.

5. Žižek, *For They Know Not*, p. 29.

6. Žižek, *Tarrying with the Negative*, p. 149.

7. Machaut, *Le Jugement du roy de Behaigne*, ll. 1672–784. The *Jugement du roy de Navarre* returns to this problematic to emphasize its gendered dimension.

8. *L'Éthique*, p. 370 (*Ethics*, p. 321). 'Je ne les distingue pas comme deux espèces humaines – en chacun de nous, il y a la voie tracée pour un héros, et c'est justement comme homme du commun qu'il l'accomplit' (*ibid.*, p. 368; 'I do not distinguish between them as if they were two different human species. In each of us the path of the hero is traced, and it is precisely as an ordinary man that one follows it to the end', *Ethics*, p. 319). Creon rather than Antigone is the model for human life.

Bibliography

PRIMARY WORKS AND TRANSLATIONS

Aristotle, *Nicomachean Ethics*, trans. David Ross, rev. J. L. Ackrill and J. O. Urmson (Oxford University Press, 1980)

Aucassin et Nicolette, ed. Mario Roques (Paris: Champion, 1925)

Caxton, William, *Here begynneth a lityll treatise spekynge of the Arte & Crafte (1490)* (Amsterdam: Da Capo Press, 1970)

La Chanson de Roland, ed. Cesare Segre, rev. edn, trans. Madeleine Tyssens, 2 vols. (Geneva: Droz, 1989)

La Chanson de Roland: The French Corpus, gen. ed. Joseph J. Duggan, 3 vols. (Turnhout: Brepols, 2005)

Le Chastoiement d'un père à son fils, ed. Edward D. Montgomery (Chapel Hill: University of North Carolina Press, 1971)

Chaucer, Geoffrey, *The Riverside Chaucer*, gen. ed. Larry D. Benson, 3rd edn (Oxford University Press, 1987)

  Troilus and Criseyde: A New Edition of 'The Book of Troilus', ed. B. A. Windeatt (London: Longman, 1984)

Chrétien de Troyes, *Le Chevalier de la Charrette*, ed. Charles Méla (Paris: Poche, 1992)

Deguileville, Guillaume de, *Le Pèlerinage de vie humaine*, ed. J. J. Stürzinger (London: Nichols, 1893). The text can be consulted at http://gallica.bnf.fr/

Deschamps, Eustache, *Œuvres complètes*, ed. Marquis de Queux de Saint-Hilaire and Gaston Raynaud, 11 vols., SATF (Paris: Firmin Didot, 1878–1903); vol. VIII, ed. Gaston Raynaud (1893). The text can be consulted at http://gallica.bnf.fr/

Epicurus, 'Letter to Menoeceus', in *Epicurus Reader: Selected Writings and Testimonia*, ed. and trans. Brad Inwood and L. P. Gerson, intro. D. S. Hutchinson (Indianapolis: Hackett, 1994), pp. 28–31

Froissart, Jean, *'Dits' et 'Débats', avec en appendice quelques poèmes de Guillaume de Machaut*, ed. Anthime Fourrier (Geneva: Droz, 1979)

  Le Joli Buisson de Jonece, ed. Anthime Fourrier (Geneva: Droz, 1975)

  Lyric Poems of Jean Froissart: A Critical Edition, ed. Rob Roy McGregor (Chapel Hill: University of North Carolina Department of Romance Languages, 1975)

Œuvres de Froissart: Poésies, ed. Auguste Scheler, 3 vols. (Brussels: Devaux, 1870–2; repr. Geneva: Slatkine, 1977)

Guillaume de Lorris and Jean de Meun, *Le Roman de la Rose*, ed. Félix Lecoy, 3 vols. (Paris: Champion, 1965–70)

Julian, 'Against the Galilaeans', in *Works of the Emperor Julian*, ed. and trans. Wilmer Cave Wright, 3 vols. (London: Heinemann, 1913–23), vol. III (1923), pp. 311–427

'Lancelot do Lac': The Non-Cyclic Old French Prose Romance, ed. Elspeth Kennedy, 2 vols. (Oxford: Clarendon Press, 1980). Trans. as *Lancelot of the Lake*, trans. Corin Corley, intro. Elspeth Kennedy (Oxford University Press, 1989)

Lancelot: Roman en prose du XIIIe siècle, ed. Alexandre Micha, 9 vols. (Geneva: Droz, 1978–83)

Lancelot-Grail: The Old French Arthurian Vulgate and Post-Vulgate in Translation, ed. Norris J. Lacy, 5 vols. (London: Garland, 1993–6)

Le Livre du Graal, ed. Daniel Poirion under the direction of Philippe Walter, 3 vols. (Paris: Gallimard, 2001)

Machaut, Guillaume de, 'Le Dit de la fleur de lis et de la marguerite', in Froissart, *'Dits' et 'Débats'*, pp. 289–301

'Le Dit de la marguerite', in Froissart, *'Dits' et 'Débats'*, pp. 277–84

Le Jugement du roy de Behaigne, in *'Le Jugement du roy de Behaigne' and 'Remede de Fortune'*, ed. James I. Wimsatt and William W. Kibler (Athens: University of Georgia Press, 1988)

Le Jugement du roy de Navarre / Judgement of the King of Navarre, ed. and trans. R. Barton Palmer (New York: Garland, 1988)

La Mort le roi Artu, ed. Jean Frappier (Geneva: Droz, 1954)

Pearl, ed. E. V. Gordon (Oxford: Clarendon Press, 1953)

Pearl, ed. Sarah Stanbury (Kalamazoo, MI: Medieval Institute Publications, 2001)

Le Roman de Thèbes, ed. Leopold Constans (Paris: Firmin Didot, 1890)

dei Segni, Lotario (Pope Innocent III), *De miseria condicionis humane [De contemptu mundi]*, ed. and trans. Robert E. Lewis (Athens: University of Georgia Press, 1978)

Sir Gawain and the Green Knight, ed. J. R. R. Tolkien and E. V. Gordon, 2nd edn, rev. Norman Davis (Oxford: Clarendon Press, 1967)

The Song of Roland, trans. Glyn Burgess (London: Penguin, 1990)

The Song of Roland: An Analytical Edition, ed. Gérard J. Brault, 2 vols. (University Park: Pennsylvania State University Press, 1978)

Sophocles, *Antigone, The Women of Trachis, Philoctetes, Oedipus at Colonus*, ed. and trans. Hugh Lloyd-Jones (Cambridge, MA: Harvard University Press, 1994)

Thomas, *Fragments du Roman de Tristan*, ed. Bartina H. Wind (Geneva: Droz, 1960)

Usk, Thomas, *Testament of Love*, ed. R. Allen Shoaf (Kalamazoo, MI: Medieval Institute Publications, 1998)

Villon, François, *Le Lais Villon et les poèmes variés*, ed. Jean Rychner and Albert Henry, 2 vols. (Geneva: Droz, 1977)

Œuvres, ed. Louis Thuasne, 3 vols. (Paris: Picard, 1923)
Poems of François Villon, trans. Galway Kinnell, new edn (Hanover, NH; London: University Press of New England, 1982)
Le Testament Villon, ed. Jean Rychner and Albert Henry, 2 vols. (Geneva: Droz, 1974)
The Vulgate Version of the Arthurian Romances, ed. H. Oskar Sommer, 8 vols. (Washington: Carnegie Institution, 1908–16)
William of Malmesbury, *Gesta regum Anglorum: The History of the English Kings*, ed. and trans. R. A. B. Mynors, completed R. M. Thomson and M. Winterbottom, 2 vols. (Oxford: Clarendon Press, 1998–9)

REFERENCE WORKS

Anglo-Norman Dictionary, 2nd edn, gen. ed. William Rothwell, ed. Stewart Gregory, William Rothwell and David Trotter (London: Modern Humanities Research Association, 2005–). A text combining the available new entries with the older can be consulted at www.anglo-norman.net/gate/
Dictionary of Medieval Latin from British Sources, ed. R. E. Latham and D. R. Howlett (London: British Academy; Oxford: Oxford University Press, 1975–)
Dictionnaire de biographie française, gen. ed. M. Prévost *et al.* (Paris: Letouzey et Ané, 1929–)
Dictionnaire des lettres françaises: Le moyen âge, ed. Robert Bossuat, Louis Pichard and Guy Raynaud de Lage, rev. edn, ed. Geneviève Hasenohr and Michel Zink (Paris: Fayard, 1992)
Dictionnaire historique de la langue française, ed. Alain Rey, 2 vols. (Paris: Robert, 1992)
Französisches etymologisches Wörterbuch: Eine Darstellung des galloromanischen Sprachschatzes, ed. Walther von Wartburg (imprint varies; 1928–)
Godefroy, Frédéric, *Dictionnaire de l'ancienne langue française, et de tous ses dialectes du IXe au XVe siècle*, 10 vols. (Paris: Vieweg, 1881–1902)
Middle English Dictionary, ed. Hans Kurath and Sherman M. Kuhn, 20 vols. (Ann Arbor: University of Michigan Press, 1954–2007)
New Catholic Encyclopaedia, 2nd edn, 15 vols. (Detroit: Thomson/Gale; Washington, DC: Catholic University of America, 2003)
Tobler, Adolf and Erhard Lommatzsch, *Altfranzösisches Wörterbuch* (imprint varies; 1925–)
Trésor de la langue française: Dictionnaire de la langue du XIXe et du XXe siècle (1789–1960), ed. Paul Imbs, 16 vols. (Paris: imprint varies, 1971–94)

SECONDARY WORKS

Aers, David, 'The Self Mourning: Reflections on *Pearl*', *Speculum*, 68 (1993), 54–73
Agamben, Giorgio, *The Time That Remains: A Commentary on the Letter to the Romans*, trans. Patricia Dailey (Stanford University Press, 2005)

Ailes, Marianne J., 'Faith in *Fierabras*', in Bennett, Cobby and Runnalls (eds.), *Charlemagne in the North*, pp. 125–33

    The Song of Roland: On Absolutes and Relative Values (Lewiston, NY: Mellen, 2002)

Alexandre-Bidon, Danielle, *La Mort au Moyen Âge: XIIIe–XVIe siècle* (Paris: Hachette, 1998)

Alter, Jean, 'L'esprit antibourgeois exorcisé dans *La Chanson de Roland*', *Romanic Review*, 78 (1987), 253–70

Andrew, Malcolm, 'Theories of Authorship', in Brewer and Gibson (eds.), *Companion to the Gawain-Poet*, pp. 23–33

Ariès, Philippe, *The Hour of Our Death*, trans. Helen Weaver (London: Allen Lane, 1981)

    Images of Man and Death, trans. Janet Lloyd (Cambridge, MA: Harvard University Press, 1985)

    Western Attitudes toward Death: From the Middle Ages to the Present, trans. Patricia M. Ranum (Baltimore, MD: Johns Hopkins University Press, 1974)

Auerbach, Erich, *Mimesis: The Representation of Reality in Western Literature*, trans. Willard R. Trask (Princeton University Press, 1953)

Avtonomova, Natalia *et al.*, *Lacan avec les philosophes* (Paris: A. Michel, 1991)

Badiou, Alain, *Saint Paul: The Foundation of Universalism*, trans. Ray Brassier (Stanford University Press, 2003)

Baltrušaitis, Jurgis, *Anamorphoses; ou perspectives curieuses* (Paris: Perrin, 1955)

Barr, Helen, '*Pearl* – or "The Jeweller's Tale"', *Medium Ævum*, 69 (2000), 59–79

Barthes, Roland, 'Textual Analysis of Poe's "Valdemar"', trans. Geoff Bennington, in Robert Young (ed.), *Untying the Text: A Post-Structuralist Reader* (London: Routledge & Kegan Paul, 1981), pp. 133–61. Originally published as 'Analyse textuelle d'un conte d'Edgar Poe', in *Sémiotique narrative et textuelle*, intro. Claude Chabrol (Paris: Larousse, 1973), pp. 29–54

    'To Write: An Intransitive Verb?', in Richard Macksey and Eugenio Donato (eds.), *The Languages of Criticism and the Sciences of Man: The Structuralist Controversy* (Baltimore, MD: Johns Hopkins University Press, 1970), pp. 134–56 (including discussion)

Bartlett, Robert, *The Making of Europe: Conquest, Colonization and Cultural Change, 950–1350* (London: Penguin, 1993)

Batany, Jean, 'Les "Danses Macabres": une image en négatif du fonctionnalisme social', in Jane H. M. Taylor (ed.), *Dies Illa*, pp. 15–27

Baumgartner, Emmanuèle, 'Géants et chevaliers', in Glyn S. Burgess and Robert A. Taylor (eds.), *The Spirit of the Court* (Cambridge: D. S. Brewer, 1985), pp. 9–22

    'Lancelot et la Joyeuse Garde', in Buschinger and Zink (eds.), *Lancelot–Lanzelet*, pp. 7–14

Beaune, Colette, *The Birth of an Ideology: Myths and Symbols of Nation in Late-Medieval France*, trans. Susan Ross Huston, ed. Fredric L. Cheyette (Berkeley: University of California Press, 1991)

Beauvoir, Simone de, *Le Deuxième Sexe*, 2 vols. (Paris, 1949). Trans. (abridged) as *The Second Sex*, trans. and ed. H. M. Parshley (Harmondsworth: Penguin, 1972); and as *The Second Sex*, trans. Constance Borde and Sheila Malovany-Chevallier (London: Cape, 2009)

Becker, Karin, *Eustache Deschamps: L'État actuel de la recherche* (Orléans: Paradigme, 1996)

Bédier, Joseph, *Les Légendes épiques: Recherches sur la formation des chansons de geste*, 4 vols., 3rd edn (Paris: Champion, 1926–9)

Bennett, Michael, 'The Court of Richard II and the Promotion of Literature', in Barbara Hanawalt, *Chaucer's England: Literature in Historical Context* (Minneapolis: University of Minnesota Press, 1992), pp. 3–20

'The Historical Background', in Brewer and Gibson (eds.), *Companion to the Gawain-Poet*, pp. 71–90

Bennett, Philip E., Anne Elizabeth Cobby and Graham A. Runnalls (eds.), *Charlemagne in the North* (Edinburgh: Société Rencesvals, British Branch, 1993)

Bersani, Leo, *Homos* (Cambridge, MA: Harvard University Press, 1995)

Besserman, Lawrence, 'The Idea of the Green Knight', *ELH*, 53 (1986), 219–39

Binski, Paul, *Medieval Death: Ritual and Representation* (Ithaca, NY: Cornell University Press, 1996)

Bloch, Maurice and Jonathan Parry (eds.), *Death and the Regeneration of Life* (Cambridge University Press, 1982)

Bloch, R. Howard, *Etymologies and Genealogies: A Literary Anthropology of the French Middle Ages* (University of Chicago Press, 1983)

Boase, T. S. R., *Death in the Middle Ages: Mortality, Judgment and Remembrance* (London: Thames & Hudson, 1972)

Boffey, Julia, '"Twenty Thousand More": Some Fifteenth- and Sixteenth-Century Responses to the *Legend of Good Women*', in A. J. Minnis (ed.), *Middle English Poetry: Texts and Traditions: Essays in Honour of Derek Pearsall* (York Medieval Press, 2001), pp. 279–97

Bogdanos, Theodore, *Pearl, Image of the Ineffable: A Study in Medieval Poetic Symbolism* (University Park: Pennsylvania State University Press, 1983)

Boitani, Piero, 'Old Books Brought to Life in Dreams: The *Book of the Duchess*, the *House of Fame*, the *Parliament of Fowls*', in Piero Boitani and Jill Mann (eds.), *The Cambridge Companion to Chaucer*, 2nd edn (Cambridge University Press, 2004), pp. 58–77

Bouchard, Constance Brittain, *Those of my Blood: Constructing Noble Families in Medieval Francia* (Philadelphia: University of Pennsylvania Press, 2001)

Boudet, Jean-Patrice and Hélène Millet (eds.), *Eustache Deschamps en son temps* (Paris: Publications de la Sorbonne, 1997)

Bowers, John M., 'The Politics of *Pearl*', *Exemplaria*, 7 (1995), 419–41

The Politics of Pearl: Court Poetry in The Age of Richard II (Woodbridge: D. S. Brewer, 2001)

Bowie, Malcolm, *Lacan* (London: Fontana, 1991)

Braet, Herman and Werner Verbeke (eds.), *Death in the Middle Ages* (Leuven University Press, 1982)

Brault, Gérard J., 'Le thème de la Mort dans la *Chanson de Roland*', in *Société Rencesvals IVe Congrès International: Actes et mémoires* (Heidelberg: Winter, 1969), pp. 220–37

Bray, Alan, *The Friend* (University of Chicago Press, 2003)

Brewer, Derek and Jonathan Gibson (eds.), *A Companion to the Gawain-Poet* (Cambridge: D. S. Brewer, 1997)

Bronfen, Elisabeth, *Over Her Dead Body: Death, Femininity and the Aesthetic* (Manchester University Press, 1992)

Brook, Leslie C., 'Expressions of Faith in the Rhymed Versions of the *Chanson de Roland*', in Bennett, Cobby and Runnalls (eds.), *Charlemagne in the North*, pp. 145–56

'Ganelon's Path to Treachery in the Rhymed Versions of the *Chanson de Roland*', in Linda M. Paterson and Simon B. Gaunt (eds.), *The Troubadours and the Epic: Essays in Memory of W. Mary Hackett* (Coventry: Department of French, University of Warwick, 1987), pp. 169–89

'La traîtrise et la vengeance: Ganelon dans les versions rimées de la *Chanson de Roland*', in *Actes du XIe Congrès international de la Société Rencesvals*, 2 vols. (Barcelona: Real Academia de Buenas Letras, 1990), vol. I, pp. 87–101

Brown, Peter, *The Cult of the Saints: Its Rise and Function in Latin Christianity* (University of Chicago Press, 1981)

Brown-Grant, Rosalind, *French Romance of the Later Middle Ages: Gender, Morality and Desire* (Oxford University Press, 2009)

Bruckner, Matilda Tomaryn, 'An Interpreter's Dilemma: Why Are There So Many Interpretations of Chrétien's *Chevalier de la Charrette?*', *Romance Philology*, 40 (1986), 159–80

Bullon-Fernandez, Maria, 'Byʒonde þe Water: Courtly and Religious Desire in *Pearl*', *Studies in Philology*, 91 (1994), 35–49

Burger, Glenn, *Chaucer's Queer Nation* (Minneapolis: University of Minnesota Press, 2003)

Burgwinkle, William E. (Bill), '*État présent*: Queer Theory and the Middle Ages', *French Studies*, 60 (2006), 79–88

Sodomy, Masculinity, and Law in Medieval Literature: France and England, 1050–1230 (Cambridge University Press, 2004)

Burns, E. Jane, *Courtly Love Undressed: Reading Through Clothes in Medieval French Culture* (Philadelphia: University of Pennsylvania Press, 2002)

'Refashioning Courtly Love: Lancelot as Lady's Man or Ladyman?', in Karma Lochrie, Peggy McCracken and James A. Schultz (eds.), *Constructing Medieval Sexuality* (Minneapolis: University of Minnesota Press, 1998), pp. 111–34

'Which Queen? Guinevere's Transvestism in the French Prose *Lancelot*', in Walters (ed.), *Lancelot and Guinevere*, pp. 247–65

Buschinger, Danielle (ed.), *Autour d'Eustache Deschamps* (Amiens: Presses du Centre d'Études Médiévales, Université de Picardie, 1999)

and Michel Zink (eds.), *Lancelot – Lanzelet: hier et aujourd'hui* (Greifswald: Reineke, 1995)

Butler, Judith, *Antigone's Claim: Kinship Between Life and Death* (New York: Columbia University Press, 2000)

'Arguing with the Real', in *Bodies That Matter: On the Discursive Limits of 'Sex'* (New York: Routledge, 1993), pp. 187–222

and Ernesto Laclau and Slavoj Žižek, *Contingency, Hegemony, Universality: Contemporary Dialogues on the Left* (London: Verso, 2000)

Butterfield, Ardis, 'Chaucer's French Inheritance', in Piero Boitani and Jill Mann (eds.), *The Cambridge Companion to Chaucer*, 2nd edn (Cambridge University Press, 2004), pp. 20–35

'England and France', in Peter Brown (ed.), *A Companion to Medieval English Literature and Culture, c.1350–c.1500* (Oxford: Blackwell, 2005), pp. 199–214

The Familiar Enemy: Chaucer, Language, and Nation in the Hundred Years War (Oxford University Press, 2010)

'French Culture and the Ricardian Court', in Minnis, Morse and Turville-Petre (eds.), *Essays on Ricardian Literature*, pp. 82–121

'Froissart, Machaut, Chaucer and the Genres of Imagination', in André Crépin (ed.), *L'Imagination médiévale: Chaucer et ses contemporains* (Paris: Association des Médiévistes Anglicistes de l'Enseignement Supérieur, 1991), pp. 53–69

'Lyric and Elegy in *The Book of the Duchess*', *Medium Ævum*, 60 (1991), 33–60

Bynum, Caroline Walker, *Fragmentation and Redemption: Essays on Gender and the Human Body in Medieval Religion* (Berkeley: University of California Press, 1987)

Holy Feast and Holy Fast: The Religious Significance of Food to Medieval Women (Berkeley: University of California Press, 1987)

The Resurrection of the Body in Western Christianity, 200–1336 (New York: Columbia University Press, 1995)

Calin, William, *The Epic Quest: Studies in Four Old French 'Chansons de Geste'* (Baltimore, MD: Johns Hopkins University Press, 1966)

The French Tradition and the Literature of Middle English (University of Toronto Press, 1994)

Camille, Michael, *Master of Death: The Lifeless Art of Pierre Remiet, Illuminator* (New Haven, CT: Yale University Press, 1996)

Cannon, Christopher, 'Form', in Paul Strohm (ed.), *Oxford Twenty-First Century Approaches to Literature: Middle English* (Oxford University Press, 2007), pp. 177–90

The Making of Chaucer's English: A Study of Words (Cambridge University Press, 1998)

Cargill, Oscar and Margaret Schlauch, '*The Pearl* and Its Jeweler', *PMLA*, 43 (1928), 105–23

Carroll, Michael P., 'The Savage Bind: Lévi-Strauss' Myth Analysis and Anglophone Social Science', *Pacific Sociological Review*, 21 (1978), 467–86

Casey, Edward S., *Remembering: A Phenomenological Study* (Bloomington: Indiana University Press, 1987)

Cerquiglini(-Toulet), Jacqueline, *The Color of Melancholy: The Uses of Books in the Fourteenth Century*, trans. Lydia G. Cochrane (Baltimore, MD: Johns Hopkins University Press, 1997)

'Le dit', in Daniel Poirion (ed.), *La Littérature française aux XIVe et XVe siècles* (Heidelberg: Winter, 1988), pp. 86–94

L'Écriture testamentaire à la fin du Moyen Âge: Identité, dispersion, trace (Oxford: European Humanities Research Centre of the University of Oxford, 1999)

Chance, Jane, '"A Wonder Thing": The *Descensus ad Inferos* of the Female Heroes Alcyone and Alceste', in *The Mythographic Chaucer: The Fabulation of Sexual Politics* (Minneapolis: University of Minnesota Press, 1995), pp. 19–44

Chênerie, Marie-Luce, 'L'aventure du chevalier enferré, ses suites et le thème des géants dans le *Lancelot*', in Jean Dufournet (ed.), *Approches du Lancelot en prose* (Paris: Champion, 1984), pp. 59–100

Cheyette, Fredric L., *Ermengard of Narbonne and the World of the Troubadours* (Ithaca, NY: Cornell University Press, 2001)

Chiffoleau, Jacques, *La Comptabilité de l'au-delà: Les hommes, la mort et la religion dans la région d'Avignon à la fin du Moyen Âge (vers 1320 – vers 1480)* (Rome: École française de Rome, 1980)

Cholakian, Rouben C., 'The (Un)naming Process in Villon's *Grand Testament*', *French Review*, 66 (1992), 216–28

Clark, James M., *The Dance of Death in the Middle Ages and in the Renaissance* (Glasgow: Jackson, 1950)

Cohen, Jeffrey Jerome, 'Masoch/Lancelotism', in *Medieval Identity Machines* (Minneapolis: University of Minnesota Press, 2003), pp. 78–115

Of Giants: Sex, Monsters, and the Middle Ages (Minneapolis: University of Minnesota Press, 1999)

Cohn, Norman, *The Pursuit of the Millennium: Revolutionary Millenarians and Mystical Anarchists of the Middle Ages*, rev. and expanded edn (London: Temple Smith, 1970)

Coleman, Joyce, '"A bok for king Richardes sake": Royal Patronage, the *Confessio*, and the *Legend of Good Women*', in R. F. Yeager (ed.), *On John Gower: Essays at the Millennium* (Kalamazoo, MI: Medieval Institute Publications, 2007), pp. 104–24

'The Flower, the Leaf, and Philippa of Lancaster', in Collette (ed.), *Context and Reception*, pp. 33–58

Collette, Carolyn P. (ed.), *'The Legend of Good Women': Context and Reception* (Woodbridge: D. S. Brewer, 2006)

Connerton, Paul, *How Societies Remember* (Cambridge University Press, 1989)

Cook, Robert Francis, *The Sense of the Song of Roland* (Ithaca, NY: Cornell University Press, 1987)

Copjec, Joan, *Read My Desire: Lacan Against the Historicists* (Cambridge, MA: MIT Press, 1994)

Cowen, Janet M., 'Chaucer's *Legend of Good Women*: Structure and Tone', *Studies in Philology*, 82 (1985), 416–36

Cox, Catherine S., '*Pearl*'s "Precios Pere": Gender, Language, and Difference', *Chaucer Review*, 32 (1998), 377–90

Crofts, Thomas H., 'Perverse and Contrary Deeds: The Giant of Mont Saint Michel and the Alliterative *Morte Arthure*', in Amanda Hopkins and Cory James Rushton (eds.), *The Erotic in the Literature of Medieval Britain* (Cambridge; Rochester, NY: D. S. Brewer, 2007), pp. 116–31

Cropp, Glynnis M., 'La "Ballade des seigneurs" de François Villon et les chroniques', *Moyen Âge*, 100 (1994), pp. 221–36

'Les trois ballades du temps jadis dans le *Testament* de François Villon', *Académie Royale de Belgique: Bulletin de la Classe des Lettres et des Sciences morales et politiques*, 5e série, 57 (1971), 316–41.

Crowell, Steven, 'Existentialism', in Edward N. Zalta (ed.), *The Stanford Encyclopedia of Philosophy (Spring 2006 Edition) (SEP)*, http://plato.stanford.edu/archives/spr2006/entries/existentialism/ (accessed 19 February 2010)

Davies, Norman, *Europe: A History* (Oxford University Press, 1996)

Davis, Natalie Zemon, 'Ghosts, Kin, and Progeny: Some Features of Family Life in Early Modern France', *Daedalus*, 106 (1977), 87–114

Deleuze, Gilles, *Coldness and Cruelty*, in *Masochism*, trans. Jean McNeil (New York: Zone, 1989), pp. 7–138

Delisle, Léopold, *Recherches sur la librairie de Charles V*, 2 vols. (Paris: Champion, 1907)

Delpech-Ramey, Joshua, 'An Interview with Slavoj Žižek: "On Divine Self-Limitation and Revolutionary Love"', *Journal of Philosophy and Scripture*, 1.2 (2004), 32–8, www.philosophyandscripture.org/SlavojZizek.pdf

Delumeau, Jean, *Le Péché et la peur: La Culpabilisation en Occident* (Paris: Fayard, 1983)

Derrida, Jacques, *Glas* (Paris: Galilée, 1974)

Speech and Phenomena, And Other Essays on Husserl's Theory of Signs, trans. and intro. David B. Allison (Evanston, IL: Northwestern University Press, 1973)

Dinshaw, Carolyn, *Chaucer's Sexual Poetics* (Madison: University of Wisconsin Press, 1989)

Douglas, D. C., 'The *Song of Roland* and the Norman Conquest of England', *French Studies*, 14 (1960), 99–116

Douglas, Mary, 'Passive Voice Theories in Religious Sociology', in *In the Active Voice* (London: Routledge & Kegan Paul, 1982), pp. 1–15

Purity and Danger: An Analysis of Concepts of Pollution and Taboo (London: Routledge & Kegan Paul, 1966)

Dover, Carol R., 'From Non-Cyclic to Cyclic *Lancelot*: Recycling the Heart', in Sarah Sturm-Maddox and Donald Maddox (eds.), *Transtextualities: Of Cycle and Cyclicity in Medieval French Literature* (Binghamton, NY: Medieval and Renaissance Texts and Studies, 1996), pp. 53–70

'Galehot and Lancelot: Matters of the Heart', in Kathryn Karczewska and Tom Conley (eds.), *The World and Its Rival: Essays on the Literary Imagination in Honor of Per Nykrog* (Amsterdam: Rodopi, 1999), pp. 119–35

Doyle, William, *The French Revolution: A Very Short Introduction* (Oxford University Press, 2001)

Draskau, Margaret Jennifer Kewley, *The Quest for Equivalence: On Translating Villon* (Copenhagen: Atheneum, 1986)

DuBruck, Edelgard E., *The Theme of Death in French Poetry of the Middle Ages and the Renaissance* (The Hague: Mouton, 1964)

— and Barbara I. Gusick (eds.), *Death and Dying in the Middle Ages* (New York: Lang, 1999)

Duby, Georges, *The Knight, the Lady and the Priest: The Making of Modern Marriage in Medieval France*, trans. Barbara Bray (New York: Pantheon, 1983)

— *Mâle Moyen Âge: De l'amour et autres essais* (Paris: Flammarion, 1988)

Dufournet, Jean (ed.), *Approches du Lancelot en prose* (Paris: Champion, 1984)

— 'Une ballade méconnue de Villon: la Ballade des seigneurs du temps jadis', in *Nouvelles recherches sur Villon* (Paris: Champion, 1980), pp. 29–46

— 'Deux poètes du Moyen Âge face à la mort: Rutebeuf et Villon', in Jane H. M. Taylor (ed.), *Dies Illa*, pp. 155–75

Duggan, Joseph J., 'L'épisode d'Aude dans la tradition en rime de la *Chanson de Roland*', in Bennett, Cobby and Runnalls (eds.), *Charlemagne in the North*, pp. 273–9

— 'Franco-German Conflict and the History of French Scholarship on the *Song of Roland*', in P. J. Gallacher and H. Damico (eds.), *Hermeneutics and Medieval Culture* (Albany: State University of New York Press, 1989), pp. 97–106

Eagleton, Terry, *Trouble with Strangers: A Study of Ethics* (Oxford: Blackwell, 2009)

Earl, James W., 'Saint Margaret and the *Pearl* Maiden', *Modern Philology*, 70 (1972), 1–8

Edelman, Lee, *No Future: Queer Theory and the Death Drive* (Durham, NC: Duke University Press, 2004)

Edwards, Elizabeth, 'The Place of Women in the *Morte Darthur*', in Elizabeth Archibald and A. S. G. Edwards (eds.), *A Companion to Malory* (Cambridge: D. S. Brewer, 1996), pp. 37–54

Edwards, Robert R., 'Ricardian Dreamwork: Chaucer, Cupid and Loyal Lovers', in Collette (ed.), *Context and Reception*, pp. 59–82

Ellmann, Maud, 'Blanche', in Jeremy Hawthorn (ed.), *Criticism and Critical Theory* (London: Arnold, 1984), pp. 99–110

Evans, Dylan, *An Introductory Dictionary of Lacanian Psychoanalysis* (London: Routledge, 1996)

Evergates, Theodore (ed.), *Aristocratic Women in Medieval France* (Philadelphia: University of Pennsylvania Press, 1999)

Fein, David, *François Villon and His Reader* (Detroit, MI: Wayne State University Press, 1989)

Feldstein, Richard, Bruce Fink and Maire Jaanus (eds.), *Reading Seminar XI: Lacan's Four Fundamental Concepts of Psychoanalysis* (Albany: State University of New York Press, 1995)

Field, Rosalind, 'The Heavenly Jerusalem in *Pearl*', *Modern Language Review*, 81 (1986), 7–17

Fleming, Katie, 'Fascism on Stage: Jean Anouilh's Antigone', in Zajko and Leonard (eds.), *Laughing with Medusa*, pp. 163–87

Fletcher, Alan J., '*Pearl* and the Limits of History', in Anne Marie D'Arcy and Alan J. Fletcher (eds.), *Studies in Late Medieval and Early Renaissance Texts in Honour of John Scattergood: 'The Key of All Good Remembrance'* (Dublin: Four Courts Press, 2005), pp. 148–70

Flori, Jean, 'L'épée de Lancelot: adoubement et idéologie au début du treizième siècle', in Buschinger and Zink (eds.), *Lancelot – Lanzelet*, pp. 147–56

Forty, Adrian and Susanne Küchler (eds.), *The Art of Forgetting* (Oxford: Berg, 1999)

Foucault, Michel, *The History of Sexuality, vol. I: An Introduction*, trans. Robert Hurley (London: Allen Lane, 1978)

Fox, John, 'A Note on Villon's "Ballade des Seigneurs du Temps Jadis"', *Modern Language Review*, 55 (1960), 414–17

Fradenburg, L. O. Aranye, '"My Worldes Blisse": Chaucer's Tragedy of Fortune', *South Atlantic Quarterly*, 98 (1999), 563–92

Sacrifice Your Love: Psychoanalysis, Historicism, Chaucer (Minneapolis: University of Minnesota Press, 2002)

'"Voice Memorial": Loss and Reparation in Chaucer's Poetry', *Exemplaria*, 2 (1990), 169–202

Fraisse, Simone, *Le Mythe d'Antigone* (Paris: Colin, 1974)

Frappier, Jean, *Amour courtois et Table Ronde* (Geneva: Droz, 1973)

'Le personnage de Galehaut dans le *Lancelot en prose*', *Romance Philology*, 17 (1963–4), 535–54

'Les trois Ballades du temps jadis dans le *Testament* de François Villon', *Académie Royale de Belgique: Bulletin de la Classe des Lettres et des Sciences morales et politiques*, 5e série, 57 (1971), 316–41

Freeman, Michael, *François Villon in His Works: The Villain's Tale* (Amsterdam: Rodopi, 2000)

'The Snows of Yester-Year: An Update', *French Studies Bulletin*, 27 (2006), 54–8

and Jane H. M. Taylor (eds.), *Villon at Oxford: The Drama of the Text* (Amsterdam: Rodopi, 1999)

Freud, Sigmund, *Beyond the Pleasure Principle* (1920), *SE*, vol. XVIII (1955), pp. 1–64

Civilization and Its Discontents (1929), *SE*, vol. XXI (1961), pp. 57–145

'Fetishism' (1927), *SE*, vol. XXI (1961), pp. 152–7

The Standard Edition of the Complete Psychological Works of Sigmund Freud, trans. under the general editorship of James Strachey, 24 vols. (London: Hogarth Press, 1953–74)

Totem and Taboo (1912–13), *SE*, vol. XIII (1955), pp. 140–6

Gaunt, Simon, 'Bel Accueil and the improper allegory of the *Roman de la Rose*', *New Medieval Literatures*, 2 (1998), 65–93

Gender and Genre in Medieval French Literature (Cambridge University Press, 1995)

Love and Death in Medieval French and Occitan Courtly Literature: Martyrs to Love (Oxford University Press, 2006)

Re-Telling the Tale: An Introduction to Medieval French Literature (London: Duckworth, 2002)

Troubadours and Irony (Cambridge University Press, 1989)

Geary, Patrick J., *Living with the Dead in the Middle Ages* (Ithaca, NY: Cornell University Press, 1994)

Geremek, Bronisław, *The Margins of Society in Late Medieval Paris*, trans. from the French (itself a translation from the original Polish) by Jean Birrell (Cambridge University Press, 1987)

Gilbert, Jane, 'Gender and Sexual Transgression', in Brewer and Gibson (eds.), *Companion to the Gawain-Poet*, pp. 53–69

Gilson, Étienne, 'De la Bible à François Villon', in *Les Idées et les lettres* (Paris: J. Vrin, 1932), pp. 9–38

Girard, René, *Deceit, Desire, and the Novel: Self and Other in Literary Structure*, trans. Yvonne Freccero (Baltimore, MD: Johns Hopkins University Press, 1965)

Gluckman, Max, 'The Frailty in Authority', in *Custom and Conflict in Africa* (Oxford: Blackwell, 1965), pp. 27–53

Green, Richard Firth, 'Chaucer's Victimized Women', *Studies in the Age of Chaucer*, 10 (1988), 3–21

Greene, Virginie, 'The Knight, the Woman, and the Historian: Georges Duby and Courtly Love', in Albrecht Classen (ed.), *Discourses on Love, Marriage, and Transgression in Medieval and Early Modern Literature* (Tempe: Arizona Center for Medieval and Renaissance Studies, 2004), pp. 43–63

Le Sujet et la mort dans 'La Mort Artu' (Saint-Genouph: Nizet, 2002)

Griffin, Miranda, *The Object and the Cause in the Vulgate Cycle* (Oxford: Legenda, 2005)

Guenée, Bernard, *La Folie de Charles VI: Roi bien-aimé* (Paris: Perrin, 2004)

Un Meurtre, une société: L'Assassinat du duc d'Orléans, 23 novembre 1407 (Paris: Gallimard, 1992)

'Le vœu de Charles VI: essai sur la dévotion des rois de France aux XIIIe et XIVe siècles', *Journal des savants* (1996), 67–135

Gumbrecht, Hans Ulrich, 'Intertextuality and Autumn', in Marina Scordilis Brownlee, Kevin Brownlee and Stephen G. Nichols (eds.), *The New Medievalism* (Baltimore, MD: Johns Hopkins University Press, 1991), pp. 301–30

Guyomard, Patrick, *La Jouissance du tragique: Antigone, Lacan, et le désir de l'analyste* (Paris: Aubier, 1992)

Haidu, Peter, *The Subject Medieval/Modern: Text and Governance in the Middle Ages* (Stanford University Press, 2004)

The Subject of Violence: The Song of Roland and the Birth of the State (Bloomington: Indiana University Press, 1993)

Hanning, Robert W., *The Individual in Twelfth-Century Romance* (New Haven, CT: Yale University Press, 1977)

Hardman, Philippa, 'The *Book of the Duchess* as a Memorial Monument', *Chaucer Review*, 28 (1993–4), 205–15

Hegel, G. W. F., *Phenomenology of Spirit*, trans. A. V. Miller, with analysis by J. N. Findlay (Oxford University Press, 1977)

Heger, Henrik, 'La Ballade et le Chant Royal', in Daniel Poirion (ed.), *La Littérature française aux XIVe et XVe siècles* (Heidelberg: Winter, 1988), pp. 59–69

Heidegger, Martin, 'The Origin of the Work of Art', in *Basic Writings, from 'Being and Time' (1927) to 'The Task of Thinking' (1964)*, ed. David Farrell Krell, rev. and expanded edn (London: Routledge, 1993), pp. 143–212

'The Thing', in *Poetry, Language, Thought*, trans. Albert Hofstadter (New York: Harper, 1971), pp. 165–86

Hemming, Timothy Dominic, 'La mort dans la *Chanson de Roland*: étude lexico-syntactique', in *Société Rencesvals IVe Congrès International: Actes et mémoires* (Heidelberg: Winter, 1969), pp. 90–4

Hertz, Robert, 'A Contribution to the Study of the Collective Representation of Death', in Robert Hertz, *Death and The Right Hand*, trans. Rodney and Claudia Needham (London: Cohen and West, 1960), pp. 25–86

Horgan, A. D., 'Justice in the *Pearl*', *Review of English Studies*, 32 (1981), 173–80

Huet, Marie-Hélène, *Mourning Glory: The Will of the French Revolution* (Philadelphia: University of Pennsylvania Press, 1997)

Huizinga, Johan, *The Waning of the Middle Ages: A Study of the Forms of Life, Thought and Art in France and the Netherlands in the XIVth and XVth Centuries*, trans. Frederik Hopman (London: Arnold, 1924)

Hunt, Tony, *Villon's Last Will: Language and Authority in the 'Testament'* (Oxford: Clarendon Press, 1996)

Huot, Sylvia, 'The Daisy and the Laurel: Myths of Desire and Creativity in the Poetry of Jean Froissart', *Yale French Studies*, 80 (1991), 240–51

'From Life to Art: The Lyric Anthology of Villon's *Testament*', in Doranne Fenoaltea and David Lee Rubin (eds.), *The Ladder of High Designs: Structure and Interpretation of the French Lyric Sequence* (Charlottesville: University Press of Virginia, 1991), pp. 26–40

'Love, Race, and Gender in Medieval Romance: Lancelot and the Son of the Giantess', *Journal of Medieval and Early Modern Studies*, 37 (2007), 373–91

Madness in Medieval French Literature: Identities Found and Lost (Oxford University Press, 2003)

Hyatte, Reginald, *The Arts of Friendship: The Idealization of Friendship in Medieval and Early Renaissance Literature* (Leiden: Brill, 1994)

'Dream-Engendering Dreams in the Old French *Lancelot*', *Mediaevalia*, 22 (1999), 343–58

'Praise and Subversion of Romance Ethos in the Prose *Lancelot*', *Neophilologus*, 82 (1998), 11–18

'Reading Affective Companionship in the Prose *Lancelot*', *Neophilologus*, 83 (1999), 19–32

'Recoding Ideal Male Friendship as *fine amor* in the Prose *Lancelot*', *Neophilologus*, 75 (1991), 505–18

Inwood, Michael, *A Hegel Dictionary* (Oxford: Blackwell, 1992)

A Heidegger Dictionary (Oxford: Blackwell, 1999)

Irigaray, Luce, *An Ethics of Sexual Difference*, trans. Carolyn Burke and Gillian C. Gill (London: Athlone, 1993)

Speculum of the Other Woman, trans. Gillian C. Gill (Ithaca, NY: Cornell University Press, 1985)

This Sex Which Is Not One, trans. Catherine Porter with Carolyn Burke (Ithaca, NY: Cornell University Press, 1985)

To Be Two, trans. Monique M. Rhodes and Marco F. Cocito-Monoc (London: Athlone, 2000)

Jaeger, C. Stephen, *Ennobling Love: In Search of a Lost Sensibility* (Philadelphia: University of Pennsylvania Press, 1999)

Javelet, Robert, *Image et ressemblance au douzième siècle: De saint Anselme à Alain de Lille*, 2 vols. (Paris: Letouzey et Ané, 1967).

Johnson, Barbara, 'Poetry and Its Double: Two *Invitations au voyage*', in *The Critical Difference: Essays in the Contemporary Rhetoric of Reading* (Baltimore, MD: Johns Hopkins University Press, 1985), pp. 23–50

Jones, George Fenwick, *The Ethos of the Song of Roland* (Baltimore, MD: Johns Hopkins University Press, 1963)

Joynes, Andrew (ed.), *Medieval Ghost Stories: An Anthology of Miracles, Marvels and Prodigies* (Woodbridge: Boydell, 2001)

Jubb, Margaret A., 'Enemies in the Holy War, but Brothers in Chivalry: The Crusaders' View of the Saracen Opponents', in van Dijk and Noomen (eds.), *Aspects de l'épopée romane*, pp. 251–9

Kada-Benoïst, Danielle, 'Le phénomène de désagrégation dans les trois ballades du temps jadis de Villon', *Moyen Âge*, 80 (1974), 301–8

Kantorowicz, E. H., *The King's Two Bodies: A Study in Mediaeval Political Theology* (Princeton University Press, 1957)

Kay, Sarah, 'Adultery and Killing in *La Mort le roi Artu*', in Nicholas White and Naomi Segal (eds.), *Scarlet Letters: Fictions of Adultery from Antiquity to the 1990s* (Basingstoke: Macmillan, 1997), pp. 34–44

The 'Chansons de Geste' in the Age of Romance: Political Fictions (Oxford: Clarendon Press, 1995)

'The Character of Character in the *Chansons de Geste*', in Leigh A. Arrathoon (ed.), *The Craft of Fiction: Essays in Medieval Poetics* (Rochester, MI: Solaris, 1984), pp. 475–98

'The Contradictions of Courtly Love and the Origins of Courtly Poetry: The Evidence of the *Lauzengiers*', *Journal of Medieval and Early Modern Studies*, 26 (1996), 209–53

Courtly Contradictions: The Emergence of the Literary Object in the Twelfth Century (Stanford University Press, 2001)

'Courts, Clerks, and Courtly Love', in Roberta L. Krueger (ed.), *Cambridge Companion to Medieval Romance* (Cambridge University Press, 2000), pp. 81–96

'Desire and Subjectivity', in Simon Gaunt and Sarah Kay (eds.), *The Troubadours: An Introduction* (Cambridge University Press, 1999), pp. 212–27

'The Life of the Dead Body: Death and the Sacred in the *chansons de geste*', *Yale French Studies*, 86 (1994), 94–108.

'Le problème de l'ennemi dans les chansons de geste', in van Dijk and Noomen (eds.), *Aspects de l'épopée romane*, pp. 261–8

Keller, Hans-Erich, *Autour de Roland: Recherches sur la chanson de geste* (Paris: Champion, 1989)

Kellogg, Judith, *Medieval Artistry and Exchange: Economic Institutions, Society, and Literary Form in Old French Narrative* (New York: Peter Lang, 1989)

Kelly, Douglas, 'Les inventions ovidiennes de Froissart: réflexions intertextuelles comme imagination', *Littérature*, 41 (1981), 82–92

Kelly, John D. and Martha Kaplan, 'History, Structure, and Ritual', *Annual Review of Anthropology*, 19 (1990), 119–50

Kendrick, Laura, 'La poésie pastorale de Eustache Deschamps: miroir de mentalité à la fin du 14e siècle', *Romanistische Zeitschrift für Literaturgeschichte*, 7 (1983), 28–44

Kennedy, Elspeth, 'Failure in Arthurian Romance', *Medium Aevum*, 60 (1991), 16–32

'The Figure of Lancelot in the *Lancelot-Graal*', in Walters (ed.), *Lancelot and Guinevere*, pp. 79–104

Lancelot and the Grail: A Study of the Prose 'Lancelot' (Oxford: Clarendon Press, 1986)

'The Re-Writing and Re-Reading of a Text: The Evolution of the Prose *Lancelot*', in Alison Adams *et al.* (eds.), *The Changing Face of Arthurian Romance: Essays on Arthurian Prose Romance in Memory of Cedric E. Pickford* (Cambridge: Boydell, 1986), pp. 1–9

'The Two Versions of the False Guinevere Episode in the Old French Prose *Lancelot*', *Romania*, 77 (1956), 94–104

Kermode, Frank, *The Sense of an Ending: Studies in the Theory of Fiction*, new edn (Oxford University Press, 2000)

Kinoshita, Sharon, *Medieval Boundaries: Rethinking Difference in Old French Literature* (Philadelphia: University of Pennsylvania Press, 2006)

'"Pagans are wrong and Christians are right": Alterity, Gender, and Nation in the *Chanson de Roland*', *Journal of Medieval and Early Modern Studies*, 31 (2001), 80–111

Kiser, Lisa J., *Telling Classical Tales: Chaucer and the 'Legend of Good Women'* (Ithaca, NY: Cornell University Press, 1983)

Kline, Daniel T., 'Female Childhoods', in Carolyn Dinshaw and David Wallace (eds.), *The Cambridge Companion to Medieval Women's Writing* (Cambridge University Press, 2003), pp. 133–29

Klosowska (Roberts), Anna, *Queer Love in the Middle Ages* (New York: Palgrave, 2005)

Köhler, Erich, *L'Aventure chevaleresque: Idéal et réalité dans le roman courtois (Études sur la forme des plus anciens poèmes d'Arthur et du Graal*, trans. from the German by Éliane Kaufholz (Paris: Gallimard, 1974)

Kolve, V. A., 'From Cleopatra to Alceste: An Iconographic Study of *The Legend of Good Women*', in John P. Hermann and John J. Burke (eds.), *Signs and Symbols in Chaucer's Poetry* (University: University of Alabama Press, 1981), pp. 130–78

Kristeva, Julia, *Desire in Language: A Semiotic Approach to Literature and Art*, ed. Leon S. Roudiez, trans. Thomas Gora, Alice Jardine and Leon S. Roudiez (Oxford: Blackwell, 1981)

Krueger, Roberta L., 'Desire, Meaning, and the Female Reader: The Problem in Chrétien's *Charrette*', in Christopher Baswell and William Sharpe (eds.), *The Passing of Arthur: New Essays in Arthurian Tradition* (New York: Garland, 1988), pp. 31–51

'Questions of Gender in Old French Romance', in Roberta L. Krueger (ed.), *The Cambridge Companion to Medieval Romance* (Cambridge University Press, 2000), pp. 132–49

Women Readers and the Ideology of Gender in Old French Verse Romance (Cambridge University Press, 1993)

Kruger, Steven F., 'Dialogue, Debate, and Dream Vision', in Larry Scanlon (ed.), *The Cambridge Companion to Medieval English Literature, 1100–1500* (Cambridge University Press, 2009), pp. 71–82

Krynen, Jacques, *L'Empire du roi: Idées et croyances politiques en France, XIIIe—XVe siècle* (Paris: Gallimard, 1993)

Idéal du prince et pouvoir royal en France à la fin du Moyen Âge (1380–1440): Étude de la littérature politique du temps (Paris: Picard, 1981)

Kuhn (Mus), David, *La Poétique de François Villon* (Paris: A. Colin, 1967; reissued with author's name David Mus, 1992)

Lacan, Jacques, *Le Séminaire, livre III: Les Psychoses (1955–1956)*, ed. Jacques-Alain Miller (Paris: Seuil, 1981). Trans. as *The Seminar, Book III: The Psychoses, 1955–1956*, ed. Jacques-Alain Miller, trans. Russell Grigg (New York: Norton, 1993)

Le Séminaire, livre IV: La Relation d'objet (1956–1957), ed. Jacques-Alain Miller (Paris: Seuil, 1994)

Le Séminaire, livre VII: L'Éthique de la psychanalyse, 1959–60, ed. Jacques-Alain Miller (Paris: Seuil, 1986). Trans. as *The Seminar of Jacques Lacan: The Ethics of Psychoanalysis, 1959–60*, ed. Jacques-Alain Miller, trans. with notes Dennis Porter (London: Routledge, 1992)

Le Séminaire, livre XI: Les Quatre Concepts fondamentaux de la psychanalyse (1964), ed. Jacques-Alain Miller (Paris: Seuil, 1973). Trans. as *The Four Fundamental Concepts of Psychoanalysis*, ed. Jacques-Alain Miller, trans. Alan Sheridan (London: Hogarth, 1977)

'Subversion du sujet et dialectique du désir dans l'inconscient freudien' (1960), in *Écrits* (Paris: Seuil, 1966), pp. 793–827. Trans. as 'The Subversion of the Subject and the Dialectic of Desire in the Freudian Unconscious', trans.

Bruce Fink, in *Écrits: The First Complete Edition in English* (New York: Norton, 2006), pp. 671–702

Lacassagne, Miren, 'Rhétorique et politique de la "médiocrité" chez Eustache Deschamps', in Buschinger (ed.), *Autour d'Eustache Deschamps*, pp. 115–26

Lacoue-Labarthe, Philippe, 'On Ethics: *A propos* of Antigone', trans. Joan Tambureno, *Journal of European Psychoanalysis*, 24 (2007), www.psychomedia.it/jep/number24/lacoue.htm (accessed 19 February 2010) (originally published in Avtonomova *et al.*, *Lacan avec les philosophes*)

Laidlaw, James, 'L'innovation métrique chez Deschamps', in Buschinger (ed.), *Autour d'Eustache Deschamps*, pp. 127–40

Laurie, I. S., 'Eustache Deschamps: 1340(?)–1404', in Deborah M. Sinnreich-Levi (ed.), *Eustache Deschamps, French Courtier-Poet: His Work and His World* (New York: AMS Press, 1998), pp. 1–72

Lazar, Moshé, 'Lancelot et la "mulier mediatrix": la quête de soi à travers la femme', *Esprit créateur*, 9 (1969), 243–56

Le Gentil, Pierre, 'Réflexions sur le thème de la mort dans les chansons de geste', in *Mélanges offerts à Rita Lejeune*, 2 vols. (Gembloux: J. Duculot, 1969), vol. II, pp. 801–9

Le Goff, Jacques, *The Birth of Purgatory*, trans. Arthur Goldhammer (University of Chicago Press, 1984)

Leach, Eleanor W., 'Morwe of May: A Season of Feminine Ambiguity', in Mary J. Carruthers and Elizabeth D. Kirk (eds.), *Acts of Interpretation: The Text in Its Contexts, 700–1600: Essays on Medieval and Renaissance Literature in Honor of E. Talbot Donaldson* (Norman: Pilgrim, 1982), pp. 299–310

Leach, Elizabeth Eva, '"The Little Pipe Sings Sweetly While the Fowler Deceives the Bird": Sirens in the Later Middle Ages', *Music and Letters*, 87 (2006), 187–212

Leclercq, Jean, 'La joie de mourir selon Saint Bernard de Clairvaux', in Jane H. M. Taylor (ed.), *Dies Illa*, pp. 195–207

(Lefay-)Toury, Marie-Noëlle, *Mort et fin'amor dans la poésie d'oc et d'oïl aux XIIe et XIIIe siècles* (Paris: Champion, 2001)

   La Tentation du suicide dans le roman français du XIIe siècle (Paris: Champion, 1979)

Lejeune, Rita, 'Jean Renart et le roman réaliste au XIIIe siècle', in Jean Frappier and Reinhold R. Grimm (eds.), *Le Roman jusqu'à la fin du XIIIe siècle*, 2 vols. (Heidelberg: Winter, 1978–84), pp. 400–53

Lemaire, Jacques, *Les Visions de la vie de cour dans la littérature française de la fin du Moyen Âge* (Brussels: Palais des Académies; Paris: Klincksieck, 1994)

Leonard, Miriam, *Athens in Paris: Ancient Greece and the Political in Post-War French Thought* (Oxford University Press, 2005)

Lewis, C. S., *The Allegory of Love: A Study in Medieval Tradition* (Oxford: Clarendon Press, 1936; repr. 1977)

Liborio, Mariantonio, 'Contributi alla storia dell' "Ubi sunt"', *Cultura neolatina*, 20 (1960), 141–209

Lochrie, Karma, *Heterosyncrasies: Female Sexuality When Normal Wasn't* (Minneapolis: University of Minnesota Press, 2005)

Longley, Anne P., 'Guinevere as Lord', *Arthuriana*, 12 (2002), 49–62

'The Lady of the Lake: Lancelot's Mirror of Self-Knowledge', in Keith Busby and Catherine M. Jones (eds.), *'Por le soie amisté': Essays in Honor of Norris J. Lacy* (Amsterdam: Rodopi, 2000), pp. 311–21

Lowes, John Livingston, 'The Prologue to the *Legend of Good Women* as Related to the French *Marguerite* Poems, and the *Filostrato*', *PMLA*, 19 (1904), 593–683

'The Prologue to the *Legend of Good Women* Considered in its Chronological Relations', *PMLA*, 20 (1905), 749–864

Lynch, Kathryn L., *The High Medieval Dream Vision: Poetry, Philosophy, and Literary Form* (Stanford University Press, 1988)

MacCannell, Juliet Flower, *The Regime of the Brother: After the Patriarchy* (London: Routledge, 1991)

Macey, David, *Lacan in Contexts* (London: Verso, 1988)

Mandach, André de, *Naissance et développement de la chanson de geste en Europe*, 6 vols. (Geneva: Droz, 1961–93)

Mann, Jill, *Geoffrey Chaucer* (Hemel Hempstead: Harvester Wheatsheaf, 1991)

'Satisfaction and Payment in Middle English Literature', *Studies in the Age of Chaucer*, 5 (1983), 17–48

Marchello-Nizia, Christiane, 'Amour courtois, société masculine et figures du pouvoir', *Annales ESC*, 36 (1981), 969–82

Margherita, Gayle, 'Originary Fantasies and Chaucer's *Book of the Duchess*', in Linda Lomperis and Sarah Stanbury (eds.), *Feminist Approaches to the Body in Medieval Literature* (Philadelphia: University of Pennsylvania Press, 1993), pp. 116–41

Martin, Ellen E., 'Chaucer's Ruth: An Exegetical Poetic in the Prologue to the *Legend of Good Women*', *Exemplaria*, 3 (1991), 467–90

Martineau-Génieys, Christine, *Le Thème de la mort dans la poésie française: De 1450 à 1550* (Paris: Champion, 1978)

Matlock, Jann, 'The "Clear Visions" of "La Bele Aude": Dream Form and Function in *La Chanson de Roland*', *Pacific Coast Philology*, 15 (1980), 35–44

McCracken, Peggy, *The Curse of Eve, The Wound of the Hero: Blood, Gender and Medieval Literature* (Philadelphia: University of Pennsylvania Press, 2003)

McDonald, Nicola F., 'Chaucer's *Legend of Good Women*, Ladies at Court and the Female Reader', *Chaucer Review*, 35 (2000–1), 22–42

'Doubts about Medea, Briseyda, and Helen: Interpreting Classical Allusion in the Fourteenth-Century French Ballade *Medee fu en amer veritable*', in M. J. Toswell and E. M. Tyler (eds.), *Studies in English Language and Literature: 'Doubt Wisely': Papers in Honour of E. G. Stanley* (London: Routledge, 1996), pp. 252–66

'Games Medieval Women Play', in Collette (ed.), *Context and Reception*, pp. 176–97

McGinn, Bernard, *Visions of the End: Apocalyptic Traditions in the Middle Ages*, repr. with additions (New York: Columbia University Press, 1998)

McLaughlin, Megan, *Consorting with Saints: Prayer for the Dead in Early Medieval France* (Ithaca, NY: Cornell University Press, 1994)

Méla, Charles, '"Je, Françoys Villon . . ."', in M. J.-C. Payen and M.-C. Régnier (eds.), *Mélanges de langue et de littérature du Moyen Âge et de la Renaissance offerts à Jean Frappier*, 2 vols. (Geneva: Droz, 1970), vol. II, pp. 775–96

Ménard, Philippe, '"Berthe au grant pié, Bietris, Alis", ou la résurgence de la culture épique dans la "Ballade des dames du temps jadis"', *Romania*, 102 (1981), 114–29

'Galehaut, prince conquérant dans le *Lancelot en prose*', in Buschinger and Zink (eds.), *Lancelot – Lanzelet*, pp. 263–73

Micha, Alexandre, 'Les épisodes du Voyage en Sorelois et de la Fausse Guenièvre', *Romania*, 76 (1955), 334–41

Mickel, Emanuel J., *Ganelon, Treason, and the 'Chanson de Roland'* (University Park: Pennsylvania State University Press, 1989)

Mieszkowski, Gretchen, 'The Prose *Lancelot*'s Galehot, Malory's Lavin, and the Queering of Late Medieval Literature', *Arthuriana*, 5 (1995), 21–51

Mills, Robert, 'Sovereignty and Bare Life in Poetry by François Villon', *Exemplaria*, 17 (2005), 445–80

Suspended Animation: Pain, Pleasure and Punishment in Medieval Culture (London: Reaktion, 2005)

Minnis, A. J., with V. J. Scattergood and J. J. Smith, *Oxford Guides to Chaucer: The Shorter Poems* (Oxford: Clarendon Press, 1995)

and Charlotte C. Morse and Thorlac Turville-Petre (eds.), *Essays on Ricardian Literature in Honour of J. A. Burrow* (Oxford: Clarendon Press, 1997)

Moi, Toril, 'The Adulteress Wife', review of Beauvoir, *The Second Sex*, trans. Borde and Malovany-Chevallier, *London Review of Books*, 32.3 (11 February 2010), pp. 3–6, www.lrb.co.uk/v32/n03/toril-moi/the-adulteress-wife (accessed 18 February 2010)

Morrissey, Robert, *Charlemagne and France: A Thousand Years of Mythology*, trans. Catherine Tihanyi (University of Notre Dame Press, 2003)

Morse, Ruth, *The Medieval Medea* (Cambridge: D. S. Brewer, 1996)

La Mort au Moyen Âge, Colloque de l'Association des historiens médiévistes français (Strasbourg: Istra, 1977)

Mühletahler, Jean-Claude, 'Aux limites de la satire: changements de focalisation et stratégies persuasives dans quelques ballades d'Eustache Deschamps', in Buschinger (ed.), *Autour d'Eustache Deschamps*, pp. 171–84

Muscatine, Charles, *Chaucer and the French Tradition: A Study in Style and Meaning* (Berkeley: University of California Press, 1957)

Nesbit, E., 'Melisande, or, Long and Short Division', in *Nine Unlikely Tales for Children* (London: Fisher Unwin, 1901)

Noble, Peter, 'The Character of Guinevere in the Arthurian Romances of Chrétien de Troyes', *Modern Language Review*, 67 (1972), 524–35

Nora, Pierre, 'General Introduction: Between Memory and History', in Pierre Nora and Lawrence D. Kritzman (eds.), *Realms of Memory: The Construction of the French Past*, trans. Arthur Goldhammer, 3 vols. (New York: Columbia University Press, 1996), vol. 1: *Conflicts and Divisions*, pp. 1–20

'Preface to the English Language Edition: From *Lieux de mémoire* to *Realms of Memory*', in Nora and Kritzman (eds.), *Realms of Memory*, vol. 1, pp. xv–xxiv

Nouvet, Claire, 'The "Marguerite": A Distinctive Signature', in Palmer (ed.), *Chaucer's French Contemporaries*, pp. 251–76

Odell-Scott, David (W.) (ed.), *Reading Romans with Contemporary Philosophers and Theologians* (New York: T & T Clark, 2007)

Palmer, R. Barton (ed.), *Chaucer's French Contemporaries: The Poetry/Poetics of Self and Tradition* (New York: AMS Press, 1999)

Paris, Gaston, 'Études sur les romans de la Table Ronde: Lancelot du Lac, II: Le Conte de la Charrette', *Romania*, 12 (1883), 459–534

Percival, Florence, *Chaucer's Legendary Good Women* (Cambridge University Press, 1998)

Philippovich, Eugen von, *Kuriositäten/Antiquitäten: Ein Handbuch für Sammler und Liebhaber* (Braunschweig: Klinkhardt & Biermann, 1966)

Phillips, Helen, 'Chaucer and Dream Poetry', in Helen Phillips and Nick Havely (eds.), *Chaucer's Dream Poetry* (Harlow: Longman, 1977), pp. 3–21

'Dream Poems', in Peter Brown (ed.), *A Companion to Medieval English Literature and Culture, c.1350–1500* (Oxford: Blackwell, 2005), pp. 374–86

'Fortune and the Lady: Machaut, Chaucer and the Intertextual "Dit"', *Nottingham French Studies*, 38 (1999), 120–36

'Register, Politics, and the *Legend of Good Women*', *Chaucer Review*, 37 (2002–3), 101–28

Plummer, John F., 'Frenzy and Females: Subject Formation in Opposition to the Other in the Prose *Lancelot*', *Arthuriana*, 6 (1996), 45–51

Poe, Edgar Allan, 'The Philosophy of Composition' (1846), in *Essays and Reviews*, selected and with notes by G. R. Thompson (New York: Literary Classics of the US, 1984), pp. 13–25

Poirion, Daniel, *Le Poète et le Prince: L'Évolution du lyrisme courtois de Guillaume de Machaut à Charles d'Orléans* (Paris: Presses Universitaires Françaises, 1965)

Pratt, Karen (ed.), *Roland and Charlemagne in Europe: Essays on the Reception and Transformation of a Legend* (London: King's College London Centre for Late Antique and Medieval Studies, 1996)

Prestwich, Michael, *Edward I*, 2nd edn (New Haven, CT: Yale University Press, 1997)

Prozorov, Sergei, *Foucault, Freedom and Sovereignty* (Aldershot: Ashgate, 2007)

Quillet, Jeannine, *Charles V, le roi lettré: Essai sur la pensée politique d'un règne* (Paris: Perrin, 1984)

Quinn, William A., 'The Legend of Good Women: Performance, Performativity, and Presentation', in Collette (ed.), *Context and Reception*, pp. 1–32

Rabaté, Jean-Michel, *The Future of Theory* (Oxford: Blackwell, 2002)

Raskolnikov, Masha, 'Between Men, Mourning: Authorship, Love, and the Gift in the *Roman de la Rose*', *GLQ*, 10 (2003), 47–75

Regalado, Nancy Freeman, '*Effet de réel, effet du réel*: Representation and Reference in Villon's *Testament*', *Yale French Studies*, 70 (1986), 63–77
  'Villon's Legacy from *Le Testament de Jean de Meun*: Misquotation, Memory, and the Wisdom of Fools', in Freeman and Taylor (eds.), *Villon at Oxford*, pp. 282–311
Ricoeur, Paul, *Memory, History, Forgetting*, trans. Kathleen Blamey and David Pellauer (University of Chicago Press, 2004)
Riddy, Felicity, 'Jewels in *Pearl*', in Brewer and Gibson (eds.), *A Companion to the Gawain-Poet*, pp. 143–55
Rockwell, Paul Vincent, '"Je ne suiz mi soffisanz"': Insufficiency and Cyclicity in the Lancelot-Grail Cycle', in Sarah Sturm-Maddox and Donald Maddox (eds.), *Transtextualities: Of Cycle and Cyclicity in Medieval French Literature* (Binghamton, NY: Medieval and Renaissance Texts and Studies, 1996), pp. 71–91
Rossman, Vladimir R., *François Villon: Les Concepts médiévaux du testament* (Paris: Delarge, 1976)
Roubaud, Jacques, 'Galehaut et l'éros mélancolique', *Bulletin de l'Association Guillaume Budé* (1982), 263–82
Rowe, Donald W., *Through Nature to Eternity: Chaucer's 'Legend of Good Women'* (Lincoln: University of Nebraska Press, 1988)
Rubin, Gayle, 'Thinking Sex: Notes for a Radical Theory of the Politics of Sexuality', in Carole S. Vance (ed.), *Pleasure and Danger: Exploring Female Sexuality* (Boston: Routledge & Kegan Paul, 1984), pp. 267–319
Russell, Stephen J., *The English Dream Vision: Anatomy of a Form* (Columbus: Ohio State University Press, 1988)
Rychner, Jean, *La Chanson de geste: Essai sur l'art épique des jongleurs* (Geneva: Droz, 1955)
Salih, Sarah, *Versions of Virginity in Late Medieval England* (Cambridge: D. S. Brewer, 2001)
Salter, Elizabeth, *English and International: Studies in the Art and Patronage of Medieval England*, ed. Derek Pearsall and Nicolette Zeeman (Cambridge University Press, 1988)
Sanok, Catherine, 'Reading Hagiographically: The *Legend of Good Women* and its Feminine Audience', *Exemplaria*, 13 (2001), 323–54
Saward, John, *Perfect Fools: Folly for Christ's Sake in Catholic and Orthodox Spirituality* (Oxford University Press, 1980)
Schibanoff, Susan, *Chaucer's Queer Poetics: Rereading the Dream Trio* (University of Toronto Press, 2006)
Schmitt, Jean-Claude, *Ghosts in the Middle Ages: The Living and the Dead in Medieval Society*, trans. Teresa Lavender Fagan (University of Chicago Press, 1998)
  'Les revenants dans la société féodale', *Le Temps de la réflexion*, 3 (1982), 285–306
  'Le suicide au Moyen Âge', *Annales ESC*, 31.1 (1976), 3–28
Schultz, James A., *Courtly Love, the Love of Courtliness, and the History of Sexuality* (University of Chicago Press, 2006)

'Heterosexuality as a Threat to Medieval Studies', *Journal of the History of Sexuality*, 15 (2006), 14–29

Sedgwick, Eve Kosofsky, *Between Men: English Literature and Male Homosocial Desire* (New York: Columbia University Press, 1985)

Segre, Cesare, 'La première "scène du cor" dans la *Chanson de Roland* et la méthode de travail des copistes', in *Mélanges offerts à Rita Lejeune*, 2 vols. (Gembloux: J. Duculot, 1969), vol. II, pp. 871–89

Shaw, David Gary, 'Huizinga's Timelessness', *History and Theory*, 37 (1998), 245–58

Siciliano, Italo, *François Villon et les thèmes poétiques du Moyen Âge* (Paris: Colin, 1934)

Simpson, James R. (Jim), *Fantasy, Identity and Misrecognition in Medieval French Narrative* (Oxford; New York: P. Lang, 2000)

'The Gifts of the *Roland*: The Old French *Gui de Bourgogne*', in Pratt (ed.), *Roland and Charlemagne in Europe*, pp. 31–65

Simpson, James (W.), 'Ethics and Interpretation: Reading Wills in Chaucer's *Legend of Good Women*', *Studies in the Age of Chaucer*, 20 (1998), 73–100

Sjöholm, Cecilia, *The Antigone Complex: Ethics and the Invention of Feminine Desire* (Stanford University Press, 2004)

Sobczyk, Agata, 'La place du Moi dans les poèmes d'Eustache Deschamps', in Buschinger (ed.), *Autour d'Eustache Deschamps*, pp. 233–43

Spearing, A. C., *The 'Gawain'-Poet: A Critical Study* (Cambridge University Press, 1970)

Medieval Dream-Poetry (London: Cambridge University Press, 1976)

Readings in Medieval Poetry (Cambridge University Press, 1987)

Spiegel, Gabrielle M., '*Reditus Regni ad Stirpem Karoli Magni*: A New Look', in *The Past as Text: The Theory and Practice of Medieval Historiography* (Baltimore, MD: Johns Hopkins University Press, 1997), pp. 111–37

Romancing the Past: The Rise of Vernacular Prose Historiography in Thirteenth-Century France (Berkeley: University of California Press, 1993)

Spitzer, Leo, *L'Amour lointain de Jaufré Rudel et le sens de la poésie des troubadours* (Chapel Hill: University of North Carolina Press, 1944)

'Étude ahistorique d'un texte: "Ballade des dames du temps jadis"', *Modern Language Quarterly*, 1 (1940), 7–22

Spurgeon, C. F. E., *Five Hundred Years of Chaucer Criticism and Allusion, 1357–1900*, 3 vols. (Cambridge University Press, 1925)

Stäblein, Patricia Harris, 'L'art de la métamorphose: *Lancelot* et les effets de lumière', in Buschinger and Zink (eds.), *Lancelot – Lanzelet*, pp. 207–17

Stanbury, Sarah, 'Feminist Masterplots: The Gaze on the Body of *Pearl*'s Dead Girl', in Linda Lomperis and Sarah Stanbury (eds.), *Feminist Approaches to the Body in Medieval Literature* (Philadelphia: University of Pennsylvania Press, 1993), pp. 96–115

Stanford, Charlotte A., 'Held in "Perpetual" Memory: Funerals and Commemoration of the Elite Dead in the Late Middle Ages', *Interculture*, 2 (2005), www.fsu.edu/~proghum/interculture/ (accessed 20 December 2009)

Starobinski, Jean, 'L'immortalité mélancolique', *Le Temps de la réflexion*, 3 (1982), 231–51

Steiner, George, *Antigones* (Oxford: Clarendon Press, 1984)

Stones, Alison, 'The Lancelot-Grail Project: Text Editions', *Lancelot-Grail Project*, http://vrcoll.fa.pitt.edu/stones-www/LG-web/L-G-Text-Eds.html (accessed 21 December 2009)

Suard, François, '*La Chanson de Guillaume* et les épopées de la révolte', in Bennett, Cobby and Runnalls (eds.), *Charlemagne in the North*, pp. 437–47

'Lancelot et le chevalier enferré', in Dufournet (ed.), *Approches du Lancelot en prose*, pp. 177–96

Sunderland, Luke, *Old French Narrative Cycles: Heroism between Ethics and Morality* (Cambridge: D. S. Brewer, 2010)

Taylor, Andrew, 'Anne of Bohemia and the Making of Chaucer', *Studies in the Age of Chaucer*, 19 (1997), 95–119

Textual Situations: Three Medieval Manuscripts and Their Readers (Philadelphia: University of Pennsylvania Press, 2002)

'Was There a Song of Roland?', *Speculum*, 76 (2001), 28–65

Taylor, Craig (trans. and annotated), *Joan of Arc: La Pucelle* (Manchester University Press, 2006)

Taylor, Jane (H. M.), '"Ballade des seigneurs du temps jadis": la poétique de l'incohérence', in Freeman and Taylor (eds.), *Villon at Oxford*, pp. 35–50

'Metonymy, Montage, and Death in François Villon's *Testament*', *New Medieval Literatures*, 2 (1998), 133–58

'Un miroer salutaire', in Jane H. M. Taylor (ed.), *Dies Illa*, pp. 29–43

The Poetry of François Villon: Text and Context (Cambridge University Press, 2001)

(ed.), *Dies Illa: Death in the Middle Ages* (Liverpool: Cairns, 1984)

Tesnière, Marie-Hélène, 'Les manuscrits copiés par Raoul Tainguy: un aspect de la culture des grands officiers royaux au début du quinzième siècle', *Romania*, 107 (1986), 282–368

Toury: see Lefay-Toury

Travis, Peter W., 'Chaucer's Heliotropes and the Poetics of Metaphor', *Speculum*, 72 (1997), 399–427

'White', *Studies in the Age of Chaucer*, 22 (2000), 1–66

Uebel, Michael, 'Imperial Fetishism: Prester John Among the Natives', in Jeffrey Jerome Cohen (ed.), *The Postcolonial Middle Ages* (New York: St Martin's Press, 2000), pp. 261–82

van Dijk, Hans and Willem Noomen (eds.), *Aspects de l'épopée romane: mentalités, idéologies, intertextualités: Actes du XIIIe Congrès International de la Société Rencesvals* (Groningen, 1995)

van Emden, Wolfgang C., *La Chanson de Roland* (London: Grant & Cutler, 1995)

'La réception du personnage de Roland dans quelques œuvres plus ou moins épiques des 12e, 13e et 14e siècles', in van Dijk and Noomen (eds.), *Aspects de l'épopée romane*, pp. 353–62

'The Reception of Roland in Some Old French Epics', in Pratt (ed.), *Roland and Charlemagne in Europe*, pp. 1–30

van Gennep, Arnold, *The Rites of Passage*, trans. Monika B. Vizedom and Gabrielle L. Caffee (University of Chicago Press, 1960)

Vance, Eugene, *Reading 'The Song of Roland'* (Englewood Cliffs: Prentice-Hall, 1970)

Varty, Kenneth, 'Villon's Three *Ballades du Temps Jadis* and the Danse Macabre', in D. A. Trotter (ed.), *Littera et Sensus: Essays on Form and Meaning in Medieval French Literature Presented to John Fox* (University of Exeter, 1989), pp. 73–93

Vitullo, Juliann M., *The Chivalric Epic in Medieval Italy* (Gainsville: University of Florida Press, 2000)

Vitz, Evelyn Birge, *The Crossroad of Intentions: A Study of Symbolic Expression in the Poetry of François Villon* (The Hague: Mouton, 1974)

'Desire and Causality in Medieval Narrative: The *Roland*, Thomas's *Tristan*, and *Du segretain moine*', in *Medieval Narrative and Modern Narratology: Subjects and Objects of Desire* (New York University Press, 1989), pp. 176–212

Vovelle, Michel, *Les Âmes du purgatoire, ou le travail du deuil* (Paris: Gallimard, 1996)

La Mort et l'Occident: De 1300 à nos jours (Paris: Gallimard, 1983)

Wailes, Stephen L., *Medieval Allegories of Jesus' Parables* (Berkeley: University of California Press, 1987)

Wallace, David, *Chaucerian Polity: Absolutist Lineages and Associational Forms in England and Italy* (Stanford University Press, 1997)

Walters, Lori J. (ed.), *Lancelot and Guinevere: A Casebook* (New York: Routledge, 1996)

Warner, Michael, 'Homo-Narcissism; or, Heterosexuality', in Joseph A. Boone and Michael Cadden (eds.), *Engendering Men: The Question of Male Feminist Criticism* (New York: Routledge, 1990), pp. 190–206

'Thoreau's Bottom', *Raritan*, 11 (1992), 53–79

Warren, Michelle R., *History on the Edge: Excalibur and the Borders of Britain, 1100–1300* (Minneapolis: University of Minnesota Press, 2000)

Watkins, John, '"Sengeley in Synglere": *Pearl* and Late Medieval Individualism', *Chaucer Yearbook*, 2 (1995), 117–36

Watson, Nicholas, 'The Gawain-Poet as Vernacular Theologian', in Brewer and Gibson (eds.), *Companion to the Gawain-Poet*, pp. 293–313

Watts, Ann Chalmers, '*Pearl*, Inexpressibility, and Poems of Human Loss', *PMLA*, 99 (1984), 26–40

Weiner, Annette B., *The Trobrianders of Papua New Guinea* (Fort Worth: Harcourt College Publishers, 1988)

Wetherbee, Winthrop, *Chaucer and the Poets: An Essay on 'Troilus and Criseyde'* (Ithaca, NY: Cornell University Press, 1984)

Wilkins, Nigel, 'Review of Wimsatt, *Marguerite Poetry*', *French Studies*, 26 (1972), 441–3

Wimsatt, James I., *Allegory and Mirror: Tradition and Structure in Middle English Literature* (New York: Pegasus, 1970)

Chaucer and His French Contemporaries: Natural Music in the Fourteenth Century (University of Toronto Press, 1991)

Chaucer and the French Love-Poets: The Literary Background of the 'Book of the Duchess' (Chapel Hill: University of North Carolina Press, 1968)

The Marguerite Poetry of Guillaume de Machaut (Chapel Hill: University of North Carolina Press, 1970)

Wogan-Browne, Jocelyn, *Saints' Lives and Women's Literary Culture, c. 1150–1300: Virginity and Its Authorizations* (Oxford University Press, 2001)

Zajko, Vanda and Miriam Leonard (eds.), *Laughing with Medusa: Classical Myth and Feminist Thought* (Oxford University Press, 2006)

Zeeman, Nicolette, 'The Lover-Poet and Love as the Most Pleasing "Matere" in Medieval French Love Poetry', *Modern Language Review*, 83 (1988), 820–42

Zeikowitz, Richard E., *Homoeroticism and Chivalry: Discourses of Male Same-Sex Desire in the Fourteenth Century* (New York: Palgrave Macmillan, 2003)

Žižek, Slavoj, 'Between Symbolic Fiction and Fantasmatic Spectre: Toward a Lacanian Theory of Ideology', in *Interrogating the Real*, pp. 249–70

'Connections of the Freudian Field to Philosophy and Popular Culture', in *Interrogating the Real*, pp. 59–86

'Courtly Love, or, Woman as Thing', in *The Metastases of Enjoyment: Six Essays on Woman and Causality* (London: Verso, 1994), pp. 89–112

'The Eclipse of Meaning: On Lacan and Deconstruction', in *Interrogating the Real*, pp. 206–30

Enjoy Your Symptom! Jacques Lacan in Hollywood and Out, rev. edn (New York: Routledge, 2001)

For They Know Not What They Do: Enjoyment as a Political Factor, 2nd edn (London: Verso, 2002)

'Interlude: The Feminine Excess', in Slavoj Žižek and Mladen Dolar, *Opera's Second Death* (New York: Routledge, 2002), pp. 181–95

Interrogating the Real, ed. Rex Butler and Scott Stephens (London: Continuum, 2005)

'Introduction: Robespierre, or, The "Divine Violence" of Terror', in Maximilien Robespierre, *Virtue and Terror* (London: Verso, 2007), pp. vii–xxxix

'Introduction: The Spectre of Ideology', in Slavoj Žižek (ed.), *Mapping Ideology* (London: Verso, 1994), pp. 1–33

Looking Awry: An Introduction to Jacques Lacan through Popular Culture (Cambridge, MA: MIT Press, 1991)

The Plague of Fantasies (London: Verso, 1997)

The Puppet and the Dwarf: The Perverse Core of Christianity (Cambridge, MA: MIT Press, 2003)

'The Real of Sexual Difference', in *Interrogating the Real*, pp. 330–55

The Sublime Object of Ideology (London: Verso, 1989)

278 *Bibliography*

Tarrying with the Negative: Kant, Hegel, and the Critique of Ideology (Durham, NC: Duke University Press, 1993)

'"There is No Sexual Relationship"', in Renata Salecl and Slavoj Žižek (eds.), *Gaze and Voice as Love Objects* (Durham, NC: Duke University Press, 1996), pp. 208–49

The Ticklish Subject: The Absent Centre of Political Ontology (London: Verso, 1999)

Index

CAMBRIDGE STUDIES IN MEDIEVAL LITERATURE

Lightning Source UK Ltd.
Milton Keynes UK
UKHW02f1335150618
324288UK00007B/91/P